KU-700-578

"This is one of those rare books that may become an instant classic. Terhalle convincingly offers a framework that helps us understand the ongoing transition of global order by looking closely at the re-negotiations of the rules of the game underlying 21st Century world politics. He presents a middle-model that captures the pluralist dynamics of today's global politics, successfully navigating between the Scylla of US-centric and the Charybdis of Euro-centric tunnel visions of global order. In that the book displays a thorough understanding of the reciprocal nature of the US-China relationship in shaping order transition."

– Jochen Prantl, Australian National University, Australia

"This ambitious book makes an important contribution to our understanding of how international order is legitimated, contested, and transformed. Dr Terhalle's analysis, grounded in extensive empirical research, of how the United States and China are engaged in a process he calls reciprocal socialization should be of deep interest to scholars and policy-makers alike. This book productively integrates the insights of both material power-based and ideas-based theories of power politics and global governance to develop a comprehensive account of how the relationship between China and the United States is in the process of reshaping multiple dimensions of our international order."

– Mlada Bukovansky, Smith College, USA

"Maximilian Terhalle painstakingly examines how world politics has begun to change in the last few years in ways we all still struggling to understand fully. He arrives at conclusions which challenge many conventional wisdoms and preconceived notions about international order and global governance. Broadly based, thoroughly researched and tightly argued, his study is essential reading for anyone interested in the future of international relations, both as an academic field of inquiry and the reality with which decision-makers have to deal."

– Hanns W. Maull, Trier University, Germany

"*The Transition of Global Order* asks what may be the single most important question in international relations today: how the rise of China and other non-western powers will affect the character of the liberal international order. Professor Terhalle examines the interplay of common culture (or its lack), rules, coercion, and governance effectiveness in shaping the outcome."

– Jack Snyder, Columbia University, USA

"This original study of challenges to the global order features a dual focus on the United States and China – not only in relation to each other ('the rise of China' and its implications for the US position in the world), but also how they act vis-à-vis other states, and, especially international institutions. The author explores why China has failed to fully socialize into mainly US-dominated, or at least US-created, institutions. He pairs that inquiry with one of the US failure to become enmeshed in international institutions and fully participate in what some have called the 'constitutionalization' of international relations. Thus the study engages a systemic-level question – how international orders change – while paying particular attention to the 'agency' of the two leading powers. It represents an important and unique contribution to our understanding of international political change."

– Matthew Evangelista, Cornell University, USA

The Transition of Global Order

Legitimacy and Contestation

Maximilian Terhalle
Potsdam University, Germany

First published 2015 by
PALGRAVE MACMILLAN

Palgrave Macmillan in the UK is an imprint of Macmillan Publishers Limited, registered in England, company number 785998, of Houndmills, Basingstoke, Hampshire RG21 6XS.

Palgrave Macmillan in the US is a division of St Martin's Press LLC, 175 Fifth Avenue, New York, NY 10010.

Palgrave Macmillan is the global academic imprint of the above companies and has companies and representatives throughout the world.

Palgrave® and Macmillan® are registered trademarks in the United States, the United Kingdom, Europe and other countries.

ISBN 978–1–137–38689–2

This book is printed on paper suitable for recycling and made from fully managed and sustained forest sources. Logging, pulping and manufacturing processes are expected to conform to the environmental regulations of the country of origin.

A catalogue record for this book is available from the British Library.

Library of Congress Cataloging-in-Publication Data
Terhalle, Maximilian, 1974–
    The transition of global order: legitimacy and contestation / Maximilian Terhalle.
       pages cm
    Summary: "Why do international orders lack systemic legitimacy? This study examines the developing relationship between the US and China and explores the ways in which these two global powers are transitioning to a new global order, albeit one with significant risks and uncertainties for governance and legitimacy. Terhalle argues that the financial crisis of 2008/09 established China as the key challenger to the United States amid a process of order transition. Subsequent disagreements between these two powers about the future shape of the global order's legitimacy have manifested themselves in their intense competition with regard to spheres of influence in East Asia and the environment and ideology-related aspects of the order. In positing a new theoretical framework for understanding order and legitimacy in International Relations, The Transition of Global Order offers a significant contribution to the debate around world politics and the new global order"! — Provided by publisher.
    ISBN 978–1–137–38689–2 (hardback)
    1. United States—Relations—China.   2. China—Relations—United States.
    3. Global Financial Crisis, 2008–2009.   4. World politics—21st century.
    5. International relations.   I. Title.
    E183.8.C5T425 2015
    327—dc23   2015002147

Contents

Preface and Acknowledgments

As an undergraduate at the University of Bonn, Germany, I remember listening to lectures on the "international" order that emerged after the Napoleonic Wars and came to an end in the trenches of the Western front, if not earlier. Another world war later, Western Europe, well-protected by the United States, developed fundamentally new, supranational institutions to learn its lessons from the devastating past. Inevitably and all things being equal, this gift, whose meaning Western Europe had learned the hard way, spread material wealth and socialized most scholars into necessarily peaceful cognitive priors. The discipline of International Relations Theory was rightly relieved when the Cold War ended and henceforth many theorists delved into thinking about how to govern a world in which questions related to the overall character of the new order, its balance of power, the role of new *and* established great powers in it and its underlying values had seemingly vanished. In a sense, this peaceful socialization of the last 70 years has, if unwittingly, strengthened Western-centric views of the world in Europe (even more so in the United States) and has, consequently, led many scholars to focus on, and prioritize, theories of norm diffusion and cooperation in an undoubtedly fully institutionalized world. Editorial decisions by major journals in the field have theoretically contributed to this development, further entrenching unspoken mainstream research, often at an increasingly abstract level. Notwithstanding its impressive merits, it seems that this evolution has come at the expense of the kind of research that is historically versed, impatiently curious and original, intellectually off the beaten path and cognitively capable of putting aside one's own mental maps and socialization, if only to foster imagination.

In many ways, one kind of liberty which I have always reserved was – somewhat instinctively – to do what most scholars told me not to do (except for a few fundamentally independent minds). I have carelessly crossed disciplinary boundaries, have read widely in opposite directions, have enjoyed being carried away by the fantastic collections in some of the world's greatest libraries, have disregarded (often self-serving) fashions and (minor) trends in the so-called community of IR scholars, have lived for extended periods of time outside Europe, have benefited immensely from active involvement in the practice of global politics and repeatedly from hands-on exchanges with practitioners and policy-makers and, finally, I have enjoyed being at home on both sides of the Atlantic.

All of these experiences have fed into, or built upon, my mindset, which is deeply suspicious about the perfectibility of human beings and, subsequently, about the endurance of the arrangements of global political order and cooperation that they compose or promote. Today, we are – again – at a point in history, whose origins go back to the US–China rapprochement in the 1970s (and less so to the end of the Cold War), at which the foundations, of what the *Zeitgeist* of too many in the discipline has long believed as the irreversible status quo in international politics, have been put into question. This book is an attempt to demonstrate where crucial drivers of the "real action" in IR theory and global politics may lie in the foreseeable future.

Intellectually, I have been fortunate enough to engage with many brilliant scholars, whose standards will remain difficult to meet. They have helped me tremendously to think through what is theoretically at the heart of our times. These encounters occurred during my research fellowships at Columbia, Yale, Cornell and Oxford Universities (2007–2011, 2012). First and foremost, I would like to thank Andrew Hurrell (Oxford) and Jack Snyder (Columbia) for their rigorous skepticism and searching questions about my initial, book-related ideas. At times, I felt thrown back to my Ancient Greek literature class in high school and convinced that I was sitting in Socrates' famous academy, constantly being exposed to their analytically piercing questions and, at the same time, always encouraged and driven to counter their criticisms. Each of these one-to-one exchanges on the analytical and conceptual tools for understanding the notions of global order, contestation and legitimacy has provided me with an immense wealth of insights and unconventional thinking par excellence. The personal style and humility of these intellectual giants are deeply admirable.

But, far more scholars have been involved in straightening out my key arguments and have been kind enough to offer upfront and highly beneficial feedback on draft chapters of my book. Among them, I would like to express my gratitude to Mlada Bukovansky, Peter Katzenstein, Matthew Evangelista, Jochen Prantl, Kal Holsti and Hanns Maull. At the opening conference of Amrita Narlikar's Cambridge-based Center for Rising Powers, I was delighted to talk to Andrew Gamble. During my stint at Oxford, I also had the great opportunity to try out some of my arguments in a discussion with Rosemary Foot. At Columbia, Bob Jervis invited me to attend the IR faculty seminars (2009–2011). His deeply learned ways of thinking about the notion of power introduced me to a much better understanding of the foundations of US foreign policy and the latter's shaping of its own/international order. At Yale, Paul Kennedy was an ever-encouraging and most hospitable bastion of unsurmountable knowledge and a great inspiration to keep thinking about the "big picture" in world politics and history. Detlef Nolte, Feng Zhang, Qin Liwen, Sebastian Heilmann, Toshi Yoshihara, Robert Ayson, Robyn Eckersley, Joanna Depledge, Charlotte Streck, Thomas Hickmann, Chookiat Panaspornprasit, Miriam Prys, Markus Kornprobst, Dominic Sachsenmaier, Nele Noesselt, Matthew Stephen and Ingo Take have usefully commented on single chapters. I very much appreciate their input. Christopher Daase gave me some good advice upon my return to Germany's academe in 2011. Throughout, Greg Gause, an old-school scholar in the best sense, has been a wonderful friend.

Parts of Chapter 3 were published as "Transnational Actors and Great Powers during Order Transition" in *International Studies Perspectives* and earlier renditions of parts of Chapters 2 and 7 were printed in a *Special Issue* of *Climate Policy* 2013 (13:5), which I co-edited, as "Great-Power Politics, Order Transition, and Climate Governance: Insights from International Relations Theory". The book has, at its various stages, substantively benefited from the comments proffered by participants of my panels at the *International Studies Association*'s annual conventions (2009–2013). Luise Köcher at Potsdam University was a great research assistant in the final stages of the book manuscript. Olaf Schneider, a US-based and Yale-educated German emigree, has been a remarkable source of stylistic meticulousness and a subtle critic, who told me whenever I did not see the forest for the trees.

The comments provided by the reviewers of the book's manuscript were extremely helpful in strengthening the structure of the book. I very much appreciate their painstaking reading of the chapters. Not least, I would like to thank Eleanor Davey Corrigan and her colleagues at Palgrave Macmillan for all their work in the production of this book.

The Fritz Thyssen Foundation (Cologne, Germany) has found an interest in my scholarly undertakings ever since I left Berlin for the United States in 2007. When I received the Foundation's letter in 2013, offering me the research grant I needed to write this book, I was very excited. I still am – and would like to thank the Thyssen Foundation for its generosity.

Needless to say, anyone who has written a (or more) book-length treatise(s) knows full well that a reliable network of good friends is absolutely central to the author's well-being, especially when the subject turns out to be much more complicated than you think, if still – curiously – fascinating. To all of you and wherever you are in the world at the moment, please accept my heartfelt "Thank you" for your steadfast friendship throughout.

My beloved parents, Max and Dr. Monika Terhalle, and my dear sister Eva have unconditionally believed in me ever since I became fascinated by international politics in high school, when translating the texts of classical authors such as Cicero, Sallust, Thucydides and Platon coincided with the time of Germany's reunification. Their loving bond of unwavering trust is second to none. As such it has been the most kind foundation of my explorations throughout. I will remember and appreciate it forever.

My greatest debt is to my family, my dear wife Alexandra and my children, Felicity and Fritz, for their boundless love, patience and support. They make everything worthwhile. Work on this book has resulted in my frequent absences. It has also been the source of major preoccupation, even when I have been at home. I know I have demanded a lot from you. Please accept my sincere apologies, Team Terhalle. Your cheerleading smiles have been priceless. Your manifold encouragements of "go-fight-win" have been the greatest motivation of all. Last but not least, I would also like to send a big "Thank you" to my extended family on the other side of the Atlantic pond for supporting me and us during the great recession. We made it!

Abbreviations

ASEAN	Association of Southeast Asian Nations
ADIZ	Air Defense Identification Zone
ADMM+	ASEAN Defense Ministers' Meetings Plus
APEC	Asia-Pacific Economic Cooperation
ARF	ASEAN Regional Forum
BBC	British Broadcasting Company
BRIC/BASIC	Brazil/Russia/India/China; Brazil/South Africa/India/China
CCP	Chinese Communist Party
CDR	Common but differentiated responsibilities and respective capabilities
CIGI	Centre for International Governance Innovation
COP	Convention of the Parties
DoC	Declaration on the Conduct of the Parties
DSB	Dispute Settlement Body
EAS	East Asia Summit
ECOSOC	Economic and Social Council (UN)
ECS	East China Sea
EEZ	Exclusive Economic Zone
EPA	Environmental Protection Agency (US)
FAZ	*Frankfurter Allgemeine Zeitung*
FT	*Financial Times*
G 2/7/8/20/77	Group of 2/7/8/20/77
GDP	Gross Domestic Product
GHG	Green House Gases
HST	Hegemonic Stability Theory
ICC	International Criminal Court
IISS	International Institute for Strategic Studies
IGO/NGO	International Government Organization/Non-Governmental Organization
IMF	International Monetary Fund
ISA	International Studies Association
IO	International Organization
LDCs	Least Developed Countries
MEF	Major Economies Forum
MFA	Ministry of Foreign Affairs (China)

MERICS	Mercator Institute for China Studies
NATO	North Atlantic Treaty Organization
NIC	National Intelligence Council (US)
NSC	National Security Council (US)
NSS	National Security Strategy (US)
NYT	*New York Times*
OECD	Organization for Economic Co-operation and Development
PLA	People's Liberation Army (China)
RtP	Responsibility to Protect
SCO	Shanghai Cooperation Organization
SCS	South China Sea
S&ED	Strategic and Economic Dialogue (US/China)
SWP	Stiftung Wissenschaft und Politik (German Institute for International and Security Affairs)
TNA	Transnational Actor
TRIPS	Agreement on Trade-Related Aspects of Intellectual Property Rights
UN	United Nations
UNCLOS/ITLOS	UN Convention on the Law of the Seas/International Tribunal on the Law of the Seas
UNGA	UN General Assembly
UNDP	UN Development Program
UNFCCC	United Nations Framework Convention on Climate Change
UNSC	UN Security Council
WSJ	*Wall Street Journal*
WTO	World Trade Organization
WW I	World War I
WW II	World War II

Part I
Introduction and Framework

1
Global Orders: Contestation and Transition

Why do global orders lack constitutive legitimacy? The answer is that systemic contestation between leading great powers prevents the large-scale institutional redesign required to remove deadlocks in the existing global governance structures. The main problem in this process of order transition is the lack of a new political bargain on the material power structures, normative beliefs and management of the global order among the key players.

Since the end of the Cold War, the theretofore dominant structural view of the anarchic fear of war driving state behavior has been superseded by a global governance focus on how to identify collective action problems and how to provide global public goods (Barnett and Sikkink 2008:63). Consequently, after the demise of the Soviet Union, questions about the nature of the underlying international order were put aside. The governance structures that had been evolving from the 1970s onwards have since taken on a strongly institutionalized and norm-based character, if fragmented; since the end of the Cold War, they have been complemented by attempts to legally codify international law, global legal regimes and international organizations into a coherent body of law (Weeramantry 2004).[1] Normatively, these efforts have had a cosmopolitan connotation (Keohane 2002; Mayntz 2010; Zürn 2010). In this respect, processes of liberal institutional enmeshment and norm-based socialization have widely been predicted to help adopt the developing world into the liberal Western order. Equally, processes of enmeshment have been assumed to involve the United States more deeply into today's post-Westphalian setting. In essence, "deep globalization, the rise of transnational actors and global civil society, and increasingly cosmopolitan norms and identities" made earlier great-power-based accounts "increasingly anachronistic" and, in turn, promulgated the dawn of "the age of global governance" (Lake 2013:569, 570).

However, two developments have severely undercut the strength of this narrative. Firstly, while the international and transnational governance-related structures and processes underlying the notions of institutionalization (Ruggie 1998; Dingwerth et al. 2009:13), norm diffusion/promotion/conversion (Zürn et al. 2012:4–8; Simmons et al. 2006) and constitutionalization (Klabbers et al. 2009; Wiener et al. 2012) have persisted due to their built-in path-dependence (Young 2012:10–11), their "overambitions" (Buzan 2011:6) to socialize rising powers into the existing order have, largely, failed. The reasons for this failure are manifold. In essence, governance accounts and related theories have neglected the impact of changes in the balance of power, of pluralistic domestic politics as well as of divergent worldviews. Thus, neither has membership in international organizations implied compliance with the overall goals of the respective institution nor has an increase in Hirschman's voice opportunities precipitated a greater sense of loyalty to such organizations (Acharya 2011:867). Conspicuously, while the socializee's agency has long been downplayed by conventional theories, it has now returned with a vengeance. Reflecting this, China's new assertiveness has widely been seen to be confirmed by its international behavior since the high point of the financial crisis in late 2008 (Narlikar 2010:78–102; Bader 2012:69–83; Johnston, Chen and Pu, 2014; Shambaugh 2013).[2]

Secondly, the United States has objected both to the thickening web of global governance structures and processes and the relative power gains on the part of China, mainly because it has led to the current order's decreasing effectiveness, as viewed from Washington. To begin with, contrary to the conventional wisdom of unipolarity theory, according to which the unipole can operate almost without any barriers in international politics, the United States has had to acknowledge powerful veto players. The latter are actors "whose agreement...is required for a change of the status quo" (Tsebelis 2002) and who are "in a unique position to simply say no" (Voeten 2011:128) to any US plans to reshape the world's institutional architecture to suit its own interest. Furthermore, demand for US compliance with international institutions and regimes has precipitated the resistance of large domestic constituencies (Foot and Walter 2011; Rabkin 2005:ch. 2). In response, the US government has – in keeping with its more revisionist foreign policy tradition – applied power-based techniques in order to retain its freedom to act and to remake the environment in which it has to operate (e.g. forum-shopping (Drezner 2007)). Its key aim has been to employ instrumental measures to secure its national interest at a time when it is no longer the case that "[t]he world, in effect, [has] contracted out to the United States to provide global governance" (Ikenberry 2011:297). This attitude has been underpinned by other factors such as the "desire to preserve what one has while the advantage is still on one's side" (Gilpin 1981:239).³ In fact, leading US officials have repeatedly stated the "'resident power' status that Washington wants to maintain" (quoted in IISS 2011:414). As a consequence, while embodying the structural as well as the liberal foundations of the order (Wertheim 2010), the United States has often refused to get more deeply enmeshed in institutionalized and norm-based governance structures (Jervis 2006; Mead 2002). In turn, this means that the enmeshment of the United States has failed.

These developments have produced a somewhat different empirical picture than the one imagined by global governance accounts. It is characterized by the increasing salience of US–Chinese great-power politics, or, as Keohane soberly put it, by "more basic problems" (2012:133). Firstly, a political and military competition between China and the United States has ensued, even if their economic ties reflect a state of complex interdependence. Despite over a dozen meetings between the US president and his Chinese counterpart in the Strategic and Economic Dialogue between 2009 and mid-2014, the relationship has evolved from Chinese hedging and "biding its time", US pivoting and bilateral attempts to strengthen strategic trust, into an era of merely managing and controlling their "trust deficit", as China's new leader Xi Jinping put it (Guangjin and Yingzi 2012). The material underpinnings of this development have been enabled by a still little understood dialectic trend in world politics. Accordingly, the early differentiation among developing countries and subsequent large-scale economic growth have established China as the strongest rising power, while simultaneously, beginning in the 1970s, the Western-led process of institutionalization took root. Although an unintended consequence, this development was initially facilitated by the United States' opening of the capitalist order to Beijing in 1971. It eventually enabled China to assume a crucial system-preserving role during the financial crisis of 2008–9. This crisis and the nature of China's behavior during the crisis, it is argued, presented the equivalent to a "turning point" (Abbott 2001) in international politics⁴; however, since this "turning point" was missed, the corresponding lack of effective voice opportunities has subsequently led to China's new assertiveness. China's economic success has, tacitly, elevated it to the status of a de facto great power; or, as the British foreign secretary, Miliband, suggested with a rather unusual degree of outspokenness after the G20 meeting in London 2009, China had become one of the "two powers that count", underlining its "indispensability" (Guardian May 17, 2009).[5] Interestingly, when he mentioned those "two powers", that is, the United States and China, he referred to their exclusive bilateral meeting *during* the G20 meeting as the most important one at a time when it was a widely shared (and propagated) belief that the G20 was the new quasi-government in world politics. Secondly, the United States and China are involved in a process of reciprocal socialization (Terhalle 2011). This means that the two countries have come to mutually influence each other to the extent that each warily observes the other's behavior toward international institutions and regimes and, subsequently, draws its respective conclusions as to how this affects its own position in the global power hierarchy (Foot and Walter 2011:4). As a result, this process has made the contest between the United States and China central to world politics precisely because "the global order and the attitudes and behavior of these two important states are a mutually constitutive social phenomenon" (Foot and Walter 2011:23). Most conspicuously, this is reflected in a recent, substantial change in great-power hierarchies. While "P-5 coordination is still substantial" at the United Nations Security Council, "bilateral U.S.–China consultations outside the Council chambers have become far more important" (Prantl 2012:5).[6] Thirdly, both China's failed socialization and the United States' interest-based selectivity concerning its engagement in global governance structures have come at the expense of the post-Westphalian setting that had emerged since the 1970s and, more forcefully, after the end of the Cold War. As Keohane put it, "[a]s a generalization, it seems that...what could have been seen in the mid-1990s as a progressive extension of international regimes, with stronger rules and larger jurisdictions, has been halted if not reversed" (2012:134). This development has, in turn, further strengthened the great-power competition that has already ensued. Pointedly, "on balance", it has "eroded the willingness of both to accept global normative frameworks as legitimate standards of appropriate behavior" (Foot and Walter 2011:294). Signposts of this evolution toward great-power-based politics can be observed in both countries. Since 2012, Chinese leaders have conceived global governance as a "new type of great-power relations" (Economist June 8, 2013:10). Moreover, such thinking is reflected in China's scholarly research agendas being strongly committed to great-power relations.[7] In fact, the "highest grant for state-sponsored social science research" was received in November 2011 by a Chinese university undertaking "[s]tudies on the evolution of the international structure and great-power interactions in the twentieth century" (Liang et al. 2012:19).[8] As for the United States, the National Intelligence Council's 2012 report for the new administration believed that the "underpinnings of the current post-Cold War equilibrium are beginning to shift. . . . If the international system becomes more fragmented and existing forms of cooperation are no longer seen as advantageous to many of the key global players, the potential for competition and conflict also will increase" (2012:82).[9]

Such observations led to the central arguments explored in this book. It will be argued that, in contrast to the more unilinear assumption of an increasingly cosmopolitan order with its focus on the provision of global public goods, the resurgence of great-power politics has precipitated a new process of order transition understood as system-relevant changes in the main practices pertaining to the nature of the global order's governance. The great-power contestation underlying the order transition has prevented large-scale institutional redesign or readjustment in order to break up existing deadlocks precisely because of the lack of a new political bargain on material power structures, normative beliefs and the management of the order among the key players. This is why, in essence, the current order lacks systemic legitimacy. In turn, this highlights the fact that, while the (unresolved) consequences of order transition are most tangible at the regime and institutional levels, the deadlocks and impasses international regimes and organizations have undergone do not only present collective action problems. Rather, a closer look reveals that the deadlocks reflect the great-power disagreements underlying the contestation of the Western order. This is precisely why leading practitioners of global governance and scholars alike hold "one broadly accepted view", according to which "existing institutions and arrangements are mostly deadlocked in the attempt to solve some of the outstanding global issues", while notwithstanding the varying degree of contestation among those issues (CIGI 2012:28; Foot and Walter 2011:6).[10] Effectively, what is currently contested and is most tangible at the regime level is the liberal economic, financial and environmental governance structure of world politics (e.g. the World Trade Organization, International Monetary Fund, United Nations Framework Convention on Climate Change),[11] albeit within a capitalist framework; equally, a great-power competition for key spheres of influence has ensued (e.g. ASEAN, East/South China Sea); finally, opposing exceptionalist worldviews reflect a highly intricate search for common sets of values (e.g. Responsibility to Protect, global aid regime). While the attribution of the roles of the hegemon and the challenger in the different theaters of contestation might be clear-cut on the surface, both states need, in fact, to be regarded as revisionist powers, each pursuing an instrumental path to securing their sovereignty within a highly institutionalized and regulated world.

What then does the argument – that the existing deadlocks have exposed the vast degree to which the current order is lacking systemic legitimacy – imply in disciplinary terms? It underlines the need to shift the research focus away from the currently predominant views, which are inherently linked to a frame of reference set by today's theories of the existing institutionalized world. Thus, while the prevailing strand of research is partly determined by the output bias of analyses narrowly focusing on legitimacy-related concerns, which pertain to the of issue-specific regimes (Koskenniemi 2009), the argument makes it necessary to shift the research focus toward generating new theories about the search for a consensus on the "basic rules of the system" (Gamble 2011:36).[12] While there is some overlap between this study and theories of global governance and liberal institutionalism, in order to theoretically capture the underlying notion of systemic legitimacy, this analysis is broadly, but not exclusively, framed by English School Theory with its key focus on the notion of *order*.[13]

Ian Clark's and Robert Gilpin's complementary accounts, both combining material and ideational aspects, serve as two theoretical starting points. The former explains the elements that shape the politics of legitimacy, referring to the dynamic interplay between the notions of legality, morality, constitutionality and balance of power, while the latter provides the key patterns that need to be renegotiated during order transition (e.g. rules concerning the economic- and security-related aspects of an order, its underlying worldview, the special rights great powers are endowed with, agreement on key spheres of influence and on the overall balance of power). This helps immensely in adopting an overall more accurate perspective on the topic of order transition and systemic legitimacy than those available in current theoretical accounts.

By unpacking some of Clark's underlying assumptions and, subsequently, conceptually adapting his account to the current order transition, the scope of its theoretical application to and usefulness for analyzing the dynamics of systemic legitimacy is increased in three important and interrelated ways. The three adaptations refer to the notions of (today's) hybrid environment, common culture and effectiveness. They are briefly outlined here.

Firstly, building on the English School's broad spectrum-based view on changes in practices opens up space for a hybrid global environment oscillating between solidarist global multi-level governance and more pluralist and increasingly salient, dynamics of great-power-based politics (Buzan 2004:49). Therefore, the revised model should be able to explain to what extent the processes and structures of global governance have been able to retain a degree of their supposed, and path-dependent, autonomy. *Secondly*, broadening Clark's notion of morality by drawing on the English School's principal suggestion of a plurality of values and historical identities, that is, worldviews, helps to better account for whether or not the absence of a "common culture" among (today's) great powers inevitably leads to the impossibility of peaceful order transition and, therefore, the instability of the global order. *Finally*, order transition also makes it necessary to rethink the notion of effectiveness in a hybrid environment. The latter is usefully juxtaposed with Clark's original parameter of constitutionality. The revised model of effective management may then answer the following question: "What kind of hegemony is needed to provide effective leadership and how, if at all, this may be reconciled with the ideas of proponents of global governance?"

Inevitably, having put forward a new set of conceptual parameters requires the analysis to pause and to raise questions as to what kind of theoretical framework is employed in the book. Building on a recent sociology of knowledge provided by Buzan and Hansen (2009) helps to clarify the problem. Since the book theorizes the parameters "as interplaying rather than as distinct and free-standing" (Buzan and Hansen 2009:48), it runs the risk, some might say, of becoming more of a framework and less like a falsifiable theory. The latter would seek to "make causal explanations where the impact of one... [parameter] is tested against that of the others" (ibid.:41). However, precisely because the nature of systemic legitimacy and the (contested) search for consensus thrive on the dynamics of the interplay between the parameters, singling out one of them, respectively, and testing it against the others would necessarily distort the characteristic tensions between them. Instead, the book willingly accepts the above risk and relies on the conceptual framework provided by the offered set of parameters. In fact, they "have a heuristic explanatory quality that allows us to produce a structured, yet... empirically sensitive analysis" (ibid.). The case studies undertaken in Chapters 6–8 will reflect this approach.

The key tension that runs through the entire book is that between the resurgence of (US–Chinese) great-power politics and how this development is reshaping established patterns of international order, on the one hand, and those post-Westphalian regime complexes, institutions and non-state actors that have become an integral part of world politics, on the other. If operating under strain, the latter ones do not allow us to view today's environment as the kind of blank slate on which the United States could have built its order in the West at the end of World War II. Rather, it is more accurate to see the developments of the last six years as (still) being embedded in a solidarist environment. This is underlined by the fact that leading practitioners, representatives of international institutions and scholars of global governance have, somewhat unsurprisingly, continued their unabated commitment to the notions of complex governance and legalization. For instance, the International Criminal Court's 2010 review conference further strengthened the idea of legal universalism. Notably, it engaged in banning the notion of aggressive war with such determination that some scholars felt "as if the ink were not [yet] dry on the 1928 Kellogg-Briand Pact, which so successfully prevented a second world war" (Snyder 2012:293–294). Finally, theorists of international law see "some basis for optimism", based on the historical development of human rights law; in fact, they believe that, due to the "unanticipated results so far of the normative dynamics initiated by rule of law promotion", it "may be possible to develop a more universally acceptable conception of rule of law and a set of laws... [and] standards applicable to all states and transnational actors and activities" (Peerenboom et al. 2011:316).[14] Nevertheless, the fact that there are very real tensions between the two strands cannot be denied. Therefore, carefully identifying the layers and shapes of those tensions is the key task that stands at the heart of this endeavor. Whether the analysis leads us to succumb to the powerful and universal "desire for some minimum order", kept up by the great powers as being "preferable to a breakdown of order" (Hurrell 2007:87), or whether post-Westphalian patterns have successfully withstood the tangible strain evinced by great powers or, finally, whether some interim solutions can be found between those two realms remains to be seen.

Finally, three notes of caution are in order with regard to the so-called G2 model.[15] Firstly, despite the fact that the United States and China build the "most significant and complex bilateral state-to-state relationship in the global order" (Foot and Walter 2011:15), the elaborations which follow below do by no means imply advocating such a model. Both, China and the United States are linked into other critical governance relationships, too. For instance, the United States possesses a strong institutional network throughout the globe (Ikenberry 2011), including the North Atlantic Treaty Organization and the G7/8, and enjoys particularly good ties with the European Union, Japan and India, while China has built up strong economic ties with the BRI (Brazil, Russia and India) states. Moreover, both states are engaged in the G20 process. Secondly, suggestions made to the effect that global politics should be viewed through a Waltzian bipolar prism are equally mistaken. Bipolarity theory in its Waltzian version is exclusively shaped by an adversarial view underlying security matters and thus cannot take into account the possibility of changes in the normative structure of balance of power politics (Little 2007; Terhalle 2011:318–319). The narrow focus on hard security, as adopted by realist security studies (Buzan and Hansen 2009:50–53), also fails to capture the importance of US–China relations for a broad range of global governance aspects (e.g. economic, financial, environmental ones). Thirdly, in contrast to Waltz's logic, the degree of US–Chinese economic interdependence has *not* sharply declined (1979:168; Grieco 1990). Rather, whereas conventional theories of economic interdependence focus on the pacifying effects of world trade and economic integration and how they help to overcome great-power rivalries, the United States–China relationship has already been characterized as extremely interdependent. Today, the essential, reverse, question is "whether their economic interconnectedness is great enough to ward off political-military conflict" (Khong 2014:163).[16]

Definitions, concepts and scope conditions

This section highlights the understandings attached, respectively, to the notions of power, legitimacy, global governance and deadlock, as employed in the book. Other key concepts, such as socialization, enmeshment and constitutionalization, are made explicit in the first section of Chapter 2.

To begin with, the term "order transition" is used in order to provide a terminology that is semantically familiar to International Relations (IR) theorists, though used much differently than in power transition theory. The latter defines "power shifts" as the critical moment when rising powers take over from the hegemon in material power terms, usually held to have acquired 80% of the dominant state's power (Tammen et al. 2000:197 n. 17).[17] In contrast, the term "order transition" denotes the contested negotiation process beginning with the missed turning point of 2008, reflected in the largely deadlocked state of today's global politics and stretching into the (unpredictable) future, when a new bargain may have been negotiated (or not). In theoretical terms, order transition is understood as system-relevant changes in the main practices pertaining to the nature of the global order's governance.

In this respect, the book adopts a social concept of power, which combines aspects of the balance of material power, of legal norms and of ideational aspects of worldviews (Scheuermann 2009:46; Schmidt 2007:49) and thereby distinguishes itself from purely material and polarity-based concepts used in IR theory, for instance, by power transition theory (Ross and Feng 2008; Tammen et al. 2000:195 n. 8).[18] In the context of order transition, the politics of legitimacy are underpinned by an understanding of power according to which the contested search for consensus on the system's basic rules occurs against the background of the prevailing balance of power.

Relatedly, systemic legitimacy is not treated as "a property of individual actions" (Clark 2005:254) to which an independent legitimacy scale can be applied, that is, it is "not about operating an algorithm" (Koskenniemi 2011:vi). Rather, it is a social property that is based on the actor's choices and the perception of these actions by his/her peers. Crucially, existing appropriate standards may suggest whether an action is morally, legally or constitutionally acceptable for some, but those very standards may be contested by others. In any event, none of this should be confused with its "degree of legitimacy" (ibid.).[19] Those (contested) standards influence the perception, but they do not determine them "alone. When they enter the realm of the practice of legitimacy, these norms encounter a complex universe of politics, consensus, and power" (ibid.). Unwittingly repeating Karl Mannheim's and Max Weber's distinction between regulated/rationalized areas and the non-regulated sphere where the latter requires action (1995 [1929]:99–100), Ian Clark has underlined the open political nature of the politics of legitimacy. "To imagine that this [encounter] can be wholly governed by appeal to a set of principles is to impose a rationalist paradigm upon a politically indeterminate sphere" (Clark 2005:254; Mayntz 2010:5).[20] The in-depth exploration of the dynamics pertaining to the notion of systemic legitimacy will be undertaken in the third section of Chapter 2.

Concerning the use of the term "global governance", it follows the distinction made by Zürn et al. (2011:2 n. 2). It denotes both regulatory activities taking place between states (international) and the degree of self-regulation among societal cross-border activities (transnational).

As regards deadlocks, the degree of contestation and the variables explaining it vary across regimes and institutions. The deadlocks mentioned above do not imply the inevitable end to any negotiations. Deadlocks leave room for negotiations to be potentially resumed, continued or transferred to a higher level. Despite the differences among the deadlocks, their respective intensity can be categorized into three types: stalemate, delay and breakdown. Stalemate refers to an "impasse in terms of movement and offers no more possibilities for escalation" in the existing negotiation format, but it may be broken by precipitating events (Narlikar 2010:3). Deadlocks can assume the shape of extended delay where a disagreement "persists for a long time, or even worsens...beyond the landmark moments through missed deadlines...and failed summits" (ibid.:5). Finally, deadlocks may occur as "complete breakdown in the negotiation process...for so long that negotiators walk away from the negotiating table" (ibid.). Turning points, if missed, are also considered deadlocks.[21] Importantly, systemic deadlocks need to be distinguished from regime-level deadlocks. Systemic deadlocks, reflected in the contestation of the international order's underlying normative and power structures, exacerbate regime-level negotiations and, thus, account for the latter's persistence.

Finally, regarding scope conditions, the time frame within which this analysis operates are the years between 2008 and 2014, marking the first six years of Barack Obama's presidency, the last four years of Hu Jintao's tenure as President and Secretary General of China's Communist Party and the first two years of China's new leader Xi Jinping. Implicit in the analysis is the assumption that, during these years, China has been rising materially and politically, while the United States has been declining in relative economic terms. It may very well be the case that this trend will be further strengthened, reversed or slowed down in regard to either party in the future. However, the book's deliberately tight time frame prevents the analysis from falling victim to changing circumstances with respect to the argument concerning systemic legitimacy.

Contribution of the book

Situating the book in the existing literature, it is distinguished by three features. Firstly, neither does it adopt a US-centric perspective focusing on the sustainability, openness, stability or decline of the American order (e.g. Ikenberry 2011, 2001; Wohlforth 2012; Layne 2012), nor does it view world politics through the lens of China, be it by treating it as a "social state" (Johnston 2008) or, conversely, as the state that will "rule the world" (Jacques 2011). Secondly, it is not an analysis of the nature of the US–Chinese bilateral relationship, how it has evolved over the last decades (Foot and Walter 2011) and whether it conforms to theories of power transition (Chan 2008; Ross and Feng 2008). Thirdly, the book does not assume, as most parts of the global governance literature seem to imply, that providing global public goods is, largely, a technical procedure which, naturally, serves the (inherently normative) "common good". Neither does it agree with the relative neglect of (US and Chinese) state power by these theories.

Much rather, while China and the United States as well as their respective foreign policies with respect to the so-called global public goods critically matter to the analysis in empirical terms, these perspectives are, in one way or another, considered to be too narrow. Curiously, to the extent that the above research strands represent the frequently separate ways in which international politics are analyzed, unwittingly, they are all inter-related, in that they all have overlooked the ways in which the international order is currently, if tacitly, renegotiated right in front of their respective turfs. Put differently, the book attempts to circumvent the "disciplinary fragmentation", in that it aims to "avoid seeing the subject as a series of disparate and disconnected, if evermore theoretically sophisticated, domains with no clear sense of how they might relate to each other" (Hurrell 2007:20). The book adopts a broad global order perspective mainly because it posits that key negotiations are deadlocked on the international plane due to the lack of an underlying political great-power bargain, that is, due to a lack of systemic legitimacy. Since the prevailing, regime-specific literatures are inherently limited to the "sectoral publics" of an institutionalized world (Zürn 2010:740; Schimmelfennig 2013:96), the order perspective, in contrast, allows us to identify some of the "deeper and more lasting causes" of why the negotiations have stalled in the first place (Narlikar 2011:15). The analysis, therefore, focuses on first-order negotiations which "concern the basic rules of the system and whether or not these are still legitimate or effective in securing the objectives for which they were instituted" (Gamble 2011:36). Second-order negotiations, in contrast, "emerge within negotiations over particular issues, such as trade or climate" (ibid.). Though the analysis does not draw exclusively from English School Theory, one of the latter's main benefits is that it permits the synthesis of power-related and worldview-related aspects that are considered critical at times of renegotiating an order. This, in turn, enables the analysis to much better capture the ongoing order transition, understood as system-relevant changes in the main practices pertaining to the nature of the global order's governance. While existing accounts have shed light on the results of "ordering moments", usually following great wars (Ikenberry 2011, 2001; Clark 2005), none has interpreted today's manifold deadlocks as a systemic crisis; neither have they tried to account for it by employing an order perspective.

Methods

In 1990, Kenneth Waltz argued that "[m]ethodological presuppositions shape the conduct of inquiry. The political science paradigm...is preeminently behavioral. The established paradigm of any field indicates what facts to scrutinize and how they are interconnected" (2008 [1990]:77). Today, looked at from a more global perspective, such method-laden times seem to have passed, notwithstanding the fact that neo-positivist texts, such as the well-known volume by King/Keohane/Verba (KKV) on Political Science methods, remain "perhaps the most widely used text in North American graduate schools and methods courses" (Lebow 2011:1219; Jackson 2010; Buzan and Hansen 2009:5–6). In any event, some substantial rethinking in favor of more problem-oriented and methodologically diverse ways of conducting social science inquiry has now been underway for a considerable time (Daase and Junk 2011).[22] In fact, there is now an increasingly strong trend toward a methodological understanding of the social sciences that has already conceived a time "After KKV" (Mahoney 2010).

In particular, this book is based on a problem-driven approach as opposed to a method-driven one. As Albert Hirschman reminded us, the latter embarks on a "search for paradigms" and is, as such, destined to become "a hindrance to understanding" (1970). Thus, being more interested in middle-range theories, rather than meta-theories and their underlying principles, the approach employed here is built upon "eclectic theorizing" (Katzenstein and Sil 2010; Barnett and Sikkink 2008). While the discipline has deepened its understanding of how to think about the (still) existing dividing lines between rationalist and interpretive research methods (Dessler and Owen 2005), and despite single advances to substantially broaden the methodological debate (Jackson 2008), only recently have proposals tried to transcend the existing boundaries. According to some of its key proponents, such theorizing "calls for the accommodation of eclectic modes of scholarship that trespass deliberately and liberally across competing research traditions", aiming at "defining and exploring substantive problems in original, creative ways, selectively drawing upon a variety of existing and emerging research traditions" (Katzenstein and Sil 2008:110). By proceeding in this manner, "eclectic scholarship is in a position to contribute to both a deeper understanding of a critical problem and theoretical progress for international relations as a whole" (ibid.:118).

Before elaborating on the extent to which this way of theorizing underlies the analysis in this book, it is beneficial to outline the pragmatist character of the approach, originating from the works of William James and John Dewey (Katzenstein and Sil 2010). Situated between objectivism (e.g. neo-liberalism and neo-realism based on neo-positivism) and subjectivism (e.g. variants of theories of constructivism based on discourse analysis), pragmatism can be said to converge on three main tenets. Firstly, it runs counter to "excessively abstract ontologies and rigid principles" and prefers "useful interpretations that can be deployed to cope with concrete problems" (Katzenstein and Sil 2008:113); secondly, the "production of knowledge is seen as a process of integrating different aspects of knowing and doing through creative experimentation" (ibid.:114); thirdly, it stresses the centrality of "dialogue among a more inclusive and democratically structured community of scholars" (ibid.).

Overall, the pragmatist underpinnings point into a direction that reflects the need to transcend ontological and epistemological boundaries whose impact had been strikingly (and unfruitfully) evident during the so-called fourth debate in the 1990s. The key is to separate theories, built on distinct methodologies, "from their respective foundations" (Katzenstein and Sil 2008:111) and thereby allow academics to return to something seemingly simple, which is to "thrive on argument" (Buzan and Hansen 2009:57). In turn, this underlines the preference increasingly given to stimulating research questions over method-driven accounts today (Daase and Junk 2011:125). Certainly, this approach has encountered myriads of obstacles, because it faces "very large intellectual, financial, professional, and psychological investments that go into producing and sustaining a research tradition and these investments militate against addressing important aspects of problems that are not easily represented in the conceptual apparatus and analytical frameworks privileged in that tradition" (Katzenstein and Sil 2008:117; Kuhn 1962). By no means is this meant to promote the notion of "anything goes". Rather, it presents an attempt at carefully removing those methodological parts of a theory that prevent its otherwise beneficial synthesis with other available frameworks and their application to complex problems in international politics (Hellmann 2003:149). As a result, the problem-driven approach, together with its pragmatist underpinnings, presents a valuable tool for providing complex explanations, which draw from various research traditions.

In the case of this analysis, since pragmatism invites "eclectic theorizing", it allows us to cut across those ontological divides, which the concept of systemic legitimacy, by synthesizing materialist and ideational theories, would seem to make inconceivable – if viewed from a more rigid perspective. In this respect, English School Theory provides the necessarily broad framework into which the distinct theoretical as well as ontological approaches can be "pragmatically" condensed. Its boundary character, situated between the logics of consequences and the logics of appropriateness, is especially useful because it is conducive to implementing the pragmatist approach to methodology. In fact, it is precisely because "[a]ny particular action probably involves elements of each" that "political action generally cannot be explained exclusively in terms of a logic of either consequences or appropriateness" (March and Olson 1998:952).

Furthermore, giving preference to pragmatist methodology and eclectic theorizing over the mainstream position, still embodied in "KKV", is also strengthened by a growing body of criticisms in IR. In particular, critics argue that mainstream approaches have come at the expense of original theorizing, which has consequently led to the neglect of critical problems in world politics. For instance, Mearsheimer and Walt have criticized the "increasing[.] focus on 'simplistic hypothesis testing,' which emphasizes discovering well-verified empirical regularities"; such an approach "is a mistake, however, because insufficient attention to theory leads to misspecified empirical models or misleading measures of key concepts. In addition, the poor quality of much of the data in International Relations makes it less likely that these efforts will produce cumulative knowledge" (2013:1). Strikingly, Ole Waever concurs with them when he states that "the mainstream has drifted back to a more empiricist, almost inductivist view of theory (more as advocated by King et al. 1994). When simultaneously theory debate weakens,..., fewer new scholars enter the field as theorists and the 'new normality' is large N work"; he concludes, somewhat provocatively, that such methodology has culminated in "testing...uninteresting questions...devaluating the concept of 'theory'" (2013:323).[23] This analysis, in contrast, deliberately has taken on a broad, indeed, systemic political problem of our times and benefits, therefore, from pragmatist methodology, which integrates divergent aspects of knowing and doing "through creative experimentation", as Katzenstein and Sil put it (2010:114).

Finally, the three reconceptualizations of Clark's original model, which are provided in Chapters 3–5, as well as the overall nature of this book stand in the conceptual as well as historical tradition of works by scholars such as Hurrell (2007), Foot and Walter (2011), Clark (2005, 2011), Goh (2013), Wohlforth et al. (2007), Bukovansky (2002) and Ikenberry (2011, 2001). In epistemological terms, they originate from a problem-driven approach to global affairs and heavily lean toward the qualitative side (Collier et al. 2010; Brady and Collier 2004).

Sources of evidence

The three case studies draw from two distinct sources of evidence. The first one can be found in some 40 semi-structured interviews (Rathbun 2008; Rubin and Rubin 2005); the second one in discourse analysis (Gerring 2007).

Regarding the former, active and retired state officials (e.g. diplomats, senior military officers) from China and the United States were interviewed at conventions and receptions accompanying visits of heads of state or senior cabinet members to Germany, at their embassies, at the sidelines of international conferences as well as at smaller exchanges and briefings at think tanks and research institutes. Similarly, living in Berlin, the author took advantage of plenty of opportunities to talk to German state officials at formal and informal gatherings. The officials were posted at the Federal Chancellery, the Foreign Office and the Defense Department. Likewise, the author's three-year stay at New York's Columbia University (2008–11) provided him with an unaffordable wealth of opportunities to engage Chinese and US top officials at and after conferences, workshops and background talks. Inevitably, some 60 one-to-one conversations and lunches with faculty members, professors of practice and Chinese visiting fellows immensely helped the author to get a good sense of the roles which the United States and China had come (and intended) to play in world affairs, especially during those crucial years. If shorter, the author's stint at Oxford (2012) equally provided manifold opportunities, often at random, to ask the specific questions driving this book.

The fact that the interviews turned out not to follow a rigid pattern often revealed itself not only as necessary for the flow of the respective interviews and, critically, for the openness of the interviewees; it also made the interviews extremely productive (in two-thirds of the cases). Unsurprisingly, most interviewees wanted to remain anonymous. Some of them requested that the content of the interviews should be absorbed into the book's overall flow, if at all, but not referenced. In a small number of cases, and after critical examination, this has happened, albeit mainly in the context of contrasting perspectives.

The second way of retrieving information was based on text analysis, that is, on the thorough analysis of texts that were openly available to the public. Most of the useful information was taken from international and German newspapers as well as from Chinese online media. In addition, the analysis relied on special reviews of US and Chinese expert debates (e.g. provided by the Mercator Institute for China Studies (MERICS), on the German Institute for International Security's foreign newspaper reviews [SWP]), on originally confidential documents that were available online for a short period of time (e.g. Wiki-Leaks, 2009–10), on the publicly available summaries of partly confidential meetings of German, US and Chinese officials, scholars and journalists (e.g. Center for American Progress, Körber International Dialogue, Chatham House, Ditchley Foundation) and, crucially, on speeches and remarks by the presidents of both states as well as by leading state officials that were available online (e.g. White House, both defense departments, the US embassy in Beijing and the Chinese embassy in Washington).

Structure of the book

Chapter 2 is central to the structure of the book and develops its main arguments. It is divided into three sections. The first section asks why conventional theories, which predicted China's socialization and enmeshment, have failed and why theories of enmeshment have not been able to account for either why the United States has not been more deeply drawn into existing governance structures or for why China's interests and its identity have not been redefined during the process. The second section analyzes the consequences of these failures; instead of an increasingly cosmopolitan order, deadlocks characterize the current international environment. The section starts by offering a new theoretical interpretation of the recent financial crisis. It is suggested that, since China substituted for the United States, even if temporarily, as the provider of global economic goods in late 2008, the maintaining of the system by an actor other than the incumbent hegemon needs to be viewed as a "turning point" or the functional equivalent to the end of a major war. The lack of effective voice opportunities, traditionally provided at peace conferences, has since led to China's new assertiveness and, in turn, further strengthened by US revisionism, to various US–China deadlocks. Liberal rationalist accounts readily admit their explanatory limits and refer back to the contested power structures. However, without adducing notions of world order the current deadlocks cannot be explained. At the same time, this development highlights the United States' and China's exceptionalist worldviews during a period of order transition which entail antagonistic potential. The third section identifies the notion of systemic legitimacy as a suitable theoretical framework to capture the (material and normative) contestation of the existing order. Ian Clark's (2005) and Robert Gilpin's (1981) complementary accounts serve as two theoretical starting points. The former explains the elements that shape the politics of legitimacy, referring to the dynamic interplay between the notions of legality, morality, constitutionality and balance of power, while the latter provides the key patterns that need to be renegotiated during order transition (e.g. economic and security-related rules, the underlying worldview, the special rights of great powers, agreement on key spheres of influence and on the overall balance of power). By conceptually adapting Clark's account, which is based on US hegemony, to the current order transition, its theoretical usefulness for analyzing the dynamics of systemic legitimacy is improved in three important and interrelated ways. The three are today's hybrid environment, common culture and effectiveness.

Chapters 3–5 provide conceptual explorations of these three variables, respectively.

Chapter 3 examines the notion of hybrid environment. This is critical since Clark's exclusively state-based understanding of the global environment does not reflect the hybrid realities that mark today's global order, that is, the existence of and tensions between solidarist global multi-level governance and more pluralist and increasingly salient great-power-based politics. It is assumed that the two cannot exist independently and thus cannot simply complement each other. Rather, they compete with each other for governance. This is because, as has been suggested, solidarist notions of global governance "will often depend on the willingness of particularly powerful states to promote them" (Hurrell 1999:291). The chapter, *firstly*, outlines why scholars have strongly committed themselves to the analysis of the role of Transnational Actors (TNAs), understood as a key part of the hybrid environment. *Secondly*, it more specifically examines how the degree of importance, which has widely been attached to TNAs, may be accounted for. The *third* and longest section takes the important results of transnational research as its starting point and, subsequently, raises the question of what exactly this importance, which the global governance literature has attributed to TNAs, means in relation to patterns of global order transition. In particular, two aspects are drawn out: their relation to the contested nature of the search for global legitimacy, as well as to power, understood as material inequalities, leadership and interests. The *fourth* section reviews the standard governance depiction of realist propositions. It identifies a weakness that flows directly from its focus on "access", presupposing well-functioning institutions while, consequently, overlooking the existing deadlocks in international politics. The key argument put forward is that the influence of non-state actors is dependent on a particular institutional context in which the key political questions framing a social order are settled. Large parts of the related literature on international institutions simply assume that this is the case. In contrast, this analysis suggests that, unless these framing patterns are agreed upon by major powers, the respective order and its elements (i.e. institutions and regimes) remain contested or deadlocked. When this happens, the political impact of non-state actors is largely neutralized or significantly weakened and their effective autonomy from great powers minimized. Such a broader perspective helps to explain why the existing literature on TNA influence in global governance, which sees "institutional access...as a central determinant of TNA influence" (Tallberg et al. 2013:50), has consistently overlooked the process of neutralization which this analysis, in contrast, has exposed. *Finally*, the conclusion links the findings back to Clark's model.

Chapter 4 revises Clark's original notion of morality. The *first* section reviews the arguments widely made to the effect that there is no need to contemplate the impact of distinct worldviews precisely because there is no ideological competition today. Following the refutation of this line of thinking, the *second* section begins by providing definitions of two concepts that are central to the chapter, that is, common culture and worldview. The following question is then raised: "What are the theoretical implications of a 'common culture' that is, to different degrees, no longer 'commonly accepted' by established and rising great powers?" In order to address this question, the section examines two aspects. It looks into the thus far underspecified dynamics of the relationship between the notions of worldview and common culture; next, it analyzes the underlying assumption that the nature of the common culture, as accepted by the predominant actor, remains basically unchanged over time. After this has exposed the role of exceptionalist worldviews more broadly, the *third* section looks into the actual nature of exceptionalist worldviews. As a first step, it provides a brief definition of the term. It then goes on to raise three conceptual questions that need to be engaged when comparing exceptionalist worldviews. In order to illustrate the importance of the empirical nature of this relationship, the key patterns of the United States' and China's worldviews are presented in the form of a brief comparative outline. The *fourth* section takes a close look at the implications of the relationship between the two exceptionalist worldviews for the notion of order transition. Against this backdrop, the question as to whether the exceptionalist nature of US and Chinese worldviews makes them incommensurable and, consequently, whether it renders peaceful order transition impossible is raised. The *conclusion* indicates the implications that the results of this chapter have for the revision of Clark's original model.

Chapter 5 rethinks the notion of effectiveness. Essentially, it addresses the shortcomings of Clark's understanding of effectiveness which is bound up with US hegemony. The *first* section scrutinizes a powerful historical myth that has, partly unwittingly, biased theoretical debates on hegemony. Its key assumption is that for the last 200 years the United Kingdom and the United States have acted as successive hegemons. A more accurate reading reveals the prevalence of collective hegemonies for most of the time. Debunking this myth informs the background of the conceptual analysis that follows. The *second* section sets out the key conceptual changes that help to revise Clark's idea of a prevailing single (US) hegemony. The first step is to break the central notion of power down into its materialist, social-relational and managerial components. The focus is then on the latter one, which is viewed as a subcategory of the relational component. An examination of the underlying assumptions of managerial theories shows that those theories have failed to address what is here introduced as the hierarchical relationship between the internal (among the great powers) and external (between the hegemons and the remainder of international society) layers of great-power management. Focusing on the former demonstrates two things. First, it shows that there are no special responsibilities without the agreement within the peer group. Second and related, it finds that an outstanding agreement on special responsibilities prevents any proper steering of international society as such. The *final* section shows how the new shape of effective management integrates formal and informal aspects of great-power politics. It highlights the operating contours of special responsibilities which occur in formal and informal shapes, regardless of the degree to which the respective environments are institutionalized or rule-based. The *conclusion* again indicates the implications that the results of this chapter have for the revision of Clark's original model.

Taken together, making these conceptual revisions is deemed necessary in order to carefully adapt Clark's original dynamic parameters of global legitimacy to a political environment that has undergone, and is still undergoing, fundamental changes.

Chapters 6–8 provide three case studies. The nature of the selected case studies is partly adopted from Gilpin's catalog of classic Westphalian patterns that are at stake when a contested order is being re-negotiated. They have gained renewed relevance. Partly, they go beyond Gilpin and include global public goods that have recently attained more salience. The cases illustrate the extent to which the parameters of Clark's revised model help to sharpen our understanding of the dynamics of order transition. The selection of the case studies is based on qualitative methodology (Gerring 2007).

Chapter 6 addresses some of the security-related rules of the contested order. In particular, it is interested in the re-negotiation of spheres of influence in East Asia. The political tensions, which have made a bargain between the United States and China thus far impossible, can be measured by the heightened difficulties that regional governance organizations (e.g. ASEAN) and international regimes (e.g. UNCLOS) have experienced in recent years. With regard to ASEAN, China has worked through the existing regional organizations in the South China Sea (SCS) and has employed its burgeoning economic power in order to gain leadership in the region. At the same time, however, it has partly undercut these attempts by conveying the message of an emerging military giant that uses intimidating measures toward its smaller neighbors. Consequently, many states in the region have strengthened their military links with the United States. At a fiercely contested summit in mid-2012, it turned out that the key dividing line among ASEAN members ran between those parties who backed China's position in the SCS and others who favored US support for their positions. As a result, after 45 years of existence, ASEAN had, uniquely, failed to produce a "consensual" communiqué that would have brought together all of its ten member states. Concerning UNCLOS, the main aim of this legal regime was to settle outstanding sea-based disputes between states. As the case study demonstrates, China has had manifold disputes about sovereign rights over various islands with smaller states in the SCS. Precisely because of the overarching US–China contest over maritime spheres in the region, their preferences for bilateral security treaties (US) and bilateral regional diplomacy (China) have undercut UNCLOS' rationale. Moreover, while the United States has never been a member of it, China's instrumental use of its membership was based on its opt-out option (Article 298), which it has used when smaller states, such as the Philippines, filed a case against it at the International Tribunal for the Law of the

Sea. Effectively, the war-prone great-power tensions about the SCS and ECS have come at the expense of the mediating functions of both governance institutions.

Chapter 7 extends the empirical analysis of classic Gilpinian patterns and looks at the re-negotiations taking place in relation to the environmental rules of the global order, as embodied in the climate regime (UNFCCC). The latter regime has equally suffered from the tensions underlying its negotiation. For instance, the Copenhagen summit in 2009 revealed the large degree to which the manifold initiatives, networks, market mechanisms, efforts of private governance and public–private partnership remained ineffective and have, partly therefore, led to the meager results of the summit. One of the deeper causes of the largely failed negotiations was that the Chinese side did not accept the underlying foundations of the negotiations. From their perspective, Copenhagen was not just about detailed standards of climate protection but an occasion where the "leadership" and the "new political and economic world order" as such were at stake. Thus, systemic reasons, such as power-related as well as worldview-based concerns, underpinned the Chinese position. With the United States remaining extremely hesitant about the promotion of any binding obligations concerning global governance, these issues only underlined and exacerbated the deadlocked nature of the regime.

Chapter 8 looks into the contested re-negotiations of the ideology/worldview underlying the international order. While ideology permeates the rationale of the first two cases as well, there is one main reason why the so-called Responsibility to Protect regime is here assumed to crystallize ideological differences and is, thus, used as a case study. Partly intended as such and, in turn, criticized for exactly the same reason, the liberal character of the regime clearly states what it deems "*good* governance" and what it does not in today's global politics. The rationale of the "Responsibility" is to identify a global framework that clearly establishes the responsibility of individual states toward their citizens as well as the responsibility of international society to address four crimes: crimes against humanity, genocide, war crimes and ethnic cleansing. Surprisingly, to those who had watched its universal adoption by the UN General Assembly in 2005 (including the United States and China), the contestation that has ensued concerning it, which has prevented the norm from becoming customary law, has not always confirmed the expected dividing line between liberal interventionists and autocratic guardians of sovereignty. Effectively, while the normative ambition of the norm affected some of the rhetoric used, most of the time the interpretations where driven by national interests and converged on the non-interventionist end.

Chapter 9 summarizes the key arguments made in the book. Crucially, it goes on to argue why the conventional research agenda on global governance has failed in light of the political dynamics of order transition and suggests which features may provide a more accurate characterization of future theoretical needs.

2
Order Transition, Systemic Legitimacy and Institutionalization

The structure of this chapter is as follows. The first section shows why existing theories have failed to account for both China's non-socialization and the United States' (and China's) evasion of enmeshment in global governance structures. The second section looks into the consequences of these failures, that is, the deadlocks prevailing on the global plane. It starts by offering a new theoretical interpretation of the recent financial crisis. It is suggested that, since China substituted for the United States, if temporarily, as the provider of global economic goods in late 2008, the maintaining of the system by an actor other than the incumbent hegemon needs to be viewed as a "turning point" or the functional equivalent to the end of a major war. The lack of effective voice opportunities, traditionally provided at peace conferences, has since led to China's new assertiveness and, in turn, further strengthened by US revisionism, to various US–China deadlocks. Liberal rationalist accounts readily admit their explanatory limits and refer back to the contested power structures. However, without adducing notions of world order, the current deadlocks cannot be explained. At the same time, this development highlights the United States' and China's exceptionalist worldviews during a period of order transition entailing considerable antagonistic potential. The third section identifies the notion of systemic legitimacy as a suitable theoretical framework to capture the (material and normative) contestation of the existing order. Ian Clark's and Robert Gilpin's complementary accounts serve as two theoretical starting points. The former explains the elements that shape the politics of legitimacy, referring to the dynamic interplay between the notions of legality, morality, constitutionality and balance of power, while the latter provides the key patterns that need to be renegotiated during order transition (e.g. economic and security-related rules, the underlying worldview, the special rights of great powers, agreement on key spheres of influence and on the overall balance of power). By conceptually adapting Clark's account, which is based on US hegemony, to the current order transition, its theoretical usefulness for analyzing the dynamics of systemic legitimacy is improved in three important and interrelated ways. The three are today's hybrid environment, common culture and effectiveness. The insertions advance the scope of Clark's original variables and, consequently, feed back into the dynamics characterizing their relations to one another.

The failures of socialization and enmeshment

The following section examines those liberal and constructivist theoretical frameworks that have been thought to explain major trends in international politics of the last 20 years. Theories of socialization are only applied to China, while theories of enmeshment and constitutionalization are applied to both China and the United States. The section makes two larger points. Firstly, it provides an answer as to why those theories have failed to predict China's non-socialization. Secondly, it shows that theories of enmeshment have not been able to account for either why the United States has not been drawn more deeply into existing governance structures or why China's interests and its identity have not been redefined during this process. As will be shown in the following, "on balance", the two states have added a degree of cynicism as to "the willingness of both to accept global normative frameworks as legitimate standards of appropriate behavior" (Foot and Walter 2011:23). Several brief empirical examples illustrate the failures, respectively.

Socialization is here understood as the process of "taking on the identities and interests of the dominant peer group in international society" based on endogenous, suasion-induced identity change (Barnett 2006:268; Wendt 1994:384; Checkel 2005:804).[1] This reflects, as Johnston put it, "essentially, the claim made by those promoting the 'sociological turn'" (2008:xiv). To begin with, the still "dominant" (Hurrell 2006:6) IR theories of the 1990s and 2000s became preoccupied with the question of how norm- and institution-based theories could account for the socialization and institutional enmeshment of the former Warsaw Pact states into the Western order. Since the "last 20 years of liberal dominance in world politics" (Keohane 2012:127) have been critical for the outlook of IR theory, theories of socialization and enmeshment (and, concomitantly, of good governance) have been predicated on the unspoken assumption that the accompanying processes are unilinear and have followed a normatively progressive path (Finnemore and Sikkink 1998:904, 907).[2] Importantly, the differences between "leverage over weak and developing states" in Eastern Europe after the demise of the Soviet Union, on the one hand, and over rising great powers in the developing world, on the other, were thus not taken into account (Finnemore and Sikkink 1998:900). This occurred despite increasingly visible structural inequalities between the two groups due to, for instance, China's much earlier embrace of capitalism in the 1970s. Partly as a consequence of adopting the same frameworks for the analysis of both sets of states, mainstream theories have mistakenly predicted the successful socialization of rising powers into the existing order. This also reveals the extent to which earlier understandings derived from dependency/world-systems theories of world politics, which presumed that great powers existed only in the Western world and, thus, "unavoidably reflect(ed) a culturally determined view of what is important in international relations", have become a theoretical legacy that has not yet adapted itself to a new environment (Smith 1999:109).

More specifically, constructivist theories have been characterized by the attribution of a large degree of passivity to the socializee, which both explains the lack of agency attributed to them and, relatedly, the underlying assumption of unilinear norm development (Terhalle 2011:345).[3] This is remarkable in the case of social constructivism which, since the end of the Cold War, has ontologically argued for a greater role of agency in IR theory. Wendt argues that "actors acquire identities – relatively stable, role-specific understandings and expectations about self – by participating in collective meanings" (1992:397). Scholars using this theoretical lens for their analysis of China, therefore, focus on "institutional environments where the institution itself or actors within it try to transmit to new members the predominant norms of the structure" (Johnston 2008:17). Wendt's "participating" in international organizations (IOs) does not anticipate, however, that an agent would at first accept the norms put in front of him because he has no other choice or for instrumental reasons, but anticipates that after a while, potentially after an increase in material power, he would change his identity over time without showing the expected and self-sustaining signs of socialization at a later stage. China's evolution from the 1970s to 2012, though, appears to reflect just that (Narlikar 2010: 71). Striving to become a member of international organizations and regimes at first, then partly internalizing some of the prevailing norms but, eventually, becoming much more powerful, so that it is now in a position to choose what is (and what is not) in its interest (to internalize), seems to be turning Finnemore's and Sikkink's (1998:895) cascade model upside down.[4] This is confirmed by a senior diplomat suggesting that "the strong Chinese nationalism, that has re-occurred, has not emerged from a post-colonial or poverty-driven attitude decrying injustice in the world. Much rather, its powerful re-assertion of its own comeback points to the forceful process of re-establishing a status in the international system that, in effect, belongs to China naturally."[5] This narrative of "restoration" has occurred despite the fact that China has become a member of over 100 inter-governmental organizations and signatory of some 300 international treaties, as the former head of the Chinese Foreign Ministry's policy planning staff recently insisted (Le Yucheng 2011).

These arguments play into a broader debate contesting the validity of socialization which is "central to constructivists" and "the one process concept in IR that is uniquely constructivist" (Johnston 2008:xvi). Epstein has pointed out that IR theory has, essentially, framed out the socializee. By allowing socialization only to "runin one direction: from the socializer to the socializee", it cuts out other parts of the process that were originally conceptualized in a two-way sense (Epstein 2012:140; Terhalle 2011). As Epstein argues, conventional constructivism assumes that "the socializee, like the child, holds no prior legitimate identity" (2012:142). In other words, one could argue that Johnston's application of constructivist theories to institutional settings does not sufficiently take into account that the latter are based on assumptions derived from analyses of cooperation among "like-minded" and "advanced industrialized states", as Keohane had stated earlier (1984:246, 247).[6] As a result, meshing notions of one-way socialization into an institutionalist, that is OECD-based, environment has often proved to work (though not anymore today), since the actors under consideration have been what Dennis Wrong has called "oversocialized" states (1999; Mayntz 2008:48) in a homogenous system (Aron 1966).[7] Moreover, if institutions prescribe any rules of obligation and, in turn, help to socialize actors into them, existing constructivist theories accept, wittingly or unwittingly, that the status quo provides precisely the standards according to which it is to be judged. In other words, "[t]he degree to which the frame itself is part of the problem is occluded by commitment to the chosen institutional path within it" (Koskenniemi 2011:323). To a large extent, this explains why the constructivist notion of socialization cannot account for China's reflective agency deviating from the predicted path.

Early on, social constructivists began studying the then emerging process of informalization in international politics. They pointed to informal groupings that had grown up around international institutions to show that it was precisely such "informal interactions" that provided "the structural preconditions for discursive and argumentative processes" (Risse 2000:16). Since then the informal interactions between old and new actors as well as those solely among new actors have intensified, albeit at different degrees, neither level implying sustained cooperative efforts but rather ad-hoc consultations (Daase 2009; Prantl 2006). Informal groupings are characterized by their (state-) power-based and exclusionary character. Forming these groupings presents in itself a form of power since it is based on the decision of who is included and who is not (Gruber 2005). In sharp contrast to constructivist assumptions, some informal non-Western groups such as the BRICS and BASIC, in which China has assumed the default leadership position, are marked by their sheer material weight and interest-based outlook (Hallding et al. 2011). It remains difficult to imagine how constructivist processes of deliberation and persuasion can be reconciled with these club- and interest-based approaches to global politics. It is far from obvious what the new groups have in common with the disaggregate views of the state which underlie liberal and constructivist approaches (Moravcsik 2003).[8]

Relatedly, institutional enmeshment (Goh 2007–8:121) is a theoretical framework that aims at a "process of engaging with a state so as to draw it into deep involvement into international and regional society, enveloping it in a web of sustained exchanges and relationships, with the long-term goal of integration. In the process, the target state's interests are redefined, and its identity possibly altered, so as to take into greater account the integrity and order of the system." Empirical examples can be drawn from the climate regime, global aid regime as well as from Asian regionalism in order to illustrate the failure of enmeshment's theoretical assumptions.

Firstly, what enabled China, together with the other states of the BASIC group it had convened at a pre-summit held in Beijing in November 2009, to refuse its agreement to the climate negotiations at Copenhagen, after the host had put forward new guidelines regarding carbon emissions, was the increased material power it brought to the negotiation table. In effect, what drove the Chinese to reject the Danish proposal was their determined interest in furthering their coal-driven economic growth, based, domestically, on their so-called "no-regrets" reductions (Conrad 2012:446) approach. At the same time, since continued economic growth is the key to the security of China's regime, concerns related to domestic social stability and poverty reduction played into this decision as well. This was the essential reason why the ministry of state security, with its "more nationalistic... officials", instead of the "pro-détente foreign ministry", was leading the negotiations in Copenhagen (Economist 2010). Taken together, this accounts for why the US president, rather restrained about this global governance issue in the first place, was not, late at night, in a position to press the high goals set by Western states. Secondly, China lent more money (110 billion USD) to developing countries between 2008 and 2010 than the World Bank (100 billion USD) in the same period (Dyer and Anderlini 2011). Despite its self-perceived status as a Third World country, though this is increasingly doubted by Western states and the World Bank, and its support for G77 states, such a policy serves China's interests well, because it helps to extract natural resources, for instance, in Africa and elsewhere. Notwithstanding the fact that the policy often contains side-payments to secure smaller states' loyalty for its cause elsewhere, for instance, at the United Nations (Economist 2012),[9] China's approach to delivering foreign aid has meant the "effective breakdown of the global aid regime" (Hurrell 2010:14). Thirdly, whereas the 1990s and 2000s used to be considered a period of irreversible ascent of Asian regional integration, for example, ASEAN, this perception has now drastically changed. Based on its immense material growth, China has begun to claim the South and East China Seas as an integral part of its national interests. Thus, when China's foreign minister, Yang Jiechi, was confronted with accusations from regional states that Beijing's assertiveness was not conducive to building trust in its intentions, he replied quite frankly (Economist 2012): "China is a big country and other countries are small countries and that is just a fact."[10] Naturally, such thinking has come at the expense of, respectively, the UN Law of the Sea Convention, the right of smaller states to self-determination and, critically, long-standing efforts to promote Asian regionalism, embodied in, for instance, ASEAN.

Against this backdrop, it is critical to understand how enmeshment's most prolific adherents argue in its favor. John Ikenberry, for instance, has argued for more than a decade that the "American-led open-democratic political order", offering "public good provision, rule-based cooperation, and voice opportunities and diffuse reciprocity" (2011:161; 2001), has been the most successful source of enmeshment since the end of World War II. In his recent work, he has refined the concept and applied it to China. Convinced that the US order is "easy to join, but hard to overturn" (2011:9), he anticipates that countries such as China will demand more voice opportunities in some of today's critical organizations. In his view, the only way of getting there is enmeshment.

Essentially, the idea behind it boils down to (2009:93) "ultimately only one path to modernity – and that is... essentially liberal in character".[11] If this is the case, one may inquire, exactly how are rising powers to be included in international organizations and regimes if the "ultimate guardian", comprising a "liberal complex of states", is, according to Ikenberry, necessary to protect "the rules, institutions, and progressive purposes of the liberal order" (2011:10)? This line of argument points to Ikenberry's (Keohane's, Buchanan's, Slaughter's, Daalder's and Bobbitt's) underlying support for a league of democracies equipped with a sanctions regime similar to that of the UNSC. Inevitably, under the conditions set by Ikenberry, the question as to how open the "unusually integrative" order really is (2011:9) arises. In essence, the durability of the order Ikenberry defends is put into question today if it is based on the terms outlined by him (2011:333–360). Similar to global governance accounts that theorize in terms of global public goods but have not answered the question who comprises this "public" for which these goods are designed (Avant et al. 2011:365–367),[12] and which tend to overlook the inequalities of power permeating the distribution of the respective goods (Mayntz 2008:55–58), Ikenberry fails to provide an answer to a critical question that he nonetheless accurately poses: "who precisely is the international community" (2011:250)? In fact, he takes the existing order too much for granted and sees it as being beyond critique. What his account conceals, therefore, is that "[b]ehind the conventional law..., there is a whole world order, a system of empowering some and disempowering other institutions" (Koskenniemi 2011:324).[13] Regardless of whether or not it is believed that China can be enmeshed in the institutionalized setting in one way or another, here it is argued that time has already passed this stage.

For its part, the United States, never hesitant to apply its revolutionary foreign policy tradition, if deemed necessary to preserve its sovereignty, has resisted the processes of enmeshment (Hurrell 2007:67) in order to retain its freedom to act and, thus, to maintain the conditions that favor its worldview based on "just *dis*equilibrium".[14] In fact, the official guidelines of the US National Security Strategy made it abundantly clear that the (any) administration would not tie its search for effectiveness and the protection of its interests to international regimes and institutions, since "no international order can be supported by international institutions alone"; this is exactly why the United States could not only "simply be working inside formal institutions and frameworks" (2010:40–41). In addition to common great-power practices such as unilateral disengagement, creating new institutions, switching allegiance to an alternative regime or informalizing international organizations, the United States has taken advantage of, for instance, the undisputed growing thickness of international economic regimes. Thus, when US preferences in negotiating the TRIPS (Agreement on Trade-Related Aspects of Intellectual Property Rights) regime at the World Trade Organization (WTO)were not met, it chose, joined by the European Union (Drezner 2007:215), "to export their regulatory preferences through bilateral and regional free trade agreements". Thus, theories of enmeshment have overlooked the possibility of great powers "to engage in forum-shopping to select the optimal IGO to advance their preferences" (ibid.:86).[15] Equally, the United States has built informal ways of channeling power in the case of the International Monetary Fund (IMF) in order to compensate for its increasingly limiting percentage of voting rights (Stone 2011). Finally, the interventionist-state impetus underlying much of the history of (global) governance theories further undermines the likelihood that it will find acceptance in US domestic politics – in contrast to US support for such measures abroad (Mayntz 2008:47; Rabkin 2005:ch. 2).

Thus far the analysis has revealed the failure of the notions of socialization and enmeshment since 2008. In addition to the variables already mentioned, the notion of power requires further explanation. Firstly, some general disciplinary shortcomings have caused the aforementioned failures. Many views of non-neorealist scholars on the notion of power have been shaped by Waltz' focus on military capabilities. After the Cold War, when the probability of a great-power war substantially decreased, it became a foregone conclusion that the concept of security was of little use in the twenty-first century. Moving away from the state-based focus on military security, the attention of many scholars shifted, for instance, toward human security (Barnett and Sikkink 2008:67; Teitel 2011).[16] A – natural – development toward exploring new theoretical grounds, thus, initiated the withdrawal of "explicit and systematic attention to power . . . from . . . analyses of global governance" (Barnett and Duvall 2005:7). Thus, while the literature on (Hurrell 2010:7) "[g]overnance focused on the identification of collective action problems and on the question of how global public goods are to be provided . . . the alternative view was sidelined", that is, "seeing governance as concerned with the ordering and preservation of power and with answers to the question who exercises power, on whose behalf and to whose detriment".[17] However, these insights precisely reflect some of the United States' and China's power-related concerns about global politics today. It is difficult to imagine, therefore, how those deliberations can be explained by reference to a discourse free of domination (Habermas 1992). Secondly, despite being often neglected by conventional theories, neorealism's understanding of material power remains critical. It is precisely because economic globalization has increased existing inequalities that China has benefited from it and that, consequentially, their impact on global politics has grown extensively (Waltz 2008; Ravenhill 2013:183; Gruber 2011). Based on its structural power, its new role as a powerful veto-player reflects its interests and, in turn, shows the influence of domestic constituencies and their non-Western worldview. As for the United States, while it embodies the liberal values system underlying the current order, its structural power, domestic resistance against deeper enmeshment and the perception of its competition with China have contributed to the failure of the conventional theoretical predictions.

In contrast to Ikenberry (2011), who believes that the US order will essentially remain the same since it is "easy to join", to Jacques (2011), who anticipates, after a supposedly inevitable change of hegemons, a time "when China rules the world", and to Schweller (2011a:285), who asks "what sort of global order will emerge on the other side of the transition from unipolarity to multipolarity?", the next section is more modestly interested in the consequences of the above-outlined failures.

Consequences of the failures: Deadlocks reflecting a contested order

The section begins by taking a novel look at the systemic meaning of the recent financial crisis for the status of rising powers and explores its theoretical implications for the extent of the contestation of the current order. The deadlocks that have evolved between the United States and China have been further exacerbated by the lack of effective voice opportunities given to Beijing in the aftermath of the crisis. This is illustrated by drawing on examples from the climate regime, Asian regionalism, the IMF and the WTO.[18] The section then shows why conventional accounts, basing their arguments solely on material self-interest, have failed to account for the variety of those deadlocks, which have persisted despite increased material incentives for China. Although (US) liberal worldviews are deeply embedded in institutionalist theories, they are not problematized, but rather given a fixed and exclusionary character. This is well known. However, by spelling out the underlying notion of global order, the respective theories are pressed to recognize their inherent limitations which, in turn, drive the analysis into a new direction. In essence, these analytical considerations prepare the ground for a more thorough theory of systemic legitimacy outlined in the last section of this chapter.

To begin with, why is a new perspective on the theoretical meaning of the financial crisis deemed necessary? There are two branches of the Hegemonic Stability Theory. Notwithstanding the detailed criticisms the Hegemonic Stability Theory (HST) has undergone, for instance, whether the hegemon is rather self-interested while providing the global economic order or whether it adopts a truly collective stance toward goods (Norloff 2010; Calleo 1987; Ikenberry 2011), the position of the provider underpinning the order has conventionally been seen as a *steady* one.

This is what is assumed today as well. But what if the provider is – even temporarily – incapable of materially underpinning the order? This is precisely what occurred in the fall of 2008.[19] With China spending some 600 billion USD or four trillion yuan as a domestic stimulus, its economic policies assumed systemic importance and, thereby, prevented the world economy from crumbling (Lebow and Reich 2014; Noesselt 2012).[20] Its export-dependent economy reached a growth rate of 9.1% the following year (Huang 2010:39), while the US foreign secretary had to make the humbling request in 2009 that the Chinese government continue buying US Treasury bills (FT February 22, 2009). What does that mean for the status of other actors that can substitute for the material underpinnings and thereby prevent the order from collapsing? Regardless of whether it did so for reasons of domestic regime security, ultimately, the accomplishment of the system's maintenance equaled China's tacit recognition as a great power (Buzan 2004).[21] But when and how can a new great power stake its claims effectively? Conventional wisdom largely considers wars the most important expressions of "turning points" (Nye 2011:215–216). It has, thus, been widely taken for granted that the absence of a war and, subsequently, "no general meeting of states to remake the institutions of public life" (Kennedy 1994:334), that is, an "ordering moment", imply that there is no need to renegotiate the "basic rules of the system". As was shown, however, the near dysfunction of the system and inability of the incumbent provider to fulfill its responsibilities, if temporarily, can be seen as the functional equivalent to the end of a major war. It is therefore suggested that the maintaining of the system by an actor other than the incumbent or perceived hegemon needs to be viewed, in analogy, as a turning point.[22] The lack of effective voice opportunities, that is, first-order negotiations, traditionally provided at peace conferences (which sometimes follow turning points), has since led to China's new assertiveness (Kissinger 2011:500–501). Ignited by the financial crisis, powerful demands for developing a new bargain of the international order can thus be discerned in various US–China deadlocks. Four brief examples may illustrate this.

To begin with, ASEAN, until recently thought of as one of the paradigmatic examples of the notion of regionalism (Acharya and Johnston 2007; Ba 2009), has had to succumb to the increased tensions between China and the United States. Both the United States and China have reasserted themselves and conceive of the South/East China Sea as their spheres of influence, respectively. Implicitly marking out room for Chinese demands for regional primacy, General Yao Yunzhu of the Chinese Academy of Military Science suggested (Economist 2012:28): "The international military order is US-led – NATO and Asian bilateral alliances – there is nothing like the WTO for China to get into." This is why China has opened a vast naval base, for instance, on Hainan Island in the South China Sea. America responded to China's regional assertiveness, beginning in 2009, by reiterating its determination to stay in the region and considering it part of its vital interests, for example, reestablishing (Cold War) naval bases in the Subic Bay (Philippines) and in the Cam Ranh Bay (Vietnam), stationing US troops in Australia and coastal battleships in Singapore. This has reinforced the prevalence of power-based thinking and, thereby, promoted the notion of bilateralism. Moreover, both China and the United States have further entrenched this state of affairs by strengthening their respective bilateral military alliances and using foreign aid as side-payments to secure loyalty (Nye 2011:227). Secondly, the IMF is, roughly speaking, in charge of macroeconomic management among industrialized countries and the pursuit of market-oriented economic reforms in the non-capitalist world. Regarding the former, China's domestic currency policy is focused on the key goal of its "stability" and has consequently led it to undervalue the Yuan. Seeing the Yuan's exchange rate as a core domestic affair has made it impossible to translate US demands for more transparency into practice (Huang 2010:36). This has led to economic disadvantages for other large economies, for instance, the United States. As a result, the strongly diverging views of the United States and China on how to resolve their currency disputes have stalled the debates on macroeconomic policies and have made the newly set up "G20 irrelevant"; critically, it has revealed the inherent limits to the IMF's enforcement capabilities at times of protracted great-power disagreement, that is, its "essential helplessness" (James 2011:535; Bremmer and Roubini 2011).[23] In other words, while the G20 could successfully press for a revision of the rules for global banks via the Financial Stability Board (FSB), that is, Basel III, the limits of the IMF's (and the FSB's) accepted and institutional authority to assert compliance could not overcome US–Chinese differences regarding global financial policies (CIGI 2100:26; Stone 2011). Concerning the IMF's policies toward the developing world, the model prevailing thus far (and preferred by the United States) has lost its monopoly of socio-economic development. China's own economic success, its handing-out of loans without conditionality and the United States' own economic downturn after 2008 have increased the appeal of non-Western ways of socio-economic reform among Third World states. This development has played into above's debates at the IMF and has, consequently, further exacerbated its deadlock. Taken together, whereas the core point of contestation thus far has been the extent and mode according to which the IMF and the World Bank have promoted neoliberal policies, today's dispute runs much deeper, because it puts into question the IMF's overall capability to provide the sole global framework for lending policies. Thirdly, with the US holding the largest number of voting rights and, conversely, with China assuming a more defiant stance since 2008, for instance, rejecting the Lamy package, the WTO's Doha trade negotiations have now stalled completely. This state of affairs was reinforced when an "absolute deadline", set for December 31, 2011, was missed (Conceicao-Heldt 2011). This is not to say that another important factor, such as the Doha round's outdated structure, has not played a role in this (Economist 2012:10). Accordingly, leading practitioners of global governance have recently stressed this development away from the 17-year-old WTO structure (CIGIa 2011). This shift is accompanied by developed economies increasingly engaging in trade-block negotiations with each other, as well as with rising powers, such as India, outside the framework of the WTO (ibid.:12). Both reflecting the dysfunction of the WTO, on the one hand, and the emerging contestation about the economic organization of (not yet delineated) key spheres of influence, on the other, the United States has been keen on negotiating a free-trade agenda via the planned Trans-Pacific Partnership with countries of the region since December 2009 (e.g. Singapore, Chile, New Zealand, Brunei, Australia, Peru and Vietnam). Meanwhile, China has similarly pursued a regional trade agreement around ASEAN, that is, the China–ASEAN Free Trade Agreement. In fact, the WTO deadlock reveals the fundamentally political contestation underlying the US–Chinese tensions. Their irreducibly normative and material substance was anticipated early on by a Chinese ambassador negotiating the accession terms: "We know we have to play the game your way now, but in ten years we will set the rules" (quoted in Schweller and Pu 2011:54). This line may not describe today's reality in entirely accurate terms. However, it highlights the perceived need for the renegotiation of the international order. Finally, concerning the impact of the US–China relationship on the overall usefulness of the WTO' Dispute Settlement Body (DSB), the United States' response to perceived violations of WTO rules on the part of China is not forwarded to the DSB. This is because "companies worry they will face retribution from China's government if they provide evidence against it in a trade case" (Economist 2011b:54–55). Instead, according to a high-ranking US trade negotiator, America "often pushes back bilaterally rather than in Geneva" (ibid.:54). Taken together, the US–Chinese disagreement on how to resolve the respective issues presents the underlying stumbling block for progress.

Looking at these deadlocks, liberal rationalist theorists readily admit that their theories of institution-/regime-based cooperation have reached their limits and, consequently, they refer back to underlying power structures. They are therefore led to insist that the key explanation for today's central problems can only be found in "a greater divergence of interests, weighted by power" (Keohane 2012:125) since "as the distribution of tangible resources...becomes more equal, international regimes...weaken" (Keohane 1989:78). Accordingly, changes in material power *alone* can account for the current state of affairs. At first sight, the aforementioned examples appear to confirm such thinking. And yet, the underlying notion of material power is too narrow to account for why China shows little compliance with its obligations to some of the institutions and regimes of which it became a member some time ago. Most conspicuously, even though Beijing has been offered more voting rights in the WTO and the IMF, it has not changed its attitude toward the institutions.[24] Referring back to the socializee's supposed passivity, this is precisely why many observers consider it (Yongjin 2008:162) "anachronistic and even pretentious to continue to assume that rising China needs to be given a place in the new global international society". Both pointing to a deeper layer of the contestation of the order and to a broader understanding of the notion of power, notions of worldview need to be adduced to prepare a fuller answer, which will reflect the distinct historico-cultural value set underpinning the nature of China's agency or, at least, its predominant narrative. The concept of worldview is here understood as the "actors' understanding of international politics and the ways in which these understandings have been gathered into intelligible patterns, traditions, or ideologies" (Hurrell 2007:17; Osterhammel 2012).

The notion of worldview permeates, largely unnoticed, all global public goods debates. In the case of climate change, for instance, it may be said that China's position in Copenhagen did not only result from its interests not being sufficiently taken into account, or from the more restrained attitude shown by the United States (although that, too, played a role). Rather, the underlying reason for why, as one Chinese top delegate put it, the politics underlying the negotiations were "much more important" than the climate regime itself can be found in its worldview (Economist 2011a). In other words, the historico-ideological backdrop, against which the negotiations evolved, is crucial and will be briefly outlined here. Based on the widely shared historical narrative of the century of humiliation, beginning with the Opium Wars in 1839, Chinese officials and (a majority of) Chinese scholars constantly "worry that the US has a hidden agenda to prevent China from rising as a peer power" (Suisheng 2008). This is "how China sees America" (Nathan and Scobell 2012) and is the driving force behind its fear of international containment which has – to varying degrees – permeated Chinese approaches to international politics and global governance, especially since its reentry into international politics in 1971. Today, however, this attitude is combined with the material power to refuse cooperation. While such a proposition could also be read as a standard realist argument of defending one's interests, what distinguishes it from such a reading is that Beijing has molded its historical experiences into its approach to world order. Precisely because the views prevailing in China present it as a victim of Western great powers, it sees itself as a "global moral pole leading the people of the world in a better direction" (Friedman 2011:19). Hence, Chinese diplomats constantly remind their US counterparts that they are deeply committed to G77 states. Overall, as the United States has condensed its founding experience and the principles underpinning its constitution into its own notion of exceptionalism, so too has China attached a morally superior worldview to its foreign policy. Moreover, as is the case with the United States, combined with its sheer size has come a large degree of insularity as well as patronizing behavior toward smaller states, for instance, at Copenhagen – despite its G77 commitment (Friedman 2011:23). Finally, similarly to the United States, some proponents of the Chinese view of world order equate its own interests with the global public interest, propelled by notions of supreme Chinese virtue/morality and harmony (Xuetong 2011).

At Copenhagen, the more nationalistic forces, ultimately determining China's position, were echoed, among others, by Ma Xiajun, professor of strategic studies at the Chinese Communist Party's (CCP) central committee. He stressed that Copenhagen was mainly about what the "leadership" and the overall shape of the "new political and economic world order" (SWP 2010:1–2) should look like. His views are part of a powerful Chinese and, by extension, Chinese-American, discourse. Its dramatic impact is well documented by Henry Kissinger's pointed public intervention that "conflict is a choice, not a necessity" (2012). This Chinese discourse (Callahan 2012:50; Yongjin and Buzan 2012; Kissinger 2011:504–513; Noesselt 2010) "is not simply a scholarly debate because Sino-speak is heavily promoted by government officials, state media, and official intellectuals in China". The view is based on China's economic rise and rereads the American worldview on its own terms. "While the Asian century looked to Asian values to explain the region's growth, Sino-speak takes economic strength for granted and looks to culture to explain war, peace, and world order" (Callahan 2012:51). Fusing together Chinese "civil and military values", Sino-speak "discards the network-based logic of globalization . . . to assert a sharp geopolitical vision of the world instead" (ibid.). From this view, the "Sinocentric neo-tributary system [is] now challenging the Westphalian system to rewrite the wrongs of China's Century of National Humiliation (1840–1949). Likewise . . . the China model challenges the American dream in grand civilizational competition. . . . Eurocentrism is replaced by Sinocentrism, Westernization is replaced by Easternization, and American exceptionalism is replaced by Chinese exceptionalism" (ibid.; Friedman 2011:24–25). Evidence of this new discourse as part of official Chinese thinking is provided by a leaked conversation between Beijing's Vice Foreign Minister Chun Yung-woo and the US Ambassador to China Kathleen Stephens. In the discussion, the Chinese chief negotiator for North Korea was said to present, according to the Chinese Minister, views which depict China's "economic rise" as a "return to normalcy with China as a great world power" (WikiLeaks 2010).

Thus, regardless of how little appeal such a worldview might have to others, because of its centrality to Chinese domestic debates, it can be argued that international politics is not only experiencing a power-related contestation in a material sense, as rationalist theorists argue. It is also about meshing non-Western worldviews into a ground that is traditionally regarded in most IR mindsets as Western. The work of Keohane, an eminent institutionalist thinker of the present, shows the inevitable difficulties when confronted with the question of why conventional wisdom has failed to determine more precisely the nature of the current deadlocks. A few remarks might suffice. Keohane (2012:126) attributes a (non-material) social purpose to rationalist institutionalist theory, that is, the latter's social purpose is "to promote beneficial aspects on human security, human welfare and human liberty as a result of a more peaceful, prosperous and free world". Identifying such a value-based framework as underlying his rationalist approach reveals the supposedly uncontested and non-material substructure taken for granted by his approach (Amadae 2003). More importantly, though, by suggesting that the core of today's problems can only be found in the current changes in material power he accurately reintroduces the notion of power to the debate and thereby moves beyond large parts of the global governance literature, which has neglected this critical variable, as stated above. Consequently, neoliberal institutionalism is (re)united with its neo-realist sibling. Nevertheless, by singling out material power as the sole variable determining his analysis, he precludes an institutionalist understanding that is sensitive to the impact which different sets of values and historical memories might have.[25] Accordingly, any contestation of the order must be understood as power-related and occurring within the framework set by Western values. Curiously, in an essay from 1988 (165), Keohane had acknowledged that institutions were "constrained by the practices taken for granted by their members", which could be found "at a more fundamental and enduring level". That these practices have been shaped – now and then – by more than purely power-based concerns, that is, that they have been embedded in liberal practices in his case, and thus may be contested (today), remains unexplored. Unsurprisingly, Keohane has recently (re)confirmed the a-priori-second-image-based nature of his understanding of systemic legitimacy which has supposedly set the parameter for the debate. In other words, it is the "ongoing consent of democratic states" that ensures the legitimacy of global governance institutions (2006:415). In other words, without any change, Keohane's "most advanced industrialised" and "like-minded" countries (1984:246, 247) continue to represent the worldview that, in his eyes, almost naturally underlies today's multilateralism (as well as theories of collection action). The possible implication that cooperation worked because it was dominated by Western states and that this same logic might explain why this is increasingly not the case today is not explored. Thereby, China notwithstanding, he overlooks the fact that democratic states such as Brazil and India have been among the most vocal ones in resisting the Unites States in multilateral fora in recent years (Narlikar 2010). In this respect, he still clings to Ikenberry's description of the rationale behind multilateralism (2011:186): "The principles of liberal order would be global and universal, but the most important commitments and core institutions would be established within the West." In other words, today's broadening of the scope of actors in global multilateralism and the distinct worldviews that they bring with them have challenged the respective theories as well as multilateralism more specifically. Precisely for this reason, it is not quite clear why, according to Keohane, there should be only one immaterial framework of reference, even if one doubts the viability of the aforementioned Sino-speak worldview.[26]

In any event, in order to underline the liberal rationalist framework, it is furthermore often argued that there is only one universal set of values in world politics, while no competing universal set is available, as the quick demise of the debate on the Asian century and values in the late 1990s supposedly showed. Reflecting its undiminished endurance, several members of the Obama administration as well as other leading Western politicians have repeated this claim (Rudd 2012:9). For instance, Hillary Clinton (Economist 2012c) stressed the essence of US diplomacy, which is "when it's all stripped away, it's (about) American values". There is a degree of a circular logic to the argument, though. Both, understanding its own origins as universal in a classical Hartzian sense (Foley 2011:40)[27] and unwittingly pursuing a Cold-War-inspired search for a universal counter-set of values inherently prevent theorists from recognizing a distinct set of values. Jervis provides one example. By looking for a "*comprehensive* alternative" (2009:202) he misses the point that the global acceptance of capitalism does by no means imply political coherence with Western policies. From a historical perspective, it could be argued that what the Islamic Republic of Iran unsuccessfully tried to achieve, though in a non-capitalist approach, may have been accomplished by China's "unsuccessful modernization" (Westad 2006:33)[28]: the spread of a powerful Westphalian message of "national particularism, international ideological pluralism, state sovereignty, strong-state involvement, and indigenous cultural development" (Gat 2010:82). This is why, as the Chinese debate shows, its underlying worldviews cannot be assumed away. In turn, this development points to two exceptionalist worldviews at a time of order transition that both contain some antagonistic potential.

Advocates of the global rule of law have made rather more progress than their liberal institutionalist colleagues. But, their underlying theory fails, similarly to Keohane's, as they admit, when faced with the "more fundamental multi-dimensional fragmentation of global society itself" (Peerenboom et al. 2012:322). To begin with, they have come to realize that "efforts to create an international order that comports with the image of domestic liberal democratic rule of law writ large", that is, attempts at constitutionalizing world politics "grounded in shared fundamental values", have been unsuccessful (ibid.:316, 317). It is precisely because, as they acknowledge, the "rule of law diffusion . . . raises challenging questions about world order" that they now feel the urge "to try a radically different approach that does not begin with domestic rule of law as the model for rule of law at the international level" (ibid.:316, 317). Nevertheless, it is hard to believe that their liberal conceptualization can retain its original character if it is to be based "on the notion that different forms of political authority require different sources of legitimacy" (ibid.:318).[29]

Order transition and bargained consensus

What do these findings imply? It can now safely be said that the opportunity, which the "turning point" of the financial crisis offered, was missed in 2008–9. In a sense, it represents what the renowned international historian A.J.P. Taylor called "a turning point in history when history failed to turn" (Economist April 13, 2013:74). In turn, this has exacerbated the manifold impasses in international negotiations which have been triggered by China's material growth and the competition between the United States and China. As was shown in the first section, theories of socialization and enmeshment have, largely, failed because the status quo of the international order, on whose constancy they depend, has changed in systemic ways. Keohane's acknowledgement in the second section that institutionalist theories have reached their limits, precisely because they cannot accommodate structural changes, leads his rationalist approach to refer back to material power structures. While such advice is accurate to some extent (but has been overlooked by the theories reviewed in the first section), it singles out one level of analysis at the expense of other, systemic, levels and does not give an account of how the two sets might be interrelated. This is why the analysis now needs to shift its focus away from conventional views, in particular from the prevailing liberal institutionalist view, since its legitimacy concerns are inherently limited to "sectoral publics" (Zürn 2010:740). Consequently, the latter perspective is less useful here since, as global goods theorists admit, at "the global level[.] most judgments of what is desirable can only be the result of a *political process*, given the tremendous disparities in living conditions and value systems that exist" (Kaul et al. 1999:6). Thus, instead of an institutionalist or regime view, a systemic order perspective will be adopted, which helps to shift the attention to the underlying dynamics of the political contestation during order transition.

This theoretical shift is partly derived from Gamble's suggestion of a conceptual distinction between first- and second-order negotiations (2011:36). Precisely because the locus of the manifold deadlocked negotiations is situated in issue-specific negotiations, it is important to identify some of the "deeper and more lasting causes" of why these negotiations have stalled in the first place (Narlikar 2011:15). This distinction is useful in an analytical sense while not overlooking the manifold layers of negotiations occurring in global multi-level governance (Zürn 2010). The latter are, despite their varying shapes, here attributed to Gamble's second-order category since they all relate in one way or another to one, or more, of the different issue-specific regimes. His first-order negotiations "concern the basic rules of the system and whether or not these are still legitimate or effective in securing the objectives for which they were instituted" (2011:36). Second-order negotiations, in contrast, "emerge within negotiations over particular issues, such as trade or climate" (ibid.; Buzan 1993). Gamble's distinction resembles in many ways the one made earlier by Wolfers (1962:73) between "milieu goals" (i.e. first-order goals) and "possession goals" (i.e. second-order goals).

The analysis proceeds by taking three steps. Firstly, it outlines the main features of the English School framework, since it usefully captures Gamble's aforementioned distinction. Secondly, the works of two authors (Clark 2005; Gilpin 1981), who have critically contributed to the debate on legitimacy from a global order perspective (in contrast to the prevailing rationale of the manifold approaches analyzing the topic through secondary institutions, for instance, the United Nations or through other regimes), are investigated more closely. Finally, by conceptually adapting Clark's account, which is based on US hegemony, to the current order transition, its theoretical usefulness for analyzing the dynamics of systemic legitimacy is increased in three important and interrelated ways. This set of three variables comprises today's hybrid environment, common culture and effectiveness. The insertions advance the scope of Clark's original variables (2005), comprising legality, morality, constitutionality and balance of power, and, consequently, feed back into the dynamics characterizing their relations to each other.

As a first step, the analysis outlines the key components of the English School framework to the extent that they pertain to this analysis.

Overall, the theory offers insights that help to better understand the links between the notions of order transition and systemic legitimacy.[30] Moreover, the framework is useful because its synthesis of material and ideational components helps to capture the broad contestation the existing order has undergone. In this way, the theory fruitfully puts itself at the juncture of logics of appropriateness and logics of consequences and opens up the related literature on practices to our topic (March and Olson 1998:949–954; Dessler and Owen 2005:607–608; Dunne 2008:268; Adler and Pouilot 2011:6, 8, 13–14). In particular, similar to Gamble's distinction, the theory's proponents introduce the notion of primary institutions as opposed to secondary ones. The latter have taken on the shape of regimes or international institutions but since they represent "frozen decisions", which "history [has] encoded into rules" (March and Olson 1984:741), it is important to recognize that they are built on a power-political and normative consensus negotiated earlier. Precisely because they merely reflect such an earlier agreement (which may be altered under different normative and power-political circumstances), Wight has called them "pseudo-institutions" (1991:141). Buzan defines primary institutions as "fundamental and durable practices that are evolved more than designed"; they are "constitutive of actors and their patterns of legitimate activity in relation to each other" (2004a:167; Adler and Pouliot 2011). Furthermore, patterns of legitimacy are "created when a social function and status are allocated to something [i.e. legitimacy] but do not reflect its intrinsic physical properties" (ibid.:166).[31] For primary institutions, or their equivalent of habitual practices, to be considered legitimate they need to reflect "some shared principle, norm or value" (ibid.:175). Such principles or values of an order cannot display some neutral idea of stability or a purely functional agenda. Rather, social order precisely "requires the existence of a particular kind of purposive pattern that human beings have infused with meaning, that involves a particular set of goals, objectives, and values, and that leads to a particular outcome" (Hurrell 2007:2; Hurd and Cronin 2008:6; Wolfers 1962:89, 60, 154). In effect, those common understandings, similar to Ruggie's embedded (liberal) "constitutive rules" (1998:871–873, 1983) or to Reus-Smit's "constitutional structure" of international politics (1999), of what is deemed legitimate together with "some minimal common interests, such as trade... or simply the need for stability" (Dunne 2008:273) constitute an international society or order. The order reflects, thus, a (varying) degree of "shared ideas that exist between actors and that are embedded in historical practice and in historically constructed normative structures – in international legal rules and practices, in international political norms, and in the dominant ideologies and practices that animate them" (Hurrell 2007:17).[32]

This more constructivist understanding of (appropriate) norms is, however, constantly balanced by the theory's recognition of (changes in the) prevailing material conditions (Buzan 2004:251–257; Little 2007:282–283, 271–272; Hurrell 2007:17; Clark 2005:20–21). In this respect, the changes which the current order undergoes reflect this accordingly, since the global order and the attitudes of China and the United States, as Foot and Walter remind us, have become a "mutually constitutive social phenomenon" (2011:23). Inevitably, in contrast to the institutionalist theories discussed above, adopting the variable of worldview into the analysis pushes to the center the question of who comprises the "we", who is providing the definitions of what legitimate activity is. The importance of this analytical revision becomes more obvious in light of the underlying ideology of most global governance accounts which presuppose common interests and common normative ambitions, as had already been the case with their interwar predecessors in legal idealism (Zürn 2010:731; Mayntz 2008:55; Shambaugh 2013:125).[33] Finally, since primary institutions can change, the theory offers a broad spectrum ranging from pluralist to solidarist notions of international society that incorporate stronger and weaker versions of their respective kind, that is, they vary as to the "type and extent of norms, rules and institutions that an international society can form without departing from the foundational rules of sovereignty and non-intervention that define it as a system of states" (Buzan 2004:8; ch. 5).

Taken together, what does the theory offer regarding the notion of systemic legitimacy? The political search for a "bargained consensus" (Little 2007:117)[34] or a "constitutional bargain" (Prantl 2013:7) on the "basic rules" of the order during transition, not unanimity on them, depends on the perceived legitimacy of the evolving political practices on the part of key actors. Systemic legitimacy is filtered through the prevailing material power structure. Primary institutions (and the corresponding secondary institutions) that have highlighted some of the issues already touched upon in this analysis are, for instance, today's changing practices pertaining to sovereignty and its derivatives of non-intervention and international law, that is, constitutionalization and its failure in the WTO's DSB or regarding the "Responsibility to Protect" (RtP); practices related to diplomacy and its derivative multilateralism, that is, socialization and its partial failure in the United Nations or WTO;

and, finally, practices concerned with great-power management and its derivative balance of power, that is, the challenge to enmeshment by the tension between notions of regionalism and spheres of influence. As a second step, synthesizing the works of two authors, who have – in different ways – contributed to the study of the relationships between legitimacy and order transition, into the framework of systemic order helps to specify two things: it tells us what exactly is at stake during order transition and how exactly do the dynamics between the particular elements of global legitimacy play out, which shape the renegotiations. Both, the pragmatist methodology and the eclectic approach to theorizing facilitate such a synthesis.

To begin with, for a long time both mainstream and non-mainstream IR theorists have habitually built their arguments against the foil of Waltz' parsimonious structural account. This has come at the expense of another important theorist, often (mistakenly) added to the neorealist school. The latter framework has often insisted that "legitimacy has no place in the study of world politics" (Gelpi 2003:12). A closer reading of Gilpin reveals, however, his firm interest in the politics of legitimacy. For instance, from his perspective, legitimacy played a "central role ... in the ordering and governance of the international system" (1981:31) since the latter could only operate if it was "based on a general belief in its legitimacy" (1987:3).[35] In fact, he firmly rejects the notion that "the hegemon must be an imperialistic power that imposes its will on other countries" and promotes instead the idea that a hegemon should "encourage other states to obey the rules and regimes governing international ... activities" (2001:95, 100). Thus, both due to his early interest in English School thinking (1981:28, 34–35, 111) and due to recent exchanges between non-orthodox structural thinkers and English School theorists (e.g. Little and Wohlforth 2007), Gilpin has been found to be a good starting point for an understanding of the global implications of the US–China rivalry (Wohlforth 2012). For the purposes of this analysis, his main contribution outlines those patterns of a systemic order that are at stake when the respective victor of the last hegemonic war, which previously set up the settlement, encounters a "rising state [which] attempts to change" it (Gilpin 1981:187). The five patterns he suggests partly resemble some of today's "global public goods" (Betts 2009:26): firstly, the great-power bargain outlines the economic and security-related rules of the order (Gilpin 1981:187); secondly, some notion of ideology underlies the agreement (ibid.:34); thirdly, great powers are provided with special rights (ibid.:30); fourthly, the consensus is built against the backdrop of the existing balance of power (ibid.:35,

187); finally, the settlement identifies and clarifies the extent of each other's spheres of influence (ibid.:35).

The second author, Ian Clark, has identified similar patterns pertaining to the negotiation of order transition, despite minor differences (2005:19, 158, 242–243). What is more important for the purposes of this analysis are the ways in which he has extended the discussion. While the discipline has come to acknowledge the importance of legitimacy after the Cold War (Franck 1990; Hurd 2007, 1999; Mayntz 2010; Charlesworth and Coicaud; Suchman 1995), Clark's account stands out because he explains the dynamics driving the politics of legitimacy. He is fully aware that for an international system to be "effective... it must be able to adapt to environmental developments and to internal changes within its member states that affect its performance and its ability to maintain itself" (Craig and George 1995:xi). But how does he get there conceptually? He does so by drawing from two major analytical strands prevailing in the theoretical debate on legitimacy and, then, juxtaposing the pair to another cognate concept. He then goes on to explain the relationship between all three of them with the notion of power. To begin with, legitimacy is widely derived from the idea of law rationality, that is, legality (Wolfrum 2008), or from substantive value rationality, that is, morality/justice. Both imply that legitimacy is "intrinsically bound up with adherence to established rules" (Clark 2005:18). The question Clark raises is whether legitimacy is constituted by or distinct from them? In other words, what happens when "legality and morality pull apart" (2005:19)? Before answering the question, he looks at another concept, frequently referred to in debates on legitimacy (Ikenberry 2001). This concept of constitutionality suggests "a sense of what is politically appropriate, rooted in expectations rather than in rules" (Clark 2005:19). Together these three elements mark out the space that constrains prevailing conceptions of legitimacy. However, building on the English School's emphasis to combine ideational and material factors, he reminds us that "only within the context of power relations... legitimacy becomes relevant at all" (2005:20). Alluding to major debates in the discipline, he suggests that legitimacy does ratify and, thereby, constrain power relations; however, at the same time, these processes cannot be thought to exist independently from those relations (2005:21; Brooks and Wohlforth 2008; Beetham 1991). Rather, legitimacy shapes and is being reshaped by power at the same time.[36] As a result, he is now able to provide an answer to the question raised above. It is precisely because, firstly, the actors' distinct understandings of appropriate

standards of the notions of legality, morality and constitutionality[37] ...,
which shape legitimacy, regularly pull in opposite directions, and,
secondly, a process exists which is channeled through the unstable
relationship of all three parts with the prevailing balance of power,
that no single element can per se equal legitimacy.[38] Rather, the
four aspects need to be seen as complementary in that they influence each other in the contested search for a consensus among them.
There is, in other words, a "certain fluidity and contestability... in
the presence of alternative and often conflicting rules" (Koskenniemi
2011:v; Kennedy 2008). This process of contestation, then, reflects the
"inescapably political nature of legitimacy" (Clark 2005:208).[39] The
political search for a consensus among these often divergent four elements is what captures the dynamics pertaining to the politics of
systemic legitimacy. Inherently, this process is reflected in the characteristic trade-off *nature* of input and output accounts underlying systemic
legitimacy.

Such an understanding of systemic legitimacy needs to be distinguished from other conceptions, focusing only on *one* of the four
(interrelated) elements outlined above. For instance, conceptions of
legitimacy, as they are put forward by international lawyers and global
governance theorists, anchor legitimacy firmly in ideas of legality (Falk
et al. 2012; Wolfrum 2008; Zürn and Joerges 2005). A second set of
accounts of legitimacy is exclusively built on the adherence to standards of democratic accountability (Buchanan and Keohane 2006; Daase
et al. 2012:14–16).[40] Finally, regime-based theories naturally show a
degree of output bias and narrowly focus on legitimacy-related concerns
which pertain to the inside of issue-specific regimes (Miles et al. 2001;
Breitmeier et al. 2001). However, notwithstanding their respective merits, none of them can capture the dynamics of the integrated approach
provided by Clark's systemic legitimacy.

Overall, Clark's and Gilpin's accounts have added important contributions to the debate on order transition and the inherently related
politics of legitimacy. And yet, despite the fact that Clark insists that his
components of the politics of legitimacy provide "most of the substantive content... of the process of legitimation" (2005:158), and despite
the fact that Gilpin stresses (1981:187) that his patterns present the key
"rules governing the international system",[41] their picture of order transition remains incomplete. The following sets of criticisms reveal several
weaknesses of Gilpin's and Clark's accounts which, in turn, prepare
the ground for providing the elements of a revised model of systemic
legitimacy at the end of the chapter.

Gilpin argues that war will most likely resolve the increasing tensions between the contenders, but he does not believe that this step is predetermined by history, as his references to the possibility of peaceful change make clear (1981:234, 242). Nonetheless, he does not inform us about which dynamics, pertaining to legitimacy, are at play in the absence of a war or during peaceful change.[42] Moreover, his otherwise important, if underspecified, suggestion that legitimacy serves as the international system's "everyday currency" (31) reveals its analytical shallowness, since it is not clear what role it plays in times of transition. Nonetheless, the patterns Gilpin suggests for the renegotiations remain valid for the analysis.

As far as Clark is concerned, his model rests on the notion of a largely uncontested US hegemony (2005:226–229) with regard to its effectiveness and the worldview underpinning international organizations and regimes. Moreover, Clark's theory is exclusively built on a state-based view of global politics. The tensions that this creates for his theory of "contestation and consensus-building" (2005:158) can be divided into four points of criticism. They are briefly outlined here and in-depth elaborated in Chapters 3–5. Firstly and more broadly, wedded to the "*day-to-day* practice" (2005:256) of the politics of legitimacy based on US hegemony, Clark does not specify whether his model is applicable to various degrees of contestation and, if it was, what the implications of such contestation would be. As a consequence, he leaves open the question of what happens to the model when the order itself is put into question to a degree that well exceeds the hegemony-based "day-to-day" extent of contestation his account assumes. That is, however, precisely the state of the current order transition, during which the patterns suggested by Gilpin are renegotiated. In contrast to Clark's account, a challenger questions the order's structural and managerial foundations as well as its underlying normative beliefs, while the order is, at the same time, being exposed to the hegemon's own revisionist stance. In other words, order transition is reflected in (the changing practices pertaining to) the patterns introduced by Gilpin, but not yet sufficiently analytically captured by Clark's theory.

The second criticism that can be raised against Clark's model has two sources. One is, again, his exclusively state-based view; the other is his neglect of the potential offered by the English School's broad spectrum-based view on changes in practices from more solidarist ones to more pluralist ones. He thereby leaves no room for a global order oscillating between (solidarist) global multi-level governance and more pluralist (and increasingly salient) great-power-based politics. Thus, the hybrid nature of the current global environment cannot be integrated into his model. Though having undergone strong pressure, governance processes and structures remain an integral part of today's global order (Avant et al. 2011). Therefore, this chapter takes the important results of transnational research as its starting point and, subsequently, raises the question of what exactly the importance, which the global governance literature has attributed to transnational actors (TNAs), means in relation to patterns of global order transition. In particular, two aspects are drawn out: their relation to the contested nature of the search for global legitimacy and to power understood as material inequalities, leadership and interests. The chapter then goes on to review the standard governance depiction of realist propositions. It identifies a weakness that flows directly from its focus on access presupposing well-functioning institutions, while, consequently, overlooking the existing deadlocks in international politics. Essentially, the key argument put forward is that the influence of non-state actors is dependent on a particular institutional context in which the key political questions framing a social order are already settled. Large parts of the related literature on international institutions simply assume that this is the case. In contrast, this analysis suggests that, unless these framing patterns are agreed upon by major powers, the respective order and its elements (i.e. institutions and regimes) remain contested or deadlocked. When this happens, the political impact of non-state actors is largely neutralized or significantly weakened and their effective autonomy from great powers minimized. Such a broader perspective helps to explain why the existing literature on TNA influence in global governance, which sees "institutional access... as a central determinant of TNA influence" (Tallberg et al. 2013:50), has consistently overlooked the process of neutralization which this analysis, in contrast, has exposed.

Thirdly, the "morality" of Clark's model, that is, Gilpin's ideology underlying the order, reflects the "taken-for-granted nature" of US hegemony. This view is further entrenched by Clark's unitary view of the state which leaves no room to look into domestic politics. In turn, this leads him to underestimate the degree to which the worldviews, emanating from US and Chinese domestic environments, have critically shaped these states' attitude as to what their constituencies accept on the global plane. Considering his familiarity with the English School, it is difficult to see why he does not explore the (potential) implication of today's powerfully articulated plurality of values and historical identities, that is, worldviews, for the global order. This omission prevents him from raising critical questions as to whether the absence of a "common culture" or of "shared values" among (today's) great powers inevitably leads to both the impossibility of peaceful order transition and the instability of the global order.[43] Research, thus far, has mainly stressed that the availability of a "common (democratic) culture" is conducive to peaceful change and stability. Looking at today's deadlocks, the questions Clark cannot address, thus, are whether "international norms and institutions [are] sustainable under the(.) conditions" of a lacking common culture and what the implications are if they prove unsustainable (Buzan 2010:2). In other words, what are the theoretical implications of a "common culture" that is, to different degrees, no longer "commonly accepted" by established and rising great powers? In order to address this question, this section examines two aspects. It looks into the thus-far underspecified dynamics of the relationship between the notions of worldview and common culture, and it analyzes the underlying assumption that the nature of the common culture, as accepted by the predominant actor, remains basically unchanged over time. If this has exposed the role of exceptionalist worldviews more broadly, the analysis proceeds by looking into the actual nature of exceptionalist worldviews. As a first step, it raises three conceptual questions that need to be engaged when comparing exceptionalist worldviews. In order to illustrate the importance of the empirical nature of this relationship, the key patterns of the United States' and China's worldviews are presented in the form of a brief comparative outline. What follows then is an assessment of the relationship between the two exceptionalist worldviews for the notion of order transition. Against this backdrop, the questions as to whether the exceptionalist nature of US and Chinese worldviews makes them incommensurable and, consequently, whether it renders peaceful order transition impossible are raised.

Finally, in Clark's view US hegemony has endowed the global order with sufficient effectiveness. The references he makes to the topic are merely implied in the all-pervasive "power relations" which shape the politics of legitimacy and in his notion of constitutionality. Nonetheless, Clark's presupposed degree of effectiveness seems less convincing when viewed against the backdrop of the various deadlocks currently prevailing in global politics, of the power competition between the United States and China, of the diverging perspectives on world order and of the uncertain relationship between global governance activities and great-power politics. The conceptual analysis provided below will offer an account of the managerial strand of the power literature. Put briefly, a closer look at the underlying assumptions of managerial theories shows that those theories have failed to address what is here introduced as the hierarchical relationship between the internal (among the great powers) and external (between the hegemons and the remainder of international society) layers of great-power management. Focusing on the former demonstrates two things. First, it shows that there are no special responsibilities without the agreement within the peer group. Second and related, it finds that an outstanding agreement on special responsibilities prevents any proper steering of international society as such. The final section shows how the new shape of effective management integrates formal and informal aspects of great-power politics. It highlights the operating contours of special responsibilities, which occur in formal and informal shapes, regardless of the degree to which the respective environments are institutionalized or rule-based. What do these considerations concerning the effectiveness of global order imply when the former head of the IMF staunchly refuses the return to a Metternichian concert approach (Zoellick 2010) while, at the same time, even some of the most dedicated adherents of the concept of global governance admit that, after 1991, "much of the talk of global governance was a rhetorical façade" (Hurrell 2013:25)? At a minimum, it suggests that Clark's model needs to integrate a completely revised notion of effectiveness into its original design.

As a result, revising Clark's original framework in light of the points of criticism raised in the previous paragraphs will open up a valuable order perspective on the current deadlocks. This deeper conceptual analysis of the last three points, that is, common culture, hybrid environment and effectiveness, will be undertaken in the following three chapters (3–5). Clark's revised model of systemic legitimacy can then help to inject a systemic interpretation into some of today's deadlocks which, according to Gilpin, reflect what is at stake when an order is being renegotiated. In this way the variables of Clark's revised model will help sharpen our understanding of the tensions at play during the strongly contested process of the current order transition. For instance, it may then be possible to conceive of the nature of the UNFCCC deadlock not only as an issue-specific collective action problem but also as the broader renegotiation of the environmental order of world politics; the gridlock characterizing ASEAN can then be viewed as the attempt to readjust understandings of a key sphere of influence; finally, the opposing exceptionalist worldviews underlying the approaches to, for instance, the "Responsibility to Protect" can then be considered a reflection of a highly intricate search for common sets of values.

Part II
Conceptual Revisions

3
Order Transition in a Hybrid Environment

The previous chapter argued that international institutions and regimes are, largely, deadlocked due to great-power disagreements. This, in turn, revealed the lack of a *political* grand bargain among the key players. The key question this chapter poses is how the negotiation of order transition can be understood when viewed against the background of what has come to be known as the post-Westphalian environment (Linklater 1998; Rosenau 1990). Contrary to Clark's (2005) exclusively state-based understanding of global order, the current environment *also* comprises global and transnational governance activities, embodied in the institutionalization of world politics surrounded by the suasion-based politics of TNAs. The chapter aims to contribute to an important broader debate into which the criticisms, raised here against Clark, have been embedded. Put briefly, the latter debate is about the degree to which patterns of global governance have reached "autonomy with respect to . . . states" (Börzel and Risse 2010; Cohen 2012:5). In order to illustrate this, TNAs, which have become an integral part of the policy processes shaped in regime complexes, have been selected to assess their impact on questions of order transition. The chapter will do so by framing the aforementioned question in the terms set by the governance-beyond-the-state literature and will thereby assess the strengths and weaknesses of their theoretical assumptions.

This chapter is structured as follows: firstly, it outlines more generally why scholars have strongly committed themselves to the analysis of the role of TNAs. Secondly, it more specifically examines how the degree of importance, which has widely been attributed to TNAs, may be accounted for. The third and longest section takes the important results of transnational research as its starting point and raises the question of what exactly the importance, which the global governance literature has attributed to TNAs, means *in relation to* patterns of global order transition. In particular, two aspects are drawn out: their relation to the contested nature of the search for global legitimacy and to power understood as material inequalities, leadership and interests. The fourth section reviews the standard governance depiction of realist propositions. It identifies a weakness that flows directly from its focus on "access", which presupposes well-functioning institutions while, consequently, overlooking the deadlocks existing in international politics. Finally, the conclusion links the findings back to Clark's model, which, in turn, revises the common perception of the much-argued-for "autonomy" of global governance institutions, such as TNAs, from states.

Why TNAs?

In light of Clark's state-based shortcomings, why have activities, which are roughly captured by the notion of "governance beyond the state"[1], become increasingly prevalent and thus an integral part of International Organizations (IOs) (Avant et al. 2011; Florini ed. 2000; Steffek 2010; Take 2013; Tarrow 2005; Willetts 2011)? Put briefly, why should we think about TNAs at all? The short answer is that it has become a widely held belief that they are critical and influential and that their density provides the necessary evidence for their importance (Keckand Sikkink 2000:28). For instance, Risse-Kappen asserted that "[w]e cannot even start theorizing about the contemporary world system without taking their influence into account" (2002:255). With the end of the Cold War providing considerably more structural space for non-state actors to maneuver (than before 1989/91), the activities of TNAs have mushroomed precisely because of their discontent with the legitimacy and efficiency of formal IOs and state policies. The most lively and popular illustrations of the increasing political opportunities for TNAs have been provided at summits in the shape of UN conferences, WTO or G8 meetings. Thus, despite the conspicuously limited influence of TNAs, for instance, on contributing to the resolution of the financial crisis, "it is striking that political scientists are paying more attention to 'global governance' than ever" (Koppell 2013:222). It remains to be seen why "NGO innovation and activism has slowed" while "the same is not true of scholarship about nonstate actors, and especially NGOs" (Charnovitz 2009:777).

Nonetheless, there are at least four sets of reasons highlighting the growing role of TNAs in global politics: contemporary precursors strengthening civil society, macro-dynamics facilitating their growth, their rise in numbers and their new functions. Firstly, the waves of democratization, which occurred in the 1970s and 1980s (e.g. Spain, Portugal, Latin America),[2] revived the notion of civil society and, thereby, prepared the ground for its broader surge in importance later on (Hurrell 2007:99). Moreover, with a new wave of economic globalization being stimulated by the notions of democracy and "good" governance, the broader conditions were laid out under which transnational activities could develop into a critical theater of political action. Technological advances such as the INTERNET and the substantial decrease in transportation costs have significantly raised the degree of interconnectedness of people (Avant et al. 2011:4–6). Furthermore, while the specific numbers offered by scholars vary, the increase in the number of TNAs remains obvious, ranging from 21,000 to 44,000 (as opposed to 14,000 in 1985) in the early 2000s (UNDP, Human Development Report 2000; Yearbook of International Organizations 2003). Finally, states and IOs have involved TNAs in three ways. They have engaged them "in the formal process of norm creation, standard-setting, and norm development" (Hurrell 2007:101). Moreover, TNAs have often been given the responsibility to serve as compliance watchdogs and to oversee processes of implementation (Boyle and Chinkin 2007:ch. 2). Their expertise in various policy fields has been incorporated into the operation of IOs (Drezner 2007:69–70). As a result, the so-called transnational turn in global politics has conferred a considerable degree of importance to transnational activities beyond the state and has, thereby, changed the ways in which international institutions and regimes operate (Risse 2013).

Three ways of explaining the importance of TNAs

How has this new importance theoretically been accounted for? There is broad consensus among a variety of theoretical approaches to examine the importance of TNAs in terms of "understanding the factors that shape...transnational access" to international organizations and regime complexes (Tallberg 2010:45). In other words, researchers have largely been interested in "where, why and with what consequences transnational actors are granted a role in global policy making" (Tallberg and Jönsson 2010:3; Tallberg et al. 2013).[3] In a recent state-of-the-art review, Tallberg identified three theoretical bodies in the literature in particular that explain the causes of transnational access. The three are, respectively, rational choice institutionalism, sociological institutionalism and power-oriented institutionalism (Tallberg 2010:45). They are briefly outlined in order to highlight the focus of current research. Firstly, in general terms, rational choice institutionalism suggests that institutions are "created and designed to address shortcomings in the market or the political system as a means of producing collectively desirable outcomes" (Tallberg 2010:46).[4] Transposed to the context of the participation of TNAs, a distinct interpretation of the links between the state, IOs and TNAs can be derived. Such thinking "perceives states as rational actors that collectively make deliberate choices about the degree and form of transnational access to international institutions, based on assessments of the functional benefits TNAs may bring in any given context" (ibid.:47). The specific functions, which TNAs perform to the benefit of states and IOs, address governance problems such as "information asymmetry, efficiency, and credible commitments" (ibid.). Thus, the functional needs of states, which TNAs satisfy, are services in the shape of policy-relevant information, efficient implementation and monitoring of commitments (ibid.:47–48). Secondly, in general terms, sociological institutionalism is predicated on the "notion that international institutions reflect broadly shared ideas and norms of what constitutes appropriate and legitimate models of governance (Marchand Olsen 1989). In this view, institutional design is a process in which low priority is given to concerns of efficiency, relative to concerns of legitimacy. Actors adopt certain procedures and practices, not because they are necessarily the most efficient, but because they constitute collectively legitimated institutional models" (Tallberg 2010:51). The diffusion of norms and institutional mimicking are the sources of institutional design (ibid.).[5] Applied to the study of transnational access, it proposes "that the tendency of international institutions to create mechanisms of participation for TNAs reflects the spread and consolidation of a new norm of legitimate global governance. According to this norm, international institutions, because of the domestic impact of their decisions, must involve representatives of civil society in the policy-making process" (ibid.:52). The evolution and consolidation of this particular norm are not found in sociological institutionalism but in four parallel paths of norm development as reflected in empirical works on the new discourse on global democracy, the global participatory democracy, changes in international law (e.g. ECOSOC)[6] and development aid (ibid.:53). Thus, states do open up to TNAs because of the spread of the new norm which, in turn, leads to an increasing homogenization of the level and form of transnational access (ibid.:54). Thirdly, in general terms, power-oriented institutionalism's main premise is that "institutions constitute reflections of the distribution of power amongst the negotiating actors. Asymmetries in resources shape the bargaining power of actors..., which, in turn, explains the distributional terms of negotiated institutions" (ibid.:56).[7] When employed in the context of transnational access, this approach, "instead of privileging efficiency or legitimacy,... emphasizes power as the driving concern of states in shaping the terms of transnational access participation" (ibid.:56). Moreover, "[j]ust like the functionalist perspective , this approach recognizes that TNAs perform tasks that benefit states, such as offering policy expertise, providing services, and monitoring commitments. Yet unlike the functionalist perspective, this approach emphasizes that these are not neutral functions, but activities that benefit some states more than others, depending on the preferences and the distribution of TNAs.... More specifically, this approach generates expectations of three forms of dynamics with regard to transnational participation, based on concerns over relative power: support for like-minded actors, opposition to antagonistic actors, and reinforcement of existing power structures" (ibid.:57).

These research findings are indeed very important and have tremendously improved our understanding of how the operation of today's international institutions and regime complexes has changed. In fact, the theoretical analysis of this new object has further underlined the post-Westphalian character of current global politics. Nevertheless, while we might now know more about the significance of TNAs in regard to IOs and the regime complexes of which they are a part, two crucial aspects remain unclear. Firstly, what does this importance mean *in relation to* questions of global order, great-power disagreements and the lacking political bargain? In other words, how significant is the supposed importance of TNAs when looked at from an angle that is different from the mainstream governance perspective with its focus on the dynamics inside and around international regimes and institutions? Secondly, precisely *how* should we examine the importance of transnational "access" in regard to those questions of order transition?

Essentially, what these two aspects suggest is the urgent need to shift the (prevailing and often exclusive) research focus away from the new dynamics surrounding the operation of international institutions toward a closer inspection of the underlying assumptions of post-Westphalian governance theories in light of order transition. In other words, instead of analyzing Tallberg's notion of "transnational access" as if it was an entirely separate issue based on its own dynamics, it is absolutely central to situate it in the broader context in which such "access" is taking place.

Juxtaposing patterns of order transition with patterns of transnational governance

In order to steer the discussion into the aforementioned direction, it is necessary to draw out some key analytical issues that pertain to the notion of order transition and, at the same time, point to some related but largely unquestioned assumptions and weaknesses in global and transnational governance theories. Quintessentially, this section highlights the strains which the latter theories have experienced during times of order transition.

For the purposes of this analysis, two central analytical aspects related to the notion of order transition will be addressed: the element of contestation of global legitimacy and the question of state power conceived as material inequality, leadership and interests, with particular reference to great powers. Both aspects will be juxtaposed with the corresponding essences identified in the governance literature reviewed in the following. The analysis of the *nature of the linkages between the two strands* provides, thus, the core of this section.

The *first set of criticisms* stresses the argument that the global and transnational governance literatures have promoted the notion of a "depoliticized" nature of politics (Koskenniemi 2011:359). Such a depoliticized conception of global politics, which is often invoked to facilitate "the flexibility necessary to navigate the complex dynamic of global governance" (Koppell 2013:224), is diametrically opposed to the main characteristic of the current order transition, that is, the deadlocks of many international regimes that have revealed the substantial extent of contestation between China and the United States. There are at least three important aspects that have fed into the notion of this depoliticized nature.

To begin with, the various kinds of sectoral expertise of governance, prevailing in regime complexes[8] and partly embodied by TNAs (Drezner 2007:70), have presented themselves in the shape of neutral regulatory reasoning. The latter has thereby concealed the "reality of choice in international law" existing "between alternative types of action", although indeterminacy, decision and bias are "inevitable aspects of all work in international law" (Koskenniemi 2011:vi). Originally, this lack of choice emanated from a strong, mainly liberal, critique of formal international law after the end of the Cold War, embodied in sovereignty, diplomacy and state-based foreign policies. With the United

States winning the Cold War, it created the necessary space for agency, so that ideas of governance could flourish. In particular, sovereignty seemed, to many, no longer adequate to further international social and economic life. Thus, a broad variety of liberal theorists began to develop non-hierarchical governance models in order to cope with problems that went beyond national borders. Henceforth, attention was diverted away from sovereign rules and treaties toward "objectives". Serving the achievement of global common goods, problem-solving and technocratic governance modes required that "[e]verything must become negotiable, revisable in view of attaining the right outcome" (Koskenniemi 2011:319). Since then, broad regime complexes have emerged by way of amalgamating international practices and consolidating knowledge patterns. Critically, this has "created redescriptions of the world through novel languages that empower novel groups" (ibid.). This quickly evolving, issue-specific compartmentalization has divided global politics into "sectoral publics" (Zürn 2010:740). Consequently, the rule of courts and TNA experts has come to permeate the attempts at solving problems related to issues of global governance (Kennedy 2005). As a result, from the perspective of governance, Koskenniemi's "reality of choice" is not required, which is why critical aspects of social life have become depoliticized.

The second consideration pertains to the internal dynamics and consequences of the process of constitutionalization (Wiener et al. 2012).[9] The idea to constitutionalize international law in order to undercut the fragmenting effects of the dispersion of law caused by globalization has been assumed to underpin the "socializing forces of international law and its corresponding ability to generate state compliance and cosmopolitan sympathies" (Brown 2012:210). This is why leading practitioners such as Mark Malloch-Brown, a former World Bank vice president, UN deputy secretary general and co-founder of the International Crisis Group, have repeatedly urged their milieu to "finish the global revolution" of legalization (2011). The rationale behind the concept has mistakenly assumed that legal coherence is a function of codification (Goldstein et al. 2001:3; Rosenau 2007). Notwithstanding well-established modi that soften or integrate multiple jurisdictions, especially in the OECD world, the main problem with this assumption is that it aims at collapsing the existing disorderliness of a plurality of rules and principles into a broad framework, while overlooking the extent to which the unresolved "conflict between legal orders, ideas, powers and traditions" is often responsible for the disorder in the first place (Kennedy 2008:848). The two main drivers behind the notion of constitutionalization have been, firstly, the liberal cosmopolitan claim that "more constitutionalization is better and... that the more states are brought under the... influence of customary law and international institutional practice, the better this will be for the international environment in general" (Brown 2012:211). Secondly, it is often believed that "more international law and more international institutions represent a more robust form of constitutionalization" (ibid.). Accordingly, viewing TNAs as the most important conveyors of the (liberal) messages of global civil society, its theorists have suggested that "the more... NGOs exist, the better" this may be for global politics (Cooleyand Ron 2002:9). However, not only has it been shown in the case of the Economic and Social Council (ECOSOC) that even though the increase in the number of accredited NGOs was fourfold between 1989 and 2009, this concealed their "lack of both legal and financial empowerment and [the] still underdeveloped relationships with UN system actors" (Popovski et al. 2008:6). This is, in turn, why some formerly leading UN officials have pointed out the degree to which ECOSOC has been "failing miserably" to fulfill its erstwhile task of connecting civil society to IOs (Frechette 2007:4). Still more important, the underlying belief that an increase in TNAs leads to an overall improvement of global politics reveals a specific presupposition of why this would occur in the first place. While scholars working on TNAs have often based their research on the assumption that what allows TNAs to agree on collective action is their shared altruistic agenda (Gourevitch et al. 2012), Stroup (2012) has convincingly shown that it is precisely the manifold national particularities that frequently disrupt possibilities of collective TNA action. Similarly, scholars examining questions of transitional justice have cautioned against an "orientation toward dominant international norms and expectations for accountability"; this orientation has led many to "assume that we are witnessing a steady progression toward greater global consensus on international justice"; much rather, TNAs and other norm entrepreneurs should be probed about their "conflicting beliefs that motivate different networks [and] whose actors share a common but alternative conception of justice" (Boesenecker and Vinjamuri 2011:349, 348). More broadly, the approaches under scrutiny confirm that some striking similarities to the inter-war legal idealism are discernible. In fact, the latter was based on a "naturalist perspective that saw the world always already united by... the principles of 'reason'... that remained unchanging through space and time" (Koskenniemi 2012:306).[10] As a consequence, the neo-functionalist "increase hypothesis" neglects the inevitable *political* contestation among actors that needs to take place before such a process of constitutionalization can occur. This reveals that, contrary to the gist of the governance literature, there are currently no political institutions that could "make important choices on priorities in the pursuit of global common goods" (Kratochwil 2012, ms, intro:18). Instead, attempts at constitutionalizing law often carry with them a conservative bias which, in turn, explains their failures to deliver. Kennedy has captured the depoliticized nature of constitutionalizing efforts well: "Constitutionalizing...existing governance structures does aim to remove them from contestation and revision, harden their division of power and freeze their political and legal players" (2008:856).

The final and related aspect touches upon the normative bias of governance accounts. They justify themselves with reference to the "attainment of the common good", "presuppos[ing] some common...goal orientations" (Zürn 2010:741, 731). This conviction is mirrored in what high-ranking practitioners of global governance, such as the aforementioned Malloch-Brown, a former World Bank vice president, UN deputy secretary general and co-founder of the International Crisis Group, believe to be a "global social contract that builds on the emerging common values of solidarity in a shared world" (2011:13). This, in turn, raises the question of who the people are who have certain interests in *common* and whose "orientations" are reflected in these proposals. Obviously, such reasoning could not be put forward if governance theorists did not presuppose the moral neutrality of their efforts to provide global goods. And yet, as it was said earlier, no conception of social order can be imagined based on neutral political and moral grounds. As Kennedy has rightly objected, this supposed neutrality is – necessarily – why "the entire project of global legal arranging offers itself as innocent of value and ideology and cultural predisposition" (2008:856). Thus, governance approaches have been predicated on an unspoken normative understanding of their preferred view on world order, equipped with a non-debatable, apriori liberal character. The cosmopolitan implications of this aspect, that is, the further strengthening of Western standards at the expense of divergent views, are often overlooked by those theorists of transnational governance who press democratic standards onto the agenda of the politics of legitimacy. The failure to provide room for non-Western worldviews, as they are held by new powers that forcefully guard their post-colonial legacy, is thus striking. Governance theories might adopt a universal problem-solving attitude to global politics with all the deficiencies that come with it, but – similar to rationalist theories – they cannot work the "flows of belief,..., the experience of triumph and victimization" into their assumptions (Kennedy 2008:851).

Taken together, the normative bias of "neutrality", quietly built into governance proposals of world order, has driven the increasing degree of depoliticization of global politics and has thereby made it seemingly uncontested.

What has emerged, thus far, is a theoretical body in the literature that is largely oblivious to the central feature of renegotiating global legitimacy in the sense that Clark has suggested: the contested search for consensus. Rather, its framework operates in a distinctly depoliticized world. Tellingly, because of that, some of the leading scholars of international law have urged the academe to help *re*politicize global governance (idem, 2011b:66–67; Kennedy 2008:852; Koskenniemi 2011:358–360).

The *second set of criticisms* refers to the inherent neglect of power by governance theories and to the related role of great powers.[11] While this omission has already been touched upon in a broader sense in the previous chapter, here the focus is on three specific aspects of power: leadership, the implications of structurally unequal power and interests. The following remarks outline why theories of governance have neglected these power-related aspects and why they are crucial to better understand the links to the theme of order transition.

The reasons for the neglect may be uncovered by an investigation of several core assumptions of governance theories. The four assumptions that will be looked at more closely are as follows: firstly, the sovereignty of states is dispersed (Hurrell 2007:294); secondly, all states are to be treated equally (Kennedy 2008:855); thirdly, global civil society provides the main actors in international politics (Avant et al. 2011:2); and, finally, states' core responsibility is to implement the compliance demands of global governance (Zürn 2010:735).

Transnational governance theories are distinctly coherent in their treatment of the notion of power, as a brief elaboration on the four assumptions makes clear. To begin with, they have commonly presented the notion of a "global civil society", for example. non-state actors, foundations and corporations dedicated to the promotion of social responsibility, as their means of choice to achieve the far-flung goals of global governance. In this vein, some theorists have identified a new avant-garde of "global governors" providing the necessary leadership to make governance work (Avant et al. 2011:2).[12] Relatedly, according to theorists of "governance beyond the state", such thinking about actors in global politics is inherently linked to their underlying assumptions of dispersed sovereignty and explicitly non-hierarchical modes of governance. Logically then, among the existing actors, states are assumed to merely implement the policy commitments prescribed by actors and regimes of global governance (Zürn 2010:735). Finally, this theoretical picture is tightened by the proposition, deduced from international law, that all states may be treated equally; this allows governance proposals to convey a degree of even-handedness among actors. Taken together, precisely because of the compartmentalization of global politics and, concomitantly, the strictly separated issue areas adjudicated by specialized judges and administered by expert rule, the idea of more centralized decision-making resembles a contradiction in terms to governance theories. And yet, the impressive coherence of this body of literature notwithstanding, these assumptions address neither questions of power as material inequality, nor as leadership, nor as interests. Why are the latter questions important?

With regard to material terms, the supposed equality of states, which governance theories have borrowed from standard assumptions of international law, runs counter to the undeniable fact that global politics has been characterized by structural inequality among states (Tucker 1977; Waltz 2008:Chapter 14; 1979). For instance, the establishment of the WTO in 1995 was widely regarded as the "highpoint of Western dominance" (Keohane 2012:134) after the end of the Cold War and further supported in its global outreach by China's accession in 2001. Its Dispute Settlement Body (DSB) has long been seen as the prime example of how international trade disputes between great and small states can be averted through a judicialized process, even giving smaller states the formal "capacity to retaliate effectively against large advanced trade partners" (Norloff 2010:71). Big states, such as the United States, however, have been in a position to powerfully undermine the DSB's underlying logic of constraining power inequalities. It is precisely "because large states have a stronger retaliatory threat, [that] small states are not likely to restrict trade with large states in the first place. Conversely, small states depend on world markets for a wider range of products than do larger ones and they might not find it in their interest to retaliate by closing off their market" (ibid.). Using threats to deny access to its domestic market has been a powerful tool in the hands of the United States and China in order to prevent smaller states from benefiting from the DSB. As a consequence, the framework usually works well between economically equally powerful entities such as the United States and the European Union, but it has generally reinforced the power advantages of large states (Drezner 2007:215). This is why as careful an observer of international politics as Ian Hurd, after having examined the politics of the WTO's DSB, summed up the pathologies of power, which come into play more so between unequal than equal actors (2011:55): "[t]he WTO's effort to create a uniform legal framework for trade and trade disputes runs against the political and economic realities of a world with huge power disparities". It is precisely these realities, however, that determine the level of influence TNAs have on the proceedings, for instance, of the WTO during order transition.

The differences in material power among nations, thus, cannot be defused by governance proposals, as much as they present themselves as even-handed. Rather, the issues that need to be addressed flow from the implications of those power inequalities. Critically, governance accounts overlook the deeply entrenched practice of the great powers' special responsibilities; this has been employed as a compromise by the international society between the recognition of formally equal sovereignty and the free play of power inequalities. This compromise has been the key to global problem-solving. In contrast to governance accounts, states have long accepted that "special responsibilities arise when unilateral imposition of material power fails, *but so too does bargaining amongst formal equals,* leading instead to a search for a hierarchical but socially grounded politics of responsibility" (Bukovansky et al. 2012:7). Thus, if one wants to identify with "whom one expects to carry the program to victory" (Kennedy 2008:850), the problem-solving attitude implicitly attributed to the global governance approach needs to address the question of leadership.[13]

But, why then has governance theory been so oblivious to the need of leadership in the first place? The problem, it appears, is built-in into the rationale of governance accounts. Kratochwil, while referring back to the administrative compartmentalization of global politics in regimes, correctly remarked that the problem of governance is neither one of transparency nor of participation, as it is commonly thought. "The problem is rather that in all these multilevel governance structures nobody seems to be in charge of setting clear priorities, as parallel processes uneasily coexist" (2012, ms, 4th med.:17).[14] In this regard, a pervasive feature of the transnational governance rhetoric, which has often been assumed rather than explained, is its technicality. Koskenniemi has put it this way (2011:327): "the use of instrumentalist vocabulary hides this (i.e. the power-related concerns), turning political judgment into an exercise of technical skill. As a result, nobody seems to rule. While (unequal) power remains, responsibility disappears." This now helps to better understand what Kennedy's aforementioned statement intended to convey to his peers. Any global order needs to be built on forces that can successfully provide leadership, that is, establish, sustain and reform it. In contrast, cosmopolitan models of dispersed sovereignty and disaggregated power, as they are commonly held among non-state actors, networks and transnational communities, fail to offer that. In fact, as Hurrell observes, this is the "central limitation to transnational models and modes of governance": "they fail to acknowledge the necessity of... power [i.e. leadership] for social order and the promotion of common moral purposes" (2007:295). As a result, the "necessity of power" is critical in that it underpins an order in material terms and maintains it through legitimate leadership.[15]

It is striking to see, though, that the global governance literature has not thought harder about how to include the notion of power more effectively into its accounts. Ironically, despite Barnett's and Duvall's attempts at putting power back onto the agenda of IR theory (2005), seven years on, a major review of global governance theories was left to conclude that "more sensitivity about... power and wealth" was needed to compose a more nuanced picture of global politics (Brown 2012:219).[16]

This finding has an important implication. It explains that "[i]n general, the lack of powerful transnational interest groups is... common across issue areas" (Koppell 2013:224). For example, the manifold initiatives, networks, market mechanisms, efforts of private governance and public–private partnerships that have grown up around the UN Framework Convention on Climate Change (UNFCCC) failed to prevent the meager outcomes of the climate change negotiations in Copenhagen (Paterson 2009:150). The failures to mobilize resources and to ensure a degree of conformity among them have strongly undercut most TNAs' capability to deliver. Neither can they claim to possess any credible degree of global representation (despite their defense of the "global" good), nor can they implement binding rules that stretch into and link the national and local levels (Mayntz 2008:50). In turn, while the UNFCCC's global representativeness is widely considered to make it legitimate, it has turned out to be ineffective, as Copenhagen evinced. Instead, led by China, it was the informal grouping of the BASIC states, whose members were assembled based on their sheer material strength alone, that struck a deal with the United States (see Chapter 7). In contrast to what climate governance experts predicted (Paterson 2009:140), TNA policy experts as well as the thin and fragmented institutional structures of loosely coupled "regime complexes" of global governance have neither proved the degree of effectiveness necessary to govern transnationally, nor set the agendas in various policy realms, nor reflected the degree of legitimacy consciousness necessary to underpin their policies (Iriye 2002; Keohane and Victor 2011; Young ed. 2012). Therefore, accounts of transnational governance which argue that states merely serve to implement the compliance demands of governance commitments (Zürn 2010:735) present a highly reductionist view of key patterns of today's global politics.

Based on such reasoning, there are three discernible ways through which great powers have crucially shaped global politics. First, broad issues ranging from the effective negotiation of core interests to the adoption of universalist governance proposals require the backing of those states that stand out in terms of their structural inequality, that is great powers. Theorists and practitioners of global diplomacy have long supported this finding. Crucially, most IR schools, such as neoliberalism, neorealism, English School Theory and classical realism, have attributed a prominent role to great powers in their frameworks (Clark 2011:240).[17] For instance, Hurrell (1999:291) finds that "[t]he paradox of universalism is that the successful promotion of 'universal' or 'global values' will often depend on the willingness of particularly powerful states to promote them". Relatedly, Kahler shows that political ideas or prospective bargains first needed to be adopted in minilateralist procedures among key actors in order to be successfully implemented in multilateral settings (1993). This is further underscored by Louise Frechette, formerly a UN deputy secretary general, who reminds us that "[v]isionary schemes, grand bargains, bold reforms...are always hatched in smaller circles before they are promoted with the broader community and success always depends on getting key countries on board" (2007:5). Second, since the non-hierarchical mode is a key assumption of governance approaches, the respective theories have tended to identify an ever-diminishing role of the state (Mayntzand Scharpf 2005). Thereby these theories have, largely, overlooked the notion of state power. Even if limited to, mainly, OECD states, those accounts have paid too little attention to the degree to which state policies have often been "crucial in fostering the emergence of civil society in the first place and in providing the institutional framework that enables it to flourish" (Gilpin 1972; Hurrell 2007:112). Finally, since the rationale underlying governance accounts is to identify broad collective action problems and, subsequently, to provide global public goods through the functionally most appropriate institutional forms, they tend to overlook the power-related question of whose interests are being served (and whose values are being protected and promoted) by the political arrangements that are made (Kennedy 2008:856). For instance, research on institutional design reflects this deficit very clearly (Koremenos et al. 2001; Snidaland Abbott 2009). Thus, the ways in which the struggle for power among actors within regime complexes has occurred might perhaps have changed the locus of political engagement when compared to former government-to-government relations. However, the struggle itself has not: it "is still about conquering the decision-making position within one's institution and then laying out the agenda for reform" (Koskenniemi 2011:70). Applying Koskenniemi's argument to the realm of today's prevailing deadlocks sheds light on the problem of the degree to which non-state actors may influence the regime design and the core political decision-making process of regime complexes. Regarding regime design, great powers may be distinguished by their ability to object to their inclusion in a global regime (complex), because there is no reason why they would voluntarily submit to having their influence undermined. Thus, depending on the depth of intrusion a regime might demand, it is the great powers that, accordingly or preemptively, implement "safety valves", that is club rules, in the design of the respective regime in order to preserve their privileged position (Koppell 2010:128). TNAs may press states to prevent great powers from doing so only at the expense of the non-membership of the latter, thereby reinforcing the latters' inclination to forum-shop. The limited impact TNAs have is further underlined by the fact that while their advocacy/service functions and, thus, their input/participation are largely considered useful, their members are usually walked out before core political decisions are made (Boyleand Chinkin 2007:ch. 2; Ditchley 2010).[18] Thus, TNAs may contribute to shaping the "agenda for reform", but they cannot determine the actual content of the reform. Sometimes this situation is exacerbated by the (varying) lack of access to information, participation and decision-making, which citizens and TNAs are granted outside the European Union's Aarhaus Convention, for instance in the environmental realm (Krämer 2012).

Taking these two sets of criticisms together has two implications. Firstly, Tallberg's "access" perspective is too narrow because it overlooks the broader context in which the relevance of "access" is being shaped and reshaped in the first place. Secondly, it seems that the "importance" that has widely been attributed to civil society actors needs to be reviewed. Following this conceptual analysis, this pertinent question emerges: "how effective can transnational governance actors really be during today's order transition?"

The role of TNAs during order transition

Maintaining or, more precisely, reintroducing a macro-view on the topic is now crucial. Global governance accounts used to thrive on the political space that was provided by the United States as one result of the end of Cold War (Hurrell 2007:102). This state of the global structure, while conducive to transnational governance underpinned by liberal ideas,[19] has experienced considerable strain in recent years, inter alia, due to the rise of China and the United States' partly revisionist attitude. From a historical point of view, this is by no means a new transitory status in world politics, since the dynamics underlying the overlapping patterns of old and emerging orders are well known (Schroeder 2004:ch. 11). Equally, political theorists reviewing the 200-year period of the nineteenth and twentieth centuries in Europe have convincingly shown the degree to which progressive understandings of world order have "often depended on the changing international and domestic circumstances under which proposals were formulated" (Suganami 1989:6). Political theorists and historians are joined by proponents of the English School. According to them, we are living in "a world in which solidarist and cosmopolitan conceptions of governance coexist, often rather unhappily, with many aspects of the old pluralist order"; in fact, the links between the two are "close and persistent" (Hurrell 2007:9, 290). Nonetheless, currently, the older, much-reinvigorated order rationale appears to be putting the "new order" under considerable strain. Thus far, the global governance literature has had little to say about the role of non-state actors *during* times of structural change and order transition. Therefore, it seems apt to reconsider the largely unquestioned and underspecified importance which has been widely attributed to TNAs in global politics. Empirically, Charnovitz (2009:777) might therefore be right when he states: "Looking back at the decade of the 2000s, particularly during the financial crisis, one might detect an ebbing of the NGO role and the claims for its significance as compared to the 1990s."

Theoretically, if it is accepted that the "access" perspective is too limited, how can we explain the meaning and degree of the role of TNAs amidst the great-power disagreements underlying today's order transition? As mentioned above, Tallberg tells us that power-oriented institutionalists expect "support for like-minded actors, opposition to antagonistic actors, and reinforcement of existing power structures" (57). However, his outline presupposes well-functioning institutions. But what if, as Keohane (2012) suggested, the structural foundations, on which these institutions are built, are substantially changing (as they are)? Moreover, what if this development has already led to the fact that important institutions or regimes have experienced "intractable deadlocks" due to great-power disagreements (Drezner 2007:85)?[20] As mentioned, the current deadlocks are substantive in nature, since they are rooted in structural and worldview-based challenges to the current order. Inherently, rationalist theories reach their limits at this point because, while they may accurately discern existing configurations of interests and material power underpinning an order, they cannot cope with and analyze the changes those structures undergo from time to time (as they do today). The question that inevitably arises is "what happens to TNAs when institutions decline in their operability or effectiveness?" In a nutshell, in order to specify the notion of TNA importance, we need to ask how effective they can be at times of order transition.

Building his analysis on the distinction between policy process and the outcome of the policy process, Drezner concludes his analysis of TNA involvement in global economic politics with the somewhat counterintuitive finding that "there is an inverse correlation between NGO influence and the public visibility of these actors" (2007:86). In his study, he attributes service and advocacy functions to NGOs and measures their effectiveness against the backdrop of great powers' agreements and disagreements in international negotiations. Should TNAs protest against the negotiation results of great-power agreements, they will most likely attract much attention, but they have the least impact on the outcome of those negotiations. Alternatively, should TNAs apply "naming and shaming" tactics as a consequence of, or in parallel to, great-power inaction or disagreement, their own material limitations (in comparison to IOs or states) prevent them from providing effective measures. Consequently, in both cases their influence on state-to-state cooperation turns out to be low (ibid.). Drezner's distinction between process and outcome now becomes much clearer with regard to the effectiveness of TNAs/NGOs: "The service functions of NGOs are a vital part of global governance structures; the advocacy functions are peripheral" (ibid.).[21] Recently, suggestions have been made to the extent that TNAs have also increased their influence in the realm of security affairs. Similar to what Drezner concluded for the economic sphere, however, such views overlook both the dynamics emanating from and the implications of great-power disagreements for the role of TNAs in international security politics. Referring to the establishment of National Security Councils in China, Japan and Australia, a former US assistant secretary of state for East Asian and Pacific Affairs stated: "There is a larger trend across Asia to bring deliberations and decision-making into presidential or ministerial offices in an effort to better respond to the rapidly changing security environment in Asia" (Campbell 2014).[22]

Looking at the deadlocked state of global politics and order transition, it follows from Drezner's analysis that TNAs continue to play a critical role as service providers; however, the prevailing great-power disagreements render TNAs ineffective in that they cannot defuse the underlying tensions, nor can they offer solutions that have any realistic chance of implementation. This underlines the broad diffusion of TNA activities, but much less so their supposed pervasiveness. In other words, here it is argued that the influence of non-state actors is dependent on a particular institutional context in which the key political questions framing a social order are settled. Large parts of the related literature on international institutions simply assume that this is the case. In contrast, this analysis suggests that, unless these framing patterns are agreed upon by major powers, the respective order and its elements (i.e. institutions and regimes) remain contested or deadlocked. When this happens, the political impact of non-state actors is largely neutralized or significantly weakened and their effective autonomy from great powers minimized. Such a broader perspective helps to explain why the existing literature on TNA influence in global governance, which sees "institutional access... as a central determinant of TNA influence" (Tallberg et al. 2013:50), has consistently overlooked the process of neutralization which this analysis, in contrast, has exposed. In this vein, it is difficult to disagree with Hurrell on the relevance of TNAs (2013:25): the 1990s and the first decade of the second millennium were "a period in which so much was being attempted with so little. Through th[is period] the normative ambition of the international legal order continued to expand dramatically. But these expansive and expanding goals were to be achieved on the back of very thin institutional structures – lots of networks, lots of market mechanisms, lots of private or hybrid governance; but rather little in the way of serious multilateralism or institutional renewal or reform. The comparison with the world order debates of the late 1940s is instructive. Looking back it is hard to avoid the conclusion that much of the talk of global governance was a rhetorical façade. The real heavy lifting was to be done by the apparently effective centralization of power around the United States and a liberal Greater West."[23]

These remarks then suggest that state-based understandings of global politics are predominant in the context of times of order transition and lead us back to Clark. What exactly are the implications of the above analysis for the revision of his model?

Revision 1: Clark's model in a hybrid environment

The *underlying* basis of Clark's contested search for legitimacy is the English School's broad spectrum-based view on changes in practices, that is from more solidarist ones to more pluralist ones; in principle, it has, thereby, opened up space for a hybrid global order oscillating between solidarist global multi-level governance and more pluralist and increasingly salient great-power-based politics. Nevertheless, he does not spell out the characteristics of the process of oscillation in detail, which is why the nature of the main actors of Clark's theory remains exclusively state-based. What the model overlooks is that the current process of oscillation reflects the "emergence of a dualistic world order" comprising sovereign states and, "[s]uperimposed…, functionally differentiated global subsystems of world society" (Cohen 2012:5). Therefore, this chapter needed to go beyond Clark's assumptions and had to address the question of what happens to the latter's – widely claimed – influence via access of the "subsystems", and TNAs in particular, when regime complexes become deadlocked.

It turned out that there are powerful arguments to the extent that great-power deadlocks neutralize the normative and political weight of TNAs. This does not imply the inevitable return to and permanent validity of a purely state-based world/view (Koskenniemi 2011:359), as employed by Clark. What it does highlight, though, is the fact that in today's dualistic order it is critical to look at the dynamic *relationship between* the two major strands shaping the dualism. This includes the possibility that, in the event of deadlocks caused by the great-power-based strand, the other strand cannot influence the ongoing process *as long as* the key players have not arrived at some agreement on the main patterns of global legitimacy. In sum, while adapting Clark's model to today's challenges clearly requires us to take into account non-state actors, it needs to be sensitive to the specific weight these latter actors have in critical periods such as order transition. As Hay put it with a great deal of insight: "In the end neither focus is mutually exclusive. And whilst that remains the case, talk of post-international relations is somewhat premature" (2010:295).

4
Order Transition, Common Culture and Exceptional Worldviews

Clark's notion of the "morality" of global legitimacy (2005) and Gilpin's "ideological... values common to a set of states" (1981:34), which underpin an order, are both premised on and derived from the assumption of US hegemony. This understanding of a "common culture" reflects the ideological "taken-for-granted nature" of American unipolarity, common to a large majority of writings in IR theory. It is also a result of a development that, originating in the 1970s (i.e. Carter's universal human rights ideology) and the 1980s (i.e. the reality and ideology of the Information Age), left the United States in a position, especially since 1991, both to globalize its domestic political system and structure international arrangements according to its domestic values. Or, as Kurth put it, "[b]y the 1990s... the United States had become the core state, the civilizational state, for the new global civilization" (2010:64).

Such assumptions also underlie the works of prominent theorists of international cooperation. For instance, Keohane recently acknowledged that the explanatory power of his rationalist model is currently stalled since the underlying global power structures are changing. During order transition, changes in the global power structures can *only* be accounted for by "a greater divergence of interests, weighted by power" (Keohane 2012:125). For Keohane, these structural developments have *no* impact on the order's underlying ideological set of values. In fact, the supposedly globally accepted social purpose of his theory continues to be the promotion of "beneficial aspects on human security, human welfare and human liberty as a result of a more peaceful, prosperous and free world" (2012:126). In other words, regardless of the structural changes, Keohane a priori assumes that a liberal "common culture" will by default underpin and define any future global order.[1]

At a more analytical level, these remarks hint at the value bias underlying existing patterns of multilateralism. In fact, as some scholars made very clear: "It may appear axiomatic to Liberal Institutionalists that states should wish to promote economic regimes built on liberal norms and principles. And the same argument applies to the promotion of human rights, the elimination of pollution,... But this position disregards the fact that it is by no means universally agreed that liberal norms and principles should be underpinning... regimes... in the international system" (Little 2006:381). Therefore, this bias, it seems, is partly responsible for the aforementioned deficiencies and deadlocks of international regimes and partly provides the ideological underpinnings of the US–China trust deficit.

Two empirical examples further strengthen this assumption. Firstly, when a former US secretary of state realized in public that the United States had to "network[.] more effectively with a lot of *other* people and institutions" (Economist 2012c), she unwittingly showed some awareness, however marginal, of the inherent ideological bias that characterizes both today's global governance institutions and the efforts of their state and non-state participants. Secondly, anonymous top Chinese officials and Chinese scholars such as Ma Xiaojun, professor at the CCP Central Committee's School of International Strategic Studies, stressed that Copenhagen 2009 had not so much been about climate regulations; rather, viewing the events through a first-order lens, they suggested that it was "much more important" (Economist 2011 (anonymous official)) to see China's objections as reflecting a clash of views on the shape of the "new political and economic world order" (SWP 2010:1–2 (Ma)).

Therefore, it is no coincidence that among a variety of theorists such statements have fed into the perception that "embedded in the emerging power structure in the new global order is a potential structural conflict between China and the United States... because of their clashing ideologies [and] contrasting world order visions" (Yongjin 2008:155–156). The necessity to shift more research attention to questions related to the notion of worldviews has received further empirical support from the political implications and underlying tensions that accompanied the recent launch of Xi Jinping's "Chinese dream". As a leading Beijing-based news portal put it, there was "nothing short of a competition between the American dream and the Chinese dream" (quoted in Economist April 5, 2013:24). To qualify such claims, while worldview-based attitudes may permeate the US–China relationship, both powers are not exclusively guided by them. Rather, as the United

States' National Security Strategy (NSS) stated, the minimum diplomatic goal is to resolve antagonisms "on the basis of mutual interests and mutual respect" (2010:11).

With regard to the main task of reconceptualizing Clark's theory (2005), it is, therefore, important to take a closer look at the second of the three key aspects, which he has merely taken for granted in his original model, that is, the worldview underpinning the international system. In particular, the following conceptual analysis addresses *three key problems*. First, according to Clark (and Gilpin), hegemons translate their domestic values into the common culture of the respective international system. This draws our conceptual attention to two assumptions underlying their accounts: the unquestioned preconditions of the transfer rationale and the supposedly unchanging nature of common culture. Second, a closer empirical look at the above-stated competition between Chinese and US worldviews reveals that there are, in fact, two rivalling perceptions of cultural superiority. This raises several conceptual questions as to the nature of the underlying assumptions that elevate exceptional worldviews to the level of superiority and as well as to the key features of superiority itself. Third, based on the book's assumption that global politics is not, despite the US–China competition, on the brink of a war of hegemonic transition, the chapter raises the question of how to think about the relationship between the two kinds of superiority that have been identified.

The chapter is structured as follows: the *first* section provides definitions of two concepts that are central to the chapter, that is, common culture and worldviews. If, as the chapter argues, the "common culture" is, to different degrees, no longer "commonly accepted" by established and rising great powers, this raises two conceptual points. It looks into the dynamics, thus far underspecified by Clark and Gilpin, of the relationship between the notions of worldview and common culture; and it analyzes the underlying assumption that the nature of the common culture, as accepted by the predominant actor, remains basically unchanged over time. The *second* section reviews arguments made to the effect that there is no need to contemplate the impact of distinct worldviews because there is no ideological competition today. It refutes those arguments based on empirical observations as well as biases embedded in the accounts of those who put forward the proposition of a non-ideological era. If it is accepted that there is an ideological competition underway, the *third* section consequently looks into the actual nature of exceptionalist worldviews. Specifically, it asks in conceptual terms what makes worldviews exceptional, what elevates them to the level of (and distinguishes them from) superiority and what are the key features of the latter? Empirical examples underline the findings. The *fourth* section examines the implications of the relationship between the two kinds of superiority for the notion of order transition. It raises the question whether the superior nature of US and Chinese worldviews makes them incommensurable and, consequently, whether it renders peaceful order transition impossible. The *conclusion* summarizes the results of the chapter and indicates the implications they have for the revision of Clark's original model.

The concepts of worldview, common culture and their relationship

Definitions

This section provides definitions of some of the key terms used in this chapter. Throughout various literatures in IR and global history, the concept of worldview is used interchangeably with terms such as vision, image, mental map or conception of world order, ideology, *Weltanschauung* or grand strategy (Bartelson 2009; Casey and Wright 2008; Conrad and Sachsenmaier 2007; Freeden et al. 2013; Nau and Ollapally 2012; Osterhammel 2012; Suganami 1989). Only the last term differs slightly from the other ones in that it integrates an actor's power interests and means-ends calculations into its worldview (Dueck 2006:9–13). The term "worldview" denotes the images and perceptions embedded in the foreign policy attitudes which states have developed toward the global realm. For instance, Hurrell has defined worldviews as the "actors' understandings of international politics and the ways in which these understandings have been gathered into intelligible patterns, traditions, or ideologies" (2007:17). As has already been stressed, those resulting ideologies are contested and exist in plurality (Katzenstein 2010; Smith 1988, 1993). Another scholar, Hurd, suggests a similar approach to think about worldviews, but goes beyond Hurrell, in that he underlines the importance of the political environment, that is, the practices, in whose context the worldviews need to be seen to operate. Thus, for Hurd worldviews are about "how people and states think and behave in world politics [, which] is premised on their understanding of the world around them, which includes their own belief about the world, the identities they hold about themselves and others, and the shared understandings and practices in which they participate" (2008:312–313).

The concept of "common culture" has two shapes. The first one is second-image based. Its distinguishing feature draws from the similarities of domestic settings and, thus, builds upon the notion of "cultural affinity" (Holbraad 1979:149). The most widely used example of this concept is embedded in democratic peace theory (Doyle 1986; Russett 1993). In this instance, the concept implies that "cultural affinities", that is, the existence of democratically governed polities, are conducive to peaceful cooperation (among democracies). In its second shape, common culture pertains to a systemic culture of common customs and practices in global politics. Those customs and practices are underpinned by the idiosyncratic cultural values of the predominant group of states, as Gilpin suggested (1981:29, 35). Historically, both in the West and in Asia, "an accepted body of law and custom", that is, "norms, rules [and] practices" to "guide and control" the co-existence of states, has been attributed a system-sustaining role (Craig and George 1995:ix, x). Most critically, only if the respective "common culture" is "commonly accepted" by the great powers of the day do its practices translate into customary international law (ibid.:x).[2] The role of common culture has been widely acknowledged. Examples of the existence of such a common culture are the Concert of Europe, the period of the United States' "unipolar moment" after the Cold War (until 2006/8) or the tributary system in East Asia (Ikenberry 2011; Schroeder 1994, 2004; Spence 1990; Yongjin and Buzan 2012; Watson 1992). In the remainder of this chapter, common culture is understood in its second shape.

The nature of the relationship between worldviews and common culture

The next step of the analysis draws from the empirical observations made in the introduction of this chapter and poses the following question: what are the implications of a common culture which is, if to varying degrees, no longer commonly accepted by the great powers of the day. Effectively, the following analysis examines two assumptions underlying Clark's and Gilpin's models that prevent them from successfully coping with today's global environment: the unquestioned preconditions of Gilpin's transfer rationale and the supposedly unchanging nature of common culture.

With regard to the transfer rationale between the notions of common culture and worldview, Gilpin identifies a group of leading states which, commonly, turn their worldviews into the common culture of an international society (1981:34).[3] This suggests the operation of some mechanism, which unwittingly executes this transfer. Moreover, the mechanism itself implies that there is a relationship between the two concepts of common culture and worldview. Consequently, this raises the question about its underlying assumptions. Unpacking the relationship between the two concepts, therefore, helps to shed new light on what Gilpin and Clark merely assume to be the automatic translation of the leading group of actors' worldviews into the commonly accepted ideology of the system. Obviously, the logic of the transfer of the hegemon's idiosyncratic values onto the international plane remains intact only as long as the hegemon's position is beyond discussion. Logically, it is equally obvious that this changes when the preconditions for the transfer rationale change. Concerning our case, if the group of leading states is viewed as less homogenous than originally assumed by Clark and Gilpin, that is, if the number of states, whose worldviews are in various ways fundamentally different and whose sheer material weight makes them matter, increases above one, then this urges us to view the nature of the transfer mechanism as politically more amenable. As a result, the conceptual room that this opens up facilitates a more dynamic view of the nature of the transfer mechanism and, thus, of the respective order's underlying common culture.

Having said this, the relationship between worldviews and common cultures has two key characteristics. Firstly, based on a constructivist understanding of foreign policy ideas, the worldviews of great powers and the common culture underlying an international order build a reciprocal relationship (Legro 2007). The perceptions and misperceptions, which the governments of great powers hold, both about the underlying power and normative structure of international affairs, as well as the obligations and terms of their participation in them, are constantly viewed and judged against the backdrop of their particular historical experience with international society and against the background of the likelihood of success in pursuing their national interests. Quintessentially, the worldviews are constantly produced and reproduced in their culturally distinct polities, on the one hand, and are being shaped by and, in turn, reshape the patterns of the prevailing "common culture", on the other. Such reciprocity does not mean that either side is easily malleable. In fact, precisely because the worldviews of any great power reflect its national historical pathways and entrenched values, they do not offer themselves as easy targets of an already established common culture. In this sense they resemble what Lipset called "deep beliefs", as opposed to more malleable, mere, attitudes (1997:25). Inherently, while an existing common culture aims to reaffirm its practices and to project them onto all great powers and their worldviews, the successful functioning of the prevailing practices, that is common culture, can be disrupted by new great powers. Their worldviews might lead them to object to or disrupt those practices that impose an undesirable common culture, for instance, one which is derived from and driven by "cultural affinities".

The second aspect, which prevents Clark and Gilpin from conceptually accommodating today's global environment, refers to their underlying assumption that the features of the predominant actors' common culture are unchanging. In the case of US unipolarity, it is static with regard to the liberal nature of the basic patterns of their worldviews. Thus, it overlooks the degree to which new systemic processes might affect the level of the hegemon's acceptance. For instance, an increasing degree of legalization-promoting globalization may contribute new layers to the common culture, which may still be informed by the original liberal ideology, but may go beyond its practices in a way that does not necessarily cohere with the leading power's conventional understanding of the application of its worldview. This suggests that while today's global governance processes and structures are indeed underpinned by liberal worldviews, the growing institutionalization and efforts of legalization shaping those processes are often not accepted as common culture by the predominant actor. For instance, the neutrality of regime experts, which adherents of global governance often adduce in order to promote the supposed necessity of collective action, is, by nature, political (Hurrell 2007:20). Thus, what has come to be known as the "ideology" of global governance (Koskenniemi 2011:66–67) is viewed by predominant actors as a source of enmeshment that is resented. As such, the "pervasive yet very parochial American concern over the suffocating power of 'big government' is carried over into the international arena" and applied to global governance (Foot et al. 2003:11). As a result, if the notion of common culture is treated as less static, the conceptual need to accommodate the predominant actor's revisionism reveals itself.

Taken together, Clark's and Gilpin's accounts mistakenly assume both that the common culture of an order is shaped by a high degree of homogeneity with regard to the group of leading states and that the features of the predominant actors' worldviews and common culture are static. Inadvertently, it seems that their frameworks conceptually need to further open themselves to the dynamics of competing worldviews. Before we can make this analytical step, we need to engage widely held arguments made to the effect that there is no such thing as ideological competition in today's global politics.

There is no ideological competition?

Why should there be a need to think about ideological competition today? Three arguments, which are widely used in the discipline, need to be engaged in order to underline the need to think about the ideological pattern of global politics.

Firstly, with the end of the Cold War and the "end of history" the notion of ideological competition was comfortably set aside. The gist of the debate is captured by Buzan, who plainly states that today's global politics is "not ideological" (2010:25). This, it is widely assumed, was also confirmed by the quick demise of the debate on the Asian century and values in the late 1990s (Kingsbury and Avonius 2008; Koh et al. 2000). Equally, the limited appeal, which the so-called China model has had, seems to further underline this attitude (Halper 2010). Subsequently, the liberal ideology promoting democracy and market economies has since been viewed as peerless and, thus, without competition. Liberal rationalist IR theorists have only seen one universal set of values remaining in world politics while no competing universal set is available or conceivable (Keohane 2012). However, it seems that the Cold War legacy has had a much larger and psychological effect on scholars than they have, thus far, admitted. As their mindsets have led on a search for an ideological counterpart to Western ideas with a similarly revolutionary nature as the Cold War Communist ideology, they have consequently been unsuccessful. In fact, their arguments are underpinned by some circular logic. Conceiving their own ideology as universal in a classical Hartzian sense (Foley 2011:40)[4] and, at the same time, pursuing a Cold-War-inspired search for a universal counter-set of values inherently prevents theorists from recognizing a distinct set of values. For instance, by looking for a "comprehensive alternative" to the liberal ideology, Jervis (2009:202) is reassured by the obvious result that there is no such (universal) thing. What he, together with many other scholars, misses is the point that the global acceptance of capitalism does by no means imply that the worldviews, shaping the foreign policy outlook of non-Western states, cohere with their Western counterparts.[5] These worldviews are predicated on the experience of long historical paths that have little in common with liberal expectations of a coming convergence of value outlooks. They might not be revolutionary or game-changing, but they reserve a historical right for themselves to maintain a significant degree of national particularity that cannot easily be penetrated. Therefore, thinking about China in terms of its "unsuccessful modernization" (Westad 2006:33) merely reveals the inherent strength of its underlying views of the outside world and the degree of contestation that this implies. Derived from its historical experience of the century of humiliation (1839–1949), China's contestation persistently takes as its foundational starting point the Westphalian "principle of sovereignty, because it believes in diversity and mutual respect in international political life. This position rests both upon its historical past as well as its vision of the future world order" (Xue 2007:86).[6] In turn, the same majority of theorists often presents the United States' worldviews as statusquo oriented, thus neglecting the United States' reinstated preference for self-reliance, that is, for preserving its own freedom of action, during perceived times of anarchic global politics. Thereby, these theories overlook the revisionist character underlying some of the United States' foreign policy traditions, which has broadly been reflected in their preference for "instrumental multilateralism" (Foot et al. 2003:266). The ways in which US and Chinese worldviews have been translated into manifestations of superiority is outlined below, respectively.

Secondly, prominent theorists of East Asia and its relations with the United States have suggested discarding the notion of (American) exceptionalism from the debate altogether. Possibly driven by the intention to counter both the burgeoning "China-fear" and "anti-Americanism" literatures,[7] as well as accompanying nationalistic public sentiments, those arguments take as their starting point the broadly accepted account of distinct traditions in US foreign policy (Mead 2002; Smith 1988, 1993). As Katzenstein put it, "[o]ne implication of the centrality of America's multiple traditions is to let go of the cherished myth of American exceptionalism. Instead it makes more sense to underline American distinctiveness, especially when viewed comparatively and in global context" (2011:218; Bender 2006). While Smith's research and the validity of the arguments of those authors suggesting a plurality of worldviews within single entities remain out of the question (Katzenstein 2010) and, equally, while the operation of countervailing traditions may again be stronger at other times, two counter-arguments can be offered against the usefulness of a plural perspective in the *particular timeframe* of this analysis.[8] First, there is a strong degree of competition discernible in US–China relations today, which has considerably strengthened, and has been strengthened by, the impact of worldviews on their respective foreign policies. Thus, while more *and* less cooperative traditions of a country's foreign policy might alternate or compete with each other at any time, either one also hinges on "specific political conditions" (Katzenstein 2011:214). In other words, it is absolutely central to look at the overall nature of a political environment in order to understand which traditions prevail over others at specific periods in time. The more pluralist "current international climate" seems to favor less cooperative foreign policy traditions (Prantl 2006:10). Second, while favoring more cooperative traditions might be more conducive to a better management of US–China relations, it would be highly inaccurate to theoretically downplay or assume away the existence of nationalist sentiments for the sake of the analysis. Self-perceptions of superiority in the publics of both great powers, however parochial, primordial or insular, need to be taken into account, in order to arrive at a realistic understanding of the tensions arising from countervailing worldviews.[9] For instance, Drezner found that "American elites are more predisposed towards liberal internationalism than the rest of the American public" (2008:51). Similarly, as a concise analysis on the status of the cognate discipline of global history recently acknowledged: "While the changing cultures of historiography have been tied to changes within US universities and American society at large, they do not necessarily reflect clear changes in majority opinion. Among large segments of the American population there is strong resistance to deconstructing national history and world historical narratives by shifting away from topoi such as the idea of US exceptionalism or the primacy of Western civilization on the global stage" (Sachsenmaier 2011:107). Failure of heads of states to pay due tribute to such parochial connotations commonly leads to fierce public reactions, as the US president "learned to his cost in 2009" (Ignatieff 2012:1; Walt 2011). Equally, the far-ranging revival of trenchant nationalism in the Chinese public and of "Chineseness" in Chinese political science and historiography powerfully mirrors the American example (Noesselt 2010:167; Sachsenmaier 2011:198, 211). Similarly, whereas Chinese literary theory in the 1990s still showed strong tendencies toward postmodernist thinkers, such as Derrida, today it is absorbed by the cross-societal "obsession with China" (Davies 2007:8).

Finally, instead of offering revised tools to think about patterns of a new ideological competition, some theories have tried to develop devices that let us contemplate agreements on "transcultural moral principles" between founding and new members (Linklater and Suganami 2006:147). For scholars working in this direction, the quintessential obstacle to generating more of these principles still lies in the undeniable fact that "perceptions of cultural . . . superiority amongst the original members of international society have not entirely disappeared" (ibid.). Nonetheless, despite their shortcomings, these theories can be adapted for our purposes. Earlier, it was found that Gilpin had mistakenly assumed that the common culture of an international order is shaped by a high degree of homogeneity with regard to the group of leading states. In turn, this had prevented his theory to accommodate today's higher degree of heterogeneity among leading states. If it is accepted that not only are there Western perceptions of cultural superiority which continue to exist today but *also* that they have unexpectedly been complemented by worldviews that reflect *no less a degree of cultural essentialism and superiority*, then the result resembles much more closely the revisions offered for Gilpin's and Clark's models. In fact, it is imperative to shift the research perspective away from simply restating the undeniable Western bias underlying the generating of "transcultural moral principles", as Linklater and Suganami suggested, and toward a better understanding of the tensions emerging from distinct self-perceptions of moral superiority by Western and non-Western great powers *alike*.

Taken together, instead of rejecting any notion of ideological competition outright and, in light of the weaknesses of Gilpin's and Clark' models it seems more fruitful to shift the analysis to a careful conceptual examination of the dynamics operating between two worldviews that *both* contain antagonistic potential. This is all the more important during times of order transition and is extremely critical of the analytical value of the New Global IR's pursuit of the aim to, according to one ISA president, "eschew[.] exceptionalism" (Acharya April 27, 2014).

Comparing worldviews

In order to press the analysis further, we now need to improve our conceptual understanding of the nature of the relationship between US and Chinese worldviews. Among the myriads of authors who have dealt with related issues, Byron Shafer (1999) and Kal Holsti (2010) stand out as having provided the most substantive accounts of conceptual problems involved in research on exceptionalism.[10]

Useful for our purposes, Shafer set himself the task of comparing sets of exceptionalisms. He began his analysis with the observation that many analysts have viewed social phenomena as being different or distinctive but not exceptional, if viewed from a sufficient distance; therefore, the conventional belief has been that there is no such thing as exceptionalism, as shown in the previous section. What he called "operational difficulties" led him to ask exactly "what to count" as exceptionalisms in order to be able to compare sets of them (1999:449).

In order to proceed, the analysis needs to define conceptual parameters that characterize worldviews as exceptional. A critical pattern of exceptionalism that can be distilled from the literature is the application of the domestic analogy (Ninkovich 2009; Smith 1999; Suganami 1989). Briefly, the central idea behind it is that states turn their domestic value sets into the central template underlying their international visions of governance and, thereby, aim at shaping the common culture of the system. This pattern reflects the intentions of agents to permeate the political nature of the international environment according to their domestic identities. This more systemic approach aims at the underlying nature of an order's governance system and is, thus, different from, if not contrary to, the idea that great powers externally impose their domestic ideals on foreign polities. Having identified such a pattern is useful in order to distinguish it from the foreign policy outlooks of states that lack the ambition to act on exceptional terms. In turn, establishing such a key feature allows us, subsequently, to compare different kinds of exceptionalism. However, this leaves open one more question. As Nau and Ollapally (2012), among others, have suggested that between those smaller states who have lacked the ambition to act exceptionally and those that have not lacked such ambitions, there do exist various middle-power states which have portrayed themselves as ambitious and exceptional.

Therefore, while retaining the domestic analogy as a template for the international environment, we need to identify further patterns that distinguish the exceptional worldviews of great powers (such as China and the US) from these latter ones. In other words, the analysis needs to supplement Hurrell's and Hurd's definitions provided at the beginning so that they can better serve our purposes. Only then is it possible to speak of worldviews which are more than distinctive and, in particular, reflect "a vision of national greatness" (Kissinger 2011:512). In conceptual terms, two interrelated features are introduced here. Firstly, Holsti has introduced the notion of "superiority" (2010:398). It is this feature that elevates exceptional worldviews from the level of distinctiveness to the level of self-perceived superiority. "Superior" worldviews convey their message by making reference to the notion of "justice", undergirding their respective view of world politics and how the environment should be designed – "as they define it" (Waltz 1979:198).[11] Holsti suggests that we search for those assumptions that are "embedded in the [great powers'] views of superiority" (ibid.). While his advice usefully directs us to identify the cultural presuppositions feeding into notions of self-perceived superiority, it fails to take into account the material component underpinning the worldviews of great-powers. As proponents of social power theory remind us in analogy, only once material components are combined with the cultural/moral features does a fully-fledged picture of superior worldviews become discernible (Bukovansky 2002:59). The second supplement is another manifestation of the notion of reciprocity in social life. One great power's feelings of superiority may produce a morally hierarchical view of other great powers. In turn, such attitudes can be expected to evoke reciprocal implications. Thus, when Jervis notes, "states that have gained a favorable position in the international system tend to conclude that their country is uniquely wise and just and that those who are seeking to displace them are morally inferior" (2011:36), he describes exactly that kind of relationship between two sets of superior worldviews.

In sum, if we aim at comparing worldviews in this analysis, we need to leave behind the prevailing attribute "exceptional". The latter needs to be substituted for by the attribute "superior". *Superior worldviews employ the domestic analogy as do exceptional ones but infuse it with cultural/moral references of superiority, predicated on material capabilities, which middle-powers do not possess.* A superior foreign policy approach is of a revisionist nature, though, the degree of revisionism may vary.

Finally, as a methodological issue, how can we observe the impact of these exceptionalist worldviews in empirical terms since worldviews commonly neither translate into nor shape real-world politics unfiltered? Theorists have addressed this issue from two perspectives, which, indeed, support each other. Shafer stressed that superiority "is real or not, ..., depending on its motive impact. If political actors believe in it or, indeed, if they are agnostic but can nevertheless use the symbolism of difference – to move public opinion, ..., or to shape the policy process – then the [superiority] is a genuine and confirmedly empirical phenomenon" (1999:446). Holsti draws from wide-ranging empirical studies which have shown that, contrary to neorealist arguments to the effect that values merely serve as a fig-leaf for power, value-based rhetoric is "not empty but reflects deeply held ideological convictions" (Holsti 2010:382). Having said that, our new definition employs a combined three-step approach in order to operationalize answers to the methodological problem. First we need to identify manifestations of the domestic analogy, then ask if they are infused with notions of justice and, finally, spot instances where reciprocal dynamics of inferiority-superiority become discernible. Therefore, Holsti's encouragement that we search for those assumptions which are "embedded in the [great powers'] views of superiority" will be executed as an empirical undertaking (2010:398).

What the definition of superior worldviews does not entail is references to notions of special responsibilities and privileges. Despite the fact that the latter are commonly associated with the conventional notion of exceptionalism, the main concern here is to identify the core reasoning that *constitutes* Chinese and US worldviews of superiority. This needs to be analytically distinguished, and thus separated out, from the specific special responsibilities that have been *derived from* those superior worldviews.

The key features of Chinese and US worldviews

Using the three-step approach, this section offers a brief overview of the key features of China's and the United States' superior worldviews.[12] First it identifies examples that provide evidence of the domestic analogy; it goes on to search for notions of (great-power) justice that might, finally, play into the dynamics of reciprocity between superior worldviews. Clearly, these steps cannot be taken in a neatly separated way; some overlap is inevitable.

As for China, looking first at the ways in which it has employed the domestic analogy illustrates the bases of its worldviews. The domestic-societal concept of a "harmonious society"[13] is viewed by the Communist Party as providing the key guidelines for "harmony" in global politics. Basically, there are three layers of evidence that together help to clarify the rationale of harmony. To begin with, the sixth plenary session of the 16th Central Committee in 2005 officially adopted the domestic concept as its central vision of and for the international plane (Noesselt 2010:191; Noesselt 2014).[14] The speeches of former president Hu, for instance, at the CCP's 17th national congress in 2007, and the domestic debates about them, confirm the conceptual transfer that has turned the notion of the "Harmonious Society" into the "Harmonious World" (Wang 2011).[15] At its core, the transfer is intended to undercut the tensions that have arisen between China's modernization process, on the one hand, and the socio-economic, political and cultural developments in the remainder of the world, on the other (Noesselt 2010:191). In other words, the transfer is supposed to synchronize the two processes without entangling the former. Furthermore, the ways in which the idea of the harmonious society is turned into a template for international politics can be seen in Chinese understandings of the notion of democratization as well as in statements by the Shanghai Cooperation Organization

(SCO). Democratization aims at the maintenance and "respect for each other's . . . choice of social system and development path" (Jiechi 2012).[16] The SCO declaration supports the argument and adds, somewhat self-consciously, that the organization itself "has become a model of state-to-state . . . cooperation in the twenty-first century", based on "respecting each other's sovereignty, independence, . . . and non-interference in each other's internal affairs" (SCO 2012). In order to then achieve "a fair and democratic international order . . . *harmonious* . . . partnerships" are required (ibid.). Put shortly, democratization refers to sovereignty-guarding and state-based principles which provide the key modi operandi of global cooperation (Noesselt 2010:162, 175, 272), regardless of the state's real attitude toward international law.[17] The implied insistence on socio-political diversity is the key message which Chinese diplomatic parlance traditionally intends to convey when it speaks of international relations based on "mutual respect" (Jiechi 2012) and is, in turn, also supposed to confirm the ideal of the domestic "harmonious society".[18] Finally, Dai Bingguo's statement from December 2010, "Persisting with Taking the Path of Peaceful Development", similarly aims to reaffirm the peaceful connotations of the "Harmonious World" concept and repeats Hu's transfer-of-harmony logic from the domestic to the international realm.[19] China, it states, pursues a socio-economic path that has allowed its people to "bid farewell to poverty and enjoy a better life" and, thus, enjoy the benefits of a harmonious society. Internationally, Beijing's harmonious behavior has already led it to enjoy "a better life" precisely because it has acted as the "most responsible, the most civilized, and the most law-abiding and orderly member of the international community" (2010).

Taken together, the three strands show how China employs the domestic analogy in global politics. But, how does it elevate this exceptionalism to the level of a superior worldview? First, it introduces a historico-political narrative which prepares the international environment for China's rightful arrival as a leading great power, then makes this move more acceptable by clothing it as a just view of world politics and, finally, reveals its superior attitude as being embedded in racial connotations.[20]

Over the last few years, Beijing has propagated its "return to normalcy". It has associated with this return a, supposedly, unquestioned status which it had enjoyed from 1750 to the beginning of the opium wars in 1839 and 1856.[21] In this time period, the vast material inequalities between China and its neighbors shaped a tributary system and provided the economic basis of Beijing's feeling of superiority (Spence

1990). This particular period of "national greatness" has been held up against the century of humiliation that followed, a historic foil which provides support for the "return" in that the then experienced "grievance [presents] a leitmotif in China's international affairs" (Westad 2012:5). China's historical belief in its pre-humiliation status, that is, the time before the opium wars, as a default great power has now come to powerfully permeate today's official statements and discourses (Westad 2012:12; Yew 2013:3). Employing this historical narrative for contemporary purposes has been materially helped by China's material success since it has been the second strongest economy in the world since 2010.[22] Moreover, both with Beijing successfully mastering the recent financial crisis *and* with it sustaining its economic growth (in contrast to the "BRI" states) thereafter, China's self-perception as an indispensable great power in world politics, whose socio-economic model is widely admired, has been immensely strengthened in recent years (Westad 2012:5). For instance, Wu Dawei, the former head of the PRC delegation for the Six-Party talks, proclaims that "the PRC's economic rise represented a return to normalcy with China as a great world power" (WikiLeaks, cable 10SEOUL272, February 22, 2010, [then] VFM Chun on Sino-North Korean Relations). True to its legacy, the contemporary return-to-normalcy narrative reinvigorates China's historical notion of economic superiority. Importantly, with China having emerged as the number one trading partner of ASEAN, Japan, Australia and South Korea already in 2011 (Khong 2014:162 n. 17), it has resumed its traditional position as the most important economic actor in the region. Reciprocally, the economic aspects have fed back into the dynamics underpinning the "return" argument. In fact, the nationalistic symbolism that has been associated with such a notion of return has been conveyed by members of the highest echelon in the Communist party. When China's president Xi, for example, offered his vision of the "Chinese dream" in 2013, he asserted that its realization could only be thought of as starting from a position of national strength and greatness, as it had been the case before the age of humiliation (Economist April 5, 2013:11). Conspicuously, this reflected the large degree to which his thinking is guided by historical notions of politico-economic superiority.[23] Unwittingly perhaps, but nonetheless powerfully, Xi thereby confirms what John Fairbanks correctly remarked with regard to the persistence of the notion of superiority in Chinese thinking: "If its belief in Chinese superiority persists, it seems likely that the country will seek its future role by looking closely at its own history" (1968:62).

Concerned about (but not determined by) the implications that the notion of superiority holds for its neighboring countries, China faces problems that are similarly known to other leading great powers. Indeed, China knows that its insistence on the notions of equality and diversity, which characterizes the harmonious world order, is difficult to square with the regional and international ambitions reflected in the "China dream". Moreover, its leadership is aware that China's "deeply rooted superiority complex" has engendered a longstanding "hierarchical mentality", which "will not dissolve or disappear" (Jacques 2009:432). Beijing has, therefore, developed a broad, though loose, concept (or cover) which allows it to frame the politics of its worldviews such that it acknowledges and weakens concerns about its "superiority" at the same time. China, it argues, aims at "establishing a just, democratic and multipolar world architecture" (SCO 2012), that is, an international order that is "more just and reasonable" than the existing one (Keqiang 2014).[24] In other words, by publicly presenting itself as a gentle advocate of a "just world", China carves out the room needed, if not necessarily accepted by others, to advance its interests, that is, its dream. The familiar great-power reflex springing from such statements, however, has been duly marked. As Waltz reminds us, "[s]ince justice cannot be objectively defined, the temptation of a powerful nation is to claim that the solution it seeks to impose is a just one" (1979:201).[25]

This leads us to the final step which Holsti encouraged us to take. We now need to look for the underlying assumptions embedded in China's superior worldview. While the "dream" has officially been proclaimed, the assumptions of superiority driving it have – for obvious diplomatic reasons – not officially been made public. Nevertheless, the "dream" has been strongly echoed in, and disseminated by, the broader, so-called "Sino-speak", discourse, which may be seen as an expression of a larger trend in Chinese public debates (Callahan 2012).[26] While this discourse is, largely speaking, inconsequential to academic exchanges,[27] its crucial importance lies in the fact that "Sino-speak is heavily promoted by government officials, state media, and official intellectuals in China" (Callahan 2012:50).[28] For instance, as the philosopher Xu Jilin observed after the Olympic Games in 2008, the term "new worldism" had been introduced precisely because many intellectuals felt the urge to support an economically and militarily strong, as well as a culturally independent posture of China in global politics (Siemons 2013). Most importantly, Xi's notion of the "China dream", announced in May 2013, had intellectually been prepared and partly framed by what was soon to become a popular author from inside the "Sino-speak" military establishment.[29] Deliberately manipulating the public's nationalistic demands, China's new president has adopted parts of the nationalistic debate into his policies and has thereby deliberately undermined the official cooperative attributes of China's foreign policy stance.[30]

Liu Mingfu, a senior colonel of the PLA and professor at China's National Defense University, named his book the "China Dream: Great Power Thinking and Strategic Posture in the Post-American Era" (2010).[31] Straightforwardly, knowing that China needs neighboring markets to continue to grow, he argues that China needs to guard its economic rise back to normalcy; this requires, in turn, a "military rise" in order to contest US power in the region (quoted in Callahan 2012:37). This rise should provide China with the military clout to counter what is widely perceived as the US' containment of China's economic rise (Callahan 2012:38).[32] As Xi put it, "To achieve the great revival of the Chinese nation, we must ensure there is unison between a prosperous country and a strong military" (quoted in Rajan 2014). Leading us to the inner workings of his narrative, Mingfu goes on to suggest that China's rise and its role as a leading great power cannot be explained in the terms set by the analogies of the rise of Western powers. Rather, when Mingfu makes reference both to historical legacies of Chinese superiority, which have supposedly been revived through Beijing's proclaimed return to normalcy, as well as to ethno-racial connotations, his proposal proves deeply entrenched in the pertaining and wide-spread Chinese discourses (Gungwu 1991; Hughes 2006; Dikötter 1992). As he argues, China's posture needs to be viewed in light of its "Chinese characteristics" (quoted in Callahan 2012:39). While Mingfu's book adds to the "increasing Chinese preoccupation with ethnic or racial characteristics" (Johnston 2014; Westad 2012:456), its "Chinese characteristics" do not reflect some intermittent phenomenon. To the contrary, the "characteristics" have much deeper roots. His notion of Chineseness is associated with "a powerful body of opinion in China that believes in polygenism and holds that the origins of the Chinese are discrete and unconnected with that of other branches of humankind" (Jacques 2009:421). In essence, "Chinese civilization is bolstered by a widespread belief that the difference between the Chinese and other people is not simply...historical but also biological" (ibid.). Thereby, Mingfu's reasoning underlines China's self-perception as being "culturally superior", a notion which is now again deeply embedded in mainstream political thinking.[33] Subsequently, Mingfu's "Chinese characteristics" reveal their closeness to traditional Chinese thinking in that they draw on a hierarchical view of humanity.[34] Or, as Chen put it, Mingfu's and most others' Han Chinese racism is indebted to the "imperial order of things" and humans (2010:Epilogue). Unsurprisingly then, Mingfu observes the beginning of a new "Yellow-Fortune Era" that "heralds the rejuvenation of the Chinese nation to its rightful place at the center of global politics" (quoted in Callahan 2012:39). Based on the return narrative, today's new era does not resemble a traditional security dilemma but an "'identity dilemma' of competing civilizational models" (Mingfu quoted in Callahan 2012:39). Confirming widely held nationalistic-racial convictions, this "identity dilemma" characterizes the value-based competition between American and Chinese civilizations as "georacial politics" (39). Expectedly, Mingfu then concludes that, in this competition over the shape of the future international order, the Chinese race acts as the "most excellent race" and will win because it is the "superior race" that is "even better than the white race" (Mingfu quoted in Callahan 2012:40).[35]

In effect, Mingfu's notion of superiority has three interrelated layers. It is based on China's regained, traditionally immense, material inequality vis-à-vis its neighbors; its implications are framed as the pursuit of an international order that is more "just" than the existing one and, finally, the particular Chineseness of its superiority over the United States is steeped in traditional terms of Han racism.

As for the US, at the beginning of the Cold War the United States decided to implement an international political order, if limited to the Western parts of the world, whose key markers were derived from its domestic model. As Ikenberry put it, "the political architecture of openness – the emphasis on a system of multilateral rules and institutions – was ... encouraged and reinforced by America's liberal identity" (2011:182). This liberal openness guaranteed that the emerging "American-led open-democratic political order" transferred its distinguishing domestic features such as "public good provision, rule-based cooperation, and voice opportunities and diffuse reciprocity" to the international level (2011:161). In turn, "[t]he American political system – and its alliances, technology, currency and markets – became fused to the wider liberal order" (2011:2).[36]

Albeit fundamentally different from the Chinese alternative in terms of its content, the outlined transfer confirms the similarity of the ways in which the United States has employed the domestic analogy. While this makes the US worldview indeed "exceptional", as the last NSS reassured itself (2010:9), it does not yet tell us how it is elevated to the level of superiority. This section shows that the US worldview, almost axiomatically, presents itself as the only version of a "just peace" that is available in world politics. The analysis then outlines the underlying assumptions of this notion of "just peace", which, in turn, point to its "superior" features. Finally, derived from such superiority, the US' understanding of leadership reveals its inherently exclusionary aspects.

At its core, America both provides and is responsible for the upholding of the notion of "just peace" (US NSS 2010:5). Such an international order offers its members the template for a world in which individuals may strive to "achieve their full potential" (ibid.). It presupposes a degree of openness which, as Ikenberry stated, facilitates the necessary "public good provision, rule-based cooperation, and voice opportunities and diffuse reciprocity" (Ikenberry 2011:161). Despite its openness, the construction of such a "just peace" is not contradicted by the assumption that, in terms of socio-economic development, "there is only one path to modernity... and that is essentially liberal in character" (Ikenberry 2009:93).[37]

What are the sources or underlying assumptions of such stark and absolute beliefs? The literature has identified two interrelated patterns that account for the inherent superiority. First, Americanism is a "creed", as Lipset, suggested (1997:19). It is an "ideology which includes a set of dogmas about the nature of a good society"; this creed comprises "five words: liberty, egalitarianism, individualism, populism, and laissez faire" (1997:31). Therefore, absolutely central to understanding the essence of its self-perceived superiority, it must be seen through the prism of "traditionalism of the American people, the way Americans venerate the core founding documents, Founding Fathers, and founding principles of the state" (Mead 2002:96). Whereas Mingfu referred back to notions of Han Chinese racism, here the key source are nation-wide recognized, political documents such as the "Declaration of Independence". Second, as the narrative goes, it is precisely those documents that have provided the guidance that has historically made the United States into what it perceives itself to be: "by far the most successful great power in late modern times" (Deudney and Meiser 2012:21; Hunt 2007). In other words, the founding documents and the key principles they contain are history-proven in that they have laid out the templates for the great successes of the United States. Inter alia, the US victories in both World Wars as well as in the Cold War have been coalesced into this narrative.[38] Needless to say, such arguments contain economic and military aspects of superiority, too. Overall, when polls find that an overwhelming majority of Americans believes that the US is "unique" and "culturally superior", they merely confirm the justifications of superiority given thus far (Tomes 2014:28, 45).

Both, the quintessential liberal quality underpinning this version of superiority as well as its major successes in history have broad and direct implications for the United States' understanding of leadership in global politics. To begin with, precisely because America has for long been a "source of inspiration for others" (Holsti 2010:382) and because Americanism is, therefore, self-evidently of advantage to everybody, the incumbent president stated in the foreword to the NSS that its liberal character is "fundamental to American leadership" and, thus, a "source of strength in the world" (2010:ii) – which others do not possess, one could add. It is the strongly held belief, as the document continues, that "our interests are bound to the interests of those beyond our borders" which allows America to perceive of its approach to world politics as being solely driven by "enlightened self-interest" (3). From a US perspective, the latter provides the essential legitimation, so that the United States "can and should set down the terms and conditions" of any international institutional arrangement (Foot et al. 2003:268; Dueck 2006). The ways in which this "just peace" is pursued leave no doubt that *only* America can carry the responsibility for this "peace" in a successful manner. In other words, America continues to view itself as the custodian of the international order and, concomitantly, of the liberal and "just peace" that it strives to deepen in world affairs. As a former secretary of state put it, the US is *the*"indispensable nation" (Albright 1997).

While Obama's insertion (2009), that it is the liberal character of the just peace which "the United States has helped to underwrite... for more than six decades with the blood of our citizens and... our arms", reminds us of the inseparable economic and political aspects of US superiority, highlighting its exclusionary liberal aspects sheds some critical light on what has been portrayed as an uncontroversially just order of peace. Straightforwardly, the NSS distinguishes between democratic and non-democratic states with regard to necessary leadership qualities. Only the former are electable in order to *help* pursue the "just peace", if not as leaders; this is because "nations that respect human rights and democratic values are more successful and stronger partners" (5). As Ikenberry noted above, deep-seated liberal assumptions about common interests, which help to build and maintain a cooperative order, are reflected in notions of restraint and reciprocity and, in turn, make the smooth working of the order possible. In this respect, the discernible preference given to supposedly "stronger partners" and the special quality attached to cooperation among democracies as being "more successful" stand out.[39] The implications of this are crucial. Non-democratic states, even if they are essential to address global problems, cannot gain the standing of a democratic leading power. In other words, when Ikenberry insists that the US order is "easy to join", he merely suggests that China may be part of the operations set by the terms of the "just peace", but it is denied a leadership role on an equal basis. In essence, this is the message which the, much less diplomatic, term liberal "just *dis*equilibrium" conveys: there can only be *one* leader. At its core, this is the unofficial conviction held by the US government.[40]

In effect, the US notion of superiority possesses three intertwined layers. Derived from the domestic analogy, it views the supposed openness of the international order as a "just peace", which is committed to "public good provision, rule-based cooperation, and voice opportunities and diffuse reciprocity". The superiority of this Americanism then flows from two sources: the founding documents as well as the manifold historical successes that have resulted from the guidance offered in those documents. Needless to say, immense material capabilities underpin this a depiction. Finally, the "just peace" can only be led by one liberal power. Others may join as contributors in the resolution of global problems, but are denied leadership based on second-image thinking.

Necessarily, we now need to juxtapose the different components of Chinese superior thinking with those of its US counterpart. The result that emerges looks bleak. Three components of their notions of "just order", respectively, underline the great difficulties that emerge in this respect. First, the firm US belief that there is "only one path to modernity and that is liberal" seems hard to square with the "China dream" and the harmonious society's insistence on socio-economic diversity.[41] Second, whereas the US' understanding of rightful leadership, that is, just (liberal) disequilibrium, leaves no room for co-equal leaders, the Chinese "return to normalcy" narrative is diametrically opposed to that.[42] Finally, while the US' justifications for its superiority are derived from its (revolutionary) founding documents as well as its undeniable historical successes, the Chinese foundations of superiority are to be found in racial connotations that allow the Chinese to perceive themselves as "better than the white race".

The admittedly relative impact of superior worldviews on policy making notwithstanding, these examples reveal the underlying tensions which attempts at global cooperation have encountered. At least in part, they confirm Yongjin's admonition from the beginning of this chapter where he pointed to "a potential structural conflict between China and the United States...because of their clashing...world order visions" (2008:155–156). In fact, the sentiments that have exacerbated such fears are well captured in a review of the main assumptions underlying the "Sino-speak" discourse: "American exceptionalism is replaced by Chinese exceptionalism" (Callahan 2012:51). As Waltz soberly explained (1979:205): "...the common good is defined by each of the (great powers) for all of us, and the definitions conflict." This section has tried to show that this is the case because of the notions of superiority underlying such definitions.

Finally, while it is not yet clear "which nationalism is likely to become more salient for the (Chinese) regime when it faces legitimacy problems", it is even less reassuring that there is "very little political space in China for public criticism of reactionary nationalist voices and their foreign policy preferences" (Johnston 2014:182). Moreover, the fact that the United States has equally reflected "superior" attributes in their worldviews is all the more important at times when leading scholars remind us that the "renewed power of nationalism (is) no longer...containable politically or analytically in a box marked 'ethnic conflict' but (is) manifest in the identity politics and foreign policy actions of the major states in the system" (Hurrell 2013:193). The degree to which notions of "superiority" feed into domestic perceptions of one's own standing while psychologically adjusting to the other's trajectory is the (puzzling) key. Consequently, scholars draw our attention to the increasing and potentially dangerous "interaction of Chinese and American nationalism", which could lead to the "emergence of a...destructive assertiveness" on either side (Johnston 2014:182). As a result, the considerations thus far prompt us to ask the important question as to how to theorize about the implications of the relationship between competing superior worldviews.

Are superior worldviews incommensurable?

Looking at the historical record, the section's question can be answered both ways. During the Cold War[43], the worldviews underlying the foreign policies of the Soviet Union and the United States, though diametrically opposed to each other, eventually managed to co-exist. Further back in the history of the twentieth century, the same could not be said about the worldviews pursued by the Third Reich, on the one hand, and the alliance that rose against it, on the other.

At first sight, IR theory is hardly reassuring, either. For instance, Gilpin suggests that in the "absence of shared values...peaceful change has little chance of success" (1981:209). Wight states that "in the absence of a common culture" a states-system is unlikely to proceed in a cooperative direction (1977:33). Earlier, E. H. Carr had stressed the point that inter-war Britain would not have conceded a leadership role to Germany or Japan even if those two countries had come to outweigh the United Kingdom in material terms. The main reason was that democratic leadership was "preferable to *any* practicable alternative" (quoted in Gilpin 1981:209).[44] Therefore, unless an order transition were to "secure one's basic values", the incommensurability of exceptionalist worldviews would push world politics into a non-peaceful direction (Gilpin 1981:209). Prominent IR scholars have sharply underlined Gilpin and Carr. For instance, Friedberg is concerned about the fact that, should China continue to "grow(.) richer and stronger without also becoming a liberal democracy, the present muted rivalry with the United States is likely to blossom into something more open and dangerous" (2011:2).[45] In fact, a potential war implies the inevitability to have to choose between different worldviews and the eventual survival of only one of those worldviews, underpinning the next order (Gilpin 1981:34; Osterhammel 2012:421; Welch 1993).

As it was stated earlier, though, the world is not at the brink of a hegemonic war. In fact, this state of affairs is also helped by the fact that China and the US are the chief beneficiaries of global capitalist structures and networks. Nonetheless, while the transition which the global order is currently undergoing has thus far been peaceful, the competition between two superior worldviews is permeating the dynamics of US–China relations. Therefore, it is almost impossible to overlook the antagonistic features of the current relationship. Tellingly, the impact of such features is confirmed by leading practitioners. Lee Kuan Yew, the former president of Singapore, states that the "sense of cultural supremacy of the Americans will make... adjustment [to a new geopolitical era] most difficult" (2013:42). Thus, since both powers aim to "secure [their] basic values", how should we think about the issue? Existing scholarship has thought about the implications of Chinese exceptionalism, but has not addressed the issue of (in)commensurability (Zhang 2011:318–322).

Three layers of incommensurability

The degree of incommensurability may be conceived as representing a spectrum of three types: strong, medium and weak. The first, strong, one views notions of worldview as exclusive phenomena. They are not comparable with each other. This position resembles the concept of strict cultural or value relativism which leaves no room to reconcile one worldview with another. The second, medium, one does not identify any hierarchy among sets of worldviews. Instead, it accepts a variety of worldviews that may coexist based on the reciprocal understanding that each can operate autonomously. This type provides a way to undercut the tensions that might arise from the collision of sets of worldviews. In that, it is closely related to the idea of value pluralism. The third, weak, one also accepts the multiplicity of worldviews. It assumes, however, that potential differences can be absorbed by a very broad, preferably codified, framework of universal values, such as the UN convention on human rights. Its underlying cosmopolitan leanings lead it to reject incommensurability as a rhetorical construct.

Applying the spectrum to the topic of this chapter, it is argued that the first layer fits neatly into the theoretical framework of a hegemonic war.[46] During such a war, the worldview underpinning the next world order is fought out, and presents itself as, the only one available at the end of the struggle. As it was stated earlier, war is currently widely believed to be inconceivable; therefore, this layer moves into the background. The third layer represents the opposite end of the spectrum. It reflects an attitude that is still widely held by intellectuals and (former) UN officials, for example, Malloch-Brown, who sees the emergence of a "global social contract that builds on the emerging common values of solidarity in a shared world" (2011:13). However, as it was shown in Chapter 2, the deadlocks prevailing in many realms of global politics today have also revealed the impact of diverging worldviews that call into question the feasibility of cosmopolitan values. In contrast to these two types, the second one offers some measure of accommodation for the tensions arising from the parallel existence of superior worldviews.

This defense of value pluralism's revised version appears highly suitable, especially in light of the key arguments made in this book. As a quick reminder, it was argued earlier that global politics has experienced a move away from more solidarist global governance concepts to a world in which sovereignty-guarding great powers, such as China and the United States, have come to re-negotiate the key elements of the global order. Their respective approaches are mainly shaped by the pursuit of their respective national interests, though their competition is also buffered by their common support for global capitalist market structures. As Buzan put it, "the basic institutions of a pluralist, coexistent, interstate society have wide support among states", whereas efforts to reach cosmopolitan "homogenization...may not [be reached] in the foreseeable future" (2010:25).[47] Therefore, precisely because the latter view of homogenization "no longer looks plausible" (Brown 2013:488), it seems that the reasons for why the more "pluralistic dimension... is radically underplayed" have moved into the background (Little 2007:260). The analysis undertakes two steps. Firstly, the core assumptions of value pluralism are outlined to show why and how the notion of coexistence theoretically resolves the problem of incommensurability. Secondly, since adopting this overarching framework leaves open the question of how decision-making, informed by value pluralism, can be grounded in theory, two complementary approaches are offered.

The concept of value pluralism and its revision

Straightforwardly, one of the key proponents of the idea of value pluralism, Robert Jackson (2000; 2007), positions himself at the opposite end of the concept of "cultural relativism". Referring to the basic norm that secures coexistence, he argues that "[s]tate sovereignty does not liberate people from their destiny of living in a world alongside other people who are similarly organized" (2000:181). To the contrary, only by fully recognizing the natural plurality of states and, concomitantly, of their respective worldviews as the foundational, if minimalist, pattern of global political life is it possible to maintain the peaceful coexistence of a highly diverse human kind. In fact, it is this "constitutionally safeguarded territorial space" (182), however imperfectly conceived and by no means impenetrable for great powers, that has put up a considerable barrier against those kinds of political behaviors that take advantage of weaker states' vast inequalities in regard to wealth and power. In other words, "we must share the planet with many other people... unless we are determined to exterminate them, subordinate them (... colonize them), or remake them in our own self-image (convert them to our... values)" (181). Therefore, "jurisdictional pluralism is an accommodation of human diversity, via the institution of state sovereignty"; this is exactly what "makes possible value pluralism by placing political responsibility for creating and safeguarding particular values in the hands of local people who enjoy and exercise political independence" (181). In sum, by placing sovereignty at the center of his suggestions, Jackson shows how to circumvent and resolve the notion of incommensurability. However, since his theoretical operationalization of normative/value pluralism then does not go beyond broad references to "diplomatic practice, international law, and the political virtues embodied by the ethics of statecraft" (181), he leaves underspecified the question as to which mechanisms, more specifically, might facilitate the embedding and overcoming of value-based political divergences.

As a first cut, accounts of the "theory of practices", normative theorizing derived from the English School and writings of the political theorist Isaiah Berlin offer two related ways forward. The first one is grounded in Berlin's understanding of "concrete situations". The second one is informed by an understanding of practices which are "repeated, or at least reproduce similar behaviors with regular meanings" (Adler and Pouilot 2011:7). For the purposes of this chapter, both are viewed as taking their respective starting points in one specific layer of the pluralist strand of the English School. The assumption is that great powers are aware that peaceful relations among them are the precondition for the maintenance of the international system (Bull 2002); quintessentially, "[t]he key point is that efforts to preserve civility ... in the relations between states, and especially between the great powers, must generally take precedence over efforts to ensure civility ... within national borders" (Bull 2002; Linklater and Suganami 2006:142). This raises the question how a decision-making process, informed by value pluralism, but at the same time going beyond it, can be grounded in theory.

Isaiah Berlin's suggestion of how to cope with substantial value-based differences helps to clarify the nature of the approach summarized by Linklater and Suganami. Essentially, he states, "the concrete situation is almost everything" (1990:15). What he has in mind is the weighing up of two elements, that is, values and interests, in a specific situation. Such thinking underlines one central mechanism that may help to overcome worldview-based divergences, that is, the preference given to realpolitik and the preservation of core interests, in order to avoid larger political distortions on the global plane.[48] However, critics depict this as a reflection of an "anemic pluralism where conflict over values is cordoned off, and instead we see international relations as an arena governed ... by practical 'rules of the game'" (Bukovansky 2009:169–170). Such "practical rules of the game", once established, facilitate minimalistic great-power cooperation and, thus, the maintenance of the necessary degree of "civility" among them. By nature, they are tentative in their extent and short-termed with regard to their applicability as a diplomatic means. Nonetheless, the potentiality of reaching an agreement on core interests can lay the foundations for a deeper and sustained engagement between two great powers, that is, an overall agreement on mutual responsibilities as well as on constraining each others' power in a reciprocal way. In fact, this is the implication of a transcript of a discussion, classified as "secret", between two top-level officials from the US and China. " ... the critical question was whether both sides would agree to take care of each other's core interests. When considering such sensitive issues in the context of the bilateral relationship, they could be viewed either as obstacles or as core interests. It did not matter whether one side liked or disliked such matters; rather in a ... close and important bilateral relationship such as ours, the question was whether the key interests for each side would be accommodated" (WikiLeaks November 29, 2011, 09Beijing1176). And yet, establishing a more substantiated relationship requires the development of a common culture between the great powers. Thus, the conflict over values may be successfully "cordoned off" by this approach, while the need to identify a broader value-based foundation for more sustained cooperation remains.

This leads to the second set of theoretical assumptions that is employed here. It comprises parts of the normative reasoning related to the English School, as well as the literature on "international practices" (Adler and Pouilot 2011; Cochran 2009).[49] Recent normative scholarship emanating from an English School perspective has built upon Martin Wight's "middle-ground ethics", situated between "personal morality ... and raison d'etat or realpolitik" (Cochran 2009:289). Wight had earlier called such ethics "political morality" and had considered them to be deeply anchored in Western values. While not denying the frequently instrumental nature of reasoning in international politics, he had seen political expedience as being affected by the moral standards of the involved politicians. Commonly, their prudence had fed back into the practices used between states (ibid.). In this respect, Wight's suggestions are very similar to the main propositions of practice theory in that "practice ... depends on individuals' reflexive normative and instrumental judgments" (Adler and Pouilot 2011:15). They also resemble Jackson's "virtues embodied by the ethics of statecraft" (2000:181). However, the translation of Wight's mental maps, that is, ideas and beliefs in IR parlance (Goldstein and Keohane 1993; Jervis 1976), onto the international plane encounters an already familiar problem. The reliance on Western values makes the idea resemble the kind of worldview that was found earlier in a common culture which is based on "cultural affinity". Thus, Wight's "political morality" has too narrow of a value basis.

Nevertheless, despite these shortcomings, the core of Wight's ideas has considerable value, especially in light of the decreasing weight of more cosmopolitan approaches. The latter ones have rightly attributed many significant flaws to the so-called "morality of states"; however, viewing the basis for an international ethics solely in "an idea of right or wrong founded on universal moral principle" (Cochran 2009:290) has mistakenly downplayed states' substantive support for "contrary, particularist trends" (Halliday 2009:49). In contrast, Cochran suggests developing Wight's original middle-ground ethics into "ideas of right and wrong found within a practice of states" (Cochran 2009:290).[50] Those ideas of right and wrong do not presuppose any kind of a "moral community...as reflected in the...broader moral consciousness of global society" (Hurrell 2007:303). Much rather, they permit states to retain their particular views of global legitimacy. Theorists of the "practice turn" stress that the actors' understandings of a common challenge do "not create uniformity of a group or community, but organize their differences around pervasive understandings of reality" (Adler and Bernstein quoted in Adler and Pouilot 2011:16). In other words, global legitimacy may serve as a focal point of contestation, while notwithstanding the difficulties which the process of identifying similar conceptions in distinct social and cultural contexts entails. Since states internationally (re-)negotiate what they deem right and wrong, this approach adequately reflects the dynamics, that is, the practices, pertaining to the contested nature of the politics of global legitimacy. Tony Brenton, the former, long-time UK ambassador to the UN, has captured the dynamics driving the difficult process of shifting ideas of right and wrong in states-practice: "The existence of a small group of key nations around whom a particular negotiation...pivots is of real importance. While the influence of the group can only rarely alter the deeply held political positions of its members, a habit of intimacy..., even among states with widely differing positions, genuinely...increases the likelihood of finding such common ground as exists" (2013:542).

Such theorizing permits the identification of a largely non-ideological, shifting set of practice guidelines that offers to steer great-power politics around potential conflicts spurred by superior worldviews. This is not to say that the great powers currently try to devise, or that they would commit themselves to, such guidelines, as the existing great-power trust deficit indicates. Nonetheless, those guidelines usefully take off the ideological edge in times of a "trust deficit", provide practice-based room to maneuver for the ongoing renegotiations of the global order and, importantly, go beyond Berlin's rather more short-termed suggestions. While *such* practice guidelines have often been accused of not wanting to "engage with any strong conception of the good", their aim has instead been to search for the "empirical conditions for agreement", or as Hobbes put it, a set of facts "about what the world will call good" (quoted in Hurrell 2013:228). Put differently, the practices embodied in "middle-ground ethics" provide the worldview-based stability necessary to transform or renegotiate global order. The conclusion that has often been drawn in this context is that such parameters only permit a minimal-order understanding (Clark 1989; Hurrell 2007:87). The latter is then solely reduced to maintaining peaceful security cooperation and presents the default foil for neorealist theories (Buzan and Hansen 2009). In contrast, this analysis suggests that the notion of such a minimal order cannot only be attributed to a security-based order, but it can also be, as is the case today, the reflection of a transitioning global order, where its "minimal" characteristics serve as the essential – and least ideological – background to re-negotiating its foundations. As opposed to the minimal-order approach, this step is necessary precisely because the "order that embodies the values of existing great powers" (Bull 1979/80:439) has already experienced strong contestation.

Revision 2: Clark's model and exceptional worldviews

Clark's notion of "morality", that is, one set of values underpinning international order, is too narrow. The analysis showed that *not only do two superior worldviews exist today (i.e. US and Chinese), but also that they are competing with each other.* Examining the underlying assumptions of Clark's notion of "morality" demonstrated that neither was the transfer logic still valid, that is, the turning of one worldview into the common culture or morality of the order, nor remained the nature of the embedded common culture itself unchanged. Rather, it became clear that, if we wanted to re-conceptualize Clark's original model, we urgently needed to think about the *relationship between the two worldviews.* Having identified the central components of their self-perceived superiority, respectively, raised the crucial question of whether or not US and Chinese exceptional worldviews were incommensurable and what the implications were thereof. Instead of building the order's morality on fixed ideological, that is, liberal, foundations, a valuable way forward was identified in an approach that was based on "ideas of right and wrong found within a practice of states". Embedded in the pluralist tradition, this practice-oriented theory also reflected the dynamic consensus nature of Clark's original model of negotiating (components of) global legitimacy. Since those practices of states did not presuppose any liberal uniformity in the ideas that shape them, this step left sufficient room to circumvent worldview-based obstacles and, consequently, to explore or re-negotiate the boundaries of a new morality for the global order.

5
Order Transition and Effectiveness

As mentioned in the earlier chapters, Clark's account of legitimacy is firmly based on the assumption of US hegemony (2005:226–229). Similarly, a later analysis by the same author revealed the degree to which his approach remained wedded to debates about America's international standing in the wake of the last Iraq war. In his view, "arguably the key problem of contemporary international order" was "finding a stable accommodation between US power and the general interests of international society" (2011:36).[1] More specifically, he suggested that what needed to be specified were "the duties that the US must bear as the key upholder of community values; it stipulates also the duty of the remainder of international society to make full acknowledgement of the costs to the leading state entailed by this role. This is the core of the constitutional bargain to be sought" (Clark 2005: 242).[2] Consequently, Clark referred to the years 2001/2003 as "pivotal year[s]" (2011:24). Beginning in 2008, however, those years seem much less significant as a frame of reference, but his perception of a theoretical environment which is, largely, shaped by US hegemony was confirmed.

In the meantime, other approaches suggested alternative ways of providing effective global governance solutions, though they have proved to be intermittent. For instance, second-image-based attempts to establish a new foundation for global governance due to the perceived lack of legitimate and effective leadership during the last Iraq crisis proved to be rather short-lived. Prominent authors suggested a concert/league of democracies, which was supposed to substitute for the UN Security Council after its – perceived – failure in 2003. Theoretically at least, it was designed with resources and rights similar to the ones of its model (Bobbitt 2002; Ikenberry and Slaughter 2006; Keohane and Buchanan 2004, 2006). Using the same frame of reference as Clark, that is, the last

Iraq war, consequently appears to be unsuitable to capture the nature of today's leadership dilemma. More importantly, what Clark's and the league proponents' efforts point to is the unsettled and larger problem of how to conceive of effective global governance. As a result, Clark's US-focused notion of constitutionality needs to be revised.

As this study has argued throughout, central to understanding today's international politics are the China–US renegotiations of a political grand bargain. These ongoing, often stalled, negotiations underlie the deeper tensions of the emerging international order and have increasingly become more salient. Having said that, there are two recent empirical developments revealing the parameters of and, in turn, requiring revised conceptual tools for the analysis of a critical new phenomenon: firstly, contrary to what Zoellick still thought in 2005, China does no longer accept its status as a passive or responsible stakeholder. As a former Australian foreign minister and regional expert put it, China is the "Hidden Dragon No Longer" (Rudd 2013). Rather, since it views itself historically as a natural great power, it "will want to lead the 21st century as co-equal" to the United States (Yew 2013:3).[3] Thus, it will "not settle for less" (White 2012:63).[4] Secondly, a new discourse, as Chinese top leaders have phrased it since 2012, envisions a "new type of great-power relations" (Economist June 8, 2013:10). These official statements are confirmed by the prevalence of the "realist school", which is "the *dominant* one in Chinese IR discourse today (if not forever)" (Shambaugh 2013:31). Such findings also seem to underline a broader realist pattern of the US–China relationship, in that both states reserve the right for themselves to determine "which games will be played and how" (Waltz 1979:194; Williams 2005:ch. 5). In other words, when "China views globalization" it looks "toward a new great-power politics" (Deng and Moore 2004:177). The United States government has reciprocated these inclinations through calls for a "new model" of great-power politics (Economist September 11, 2013:51). Moreover, while concealing the large extent of "strategic distrust" between them, the new demands for great-power leadership are accompanied by repeated and self-interested calls of the leaders of both countries "to ensure...effectiveness in conducting global governance" (Jiechi 2012).

Clearly, in light of these developments, Clark's original assumptions of a singular, US-based hegemony have lost much of their explanatory power. Identifying major gaps in the existing literatures in the following sections then helps to emphasize the importance of this chapter's task. In particular, the fourth component of Clark's notion of legitimacy, that is, the "power relations", which routinely shape the dynamic interplay between legality, morality and constitutionality, needs to be reconceptualized. The third component of constitutionality, which Clark defines as the "political realm of conventions, informal understandings, and mutual expectations" (2005:220), is closely linked to the notion of unequal "power relations" through the intrinsic concept of special responsibilities.[5] In this sense, building upon the conventional understanding of power as comprising material and social/relational strands, the managerial strand of great-power politics is introduced as a subcategory of the relational one. In essence, the key task of this chapter is to address several sets of problems that emerge from the underlying assumptions of great-power managerialism. For the purposes of this chapter, Clark's "power relations" are understood as hegemonic management.[6]

Note that this chapter focuses on conceptual questions regarding existing theories of effective leadership/hegemony. This is analytically distinct from leadership understood as concerted political activity of one or a group of great power(s), including its/their courses of planned and executed action.[7]

The chapter is structured as follows. The *first* section scrutinizes a powerful historical myth that has, partly unwittingly, biased theoretical debates on hegemony. Its key assumption is that for the last 200 years the United Kingdom and the United States have acted as successive hegemons. A more accurate reading reveals the prevalence of collective hegemonies for most of the time. Debunking this myth informs the background of the reconceptualization of Clark's analysis that follows. The *second* section sets out the key conceptual changes that help to revise Clark's idea of a prevailing single (US) hegemony. The first step is to break down the central notion of power into its materialist, social-relational and managerial components and then to focus on the latter one, which is viewed as a subcategory of the relational component. An examination of the underlying assumptions of managerial theories shows that they have failed to address what is introduced here as the *hierarchical* relationship between the internal (among the great powers) and external (between the hegemons and the remainder of international society) layers of great-power management. Focusing on the former demonstrates two things. First, it shows that there are *no* special responsibilities without agreement within the peer group. Second, it finds that an outstanding agreement on special responsibilities prevents any proper steering of international society as such. The *final* section shows how the new shape of effective management integrates formal and informal aspects of great-power politics. It highlights the operating contours of special responsibilities which occur in formal and informal shapes, regardless of the degree to which the respective environments are institutionalized or rule-based.

The myth of a 200-yearhegemony

Among influential Western IR theorists, there is a deeply embedded and long-standing assumption of an Anglo-Saxon hegemony stretching over the last 200 years. Three examples may suffice. Firstly, Ikenberry tellingly employed the 200-year assumption as the opening line of his recent *Liberal Leviathan*: "One of the great dramas of world politics over the last two hundred years has been the rise of liberal democratic states to global dominance" (2011:1).[8] Three decades earlier, Gilpin had put it this way: "The Pax Britannica and Pax Americana ... ensured an international system of relative peace and security. Great Britain and the United States created and enforced the rules of a liberal economic order" (1981:144). Finally, in a speech at the British Parliament in 2011, US President Obama subtly pointed to the importance of America's and Britain's continued leadership in the twenty-first century. By highlighting the need for the continuation of their leading roles, he made reference to their historical legitimacy, respectively. Against the backdrop of rising powers, he rejected the argument that "the time for our leadership has passed. That argument is wrong. The time for our leadership is now. It was the United States and the United Kingdom and our democratic allies that shaped a world in which new nations could emerge and individuals could thrive.... our alliance will remain indispensable to the goal of a century that is more peaceful, more prosperous and more just" (May 25, 2011). Regardless of the historical accuracy of these statements, the common point of all three statements pertains to a narrative according to which the United States and the United Kingdom have successfully led the international order for the last 200 years, have provided it with collective goods and are entitled to do so in the future.

However, as the chapter argues, this historical narrative of two successive hegemonies is a myth. Providing a more complex historical narrative is then the key task of this section, which, in turn, will inform the conceptual debate on hegemonic leadership that follows below. The time period that is examined begins in 1815 and ends in 2008, where this book's timeframe begins. Four episodes in particular are investigated: 1815–1914, 1918/19–1939, 1945/47–1991 and 1991–2008. At its core, the two main analytical parameters, which are chosen to affirm (or falsify) the proposition that first the United Kingdom and then the United States can be portrayed as effective single hegemonies, are the provision of security-related and economic public goods. In contrast to theorists who argue that power can be disaggregated into its economic, military and soft components and that these layers can be viewed as operating largely independently (Nye 2011), the theoretical assumption underlying the two chosen parameters rejects this implied separation. In fact, it is the provision of a (non-imperial) regional/global security regime that first provides the foundation of a similar regime in economic terms and, subsequently, of a legitimate global order. As a caveat, due to space constraints, what follows can only amount to a brief review of the historical literature on managerial variances regarding the notion of effective hegemony.

To begin with, is the proposition accurate that Britain was the sole hegemon in international politics between 1815 and 1914, as it is implied in the argument of the supposed 200-year hegemony? There is a broad consensus that British economic interests overseas could only be defended as long as there was stability available on the European continent (Clark 2011:105). According to the two parameters offered above, we should be able to discern British hegemony reflected in its effective and steady provision of security-related and economic public goods. But, this was not the case. While most economic historians today argue that, if there was British economic hegemony, it could only be seen as an intermittent phenomenon in the nineteenth century, that is, the 1850s and 1860s (Darwin 2009; O'Brien and Pigman 1992), they point out two major limitations to its effective performance. Firstly, the smooth operation of the gold-standard critically rested upon the coordination of other European central banks' fiscal policies. Secondly, when the European economies decided to adopt system-wide measures of protectionism in the 1870s, the alleged British hegemon could not prevent them from following through on such policies (Pigman 1997). In regard to the security realm, the picture looks equally bleak to support the claim of a British hegemony. There are two major limitations that heavily undermine such a proposition. Firstly, while it is commonly acknowledged that the United Kingdom played a distinctive role in the diplomatic process conducted at, and the conclusions arrived at, the Congress of Vienna (1814/15), it is equally well documented that Britain was but one out of two flanking powers of the nineteenth-century concert, the other being Tsarist Russia. Moreover, while Russia served as the main actor of the European balance of power, it was first Austria under Metternich and, after the Crimean War which was to open strategic space on the continent (i.e. the so-called Krimkriegssituation), the German Empire under Bismarck that served as "key balancers" on the continent, though neither was among the strongest powers then (Schroeder 1994). Secondly and relatedly, the lack of British leverage was most openly exposed when, after the Crimean War, it could not halt the emerging power on the continent, Prussia, from completely distorting British strategic preferences during the German wars of unification (against Denmark in 1864, Austria in 1866 and France in 1870/71) (Baumgart 1999). As a result, it is difficult to disagree with Clark's – authoritative – conclusion "that there is no overarching account of British hegemony that offers a fully convincing explanation across the economic and security domains" (2011:121).

The interwar period (1918/19–1939) presents an even more troubling historical theater for trying to sustain the 200-year proposition. In the aftermath of "*the* great seminal catastrophe of this century" (Kennan 1979:3), Imperial Russia had undergone a far-reaching revolution of its domestic affairs and Britain had been economically and militarily drained. What ensued were erratic attempts, highly contested between France and Britain, to provide security-related public goods for the center of Europe. The "broken balance between the world wars", as has rightly been suggested, turned out to be an insurmountable obstacle for a hegemonic role by Britain (Taliaferro et al. 2012). The manifold failures of the League of Nations (e.g. Abessinia) and the subsequent German revisionism before the outbreak of the Second World War (e.g. Rhineland, Czechoslowakia, Austria) demonstrated all too well the lack of a military hegemon. In the economic realm, Britain's trajectory was equally flawed. Not only could Britain (or France, for that matter) not economically underpin the rebuilding of the international order based on the Treaty of Versailles without American financial support, which is why the order resembled much more an "unfinished peace" than an effective Pax Britannica (Cohrs 2006). More importantly, itself extremely weakened, Great Britain had no sway over the developments that turned the world economy into a paralyzed state during and following the Great Depression in 1929 (Kindleberger 1973). Taken together, the 200-year proposition does not hold by any means during the interwar-period, either (Steiner 2007, 2013).

The period from 1945 to 1991, for many, has become the classic example of Western, that is, US, hegemony. One of the most prominent defenders of the 200-year argument, Ikenberry, forged ahead and depicted the United States as the central "manager" of the post-World War II order (2011:2, 297). Among most IR theorists, the basis of the argument was the United States' – undeniable – preponderance in the realms of finance, technology and manufacturing. And, indeed, the United States provided both security-related and economic goods. After a period of hesitation in 1946/47, the United States tied its concept of a liberal economic order, based on its own experiences during the "New Deal" era, to the quickly developed contours of its containment order. In fact, against those arguments that have been raised to the extent that economic- and security-related aspects of US hegemony could be separated, it is more accurate to suggest that "the bipolar containment order actually stimulated voluntary compliance with Washington's preferred economic order" (Clark 2011:137; Gilpin 1973). However, none of what has been said thus far reinvigorates the claim of a 200-year hegemony. All too often, what disappears from such an account is that its assumptions were limited to the "Free World". Curiously, this overlooks the polarity-based character of the Cold War. In fact, such an account cuts out the entire sphere of the Soviet Imperium, which was organized along the line of patterns of alliances and economic zones that were based on coercion and the denial of free trade (Haslam 2011). In effect, as much as the US hegemony in the West might be regarded as a sound example of the provision of security-related and economic goods, the latter were indeed only club goods, exclusively available to the member states in the Western world.

Finally, in regard to the time period between 1991 and 2008, a more nuanced picture evolves that approximates the notion of Western hegemony more than any of the other historical examples. As for the security realm, the United States' overwhelming military power has provided the security underlying, and integral to, a widely acknowledged great-power peace (Jervis 2002). Moreover, as before, Britain during the Cold War in the Western sphere, American provision of security has served an essential goal of liberal policy. That is, US foreign policy has – with various means (and success) – tried to spread the notion of the liberal state ideal. Inextricably linked to this policy, the United States has been the key advocate capable of upholding and underpinning the notion of free trade, broadly conceived. In sum, looking at the security-related and economic realms combined, this last period is the one that is least difficult to reconcile with the notion of (Western) hegemony.

Admittedly, this empirical exercise has been reductionist in some ways. Nonetheless, its conclusion is that the claim of a 200-year Anglo-Saxon hegemony is downright spurious, except for the final period. If the analysis is centrally focused on the key parameters of providing (as opposed to supporting the spread of) security-related and economic public goods, then the result is that a single, as opposed to a multiple, hegemony, which included non-Western powers throughout, has historically been the exception rather than the (alleged) rule. In this sense, one can agree with O'Brien and Clesse that no "two interconnected hegemonies" were available that were linked through a "hegemonic succession" (2002).[9] If anything, this review should make us more cautious about the defining features of managerial devices in global politics. Now that this layer is removed from the debate on hegemonic management, the chapter can move on to the conceptual issues at stake.

Power as effective management

The aim of this section is to explore new forms of managing the global order that may more accurately accommodate the leading roles of China and the United States than Clark's attachment to a singular US hegemony. This search is necessary, because many global governance failures have exposed the critical disagreements between those two states and both states have repeatedly demanded more "effective" global governance. Foot and Walter remind us why such concerns weigh considerably more when looked at from a US–China perspective than from that of other states: "the global order and the attitudes and behavior of these two important states are a mutually constitutive social phenomenon" (2011:23). This raises theoretical challenges. While it requires us to think about the "future constitutional structure of the international society", the latter's key parameters, for instance, the modus of great-power management, have traditionally (and solely) been determined during peace negotiations after systemic wars (Simpson 2004:73).[10]

As a first cut, the power-related literatures provide several useful points of entry. At their very heart stands the multifaceted phenomenon of power, depicting the reciprocal relationship between purely material/polarity-based components and relational/social ones (Baldwin 1989:introduction,chs.6, 7; Barnett and Duvall 2005; Braumoeller 2012:7–10; Krieger and Stern 1967:8; Morgenthau 1993:84–98; Wolfers 1962:ch.7). Relatedly, though much earlier debates had prepared the ground for the "social turn" in IR (Bull 1977; Kratochwil and Ruggie 1986; Wendt 1987), it is only in the last ten years or so that the latter turn has entered discussions about the key notion of great-power politics (Lake 2013:560, 570). Viewing the material and social components as inextricably linked, as this book does, leads us straight into thinking about the key concern of this section, that is, the managerial strand of power (Bisley 2012; Bukovansky et al. 2012; Frechette 2007; Ikenberry 2001:29–32; Kahler 1993). This strand, which is linked to the structural inequalities of power through the concept of special responsibilities, can be introduced as a subcategory of the relational one. In fact, the managerial strand implies the pursuit of what Wolfers called "milieu goals", partly exercised through special responsibilities, as opposed to narrow national possession goals (1962:73–77).[11] Similarly, other scholars have viewed the managerial role of great powers as functional differentiation among states (Donnelly 2000:97).

Where should we start looking for a hint regarding the notion of effective management in a way that reflects the *evolution of the arguments made in this book* thus far? To begin with, theories of legitimacy commonly distinguish between input and output legitimacy (Scharpf 1999). While this analysis does not support the idea of a strict separation between the two strands,[12] the distinction is useful in conceptual terms because the latter one draws our attention to the notion of effectiveness. In fact, distinct literatures such as the ones on regimes, hegemonic stability as well as neo-Gramscian accounts have placed "effectiveness" at the center of their arguments (Cox 1993). Gilpin's work, for instance, views US hegemony as the key to the international order's effectiveness (1981). His theory is useful here since it moves the conceptual analysis away from the conventional regime-based view, with its sole focus on compliance from the inside of issue-specific regimes (Chayes and Chayes 1993; Koskenniemi 2009). Moreover, Gilpin accurately elevates the analysis from the cooperation and coordination levels to the level of management. In this, he was partly inspired by Kindleberger, who talked of "leadership...as the provision of the public good of responsibility" (1986:304). Broadly speaking, the new framework needs to lean more toward the social-relational/managerial branch of HST (Ikenberry 2001, 2011) than to its purely self-interested/exploitative version (Norrlof 2010). As a result, since Gilpin frames power not only as material capabilities but also as legitimate governance by the leading state, he points the analysis into the direction of global leadership.[13]

Nevertheless, while Gilpin's Hegemonic Stability Theory contains many useful considerations for our purposes, they need to be seen in light of the criticisms that have been raised against them. Gilpin, and before him Kindleberger (1973:305), conceived of leadership as being executed by *one* hegemon. Early on, though, scholars argued against Gilpin that there was no reason why only one, as opposed to two or a small group of states, should be able to lead (Eichengreen 1987; Lake 1983; Snidal 1985). To be fair, Clark acknowledged in 2005 that the management devices of global politics are "certainly not immune to shifts in the distribution of power" (221), though since then he has not comprehensively revised his theory accordingly. This did not change, either, when Clark looked into the "composition of the hegemon" in a later piece and introduced an analytical distinction between singular and collective leadership/hegemony (Clark 2011:63). His reasoning was based on a historical review whose "key point is how past hegemonies have operated" (2011:59). In other words, he inferred from his empirical analysis that there is some historical variance as to the number of hegemonic powers in global affairs. But he left two questions unanswered. While such an approach is, as Clark shows, suitable to provide a taxonomy of hegemonies, it does not allow us to identify the characteristics which turn a state into a great power that provides leadership. Neither does it provide us with insights into the relation of the core conceptual parts that make up the notion of effective great-power management.

To begin with, while US leadership ambition may be taken to be undisputed despite recent (and recurring) claims about retrenchment, the new framework needs to show first that China is indeed a great power in order to include it in a concept of great-power management. In line with the relational understanding of power employed here, the important task is to show that special responsibilities are not "little more than a social mapping of an already existing material distribution of power" (Bukovansky et al. 2012:49). Therefore, in addition to what has already been said about China's critical material support for the capitalist system during the financial crisis[14] and to what role China has claimed for itself, there are two further requirements (Buzan 2004). Firstly, a potential great power needs to rank in the upper echelon of material capabilities. In contrast to assumptions of bipolarity (Waltz 1979), though, it does not yet have to be equal to the strongest great power. Some degree of hierarchy among the members of a collective hegemony is, in fact, a common historical phenomenon. China's continued material growth underpins such stipulations and is in line with more recent arguments derived from polarity theory (Posen 2011).[15] Secondly, a potential great power constantly needs to be part of other great powers' calculations due to its political, military and economic ambitions. As Buzan put it, such a great power is "being regularly talked about and treated either as potential challenger(.) to the US and/or as potential superpower" (2004:70–71).[16] Both, China's own ambitions as well as its constant presence in the calculations of US policy planning confirm the reciprocity underlying their calculations (Foot and Walter 2011). Symbolically, the United States' ceremonial promotion of China from the status of being granted a "working visit" in 2006 to a fullyfledged "state visit" in 2011 has marked this development very well.

Taken together, in contrast to Clark's assumption of a single hegemony, here it is suggested that there are indeed two great powers
that are characterized by their combination of material capability *and*
political ambition to critically influence world affairs. By implication,
we can assume that global politics cannot be accounted for without
problematizing the leadership roles of China and the United States.
Nonetheless, outlining the preconditions of greatpowerhood does not
yet improve our understanding of the nature of and, more importantly,
the dilemmas associated with the notion of hegemonic management.
These dilemmas will be dealt with next. So far, we can suggest that, if
power/effectiveness can be framed as leadership, then the analytical category of leadership may serve as the conceptual bridge toward effective
management and the managerial strand of great-power politics.[17]

To begin with, the analysis first outlines the main assumptions of
managerial theories and, then, reassesses them in conceptual terms. The
core proposition of these theories is largely uncontested by a majority
of scholars of great-power leadership (Bukovansky et al. 2012; Claude
1986; Goh 2005; Jervis 1985, 1992; Little 2007; Miller 1995; Osiander
1994; Watson 1992, 2007).[18] Based on material capabilities, its focus is
on "exploiting asymmetries of power for collective advantage" (Clark
2011:68).[19] For example, former US Secretary of State Stettinius reaffirmed the underlying rationale when he stated in early 1945 that the
United States aimed at "a world so organized for peace that the industrial
and military power of the large nations is used lawfully for the general
welfare of all nations" (quoted in Goodrich and Carroll 1947:421).[20]
Commonly, the literature outlines a set of "managerial tasks" (Waltz
1979:204), which leading great powers subsequently take on. In this
respect, this classic statement was provided by Bull (2002:200): "Great
powers contribute to international order in two main ways: by managing their relations with one another; and by exploiting their preponderance in such a way as to impart a degree of central direction to the
affairs of international society as a whole."

However, there are a couple of problems that emerge in relation to
those managerial assumptions. Neither Clark nor the wider literature
has addressed these shortcomings.[21] *Firstly*, viewed against the backdrop
of today's global governance failures, it can be argued that China and
the United States have not "impart[ed] a degree of central direction"
precisely because they have not "manag[ed] their relations" with each
other in a way that is conducive to providing "central direction" in
global politics. In other words, when managerial theories assume that
leading great powers have "grave obligations...to each other" (Claude
1986:727), they imply that recognizing these internal "obligations"

occurs somewhat naturally between the leading great powers. This is the case, inter alia, because IR theory exclusively believes that the great powers negotiate their special responsibilities *only* in the aftermath of major wars (Bull 2002). Therefore, conceptually we need to step back to the level when such obligations are not yet determined – even though empirically no war has (as yet) occurred. *Secondly*, precisely because there has been no such sense of "gravity" recognizable among US and Chinese perceptions of special responsibilities, the crucial question, which the managerial school has not asked, is whether there is a correlation between the internal and the external layers of great-power management and how the nature of this correlation can be characterized. Here it is suggested that the two layers form a *hierarchical* relationship in which the internal one stands on top. Thus, precisely because agreement on the main features of the internal layer is the necessary precondition for the latter to function, this requires us to prioritize an assessment of the *intra*-hegemonic aspects of great-power management, that is, the internal layer. *Thirdly*, this will, in turn, help to account for why the internal layer of great-power management can render the external one dysfunctional. Consequently, since existing research has mainly focused on the politics of the external layer, that is, how claims of leadership have been made acceptable to the remainder of international society (Dunne 1998:147), it has failed to address the dynamics pertaining to the internal aspects of the managerial approach.

The focus on the external layer has theoretically and historically been a quintessential aspect in IR; however, its overemphasis looks much less imperative when put into the context of renegotiating global order and of the deadlocks that have characterized this process. Thus, while the dynamic relationship between the internal and external aspects of management retains its overall centrality, the analysis needs to shift toward the politics of the internal layer.

What exactly justifies this shift of attention? In essence, here it is argued that if there are indeed accepted special responsibilities among leading great powers, then this presupposes that those responsibilities can *only* be negotiated *exclusively between the great powers*. This means that "special responsibilities", conceived as one of the central negotiating issues of the dynamics of global order transition, have moved center stage. More explicitly, there are *no* special responsibilities *without* agreement within the peer group (Clark 2011:65). For an exemplary account, Bukovansky et al. (2012) belong to the strand of research that emphasizes the aspects of the external layer of great-power management; precisely for this reason they do not recognize the conceptual importance of the hierarchical relationship between the two layers.

Admittedly, they acknowledge "the existence of a peer constituency" and believe that great-power responsibilities are only "partly derived" from that constituency and are only "in part owed" to it (2012:45). However, this is not the case. The main reason is that, while the remainder of international society may (or may not) bestow legitimacy on the great powers' actions at a later stage, it has no impact on the actual negotiating process of foundational special responsibilities (e.g. voting rights, demarcation of spheres influence, etc.). Put differently, states *other* than the two mentioned, or other agents for that matter (e.g. TNAs),[22] are not decisive as to the (re)negotiations of special responsibilities. In this vein, when Waltz (1979) argues in his rarely read ninth chapter on "The Management of International Affairs"[23] that "others may have to worry about the credibility of our commitments, but we don't" (208), a careful reading of his arguments confirms what has just been suggested: the underlying bargain on global credibility (read legitimacy) and the subsequent commitments of great powers (read special responsibilities) are exclusively concluded between them. Similarly, Simpson agrees when he states that leading "great powers... have... prerogatives over... the whole international system" (2003:68). Those prerogatives do not merely confirm the existence of special responsibilities but, more importantly, imply that only the great powers decide about their content and scope in the first place. Put briefly, actors other than the leading great powers cannot influence this process. As a result, China and the United States are independent of third parties in their renegotiations of special responsibilities.

Two empirical observations briefly underline the exclusiveness that has characterized the renegotiations of great-power responsibilities. First, a close look at the echoes of the Copenhagen Summit 2009 shows how important it is to step back from the climate issues that were negotiated. Ma Xiajun, professor of strategic studies at the Chinese Communist Party's (CCP) central committee, stressed that the late-night Copenhagen Accord between China and the United States had mainly been part of an ongoing and unresolved process attempting to define what exactly "leadership" in a "new political and economic world order" (SWP 2010:1–2) should look like. Second, a recent development at the UNSC further underlines the salience of this point. There, the frequency of meetings taking place *exclusively* between these two Security Council members *before* major decisions are made among the P5 as a group has substantially increased since 2008 (Prantl 2012).

These considerations now allow us to better take stock of the current status of the relationship between the internal and the external layers. A remark made by Jervis shortly after the end of the Cold War gives us a first hint: "Little of the talk of a new world order asks the United States to bend its conception of the common good (presupposing special rights – Maximilian Terhalle) to that of the other members of the international community" (1991–2:68). In other words, Jervis suggests that major systemic changes should require the renegotiation of special responsibilities. In contrast, today there is no clear definition available, not even an outline, of what China considers to be its special responsibilities that would help to address Jervis' point. Neither has the United States adopted an active attitude toward reforming the political foundations of the global order in the years since 2008. Thus, these observations do not produce a clear-cut picture of how these two states intend to revise the internal management of their relations. What they do reveal, however, is that the two leading great powers have not yet successfully negotiated an agreement on the nature and specific contents of their special responsibilities. Such an agreement would indicate what exactly they would allow, or concede to, each other as peers. In turn, precisely because they have not yet done so, the conclusion can only be that the great powers have *not managed to manage* their relations properly with regard to the steering of the international system. Following our conceptual analysis, this reveals the decisive weight that the internal layer possesses in the hierarchical relationship to the external layer. Referring back to Bull's classic statement outlined at the beginning, our investigation has scrutinized his first management stipulation more deeply than has been done so far in the literature.[24]

Finally, it is suggested that the existing degree of strategic distrust in US–China relations (Lieberthal and Jisi 2012) led us into the analysis of the hierarchical relationship between its internal and external layers in the first place. Since we now know that the unresolved issues in the former have made the latter dysfunctional, how does this help to better categorize the, admittedly, small degree of intra-hegemonic cooperation that does exist? Here it is argued that the current US–China relationship is neither captured by Waltzian bipolarity nor by concert-style models.[25] This is so because the former is driven by rationalist individual actors, which completely "ignore(.) how units relate with one another (how they interact)" (Waltz 1979:80), and because, for the latter to materialize, states "must have wider concerns, a longer-run perspective, and greater wisdom" (Jervis 1992:724). In this sense, the relationship currently oscillates, rather uncomfortably, between the extremes of these two models. Though driven by decades of growing prosperity, it is leaning no more than slightly toward the latter, and the two powers have, accordingly, made no discernible efforts to pursue an overall "transformation in thinking about world politics", which is one of the two key preconditions for a concert to emerge (Jervis 1992:723; Schroeder 1994). The other precondition is a shared consciousness of caution and restraint that originates from recent war experiences (Jervis 1985). Not only has there been no recent war, but such an awareness has also been watered down by over six decades of peace since the end of the Korean War. Therefore, the – at least – publicly announced necessity to engage in the management of their relations remains merely based on "their mutual recognition that they have a shared need to restrain some of the more dangerous elements of their competition" (Ayson 2013:206). This confirms the strongly pluralist conjectures which the United States' National Security Strategy (NSS) made; remarkably close to Chinese statements, it suggested that differences should be resolved "on the basis of mutual interests and mutual respect" (2010:11).

Formal and informal aspects of great-power management

Thus far the analysis has developed a conceptual critique of Clark's US-hegemony-based model of effective management. It has offered the notion of a hierarchical relationship between its internal and external layers which has, subsequently, helped to turn his model into a broad managerial framework capable of accommodating two global hegemons. If this new conceptual construct is to be accepted, it still needs to cope with and, more importantly, incorporate the current manifestations of an emerging double hegemony. Therefore, in order to identify the *operating* contours of the emerging double hegemony, the final task of this analysis is to draw out the formal and informal aspects of the managerial concept. In all of this, the starting point is that while there are two major powers, which are essential for the management of global politics, they have *not* yet reached any kind of a broader understanding "on ways and means of sharing power", which is the "sinequanon" of their relationship (Prantl 2013:12).

For Clark (2005), those contours were easily recognizable as being manifested in formalized institutions. Today, the variety of crucial changes, which need to be worked into our reconceptualization, comprises inter alia the sheer number of official and semi-official US–China summits (if shaped by strategic distrust), US–Chinese encounters at the G20 or the East-Asia Summit, at major international institutions (e.g. UNSC, IMF, World Bank), countless informal initiatives between the two leading great powers and, most importantly, public exchanges of diplomatic notes through which varying degrees of discord vis-à-vis objected actions of the other party are conveyed. Two statements underline this point. For instance, a former Australian foreign minister pointedly underlined the multi-faceted nature of the political environment in which great-power cooperation had to commence: "There are currently more informal initiatives under way between the United States and China than there are ships on the South (and East) China Sea" (Rudd 2013). Furthermore, the US government, traditionally selective in its approach to multilateral institutions, implicitly hinted at the necessity to look at both formal and informal aspects of intergovernmental cooperation during order transition: "The United States will work with influential partners wherever these can be found, and not simply 'inside formal institutions' " (US National Security Strategy 2010:41).

How is it possible to capture these additional features of an emerging and currently negotiated US–China hegemony? A brief look into the realms of related research appears useful here, since their shortcomings provide us with a first idea of where to push our analysis. To begin with, the latest scholarship on multilateralism has reflected strong emphasis on the relevance of design-based aspects of international organizations (Koremenos et al. 2004), as well as the impact of informal networks and international regulatory regimes on shaping collective action (Woods and Mattli 2009). The criticisms that have been leveled against the focus of such forms of research apply to our concerns about great-power management as well; this is because they share a broad interest in the preconditions of effective problem-solving. As Prantl has suggested, existing research on multilateralism "misses out the key part, where formal and informal governance intersect" (2013:5).[26] In other words, formal and informal aspects of interstate governance need to be considered parts of a larger continuum.

If this is indeed the case, how can we adapt these findings for our purposes of further sharpening the understanding of great-power management? In contrast to Prantl (2013), who is more specifically interested in the nature of the preconditions of collective action embedded in the varying fabrics of regional multilateral arrangements (e.g. the ASEAN way), here the key focus is on special responsibilities as effective instruments of hegemonic management. More specifically, while the analysis has thus far established the *overall* contours of the internal layer of the managerial strand, now the aim is to provide a better understanding of the *operating* contours of special responsibilities. The shapes of those contours are formal as well as informal.

Obviously, a purely formal view of such responsibilities, as held by Clark (2005), is predicated on an accepted status quo. Since this is no longer the case today, we need to take a closer look at the nature of the relationship between formal and informal aspects of great-power management. On the one hand, a formal view can retain its relevance as long as it is conceived as non-static and, thus, amenable to changes due to systemic influences of order transition. One could argue, for instance, that this is partly the case with the processes driving the readjustment of voting rights at the IMF, if slow in the eyes of some. On the other, properly adapting the formal–informal dynamics of governance helps to make the analysis also conducive to accommodating informal aspects of great-power management. Those aspects refer to informally legitimized special rights and responsibilities (Doran 1991:30–31). For instance, the notion of a grand bargain can be broken down into regional bargains, for example, spheres of influence. The latter present the kind of agreement that is informal in nature, regardless of the degree to which the environment may be rule-based or institutionalized. In fact, spheres of influence permeate those global governance rules and are here viewed as an example of informal special responsibilities. More precisely, spheres of influence embody the key parameters of a potential political deal that needs to be struck between the leading great powers of the day, if they are to fulfill their part of the grand bargain. Constructing such an agreement rests on the expectation that the respective states, partly unintentionally,[27] eventually arrive at lasting but not formalized "tacit understandings" or "unspoken rules" in order to manage their differences (Keal 1983). It is, therefore, only by way of "tacit bargaining" (Schelling 1960) that such an informal sphere-related understanding can come into existence and may then be understood as "a definite region within which a single power exerts a predominant influence, which limits the independence or freedom of action of states within it" (Keal 1983:156).[28]

Revision 3: Clark's model and effectiveness

This chapter has suggested revising Clark's idea of a prevailing single (US) hegemony in several ways. Based on the analysis of the previous chapters as well as on a brief examination of the last 200 years of supposed single hegemonies, the chapter took a Chinese–US double hegemony as its empirical starting point. Conceptually, the next step was to break the central notion of power down into its materialist, social-relational and managerial components and, subsequently, to focus on the latter one, which was viewed as a subcategory of the relational component. Proceeding in this way opened up a host of important aspects that needed to be worked into the revision of Clark's model.

Looking at the managerial subcategory more closely, the examination of the underlying assumptions of managerial theories revealed that they have failed to address what was introduced as the hierarchical relationship between the internal (among the great powers) and external (between the hegemons and the remainder of international society) layers of great-power management. Focusing on the internal layer demonstrated two things. First, it showed that there are no special responsibilities without the agreement within the peer group. Second, it found that a yet outstanding agreement on special responsibilities prevents any proper steering of international society as such. The final revision that was offered showed how the new shape of effective management integrates formal and informal aspects of great-power politics. It highlighted the operating contours of special responsibilities which occur in formal and informal shapes, regardless of the degree to which the respective environments are institutionalized or rule-based.

*   *   *

Before the analysis moves on to the empirical chapters, it needs to clarify how the results of the three conceptual chapters have improved the overall argument of this book and, subsequently, how the latter results inform the structure of the following set of case studies.

For Clark (2005), there was no particular need to think about spheres of influence, for instance, in Southeast and East Asia, because the US presence and predominance was largely perceived as a given. Equally, when Clark wrote his book in the early 2000s, he did not have to be concerned about fundamental resistance against the global climate regime or the world trade regime (though the latter showed first signs of tension). Finally, at the beginning of the millennium there was no need to think about ideologies other than the liberal-humanitarian one that could underpin the global regime of the "Responsibility to Protect", despite all of its shortcomings. In other words, this was the time when the major institutions and regimes of global governance, *mutatis mutandis*, were largely uncontested. Resting on a widely accepted US hegemony, the United States largely supported the order but exempted itself from it when it did not see its interests preserved. In this period, the flourishing of liberal governance ideas was still in full swing or, at least, not yet in an unhealthy condition.

In contrast, since the publication of Clark's book, these governance certainties have come under very considerable strain. At the expense of notions of global governance, disagreements between the United States and China have come to dominate, or stall, global politics. As this analysis has argued throughout, since 2008 a great-power contestation has emerged that is at the core of the transition which the global order has been undergoing. The contestation between the leading great powers has prevented the large-scale institutional redesign required to remove deadlocks in the existing global governance structures. The key problem has been the lack of a new political grand bargain on material power structures, normative beliefs and the management of the order among the key players.

This, in turn, rendered necessary the three conceptual revisions provided in the preceding three chapters. Clark's revised model incorporates those crucial aspects of global politics which, consequently, permit to cope much better, though perhaps not perfectly, with the theoretical challenges of order transition.

The key parameters of the "rules of the game" that are at stake during such momentous times, that is, economic rules, spheres of influence and values of the international order, have been outlined by Gilpin (1981). They have been moderately adapted here (by substituting economic for environmental rules), since the core content of these parameters is as relevant today as it was at earlier occasions. This adapted set of key parameters presents the source from which the case studies have been selected. The empirical section in Chapters 6–8 will, thus, explore the cases in light of the three conceptual revisions.[29]

Firstly, the argument that special responsibilities are exclusively (re)negotiated among leading great powers is explored through an account of the degree to which renegotiations of spheres of influence have come at the expense of global regimes as well as East Asian regionalism (Chapter 6); secondly, the proposition that the environmental rules of today's hegemonic order need to be viewed in light of hybrid sets of actors is explored through an analysis of the degree to which the impact of transnational actors has been neutralized due to the prevailing disagreements among the great powers (Chapter 7); finally, the argument that the competitive encounter between two superior worldviews is accommodated through middle-ground "ideas of right and wrong found within a practice of states" is explored through an assessment of the degree to which the RtP has been rejected as a norm of customary international law, because the two great powers have not been able to agree on common standards to make it such (Chapter 8).

Part III
Explorations

6
Renegotiating the Security-Related Rules of Global Order

This chapter explores the ways in which China and the United States have renegotiated the security-related rules of the global order since 2008/9. In particular, it looks at the efforts of both countries to strike a bargain on the contours of their respective spheres of influence in the South and East China Seas and finds them as yet undetermined (Keal 1983).[1] In fact, both states have repeatedly claimed that the South and East China Seas (SCS, ECS) are part of their "national" or "core interests", while consistently failing to reconcile their claims.[2] In line with the overall argument of this book, the key point here is not whether the United States would ever accept a Chinese Monroe doctrine (Foot and Walter 2011:175; Mearsheimer 2014),[3] but it is that the underlying disagreements reflect systemic challenges to the global governance literature. Conceptually, the two players have not yet found an accommodation as to how to renegotiate the internal layer of great-power management, that is, how to reassemble the scope of the rights and duties *among* themselves. Such an agreement, however, is the key foundation for a *political* balance of power in Southeast and East Asia. As an authoritative observer has put it: "striking an informal understanding between China and the United States on ways and means of sharing power will be the *sine qua non* of regional stability. Without an informal or tacit bargain on the rules of the game underlying regional cooperation in East Asia, multilateral institutions will not be able to perform the functions in solving collective action problems" (Prantl 2013:12).[4]

In turn, as outlined in the first two chapters, the resurgence of heightened great-power tensions since 2008/9 has come at the expense of attempts at fostering regional cooperation. More precisely, while for many scholars the 1990s seemed to pave the way toward multilaterally regionalizing cooperation, and while the early 2000s appeared to present the heyday of this development, which was also supported by states in the region propagating the advent of the "ASEAN Community", events related to order transition have forcefully derailed such efforts since then (Buzan and Waever 2003; Emmers 2012; Fawcett and Hurrell 1995; Mansfield and Milner 1999; Roberts 2013). Concomitantly, political ambitions toward the adoption of dispute settlement procedures in the region, as applied elsewhere, have failed (Beckman 2013; Goldstein et al. 2000; Tallberg and Smith 2014). As a result, these countervailing developments have powerfully underscored the notion of strategic distrust which has characterized US–China relations in recent years. Well aware of this state of affairs and wary about the spill-over effect which it has had on the deliberate multiplication of, and competition between, regional arrangements (e.g. ASEAN ARF, EAS, ADMM+, APEC),[5] the Prime Minister of Vietnam, for instance, concluded at a conference in 2013: " what is still missing is the strategic trust in the implementation of those arrangements" (Dung 2013).[6] Conversely, since the lack of deep trust makes institutionalized cooperation all but epiphenomenal, the geographical boundaries of the future spheres of influence are negotiated and made visible through tacit understandings only (Bull 1977). The latter, thus, reveal themselves in and "through tests and probes" of diplomatic clout and military strength (Waltz 1979:209).

Two institutions have been chosen in order to provide evidence of these new tendencies in global politics. Both aim to mediate disputes either through consensual conflict management or through legal mechanisms. The Association of Southeast Asian Nations (ASEAN) has been selected because it represents the historical centerpiece of Southeast Asian regional diplomacy aimed at consensually reconciling political differences, as viewed by its member states since 1967 (Acharya and Johnston 2007; Ba 2009; Beeson 2009). The UNCLOS has been selected because it mirrors attempts at codifying legal procedures that are aimed at settling outstanding disputes between states. It has been called upon by various ASEAN states, Japan as well as the United States with regard to dispute settlement in the SCS and ECS (Beckman 2013; Damrosch et al. 2009:ch. 17; Dupuy and Dupuy 2013; Dutton 2010; Manicom 2014; Raine and Le Miere 2013). Since UNCLOS serves as the central legal underpinning of dispute-related international law in the region, it is inextricably linked to the activities of the key institutional body aimed at deepening regional cooperation, that is, ASEAN. Therefore, the remainder of the chapter follows the co-evolution of those two governance institutions between 2008 and 2014. The chronological assessment shows the large degree to which those institutions have been penetrated and, thus, rendered ineffective, by the disagreements between the two critical great powers in the region. Since the politics of both institutions significantly complement each other in their activities, their examination may not be neatly separated.

Whereas parts of the literature divide SCS disputes into those about the freedom of navigation between the United States and China and those about territorial disputes between the latter and other Southeast Asian claimants (Goh 2013:114; Raine and Le Miere 2013:14–15), this analysis does not assume that they should be strictly separated. There are three reasons for this. First, precisely because the nine-dash line,[7] which China has stringently employed to delineate and constitute its claims in the SCS, covers almost all of the pertaining sea territory, it inevitably merges the United States' "national interest" in the freedom of navigation with the security demands of those states whose SCS-based claims differ from those of China. Second, the logic of China's domestic regime security makes it one of its top priorities to increase trade with its smaller Southeast Asian neighbors. Precisely because trade and security are intimately related,[8] the freedom of navigation in the SCS is inextricably linked with concerns based on UNCLOS. Third, developments in the SCS and the ECS and their perception in the region influence each other. The behavior of China and the United States in either region is painstakingly observed by the respective counterpart and, importantly, also by smaller states. For instance, Japan has tried to use its economic power to steer economically weaker Southeast Asian states away from China in order to further delegitimize Beijing's policies in East Asia; it has also tried to manipulate ASEAN's Regional Forum (ARF) for its own interests (Yuzawa 2007). Therefore, by collapsing the two strands into one broader contest about the shape of future spheres of influence in East and Southeast Asia, the great-power tensions underlying, and spilling over into, the two regions give the *nexus* between those two instances the appropriate weight.

To begin with, ASEAN was originally established in 1967 as an intra-Asian institutional means of strengthening the sovereign independence of its members amidst the ideological and power-political pressures to commit to either camp of the Cold War. The founding members were Thailand, Indonesia, Malaysia, Singapore and the Philippines, but they quickly accepted some six more regional states into their organization, that is, Brunei, Cambodia, Laos, Myanmar and Vietnam. By 1999, it comprised ten members, which continue to represent the core of ASEAN today. In the 1990s and early 2000s, ASEAN stood as a model for other formats such as the East Asia Summit (EAS) or Asia-Pacific

Economic Cooperation (APEC), adding extra-regional players respectively. What closely links these organizations is their shared belief in a more long-run vision of developing a regional community in security, political, economic and social terms. Fundamental to their interactions is the firm belief that realizing such a vision must necessarily be based on dialog and other consensual measures (Foot 2012:135). Due to its Cold War-based traditions, ASEAN member states have, therefore, habitually tried to fend off great-power incursions into their organization. For instance, since 1991, and especially in recent years, they have done so by regularly providing opportunities for great powers to discuss their differences while ASEAN's member states themselves have remained neutral. The tensions, which this attitude has created for ASEAN's provision of effective governance, form the backdrop against which the trajectory of the Association's interactions with China and the United States needs to be viewed. A key problem seems to be that the mental maps of the global environment, as held by the various regional leaders, are still partly embedded in the iron cage of bipolarity, whereas the regional order already finds itself in the, yet undetermined, stage of its own renegotiating.

In 1994, an incident between China and the Philippines at the Spratly Islands precipitated a first move toward more substantive regional thinking about how to regulate maritime conduct in the SCS. With China intent to regain international reputation after Tiananmen 1989 and to successfully apply for WTO membership, ASEAN seemed to have good reason to celebrate the signing of the "Declaration on Conduct of the Parties" in the SCS in 2002. Indeed, to many at that time, the declaration "represented the high point of ASEAN engagement policies towards China" (Goh 2013:105). Designed as a political statement, the challenge for ASEAN over the following years was to turn the declaration into a more formal code of conduct.

At the same time, while the United States involved itself in the so-called "global war on terror", first in Afghanistan and then in Iraq between 2001 and 2011, China's economic growth continued unabatedly. China's more accommodating posture in those years was further reflected in two deals, among others, that were struck between Beijing and members of ASEAN as well as Tokyo and Beijing. Having negotiated the agreement's details since 2004, China and Japan decided to jointly develop the exploitation of maritime resources in June 2008 (Emmers 2010:111–112).[9] The second deal was closed between the Philippines and Vietnam, on the one hand, and China, on the other, in March 2005. The "Joint Seismic Undertaking" was signed by the respective state-owned oil companies and permitted limited oil pre-exploration surveys in the Spratly Islands (Emmers 2010:123–124). Further reflecting the prevailing cooperative attitudes in the region at that time, all ASEAN members signed (2007) and ratified (2008) a newly drafted "Charter". The firm commitment of the signatories to build a genuine regional community that would eventually resemble the European Union seemed to be a strong expression of political unity among smaller states in light of growing economies, such as those of close by India and China (Jetschke 2011:329).[10]

However, the financial crisis, the performance of the United States in it and the *perception* of both in China dramatically changed the climate in the regional environment.[11] ASEAN's engagement with China has since become increasingly more strained. Beijing's more robust, partly assertive, new behavior in the region derived from the perceived declining status of the United States and, in turn, China's continued successful economic rise. In other words, while global governance institutions, such as ASEAN, seemed to play an increasingly important role in regional governance questions and mediating efforts when the US security guarantee was largely unquestioned, China's bold attempts at translating its economic power into political influence revealed the Association's underlying political weaknesses and divisions. Both, the United States' and China's subsequent policies have undermined ASEAN's consensual rationale. Henceforth, disputes over sovereignty rights have been politically and nationalistically charged and have, thus, stimulated, partly fierce, competition over access to and power over the SCS and ECS.

To begin with, aware of their mutual dependence in economic terms, the United States and China convened their first Strategic and Economic Dialogue (S&ED) on July 27–28, 2009, in order to coordinate their policies more closely. The newly elected US president, Obama, and his Chinese counterpart, Hu, had already agreed to hold such a summit at the G20 meeting in London in April. For the purposes of this chapter, it is important to note that the meetings between Foreign Secretary Clinton and her counterpart, State Councilor Dai, as well as between the secretary of the treasury, Geithner, and the Chinese vice premier, Qishan, reflected high-level exercises in diplomatic cooperation aimed at channeling the financial crisis and the US–China relationship. This first dialog was followed by a state visit of the US president to Beijing between November 15 and 18, 2009. While their traditional differences on issues such as Taiwan, Tibet and human rights, unsurprisingly, did not change and no progress was made with regard to North Korea, sanctions on Iran or climate issues, for China the most crucial point in their communique was that "respecting each other's core interests is extremely important to ensure steady progress in US–China relations" (White House 2009). But none of these efforts, if important, could disguise China's growing self-confidence vis-à-vis the United States and the region, which occurred *simultaneously*. Overall, while the relationship developed fairly calmly during the first year of Obama's presidency, it was soon to "enter[.] a rocky period at the start of the second year", which immediately affected the regional political climate (IISS 2010:335).

While ASEAN's performance suffered from border skirmishes between their members Thailand and Cambodia and diplomatic rows over some of their respective top staff (Wagner 2013), its rapprochement with the United States (which had refused participation at the annual meetings since 1997 due to the ASEAN membership of Burma's military junta) before Obama's visit to China seemed to slowly improve the relationship between them. Equally, the second SE&D, held on May 24–25, 2010, appeared to reflect a sound degree of cooperative intentions among the two powers. In fact, with over 200 American officials traveling to Beijing for the talks, this SE&D was "the largest bilateral dialogue ever held between two nations" (IISS 2010:339). But then, quite unexpectedly, China's robust rhetoric fundamentally changed the setting. Possibly also influenced by the annual debate about US arms sales to Taipei in January 2010 (IISS 2010:337–339), Beijing's state councilor, Dai Bingguo, and its foreign minister, Yang, told two US top officials,[12] visiting China in March 2010, that the SCS was now part of China's "core interests" (quoted in Chen and Yang 2013:269) – a term which it had previously only applied to Taiwan and Tibet.[13] In order to underline its rhetoric more forcefully in the following months, China quarreled with Vietnam and the Philippines about territorial rights at the Paracel and Spratly Islands, using its coast guard to unilaterally mark its new territory (IISS 2011:354). The unease with which Beijing's gunboat diplomacy was received in the region was then to come to its head at the annual meeting of the ARF in July. As mentioned, the ASEAN member states had originally added this format to the ASEAN-only format in 1994 in order to facilitate exchanges between great powers in the region and thereby help defuse potential tensions among them.

While the ARF meeting in Hanoi did indeed provide an institutional way to openly put their differences on the (ASEAN) table, it, more importantly, revealed the degree to which their disagreements came at the expense of ASEAN's traditionally consensual approach of defusing tensions, thus pointing out its limitations. On July 23, 2010, partly directly encouraged by small states in the region (e.g. Singapore, Vietnam), the then US Foreign Secretary Clinton condensed the prevailing mood among regional states into a statement in which the United States not only expressed the former's concerns over China's recent maritime behavior but also insisted that the SCS was part of its "national interest" (State Department 2010). Inadvertently, having assumed the role of the spokeswoman of a majority of regional states, the United States' reaction implied that it did not accept the unilateral sea-based delineation of spheres of influence that had been attempted by China. Rather, the United States wanted China to stick to international law, which meant that uninhabited rocks and atolls did not suffice as legitimate claims to maritime space. It also implied that these disputes should be settled according to UNCLOS or in front of ITLOS, if necessary. China's foreign minister, Yang, reportedly left the meeting, if only to return after an hour to give a 30-minute response. For the purposes of this chapter, his remarks proved very interesting because they provided a short glimpse of China's underlying assumptions with regard to regional and global politics. Yang stated: "China is a big country and other countries are small countries and that is 'just a fact'" (quoted in Pomfret 2010).[14] Straightforwardly, these rarely made Thucydides-like remarks demanded that those ASEAN states that had sided with the United States should instead know their place and status and, accordingly, should yield to China's wishes. Pointedly summarizing China's openly patronizing approach, a top diplomat from the region put it this way: "*We as Asians possess plenty of wisdom to deal with the issue ourselves.*"[15]

China's response was twofold. First, within days it launched the "largest joint military drills yet undertaken by the Chinese military" in the SCS (IISS 2011:360). Second, two days after the ASEAN summit, on July 25, Yang wrote on the foreign ministry's website that the United States' attempts at "internationalizing" the disputes, that is, resolving them according to international law, presented an "attack on China" (MFA China July 26, 2010). In other words, China openly disregarded ASEAN's consensus-driven way and, instead, underlined its long-standing mechanism of conducting international diplomacy through bilateral negotiations. In this context, it immediately became clear why China had opted out of UNCLOS in 2006, referencing its Article 298.[16] The latter allowed it to opt out of any regulations that might oblige it to accept external judgment concerning its sovereign rights (Raine and Le Miere 2013:218). Moreover, what these rather bold moves revealed was China's self-image as a traditional great power that did not hesitate to use its unequal bargaining power vis-à-vis smaller powers, regardless of the extent to which the environment, in which it operated, was legalized. The classic nature of his underlying thinking becomes even clearer when acknowledging that the same foreign secretary, Yang, had addressed the Munich Security Conference just five months earlier, as follows: there he had expressed unequivocal support for the statement that "all countries, whether big or small, are to be treated as fully equal members of the international community" (China Embassy Berlin 2010).[17] That his thinking was highly reflective of the Chinese Communist Party's (CCP) leadership became clear when Yang was adopted into the politbureau in 2013.

Crucially, the Hanoi instance showed that the likeliness that ASEAN states would have to confront a situation in which they had to choose between their allegiance to China or the United States was high. In fact, this was to be the case when ASEAN states would strategically reassure themselves by refreshing their *bilateral* security treaties with the United States and when the latter would, in turn, reaffirm its security guarantees in order to limit China's attempts at extending its sea-based interests according to its nine-dash line, which covers almost the entire SCS. In other words, the tensions at Hanoi pointed at the growing governance-related difficulties which the consensual ASEAN would face in the future, if the SCS disputes and, thus, the renegotiations of the great powers' spheres of influence remained unresolved. As a consequence, China's unconditional bilateral approach and the bilateral nature of the United States' security system were foreseeably bound to undermine the multilateral and consensual character of a global governance institution such as ASEAN. Ironically, ASEAN's stated willingness to defuse great-power tensions by deliberately adopting states, such as the United States, as members into the East Asian Summit in July 2010 reflected the Association's unwitting acknowledgment that those powers would eventually determine its effectiveness in governance-related terms.[18]

The year 2011 saw similar developments and patterns in the relations between the United States and China, on the one hand, and ASEAN and the latter two, on the other. Overall, the tensions between the institutionalized layers of the Southeast and East Asian regional environments and their penetration by the disagreements among the great powers became even more clearly discernible.

Driven by the desire to play down their substantive differences in public, the Chinese president was received with all requisites available to the White House's protocol in order to facilitate a proper state visit in January 2011 (as opposed to a work visit ceremony in 2006). Moreover, the next SE&D between Washington and Beijing, held between May 9 and 11, 2011, seamlessly gave the impression that everything was well with the level of cooperation between the two. The meeting, it seemed, had helped to further entrench the communicative value of their exchanges and led to a list of 48 "Outcomes of the Strategic Track", for instance, joint military–civilian discussions on cyber and maritime issues (IISS 2011:358). In the meantime, China continued to harass its smaller neighbors. For instance, its coast guard cut the cables of a Vietnamese surveying ship exploring oil and gas on May 26, 2011 (IISS News 2011:5), and further increased submarine and surface patrols in the SCS. Nevertheless, though Vietnam was a member of ASEAN, the Association's mixed feelings about China's maritime intentions did not deter it from celebrating the introduction of guidelines aimed at implementing the 2002 "Declaration on the Conduct of the Parties" (DoC) in the SCS at the annual meeting in Bali on July 20–21. Put in place already in 2005, the ASEAN–China joint working group had eventually hammered out the final draft after six years of intermittent debates and some 21 drafts. Its key weakness was the, revealing, failure to agree on (and include) clear regulations as to how civil and military ships from claimant states were to conduct themselves in those territories that are disputed. Eager to stress the consensual element to the extent that, as the Malaysian foreign minister stated, "ASEAN and China can sit together and discuss problems", the "guidelines essentially regulate how to implement the DOC – not the code of conduct itself but on the projects" (quoted in Jakarta Post 2011). Those projects comprised future workshops on marine hazard prevention and mitigation in the SCS, on marine ecosystems and biodiversity, and on marine ecological environment and monitoring techniques (ASEAN 2011). Conspicuously, China had succeeded in retaining its traditional position to the extent that the involved parties needed to resolve sovereignty-related and jurisdictional disputes bilaterally only. Thereby, it had pierced through, and virtually displaced, ASEAN's key principle, which stipulated consultations among its members *prior* to negotiations on the guidelines with China.

The celebration of the "guidelines" as a "milestone achievement for the region", as the Malaysian foreign minister put it (quoted in Jakarta Post 2011), therefore, helped to gloss over the deep political divisions that underlay the document. In fact, the document's face-saving character helped to sustain ASEAN's self-perception as the central multilateral negotiating forum in the region, capable of producing major political communiques. In reality, however, there was no overlooking of the fact that in 2010 the majority of ASEAN states had voted for the internationalization of the maritime disputes and had thereby tried to contest China's unilateral decision of making the SCS its "core interest". In this vein, speaking at a regional conference in June 2011, the Vietnamese defense minister, Thanh, explained why most ASEAN states were opposed to China's behavior (quoted in IISS News 2011:5): "We constantly hope that China will follow its declarations (of peacefulness) to the world. We also strongly hope that China's declarations become reality. We look forward to seeing action that corresponds to China's declarations."

Moreover, while the United States conveniently employed international law to support ASEAN member states (against China), at its core, its national interests were geared at the defense of its sphere of influence, which it had established during the Cold War.[19] Mainly in this narrow sense of national interests and much less in the sense of upholding ASEAN as an important governance institution, US interests were diametrically opposed to what the Chinese character of the "guidelines" conveyed. Therefore, it can be said that the guidelines only superficially concealed the real disagreements that had surfaced in 2010. This is also why the document contained no definitions and no specific rules as to how to resolve the existing disputes. That the guidelines had, in fact, hollowed out the notion of the "ASEAN way" was subsequently made unmistakably clear when an article in Beijing's mouthpiece *on the day of* the publication of the "guidelines" stated that the pertaining disputes were "exclusively bilateral in character regardless of the multilateral setting in which they had occurred" (quoted in Buchsteiner July 21, 2011:7). As a diplomat from the region put it, China continuously employed a purely instrumental, that is, self-interested, understanding of multilateral gatherings such as ASEAN.[20] Moreover, as if any further clarification was needed regarding the direction which China's diplomacy was taking, the article hastened to add that the disputes would be handled "without the interference of foreign powers", that is, without the United States (ibid.).[21] In part, China's distrust of international law was due to its (not wholly inaccurate) perception that the United States itself had displayed an ambivalent record in regard to or, at least, an often instrumental relationship to it in the last decade or so. For instance, while the United States had never signed and ratified UNCLOS, it now insisted that the convention had to be applied as a means of legal arbitration.[22] As a result, since the deeper disagreements had not been solved, it was only a matter of time before the underlying positions would clash again.

Within the region, it became clear to many, if only reluctantly recognized, that while some ASEAN states had already been the first ones in line to be directly affected by China's maritime policies, in the larger picture the regional controversies were but a reflection of the rivalry between the United States and China. As Rizal Sukma, a leading Indonesian analyst, drily observed: "With regard to ASEAN, everything political is about the long-term relationship with China – and, critically, which role the United States... will play in it" (quoted in Buchsteiner July 25, 2011:10). Pointedly, while ASEAN member states clearly tried to keep alive the notion of the "guidelines" as a breakthrough and major achievement of ASEAN regional diplomacy and, therefore, kept quiet about their inherent weaknesses at the subsequent ARF meeting on July 24–25, it was US Foreign Secretary Clinton who explicitly addressed the shortcomings and, implicitly, reasserted the United States' sphere of influence vis-à-vis China (Buchsteiner July 25, 2011:10).

Further contributing to the tensions undermining ASEAN's role in regional governance, the United States introduced the "pivot to Asia", which powerfully combined its (renewed) military and political commitment to the region. After having underlined the United States' more traditional commitment to Taiwan by agreeing to modernize the latter's air force on September 21 (FAZ September 23, 2011:6), the US president announced at the Australian Parliament on November 17 that the United States was "here [in Asia] to stay" and that it would therefore station some 2,500 US troops in Australia – only days ahead of the East Asian Summit in Bali (White House 2011); furthermore, Singapore invited the United States to station up to four littoral war ships, and Vietnam and the United States began first steps of military cooperation (IISS 2012:335); finally, and parallel to the US president's announcement, Foreign Secretary Clinton stated a day earlier on the deck of a US Navy destroyer in the Philippines' Manila Bay that the key US goal was to strengthen its military ties with Manila and also to "update" its relations with Australia, Japan, South Korea and Thailand (Economist November 19, 2011:56). The immediate and unchanging reaction and (accurate) perception in China was that the pivot was intended to contain Beijing.[23]

Furthermore, having just become a member of the EAS, the US president decided to use the opportunity of the summit to support American SCS-related utterances made thus far with his personal authority. His statements, though highly appreciated by the majority of member states, were to further undermine the effectiveness of ASEAN. China's response had a very similar effect. To begin, when the heads of states convened on November 18, the vast majority of them, as in the past, made it clear that they preferred a "multilateral solution" to the SCS-related conflicts. China, in contrast, insisted right from the beginning of the summit that the topic should not be talked about at such a venue, but it should rather be left to bilateral negotiations. Disregarding China's wishes, though, Obama gave a short speech in which he laid out the rationale behind the United States' continued involvement: the Asia-Pacific was its sphere of influence. In his words, the United States had an "overwhelming interest in the security of the seas and the SCS in particular" because it was a "pacific nation, a sea-based nation, a trading nation, and the *security guarantor of the Asia-Pacific*" (quoted in Buchsteiner November 20, 2011). The Chinese president, Wen, promptly intervened and restated his claim that this was not the right place to discuss such matters; however, he had to recognize quickly that, except for Burma and Cambodia, all other attendees, that is, 15 states, remained extremely critical about China's bilateral approach in their statements (ibid.). Quintessentially, the "guidelines", on which ASEAN had recently agreed with China and thus, implicitly, the Association's impact on regional governance, were officially and authoritatively disregarded by all sides. The main reason for this continued to be the underlying US–China disagreements about the SCS as a sphere of influence, both in the all-encompassing sense of the Chinese nine-dash line and the more traditional and habitual sense of the United States. Facing this dilemma of the summit, critical voices from the region reminded the attendees of the constituting *consensual* element in ASEAN diplomacy and tellingly warned that the break-up of the Association might not be inconceivable if the present course of action was not turned around (FAZ November 20, 2011).[24] In fact, while the idea behind the great powers' inclusion in ASEAN (and in its off-springs) used to be that they could use the forum to negotiate their differences, now those powers and their differences were about to determine the effectiveness of the Association itself. This is why some theorists have correctly attributed only a "limited 'brokerage' role" to ASEAN (Goh 2011).

The year 2012 was to lead to the culmination of the tensions that had undermined ASEAN's governance output in the years since 2009. Whereas in previous years the SE&D had managed, if cryptically, to sustain the idea that the United States and China would find ways to cooperate, 2012 marked a substantial change in this respect. The tensions that had accompanied the bilateral relationship elsewhere now spilled over into the dialog as well.

In April, the maritime forces of the Philippines intercepted Chinese fishing vessels at Scarborough Reef/Huangyan Islands claimed by

Manila. When the Chinese side succeeded in preventing the detainment of its fishermen, a brief stand-off between Philippine and Chinese coast guard and surveillance ships began. In the end, no shot was fired and the Philippines withdrew from the Reef. China's success remained contentious, however. Only a few days later, the Philippines suggested to China that the case be decided by the International Tribunal of the Law of the Seas (FAZ April 26, 2012). Knowing full well that China would reject such an offer (which it promptly did), Manila received support from the United States, in that the latter accepted to undertake military exercises, which were deliberately designed to train the recapturing of smaller pieces of Philippine sea-based territory, with the Philippines at the end of April (Economist April 28, 2012:32).

Already in February and days before his visit to the United States, the then president-in-waiting, Xi, had one of his diplomats suggest that China and the United States were suffering a "trust deficit" (quoted in Reuters February 7, 2012). The subsequent SE&D, which took place on May 3 and 4, precisely reflected this atmosphere, though not in official statements. One of the key sources of the trust deficit was the tensions in the SCS. After the Chinese–Philippine stand-off in April, another ASEAN member, namely Vietnam, challenged China in June. In fact, its parliament signed a law on June 21, according to which the Spratly and Paracel Islands were possessions of Hanoi. China immediately responded in kind and charged Vietnam's decision as a "serious violation" of Beijing's sovereignty; moreover, on June 28 it added in public that it was about to launch "combat-ready" patrols in the SCS (Economist July 7, 2012).

These instances were the closely linked global and regional theaters which provided the political background against which ASEAN met for its annual meeting on July 9–13 in Cambodia. While the Association's diplomats wanted to discuss the issue of how to make progress with regard to the notion of a coming economic ASEAN bloc, it soon became clear that this was not the direction the summit was going to take. Instead of what some members thought would soon become an EU-like format, the tensions between the different SCS-related claimant states quickly surfaced. When the heads of states wanted to conclude the key terms of the code of conduct in the SCS, the ASEAN way of doing diplomacy reached its, power-political, limits. The latter way, described by one of the attendees as resolving disputes "quietly amid the rustle of batik silk" (quoted in Economist July 21, 2012:47), was supposed to help decide on the rules of engagement when naval vessels meet in contested territories. In reality, the atmosphere behind closed doors was reportedly poisonous. The key dividing line, it turned out, ran between those parties who backed China's position in the SCS, that is, those who did not want to condemn Beijing (e.g. Cambodia, Laos), and others who favored US support for their positions (e.g. Vietnam, Philippines, Singapore, Malaysia). Not even Indonesia's 18 attempts to offer changed drafts for the concluding communique were successful in mediating the differences (ibid.). As a result, Cambodia, as the host (supported by Laos), blocked any suggestions that would have mentioned China directly as being responsible for much of the SCS-related tensions.[25] After 45 years of existence, ASEAN had, for the first time, failed to produce a "consensual" communique, bringing together all of its ten member states.

The underlying contest between the United States and China had clearly played out as the key driver separating ASEAN members to an unprecedented degree. ASEAN did not have any experience dealing with this new quality of (great-power-related) problems; neither did it have the political capacity to cope with it. Thus, when the Philippines declared the Cambodian ambassador a *persona non grata* in August, this was a mere symptom of the much larger problem at hand. As a senior advisor to the Indonesian government put it (quoted in Economist August 18, 2012:42), the diplomatic clash over the South China Sea "is a lesson for ASEAN, about living in the real world, with big players and big issues. It's part of growing up."

ASEAN's immediate response to its own *malaise* was reflected in Indonesia's shuttle diplomacy, aimed at restoring some degree of consensus among its members. Though China's participation remained central, ASEAN states committed themselves to (thus far politically highly contested) formal regulations, such as the 2002 "Declaration on the Conduct of the Parties" in the SCS, to the early implementation of a "Code of Conduct" and the peaceful resolution of disputes according to UNCLOS (CFR 2012). These face-saving efforts could not, however, hide the fact that the underlying great-power rivalry had, effectively, divided ASEAN into four groups: those averse to China's ambitions (Philippines, Vietnam), those heavily affected by Chinese advances (Cambodia, Laos, Thailand, Myanmar), those willing to appease (Brunei, Malaysia) and those without sea-based claims but intent to, above all, maintain stability in the region (Indonesia, Singapore).

China, which after the fall-out at Phnom Penn had drily suggested that it would discuss the issue "when conditions are ripe" (quoted in ibid.), showed no concern about the erosion of ASEAN. In fact, it went on and created those very conditions itself, regardless of the outcome at the ASEAN meeting. Only seven days after the meeting,

China established the prefecture-level "city" of Sansha (an upgrade to the former county level) on the largest Paracel Island, Woody Island, in order to administer the Paracels, the Spratlys and other entities in the SCS. In addition, the CCP's Military Commission deployed a small contingent of soldiers to the island. Having done that, on August 8 it declared per law that the Paracel and Spratly Islands now belonged to the new Chinese administrative district of Sansha. Intended as a reaction to Vietnam's opposite claim in June, ASEAN's underlying division was thereby further cemented. The United States, on the other hand, did not try to mediate the disputes either; rather, as Clinton said, it assumed a seemingly passive stance to the extent that ASEAN was simply "wrestling with some very hard issues here" (quoted ibid.). It was much closer to the point, however, that the United States was conveniently disguising its national interest in sustaining its sphere of influence, regardless of the costs which ASEAN encountered in the meantime. Succinctly summarizing the relationship between all three, that is, China's challenge to the regional order, the US advantage in the latter and the very limited meaning of modes of institutionalized governance in it, a Chinese general stated: "The international military order is US-led – NATO and Asian bilateral alliances. There is nothing like the WTO for China to get into" (quoted in Economist April 7, 2012:28). In other words, in 2012 it became clear that the political disagreements between the great powers about the foundations of a new global order had come at the expense of regional governance institutions. Goh succinctly summarized it: "ASEAN authority (had) suffered a body blow" (2013:107).[26]

In 2013, China extended the nine-dash line, with which it has tried to establish its sphere of influence in the SCS, along its shore into the north in order to establish an Air Defense Identification Zone (ADIZ). This unilateral move to enlarge its claimed sphere of influence saw a geographically and politically related north-bound shift of international attention in the region, which required this analysis to include Japan's role in the contestation.[27] While ASEAN's decision-making process remained elusive due to the continued great-power disagreements, the decision of Japan's government to purchase the Senkaku and Diayou Islands from private Japanese owners in September 2012 now led to serious repercussions in the ECS.[28] The growing war-proneness of the situation at sea was to become a considerable international concern. Again, while the sea-based confrontation occurred between Japan and China on the surface, the former's treaty with the United States as its security guarantor really turned it into a contest between the United

States and China. When China pushed against Japan in 2012, it did not only want to signal its newly gained strength to Tokyo but also wanted to reiterate its determination vis-à-vis those ASEAN states with which it continued to have substantive disagreements about claims in the SCS. From a regional perspective, the (unsuccessful) handling of diplomatic and legal disputes in one region and the role of military force in them inevitably had an impact on neighboring regions. The reciprocity of this process demonstrates why the ECS and the SCS need to be looked at in parallel. To be clear, none of the renegotiations of East Asian spheres of influence took place as settlement conferences, but, rather, they were reflected in tacit understandings of where the limits of their positions were, respectively.

To begin with, after Japan's island purchase some 124 miles northeastwards of Taiwan in 2012 and the outgoing president Hu's subsequent admonition that China had to "build itself into a maritime power" (quoted in Economist January 19, 2013:40), the ECS experienced a string of incidents that would culminate at the end of the year. Already in December 2012, an aircraft of China's State Oceanic Bureau flew over Japan's territorial airspace at the Senkaku Islands. Tokyo responded by sending surveillance airplanes to monitor the islands. When on January 10 two F-15 jets intercepted a Chinese military aircraft flying near the islands, Japan publicly raised the question whether it should fire in the future if similar incidents occurred (FAZ January 12, 2013). The tone for the confrontation was then set by China's official *Global Times* calling Japan the "vanguard" in the US strategy to "contain China" (quoted in ibid.), which was why official, televised Chinese news shows as well as the People's Liberation Army's (PLA) mouthpiece stressed that the PLA was "prepared for war in 2013" (quoted in FAZ January 23, 2013). Consequently, China's sabre-rattling was again visible on January 30 when a Japanese naval boat was painted by the fire control radar of a Chinese navy vessel, according to the Japanese government (IISS 2013:12).

Certainly, the changing of the Chinese CCP guard in the spring contributed to heightened nationalistic sentiments which might therefore have led to exaggerated gestures. Nonetheless, the new deputy chief of China's general staff, Qi Jiangguo, left no doubt that it was the sea where China saw its interests threatened. Clarifying Hu's speech cited above, he said: "Our attention must be focused on the sea. It is from there that we have to expect the threat to our interests" (quoted in FAZ February 7, 2013). Importantly, President Xi himself was in charge of coordinating the Chinese activities with regard to the islands. In fact, contrary to assumptions that Chinese foreign policymaking was simply uncoordinated, a new office, presided by him, was established to manage the activities (Economist February 9, 2013:45).

Further sea-based incidents continued to occur in the following months. On January 30, a Chinese warship beamed "fire control" radar onto a Japanese destroyer (Economist February 9, 2013:45); on April 17, two Chinese warships moved into the area around the Senkaku Islands, preceded by three Chinese patrolling boats telling Japanese vessels to leave the area instantly, a demand to which the Japanese did not respond (FAZ April 18, 2013). Xi also used other opportunities to underline China's claims of an unspoken sphere of influence. First, China's White Book 2013 reiterated the claim that the islands historically belonged to Beijing; second, during a visit to Germany, he symbolically chose Potsdam to suggest that the Senkaku Islands were, among other things, the "hard-won fruit of the Second World War" (quoted in FAZ May 27, 2013).[29]

Conversely, the United States, which officially did not take sides in the disputes over sovereignty, publicly agreed with Japan that China's assertions were "incompatible with existing international law" (quoted in FT July 10, 2013:3) and thereby implied that what was at stake were its own interests (which the United States could and would naturally protect). Over the following months, the escalation was furthered by Japan launching its (close-to) aircraft carrier[30] and, conversely, China making public that its own carrier was soon to depart its port for training missions in the SCS (Economist August 10, 2013; FAZ December 14, 2013). When, on October 29, Japanese and Chinese fighter jets yet again encountered each other at the Senkaku Islands, clashes between them were avoided only at the last minute.

On November 23, China undertook a bold move, which must have been orchestrated by Xi himself. On that day, Beijing announced a so-called Air Defense Identification Zone, which stretched from its Eastern shores down south and covered the Senkaku Islands. Formally established to "protect its state sovereignty and territorial and airspace security . . . with defense acting as the key point" (Defense Ministry December 3, 2013), it demanded from any state that its aircrafts had to declare themselves and had to follow the instructions of the Chinese air force; otherwise, its military, as it was put, would take action against them. The reaction of Japan and the United States was predictably unequivocal. Despite the fact that China's summoning of the US ambassador included the admonition to "avoid making any further irresponsible remarks in this regard" (quoted in FAZ November

25, 2013), both the US and Japan the ADIZ within a few hours as a unilaterally imposed change of international law.

Only two days later, the United States responded to China's action by flying two B52 bombers, though unarmed, through the ADIZ without having given notice to the Chinese in advance (FAZ November 25, 2014). In other words, the United States had made it clear that it did not accept the changes imposed on its sphere of influence. The fact that China, in turn, did not try to enforce the ADIZ against the United States turned the two-day event into a classic example of a "tacit understanding" between the two antagonists about the scope of their spheres of influence. For now, it was tacitly agreed, the status quo was not to be changed. This result was further underlined when US, South Korean and Japanese military aircraft passed through the ADIZ without telling the Chinese authorities in advance and, more importantly, without facing any resistance from the Chinese air force when they did so on November 28 and 29.[31]

In sum, the contest between China and the United States over their respective spheres of influence was halted for the moment. The tacit understanding, which the two powers had reached through diplomatic and military "tests and probes", as Waltz put it, revealed that the room to maneuver was minimal and the status quo, therefore, unchanged. At the same time, it showed that the existing global governance institutions, such as UNCLOS/ITLOS, inevitably remained without influence in a situation where the new rules on the foundations of material power distribution were at stake. Similarly, ASEAN's muted response not only revealed the silencing impact of its internal rifts but also the conspicuous limits to its influence in view of the ongoing great-power crisis in the region.[32]

The year 2014 saw the continuation and further deepening of the tensions in the interrelated regional theaters of the ECS and the SCS. With regard to the latter, the Philippine president uttered his concerns about Chinese intentions in a drastic and telling manner in February. He found that Beijing's behavior in recent years was geared at confronting resistance and absorbing foreign territory in a fashion that resembled Hitler's behavior in the late 1930s. In fact, he drew parallels to the failed appeasement policy of the European powers in the inter-war period and explicitly pointed out Hitler's annexation of the "Sudetenland" in 1938. As President Aquino put it, "If we say yes to something we believe is wrong now … [A]t what point do you say, 'enough is enough'? Well, the world has to say it – remember that the Sudetenland was given in attempt to appease Hitler to prevent World War II" (quoted in NYT,

February 4, 2014). Moreover, the long-standing Philippines–China quarrel about territories in the SCS was furthered when Chinese vessels used their water cannons to prevent Philippine boats from delivering supplies to some of their soldiers. In particular, the soldiers were stationed on a grounded boat in the disputed area which Manila used to underwrite its claim that it lay within its Exclusive Economic Zone (EEZ) (Economist March 22, 2014:50). Simultaneously, while further criticisms were raised against China's behavior by Vietnam, Malaysia and Indonesia, China and ASEAN held the tenth meeting of their Joint Working Group on guidelines for a code of conduct on March 18 (MFA Thailand, March 19, 2014). At this venue, China insisted on its historical rights, embodied in the nine-dash line, whereas the Philippines made reference to UNCLOS, according to which any country's claims, that is, territorial waters and EEZs, need to originate from the land over which it has sovereignty. Unsurprisingly, the parties could not reconcile their diverging (and long held) points of view. This result did not only resemble the record of recent years; China had also contributed to its failure by making the unmistakable statement that, should Manila present the case in front of ITLOS, it would ignore it altogether (Economist March 22, 2014:50). This was, however, exactly what the Philippines had suggested since 2012 and which now made them file and submit their claims to the Hamburg-based court.

The following weeks again provided evidence of how deeply the United States, if formally neutral on sovereignty issues, was politically involved in the issue. First the Philippines escalated their stand-off at the Reef with the Chinese, when they broke through the latter's sea-based blockade on March 29 (FAZ March 29, 2014). Less than a month later, President Obama, visiting the region, reassured Manila of its safety by renewing the ten-year security treaty between the two states. Whereas the Philippine population's resistance against similar former treaties had led to the removal of US troops in 1992, now there was widespread support for American forces (FAZ April 24, 2014). The Philippine case, therefore, most clearly indicated the large extent to which the United States was integral to the dynamics of the underlying tensions in the SCS.

In the ECS, the rivalry over the scope of the sphere of influence equally continued. After China's contested implementation of the ADIZ in November 2013, the US secretary of defense traveled to East Asia in April. Diplomatic conventions of politeness notwithstanding, two instances in particular starkly highlighted the deeper contours of the relationship between China and the United States.

First, when the US Secretary of Defense Chuck Hagel arrived in China, he was given the otherwise rare opportunity to go on board China's new (first) aircraft carrier at Qingdao. However, after a two-hour exchange between him and his titular counterpart, that is, Defense Minister Chang Wanquan, their diverging views on regional security issues stood out in sharp relief during a press conference. While Hagel's summary of his conversation with Wanquan touched upon the security issues in the region in a diplomatic fashion, the latter's remarks with regard to Japan and the Philippines and Hagel's response showed the real differences between the two states. The Chinese defense minister, quite unusual in a diplomatic setting such as this, explicitly pointed the finger at Japan's "Abe administration ... causing severe difficulties in China–Japan relations"; in fact, he believed, "Japan takes the reversed course of history and confronts the right with the wrong" (quoted in Pentagon 2014). Equally unusually, he went on to suggest that the Philippines "illegally occupies part of China's islands and reefs in the South China Sea", repeating Beijing's default position that "it does not accept and will not participate in the international arbitration initiated by the Philippines". Referring to Japan and the Philippines, he left no doubt that "China's position ... is clear and consistent. China has indisputable sovereignty over Diaoyou (Senkaku) islands, Nansha islands, and their adjacent waters" (quoted in Pentagon 2014). Precisely because "territorial sovereignty ... is China's core interest ... we will make no compromise, no concession, no trading, not even a tiny bit of violation is allowed" (quoted in Pentagon 2014). Finally, in order to underline the importance of the last point, he added that the PLA's "mission [was] to safeguard national sovereignty ... (Therefore), the Chinese military can assemble as soon as summoned, fight immediately ... and win any battle" (ibid.). As a response, Hagel used another journalist's question to address Wanquan's strong message. Referring to China's imposition of the ADIZ last November, he said that, indeed, "every nation had a right to establish air defense zones, but not a right to do it unilaterally, with no collaboration and no consultation" (quoted in ibid.). Unsurprisingly, the real clash then came over the Philippines and Japan. At this point, the US defense secretary could hide neither his impatience nor disagreement any longer. By vigorously wagging his finger, he made it even more obvious that China's and the United States' viewpoints were irreconcilable. He stressed that the Philippines and Japan were "long-time allies of the United States. We have mutual self-defense treaties with each of those two countries. And we are fully committed to those treaty obligations" (quoted in ibid.). The shaky grounds on which the tacit agreement of last November was based could not have been exposed more strongly.[33]

Second, Hagel's visit was, among other things, meant to test the waters of what Xi and Obama had earlier called "a new model of major country relations", so that when the US president arrived in the region at the end of April, the undetermined disputes between the two great powers figured centrally on his diplomatic agenda. The nature of the tacit agreement between the United States and China, which had resulted from the events of the previous November and December, remained intermittent and tentative. In fact, since China saw the establishment of the ADIZ as a rightful reflection of its sovereignty and, thus, the US contestation of the zone as a violation of both China's non-interference policy and its historical rights,[34] it showed no signs of giving up its claim to the ADIZ, including territory claimed by Japan, but merely held back its ambitions. Thereby, the agreement remained ex-negativo in its status and, thus, could not prevent renewed unilateral attempts at changing it. The exact nature of such unilateral moves could, in turn, exacerbate the war proneness of the issue, soften the tensions or further test out the other's commitment.[35] When he arrived, the US president did not choose any of these options but, instead, indicated that its policy was about proactively underlining the status quo. In fact, at the beginning of an informal meeting in Tokyo with Japan's Prime Minister Abe, Obama made it explicit in public that the islands, which were disputed between Japan and China, were militarily fully covered under the umbrella of the security pact that had existed between Tokyo and Washington since 1972 (FAZ April 24, 2014).[36] Certainly, US top officials had made it clear at various earlier occasions that the islands were covered by the treaty;[37] most noteworthy, Obama and Xi had already had a short but rather sharp exchange about exactly this issue at their private Sunnyland dinner in June 2013.[38] Nonetheless, not only was the extent of clarity with which the US president *himself publicly* promulgated his strategic commitment *in the region* unprecedented, but he also further underlined the United States' view of the last year's tacit agreement. Put differently, the sphere of influence, as read by the United States, was barred from geopolitical change. Knowing that China would/could not back down, he took into account that the contestation was bound to continue.[39] Inadvertently, his move implied that UNCLOS was in no position to determine, or merely shape, the politics underlying the great-power dispute in the region. Equally, a Chinese judge at ITLOS, who was also the executive director of the China Institute of Maritime Affairs (Beijing), together with another Beijing-based scholar of law, argued that the politics related to the SCS had to be given preference over the legal aspects to the issue. Turning the debate from legal into (self-attributed great-power) political rights, they suggested: "The Chinese people have without challenge enjoyed and exercised certain rights in the South China Sea throughout recorded history. *Those rights do not derive from UNCLOS* [author's emphasis]" (Gao and Jia 2013:121).[40] Similarly, the fact that neither side even mentioned or showed minimum confidence in the potentially mediating role which global governance institutions, such as ASEAN, could play in the SCS theater demonstrated that neither great power attributed them with a credibly effective function. Put differently, notwithstanding the United States' and China's participation in manifold ASEAN-related meetings, their negotiations of the scope of the East Asian sphere of influence were exclusively undertaken *among* them. If observing from alternative perspectives, both great powers agreed "that (ultimately) ASEAN has no role in territorial issues" (Economist December 3, 2011:51).

In sum, none of this is to say that, because of China's partly assertive behavior, the United States managed to draw the majority of the ASEAN members into its camp. While its role as security guarantor was now much more appreciated than before 2008/9, this did not change the value that those states attributed to their political non-partiality vis-à-vis great powers. Except for the Philippines, and maybe for Vietnam, most other states had to take into account both their economic links to China and the domestic constituencies that required a more cautious embrace of the United States. In this sense, they kept alive "[t]he (ASEAN) idea that will not go away" (Ba 2009:193). However, this case study did also show that, in 2015, it would be difficult to maintain that "ASEAN... [was] a cohesive diplomatic force exerting its influence on the great powers" (Sing 1994:451). Rather, and more broadly, the region and its governance-related institutions increasingly appeared to be "on [their] way to becoming a cockpit of major-power rivalry", reflecting the renegotiations of spheres of influence in it (IISS 2013:355; Raine and Le Miere 2013:22). In fact, a very senior diplomat of the region suggested that the US–Chinese political tensions presented the litmus test for ASEAN's long-standing insistence on maintaining the sovereign independence of its member states.[41]

7
Renegotiating the Environmental Rules of Global Order

This chapter outlines the ways in which China and the United States have been renegotiating the environmental rules of the global order since 2008/9. More specifically, since Clark's purely state-based views do not reflect the hybridity of actors operating today (see Chapter 3), the global order's environmental rules (e.g. UNFCCC) and their renegotiation need to be explored in light of this hybridity. Further evaluating the main argument of this book, the focus of this case study is on the degree to which the impact of TNAs has been limited by the disagreements prevailing among the great powers. In fact, it is the irreconcilability of the latter's viewpoints which has led to the UNFCCC's continued and overall failure to reach a legally binding treaty on reducing and limiting carbon dioxide emissions.[1] The great powers' stances have powerfully undermined the goals that the UNFCCC's head recently summarized (and repeated) for the Durban Platform since 2011: "To adopt a universally inclusive and legally binding agreement by 2015 (which is) to come into effect from 2020" (Figueres 2013:539).

Curiously, this failure stands in sharp contrast to an important and broad strand in the literature. Its key argument has been that TNAs have already managed to attain so much political weight so that they can effectively steer governance processes. For instance, Haufler suggested that "private actors do influence the negotiations between public actors but, more importantly, they *directly govern* in some areas", and "in a surprising number of cases, particular issues have been addressed through collaboration between the private sector and advocacy organizations" (2009:122, 124). Similarly, Avant et al. have prominently argued that the emergence of non-state "global governors" has already evolved into the successful occupation of governance areas by TNAs (2010). In fact, those governors "are active agents who want new structures

149

and rules ... *to solve problems, change outcomes and transform international life*" (2010:1). Having condensed the various layers of the related literatures into a definition, Bulkeley et al. describe transnational governance processes as being "concerned with *realizing public goals* through the process of *steering* a particular constituency of actors (which) is regarded as authoritative" (2012:594).[2]

Against this theoretical background, this chapter aims to illustrate the extent to which NGOs and transnational climate-related initiatives have actually been able to effectively govern the issue in light of US and Chinese climate policies vis-à-vis the UNFCCC. The two countries are quintessentially important here since the latter is both the world's largest emitter of carbon dioxide as well as the largest consumer of energy resources while the former follows closely and is ranked second on both accounts.[3] Together they produce over 40% of the worldwide emissions of greenhouse gases. Moreover, coal-driven/-reliant China alone accounts for 71% of the worldwide increase of energy consumption (Tellis and Tanner 2012–13:385) and will, by 2035, have produced more carbon emissions than all European states together since 1990 (FAZ December 1, 2011).

The chapter is structured around the 2009 Conference of the Parties (COPs) at Copenhagen, which immensely raised the public's awareness of the deadlocks prevailing in global governance negotiations.[4] Employing a rarely used double lens, that is, one that combines the views of great powers and NGOs on the global climate regime (Terhalle 2015), the event can be divided into two complementary lines of development. In both cases, the dynamics between the NGO-strand and the great-power strand build the analytical core of examining UNFCCC-related events since 2009. The first section reflects the activities of NGOs trying to directly influence the negotiations at Copenhagen. Looking at the results of the COPs more closely helps to highlight the problems related to the effectiveness of vast numbers of NGO observers in the negotiation processes. The second section outlines the subsequent changes to NGO tactics, since many NGOs felt uneasy about the minimal impact they had had at the COPs.[5] After Copenhagen, a sizable number decided to pursue the alternative path of launching transnational initiatives to facilitate more efficient governance output.[6] Nonetheless, the ongoing state-based negotiations at UNFCCC and, accelerated by Copenhagen, the steady erosion of the Kyoto Protocol during the first (2008–12) and second (2012–[2020]) phases of its implementation present the necessary foil against which the activities of non-state actors need to be viewed. Therefore, those activities are juxtaposed with the impact of the disagreements and the ensuing strategic competition between China and the United States since 2008/9.

The impact of NGOs at COP-15

In October 2009, 350.org, a global grassroots campaign to reduce atmospheric concentrations of GHG emissions from currently 392 to below 350 parts per million, managed to coordinate some 5,200 simultaneous rallies and demonstrations in 181 countries in order to politically prepare the grounds for the Copenhagen Summit two months later (Christoff and Eckersley 2013:167). There, the Conference of the Parties (COP), that is, the UNFCCC's summit, brought together some 30,123 officially registered participants in 2009 (COP 2008:9252). Two-thirds of them, that is, 20,611, were accredited as NGO observers (COP 2008:3869).[7] During the two-week-long gathering, a small number of those observers were active as legal and policy advisors to their national delegations, joined by others who helped disperse the available evidence from the summit online via ECO, the Climate Action Network's publication.[8] At the same time, precisely because only a very limited number of those observers were invited to the final government-to-government negotiations,[9] a practice that combined NGO activities inside and outside the negotiations halls (Carpenter 2001:320; della Porta and Tarrow 2004) had evolved in the last ten years. Commonly, this meant that NGOs would organize events parallel to the COP-15's official summit meetings; more specifically, on the Saturday between the two weeks, environmental NGOs reportedly mobilized between 60,000 and 100,000 demonstrators in order to reinforce their policy claims in public. Carefully orchestrated, the demonstrations were part of the "Global Day of Action" around climate change, simultaneously taking place in 108 countries (Fisher 2010:14). However, when the governments of the United States and China (leading the G77)[10] failed to agree on "any peaking year for emissions, or collective mitigation target (either global or for Annex I parties)" and could only find a common position on holding further negotiations in the future besides new technology mechanisms (Depledge 2010:20), widespread disappointment about the UNFCCC's capability to deliver was the predictable result.[11]

Looking at the meager results of Copenhagen raises the question of how to characterize the influence of NGOs more accurately. Their overwhelming presence inside and outside the convention center, their widely acknowledged expertise and the attention they paid to furthering their media publicity had not been sufficient to prod the key states to find the political will for a more substantial compromise in the negotiations. Thus, their capability to deliver or to "directly govern" climate issues turned out to be woefully underdeveloped. Strikingly, the results of the UNFCCC's COP-15 confirmed Drezner's assumption mentioned in Chapter 3. He had found that "there is an inverse correlation between NGO influence and the public visibility of these actors" (2007:86). Thus, both the ways in which environmental NGOs dominated the public sphere and perception and the ways in which they offered their service functions could not alter the diametrically opposed positions of the key states. Indeed, it was precisely Drezner's notion of "inverse-ness" that helped to deflate the notion of the often-exaggerated impact of non-state actors and, thus, put them into the more sobering, eventually, more accurate context of deeply seated disagreements between the leading great powers during order transition.

To be sure, disagreements between the major powers had long characterized the evolution of the climate regime and had, in fact, tended to resurface whenever the attempt was made to turn the more general stipulations of the UNFCCC into more obligatory rules. Put briefly, states (have) remained divided in their assessment of the problem's severity: they vary as to how much they contribute to it; their material ability to address the consequences; and their capacity to adapt to climate change accordingly (Mitchell 2010). Nonetheless, Copenhagen was different in that it added a new and crucial layer to the disagreements. In particular, it hardened the respective positions (especially of China and the United States) because of emerging and "much wider political and ideological concerns that extend[ed] way beyond the specific issue of climate change" (Depledge 2010:18). Foreshadowing the reciprocal nature of their strategic competition, China's government saw the summit in the wider terms of a global great-power contestation. As the chief correspondent of the Chinese newspaper *Xinhua* stated: climate change was above all *not* a technological or economic problem; much rather, addressing the United States, it represented a "deeply political problem in that it was but a part of the much larger problem of re-organizing the global order" (quoted in Bräuner 2010:2).

What was the reaction of TNAs to the procedure and results of Copenhagen? Leaving aside the unsurprising and often partial charges, one of the more interesting consequences was that it prompted a large number of those actors to organize transnational initiatives "in the shadow of the international regime" (Bulkeley et al. 2012:603). The next (longer) section empirically addresses the nature and impact of this informal phenomenon on the UNFCCC; it shows how the new initiatives fared at COPs 16–19 and the political turn the UNFCCC began to take before Durban; finally, it outlines more broadly the key reasons for US–China disagreements, causing the UNFCCC's disarray in the first place.

Transnational climate initiatives and US–Chinese strategic competition

In the wake of the Copenhagen Summit, TNAs began to review and revise their approaches to the problem of climate change. Discontent with the results of mega-multilateralism, a sizable number of NGOs decided to complement those non-state actors who worked closely with state delegations.[12] In particular, NGOs launched manifold initiatives that mainly aimed at governing mitigation through rule-setting and the provision of funding on the transnational level (Bulkeley et al. 2012:593, 599).

Drawing from an international survey of some 60 such initiatives (Bulkeley et al. 2012),[13] environmental NGOs were the key drivers behind the revised focus on mitigation. Operating outside, though complementing the UNFCCC framework, those NGOs "establish(ed) initiatives in order to advance a set of norms as a basis of governance" (Bulkeley et al. 2012:600). Some 50% of them promoted such norms through rule-setting (ibid.:604). In order to arrive at a higher degree of (voluntary) compliance with mitigation-related rules, the initiatives overwhelmingly advanced the provision of "information sharing" as the "most common function amongst" them, that is, 93% (ibid.:604). At its core, the mainly Northern initiatives (87%) sought to "shape the subjectivity of those they govern" "by changing the informational context" so "that actors internalize more deeply norms about how to act on climate change" (ibid.:605). In other words, the new initiatives created considerable informal space in order to reinforce their well-known normative goals in relation to climate change. The key difference to pre-Copenhagen standards and, in one way or another, the lesson learnt was that "a dominant cluster of initiatives" wanted to employ their readily available and expertise-based knowledge in the "pursuit of *efficiency*" (ibid.:608).

The compartmentalization of international environmental politics has portrayed these new initiatives as valuable, and in many ways necessary, informal development that was created in the wake of the failure of UNFCCC's COP-15. Nevertheless, the empirical picture would remain incomplete if the relationship between those initiatives and the post-Copenhagen developments was not taken into account. In other words, what were the consequences of the new initiative-based "efficiency" in relation to the trajectory of the UNFCCC? Have the informal initiatives managed to fill the gap that has existed in the formal UNFCCC process since, at the latest, 2009?

One straightforward way of measuring the implied progress in this instance is to look at the core results of the UNFCCC summits between 2010 and 2013, notwithstanding the salience of national commitments such as mandatory annual reports[14] to be sent to the United Nations and the pledge to provide funding to the most underdeveloped states. Due to space constraints, this cannot be the place to give a full and detailed empirical account of COPs 16–19. Therefore, at this point it is crucial to concentrate on the *key political results* of the four summits and their implications for the overall coherence of the state-based regime.

The four summits

In a nutshell, none of the four summits in Cancun, Durban, Doha and Warsaw reached a breakthrough toward the overall goal of a legally binding treaty for all signatories. Neither did those COPs lay any substantive foundations for a future treaty. In fact, most of the achievements remained procedural as they merely kept the overall process alive by agreeing to new rounds of negotiations; however, they did not produce any new and tangible commitments. Even worse, with the largest emitters, that is, China and the United States, not even bound by the UNFCCC's Kyoto Protocol, the future coherence of the latter's members could not be taken as a given before the end of the first commitment period on December 31, 2012.

To begin with, while Cancun 2010 saw the adoption of the loose Copenhagen Accord into the formal UN process,[15] the summit in Durban in 2011 revealed the deeper underlying political tensions of the UNFCCC process. Three important states, that is, Canada, Russia and Japan, announced that they were determined to leave the Kyoto Protocol before the beginning of the second commitment period on January 1, 2013.[16] Their decisions further played into the increasingly more national and unilateral challenges that the global environmental regime came to face at Durban. Moreover, China and the United States, neither of which was bound by the Protocol, accused each other of derailing the overall process precisely because each insisted that the other should take the first step to show more commitment (Never 2013:222). Such exposure of the hard-nosed defense of their respective national interests further exacerbated the already ongoing erosion of the climate regime (FAZ November 29, 2011; January 12, 2011).[17] Two brief examples may underpin this strand of development. First, members of NGOs were openly questioned at Durban for why they still promoted transnational solutions when, at the same time, major states were adopting effective national measures to counter climate change domestically.[18] In fact, this was precisely what the World Bank's special envoy for climate change, Andrew Steer, had in mind when he stated: "The world of action on climate change is a long, long way ahead of the world of negotiation" (quoted in Economist November 5, 2011:87; FAZ December 11, 2011). Second, the US president, aware of the domestic obstacles he faced in Washington but, equally, unsatisfied with the outcome of recent COPs began to "approach[.] this [problem] creatively", "thinking strategically about using other forums", as his top advisor on climate, Heather Zichal, put it in retrospect (quoted in NYT January 3, 2014). Moving away from the UNFCCC, Zichal implied that Obama had decided to engage groups such as the G8, G20 and the Major Emitters Forum (MEF).[19] While political differences were by no means resolved in these formats, the direction toward smaller circles of countries and fewer to no NGOs participating in them was in itself a clear indicator of the strong tensions that existed within the hybrid order of global environmental politics.

Seen from the broader political perspective, as it is adopted here, Doha 2012 brought no progress. No agreement that limited greenhouse gases was concluded.[20] Even though the leader of the Chinese delegation praised the nature of the UN process as such, his insistence on China's status as a developing state made clear that it showed no intention to agree to binding obligations in the coming round of talks (Guardian December 12, 2012). Pointedly, it was the former prime minister of Denmark, Rasmussen, who pierced through the large negotiation rounds when he stated that there was some "blame game – who is to blame for climate change" – going on in which "people (were) pointing their fingers at each other" (quoted in Guardian December 12, 2012). Mistakenly, though, he believed that "it is crystal clear that...[this game] is over" (ibid.). To the contrary, both China and the United States continued to point at each other in order to distract from the fact that neither was interested in accepting legally binding emission reduction commitments during the second commitment phase of Kyoto (FAZ December 8, 2012).

After the dropout of the three aforementioned states from Kyoto at the 2012 Doha meeting, the Conference of the Parties reconvened one year later in Warsaw. The parties not only concluded that member states would make "contributions" to climate-change reduction by 2015, but also said that this applied only "to those who are ready" (Economist November 30, 2013). Quintessentially, the diplomatic formula that was found concealed the underlying tensions that had characterized previous COPs and, thus, no substantive progress toward the binding agreement, which was aimed at for 2015, was made.

As a result, the failure of the COPs after Copenhagen to conclude a universal and legally binding treaty or, at least, to produce tangible results that could have laid the foundations for such a treaty was now indisputable. Instead, the further erosion of the Kyoto Protocol, reflected in the exiting of the aforementioned states, was only the latest, though most revealing, symptom for the UNFCCC's lack of normative pull on governments. Consequently, a major implication of these developments was that a growing number of states unwittingly joined the two largest emitters, that is, the United States and China, in trying to tackle the challenges of climate change on a national and unilateral basis. As it was said regarding the latter two: "After years of fruitless wrangling to negotiate a global treaty for all, the big polluters have decided to go it alone" (Economist June 29, 2013:14). Conspicuously, NGOs and their transnational initiatives had not been able to prevent this diplomatic outcome.

Commonly, the literature on transnationalism assumes that, since NGOs are critical both "at the beginning...for putting...issues on the agenda and shaping the ways those issues are understood" and "at the end" when they "help to implement global accords", the politics of "the classic stages of diplomatic negotiations between governmental representatives" (Downie 2014:182–183; Hochstetler 2013:176)[21] are a merely passive transmission belt for global issues. However, the recent history of the COPs has proved this literature plainly wrong. In fact, the new "efficiency" attributed to transnational initiatives turned out to be heavily dependent on the states from which they operated. In this regard, Hickmann (2014) has provided an in-depth examination of three initiatives, focusing on rule-setting (e.g. Cities for Climate Protection (ICLEI); the Gold Standard; the GHG Protocol). In the case of the ICLEI, members of local governments admitted that, precisely because there was no global climate regime available, governments were not legally bound to mitigation measures. In turn, this meant that international funds for more local climate projects, that is, initiatives, were held hostage. Concerning the Gold Standard, members of the staff acknowledged that their initiatives were strongly reliant on a well-functioning global regulatory structure that creates an incentive for buyers of carbon offsets to go ahead and invest more securely in mitigation projects. Finally, the GHG Protocol most clearly suffered from the lacking global treaty on mitigation. Without the latter, the guidelines produced by the Protocol cannot get firms to conduct and complete falsifiable documents of their emissions.[22] Taken together, these observations convincingly show that bottom-up governance is not simply and "intimately connected" to state policies but, rather, it is "highly dependent" (Bulkeley et al. 2012:603) on the existence of an international rule-based framework negotiated by nation-states in international settings.[23] For instance, as a former top-rank diplomat succinctly summarized his experiences at the United Nations: "it remains true that most of the running has been made by the Great Powers... It has been on their *ability* to craft agreed solutions *that the success, or otherwise,* of the negotiations has *depended*" (Brenton 2013:543). Precisely because this has been the case, disagreements among the great powers have necessarily led to the freeze of transnational activities, as former UNFCCC staff members openly admit.[24]

As the next section shows, at a fundamentally systemic level, it was the fierce contestation about the underlying political parameters of the environmental world order which was at the very heart of the UNFCCC's failure. The following section outlines and analyzes the strategic great-power disagreements between China and the United States. Their disagreements showed no sign that they could be resolved by innovative transnational means.

Great-power disagreements

In order to better contextualize the failures of transnational initiatives to evince support for the establishment of binding climate obligations, this section first outlines the key reasons behind US and Chinese objections to the core goals of the UNFCCC, respectively, and then shows how their relationship, shaped by strategic competition, has come to further exacerbate the fortunes of the global carbon mitigation efforts.[25]

To begin with, the United States' ambivalence toward the global climate regime derives from three factors: the confluence of domestic values and its political institutions as well as from the particular shape of US power which allows it to act outside existing frameworks (Foot and Walter 2011:212). As in the case of China, Washington has given preference to factors such as economic growth and national competitiveness. In turn, these factors have, more often than not, come at the expense of accepting international and legally binding obligations. This is not to say that the United States has not produced advocates of climate protection such as former (Democratic) Vice President Al Gore, who started a massive film campaign to change public awareness in favor of the climate regime after having left office.[26] Nonetheless, while still in office, President Clinton canceled the idea of taking his vice president's policy plan, which suggested a carbon tax, to Congress; this was a powerful indicator of where the political limits of environmental policy issues began (Hovi et al. 2012). Despite their in many ways vast differences, the concerns behind Clinton's interference have been reflected in his successors' policies, too.

Regarding domestic values, though the United States has been home to a very broad environmental movement since the 1960s, the latter has failed to effectively convince the public (and its media awareness) that concerns related to national health, the natural habitat and the protection of the global climate are in fact interconnected. Not the least, climate matters have consistently not been ranked as a major concern among the US population. For instance, while US presidents signed some 11 major multilateral environmental agreements between 1989 and 2011, none was ratified by the US legislative branch (Bang et al. 2012).[27]

Undoubtedly, the United States has been one of the most science-friendly and science-driven countries on the globe. However, the seemingly scientific cause of environmentalists to the extent that the rise of temperature is a scientifically proven development and that, in turn, international measures must be taken to prevent global warming stepping over the mark of two degrees Celsius has not generated the expected mass support. Rather, when it was demonstrated that the surface temperature had risen only 0.04 degrees between 1998 and 2013 (1990s:0.18 degrees), the already existing suspicions against those scientific predictions fell on fertile grounds (Economist March 8, 2014:66; March 30, 2013:14). Propelled by US businesses, those suspicions could successfully draw on the overwhelming societal support for economic growth, both in purely economic terms and also in a very American sense, in intra-societal, competition-based terms of measuring personal success. For instance, the US Chamber of Commerce and the National Association of Manufacturers successfully lobbied against extending any regulatory rights to the EPA (US Environmental Protection Agency) concerning greenhouse gas emissions and to cap and trade legislation. This way the US president, aware of the climate-related obstacles in Congress, was prevented from using executive directives to circumvent exactly those obstacles in 2009 (Foot and Walter 2011:215).[28] This does not imply that the CEOs of US businesses have without exception been hostile to public mitigation efforts; rather, it is more accurate to suggest that while their broad majority continues to successfully lobby against costly emissions regulations, there is a tendency, discernible among them, to back multilateral treaties "only if these internationalize domestic regulations" or "if they offer competitive advantages" vis-à-vis international competitors (Foot and Walter 2011:213). The overall domestic political climate and, accordingly, the popular mood were further geared toward this direction when the so-called fracking revolution, that is, new ways of extracting energy resources in the United States, started to considerably lower national carbon emissions in 2012.

Regarding political institutions, they have reflected, if not unanimously, the objections that have been deeply embedded in the population. To begin with, the US constitutional structure provides both chambers of Congress, House and Senate, with huge influence on environmental politics. The openness of the legislative process also allows lobby groups manifold ways to influence policymaking. Most importantly, however, any urgency of global concerns, such as climate protection, is severely "mitigated" by the local concerns of congressmen of both parties. As one senator put it: "All of us know that fighting for our individual states is that responsibility which is foremost" (John Warner quoted in Bang et al. 2012:757). Together with their lobbying groups, the vast interests of those members of Congress who came from coal-dependent and rural states have prevailed over those who preferred a more climate-friendly position. Similarly, a large majority of Senators had opposed Kyoto early on; in fact, some 16 states objected to the Senate's ratification of the Protocol, with California being the exception. Again, the bedrock of resistance against any environmental enmeshment originated from states with high numbers of carbon emissions per capita (Lee 2000).

Regarding the international impact of US power in climate negotiations, US negotiators have not only had to represent the aforementioned majority opinion. In contrast to European governments, they have also shown a significantly different take on the issue of "common but differentiated responsibilities and respective capabilities" (CDR). Conspicuously less worried about (contested) responsibilities emanating from the historical past, American state officials have tended to predicate the defense of their self-interest on more current concerns. In particular, they have not viewed the imbalance that was built into CDR[29] as being politically accurate; rather, they have strongly disagreed with the entrenched interpretation of, as they saw it, the allegedly historically grounded and distributional fairness of the responsibilities. In other words, the US position has been to participate in negotiations while not accepting the imbalance as a basis for future decisions. The founding or, rather, crystallizing document of this policy remains the Senate's Byrd–Hagel resolution of 1997, which was passed with 95 votes for and no votes against it. At its core, it states: "The United States should not be a signatory to any protocol...which would...mandate new commitments...unless the protocol...also mandates new...commitments...for Developing Country Parties...; or result in serious harm for the U.S. economy" (105th US Congress, July 25, 1997). For instance, President Obama, while committed to the issue of global climate protection, has failed to convince Congress to adopt a more internationally compatible posture, precisely because of the bipartisan resentment that is reflected in the Byrd–Hagel resolution.

In the case of China, its ambivalence toward the climate regime mainly derives from two interrelated factors: domestic stability and the impact of the former on institutional capacities. To begin with, as has been argued throughout, the survival of the Communist Party's rule is exclusively dependent on the provision of economic growth. Economic growth facilitates the continued improvement of the regime's efforts to lower the countrywide poverty rate and, thus, underpins societal stability and prevents domestic disorder. Furthermore, poverty reduction is critical for its self-perception as the developing world's leader of the G77. It is these interest-based drivers that have been the most crucial ones for the politbureau's policy planning process.[30]

This is also why Beijing has consistently argued that it cannot accept obligations with regard to cutting carbon emissions. In fact, it has made sure that, at its core, neither the UNFCCC as such nor the Kyoto Protocol have been changed to that end. Its proven record remains obvious in this instance. For the same reason, China's practice of implementing the legislative and verbal commitments, which it has made on a national level, has been highly ambiguous (Hallding et al. 2011:72–74). Two examples may help to illustrate this. First, one of China's leading lawyers of environmental issues suggested that "barely ten percent of the country's environmental laws and regulations are actually enforced" (quoted in Foot and Walter 2011:195). Second, the Chinese Academy for Environmental Planning concluded that a mere 1.3% of the annual budget that was dedicated to environmental protection between 2001 and 2005 was actually used for its intended purposes, that is, for legitimate environmental projects (ibid.).[31] In this vein, while China's persistent unwillingness to allow international monitoring of its activities reflects its conservative understanding of sovereignty, it also unfavorably strengthens the international perception that its actions do not live up to its rhetoric. Its declaration of "Nationally Appropriate Mitigation Actions" (NAMA), which it submitted to the UNFCCC after Copenhagen, outlining the sets of targets or policies that it intends to carry out voluntarily in order to reduce its carbon emissions, may have inspired prominent economists, such as Hu Angang, to portray China's efforts as the dawn of a "green revolution" (Held et al. 2013:330); however, they have not changed the overall perception held by others.

The politics of the unequal relationship between economic and environmental policy objectives have further been reflected in the common diminishing of the capacity of environmental bodies in China. For instance, officials at the Ministry of Environmental Protection have often been sidelined by their counterparts at the National Development and Reform Commission. More precisely, since the (8%) growth priority has been the guideline for China's overall policy process, local and provincial party officials aiming at the fulfillment of the expected growth rates have constantly gained the upper hand vis-à-vis the directives proclaimed by environmental officials. In one instance, the national statistics bureau denied publishing numbers regarding China's green GDP. The reason given was that this would yield an "unfavorable reaction from provincial governments", because "pollution data would hurt their performance assessments" (quoted in Foot and Walter 2011:197).

Taken together, China's key national interest of economic development quintessentially presides over any other policy concerns. Global environmental concerns have consistently been made to submit to this national interest. The similarities to the United States are striking in terms of the explicit preference given to economic growth.

Strategic competition

Building on what has been suggested thus far, it is important to take another layer into account that has in many ways sharpened the already existing disagreements between the two great powers. In other words, the aforementioned national positions in environmental politics have strongly influenced, and have been influenced by, the strategic competition that has emerged between the United States and China since 2008/9. In a quite Gilpinian manner, the hegemon has continued to manipulate the international system in its favor, as long as it can, in order to slow the challenger's rise to the top (1981).[32]

While both states had signed the UNFCCC's Rio declaration of 1992, in the years thereafter, the Kyoto Protocol with its legally binding obligations for the developed world became the most outstanding point of contestation. In particular, the notion of distributive fairness, embodied in the "common but differentiated" responsibilities between Annex 1 and non-Annex 1 countries, crystallized the diametrically opposed views. There have been two main issues, both of which are intimately related, that build the core of the strategic competition. First, China's supreme interest in economic growth has several layers. While it is central to the Chinese Communist Party (CCP)'s concerns over domestic and social stability for China, as stated above, it is also the central pillar in the overall contest with the United States. Thus, China's reluctance to accept more climate-related obligations at the COPs was partly based on the suspicion that the United States has attempted to undercut the terms set by the Kyoto Protocol (Foot and Walter 2011:223). In other words, Beijing fears that Washington has undermined the Protocol for the sake of its own economic interests. In fact, these fears have been intensified by the boldness with which US congressmen justify this position, making reference to China as being unwilling to adopt similar obligations (Lieberthal and Sandalow 2009:38). Therefore, the "[c]ompetitiveness concerns [between the US and China] are essentially zero-sum: China's are mirror-image of those that are prominent in the United States and are also framed in terms of fairness" (Foot and Walter 2011:223).

Second, precisely because developed states have already passed through their inevitably emissions-intensive phase of urbanization and industrialization, China is not only sensitive to any obligations and demands to curb its emissions in economic terms; more importantly, the Chinese "voice suspicions [that are] based on strategic calculations" (Foot and Walter 2011:223). In fact, there is a deeply embedded fear prevailing in China to the extent that the hegemon, that is, the United States, tries to contain the challenger's rise. The (Gilpinian) suspicion holds that the United States, while it is still in the powerful position, tries to slow China's growth by prodding it to accept the Kyoto targets and thereby raising the economic costs for its further development (ibid.). Put differently, the hegemon, that is, the United States, has manipulated the climate regime for its own purposes because it is afraid of China's immense economic growth, its vast increases in military spending and great surpluses in their bilateral trade (ibid.:225). In this respect, precisely because the United States does not want China to improve its climate record, Washington has been unwilling to transfer the technology necessary to support Beijing's capacity to reduce emission levels (Hallding et al. 2011:73–74). This is also why the head of the CCP's School for Strategic Studies suggested that the failure of the climate negotiations was a mere symptom of a broader process in which the "great powers' special responsibilities [in relation to the environment] were newly constituted" (Bräuner 2010:1). In this sense, the two powers have been engaged in a process of strategic and "reciprocal socialization" (Terhalle 2011), which has ultimately come at the expense of the tightening grip of the UNFCCC.[33] For instance, in 2001, when President G.W. Bush announced that the United States would withdraw from Kyoto, the Chinese side cheerfully acknowledged that this move had taken the pressure off China for the next eight years (Zhang 2009).

As a consequence, if detrimental to the climate regime, the evolution of the US–China strategic competition has led to a state of affairs in which the highly self-interested behavior of both sides prevents any progress of the regime "*unless* the other accepts that it too must play its part" (Foot and Walter 2011:175). Needless to say, the inherent dynamics of such thinking have conveniently made the other's position a scapegoat for the failure of the overall regime as well as the other's implied irresponsibility. In sum, while it remains an open question whether "China and the US hold the key to a new global climate deal" (Guardian December 12, 2012), so far the key has only worked to shut down progress in transnational climate governance.

To summarize, Bulkeley et al.'s indirect question – "it will be interesting to assess what the effect of prolonged stalemate in the climate negotiations will have on the further evolution of transnational climate change governance" (2012:610) – was already outdated when asked. Straightforwardly, it can be suggested that the continued and repeated deadlocks at the UNFCCC's COPs have been caused by the deep political disagreements, inter alia, between China and the United States that have further been exacerbated by the strategic nature of their competition.[34] In turn, this implies that precisely because progress in climate politics "*depends upon* effective and courageous political leadership" (Edmondson and Levy 2013:x),[35] the impact of activities in transnational climate governance has almost been neutralized. Or, as two experienced observers, who are overall sympathetic to the notion of transnationalism, caustically remarked on whether networks of civil society actors (which includes the aforementioned initiatives) have made any difference through their "pursuit of efficiency": "...yes, but not much" (Christoff and Eckersley 2013:168).

8
Renegotiating the Ideology-Related Aspects of Global Order

This case study looks at the ongoing process of renegotiating Clark's "morality" of the global order (2005) and Gilpin's "ideological...values common to a set of states" (1981:34) with reference to the "Responsibility to Protect" (RtP). As it was shown in Chapter 4, Keohane's (2012) underlying assumption to the effect that any future order, despite changes in the material structure of international politics, will be underpinned by a liberal "common culture" was put into question. This was the case precisely because the "diffusion of ideas and values, with a reopening of the big questions of social, economic and political organization" has accompanied the diffusion of material power (Hurrell 2013:21). Furthermore, the absence of a common culture, embodied in the overall incommensurability of US and Chinese superior worldviews, as Chapter 4 concluded, could analytically only be channeled through the pluralist competition between "ideas of right and wrong found within a practice of states" (Cochran 2009:290). For this reason, in order to better illustrate the features of this competition, the case study breaks down the notion of ideology into contested understandings of sovereignty.

In line with the overall argument of this book, this case study finds that, while it is often assumed that the more conservative interpretation of sovereignty is a preference of (great) powers with a colonial past, in fact *both* China as well as the United States hold strong sovereignty-based reservations against the Responsibility to Protect (RtP).[1] Though the two states differ in terms of the origins of their sovereignty-protecting attitudes, their often very Westphalian positions with regard to the practice of RtP have come at the expense of establishing the norm as customary international law. In other words, while chief advocates of the norm maintain that it "is now overwhelmingly accepted"

(Evans and Thakur 2013:201),[2] Chinese and US political attitudes have continued to undermine the strength of the underlying theoretical assumption that global governance institutions and norms can guide great powers to act in ways in which those institutions and norms believe they should. In fact, the two states' combined objections to deepening enmeshment (United States), on the one hand, and to perforating the principle of non-interference (China), on the other, have exposed the weaknesses of this assumption. In turn, the following empirical observations help pierce through, as Koskenniemi critically suggested, the "mystery of legal obligation" (2011). Unsurprisingly, the United States and China had agreed to the universal adoption of RtP by the UN General Assembly in 2005. Therefore, it can be said that the RtP is but one more example of what Jackson's earlier remarks correctly criticized as a propensity for the cheap talk of the great powers' "declaratory tradition", which deliberately endorses high-aiming ideals, such as RtP, precisely because "they do not carry as much weight as obligations" (2000:128).[3] Finally, whereas global governance theorists could point to the degree to which the issue of responsibility was truly globally discussed at the UN General Assembly before 2011, the critical debates on Libya and Syria showed that a substantive shift to the exclusive realm of the P5 had taken place.

The structure of the chapter is as follows: after a short introduction to the origins of the norm as well as to the three pillars supporting the concept of RtP, the chapter examines in-depth two recent cases which display the political dilemmas surrounding the norm internationally, for example, in Libya (2011) and Syria (since 2012).[4] It concludes by suggesting that China's and the United States' political practices have been based on conservative understandings of sovereignty and have, thus, prompted a degree of pluralist expediency, which has been detrimental to the furtherance and adoption of the new norm into the accepted fabric of international law.

RtP: Origins and pillars of a new concept

It is well known that with the collapse of Soviet and Yugoslav states after the end of the Cold War considerable political space was unwittingly created for failing and failed states to occur. Equally, the onset of the US-driven "liberal moment" after 1991 permitted more conceptual thinking about how to cope with the often dramatic events involving mass killings.[5] Put briefly, the ascendance of the new concept was affected by the course of international humanitarian crises which, in turn, laid bare, at an early stage, the tensions that would shape the emerging norm in the future.

While the breakdown of state structures in Somalia led to a broad military intervention by the United Nations, the media coverage of the death of American soldiers had a lasting impact on US domestic politics. More precisely, in 1994, when the Rwandan genocide saw the killing of some 800,000 human beings within a few weeks, the United States' government was politically unwilling to intervene militarily in the Central African state precisely because of what had happened in Somalia a year earlier. These developments spurred a new process of conceptual thinking, culminating at first in the pioneering work of Francis M. Deng et al., which stressed the notion of responsibility as the most fundamental part of classic understandings of sovereignty (1996). While Deng and his co-authors were centrally concerned with the African continent, the Bosnian civil war and the atrocities committed against the inhabitants of neighboring Kosovo made it abundantly clear that the problem was not limited to developing states. NATO's controversial intervention on the Balkans in 1998 triggered the broadening of the previously completed conceptual work. At the end of 2001, the Report of the Ottawa-based "International Commission on Intervention and State Sovereignty" presented some of the features of what is now entitled the "Responsibility to Protect". Tellingly, the members of the commission did not make reference to notions of legal obligation, but they held that the new norm was "predominantly a moral imperative" (Welsh 2011b:105). If perhaps unwittingly, by adopting a more cosmopolitan belief the commissioners predicated their understanding of norm adherence on appeals to a presumed "common humanity" (ibid.). Regardless, the timing of the presentation was unfortunate in relation to the wider developments of international affairs. Presented three months into the military campaign launched by the United States (and others) after 9/11 and the run-up to the Iraq War in 2003, these events withdrew much of the attention that the project had previously received. In fact, foreshadowing the salience of (great-power) preferences and vagaries of action and inaction vis-à-vis the potential impact of the norm, the atrocities of the civil war in Sudan's Darfur region, which started in February 2003, were not sanctioned.[6] Nonetheless, the Darfur example at least helped to keep the issue on the (sidelines of the) international political agenda and was instrumental to the provision of a report by a high-level UN panel on threats, challenges and change at the end of 2004. The latter eventually produced the key conceptual foundations for the United Nations General Assembly's debate on September 16, 2005. Unanimously accepted by the World Summit of heads of state, its Outcome document spelled out the essential elements of the new "Responsibility to Protect" (2005).[7]

In short, embedded in Paragraphs 138 and 139 of the Outcome document, the concept of RtP consists of three pillars (2005:31, all quotes). Pillar one defines the prevention and protection of a state's inhabitants "from genocide, war crimes, ethnic cleansing and crimes against humanity" as the respective authorities' core responsibility. The second pillar addresses the responsibility of the international community to "encourage and help states to exercise this responsibility" through capacity building, derived from concepts of good governance. The third pillar introduces an international responsibility to react to the four aforementioned crimes. In particular, the "international community, through the United Nations, ... has the responsibility to use appropriate diplomatic, humanitarian and other peaceful means, in accordance with Chapters VI and VIII of the Charter, to help protect populations ... [and] to take collective action, in a timely and decisive manner, through the Security Council".

More broadly, the new norm of RtP has attempted to recalibrate the notion of agency in relation to the classical theme of intervention. As Evans and Thakur straightforwardly suggested, RtP is "victim- and people-centered, whereas 'humanitarian intervention' privileges the perspectives, preferences and priorities of the intervening states" (2013:202). As this chapter will show, a key difficulty which RtP encountered was the fact that the underlying assumption of Evans' and Thakur's thinking has not prompted the political resolution of what, more accurately, remains a powerful tension in which the "intervening states" have retained considerably more influence than the authors want to admit. Strikingly, Evans' and Thakur's analytical dichotomy entirely overlooks actors that do not want to intervene in the first place (e.g. China).[8] The case study will highlight the implications of this omission.

Following this short introduction, the next two sections investigate the empirical record of the norm in light of the US–China relationship and with particular reference to the cases of Libya and Syria. The empirical focus is on the outbreak of the crises and the subsequent process of decision-making in both countries. The case studies do not address the overall trajectory or unintended consequences of the crises; nor do they explicate the regional implications, respectively.[9]

The politics of RtP 1: Libya

As for the purposes of this chapter, the Libyan crisis of 2011 and the role of RtP in it need to be viewed against a three-layered background.

First, due to the mainly negative reactions to its more assertive regional behavior in 2010, China had become slightly more sensitive to factors affecting its international image. Second, the United States was almost exclusively concerned with its domestic economic rebuilding and saw a president relentlessly aiming at the full withdrawal of US troops from Iraq. Quintessentially, the administration (and the electorate) had become extremely self-conscious about the 2003 intervention in Iraq and showed no interest in any new commitments abroad. Finally, the so-called Arab Spring in North Africa and the Levant (but much less so in the Gulf) had just ousted the presidents of Egypt, Mubarak (February 11, 2011), and Tunisia, Ben Ali (January 14, 2011) from power, after both had led their countries for more than three decades.

Social and other media ensured that Libya, located between Tunisia and Egypt, was affected by the mass upheavals as well. Bringing to the surface the massive extent of political tensions that its president Gaddafi had both fostered and repressed, often brutally, for over forty years, eastern Libya turned out to be the stronghold of the demonstrators and soon-to-be rebels. Early protests in Cyrenaica (2–15), Benghazi (2–17) and Bayda (2–18) were, as Gaddafi had already warned in a public speech after the downfall of Ben Ali in January, heavily suppressed (IISS 2011:67). When protesters, on February 18, nonetheless demanded that the president step down, state authorities indiscriminately shot unarmed citizens, using machine guns and reportedly killing several hundred people in the following two days (IISS 2011:14). A civil war was now in full swing with the rebels and loyalist forces fighting over various cities (e.g. Misrata, Zawiya, Ajdabiya). When, on February 25, state forces opened fire on protesters after their Friday prayers, Gaddafi's actions only confirmed what he had said in a speech three days earlier. Speaking on TV, he had made it unmistakably clear that he would hunt down protesters "door by door" and that "officers have been deployed in all tribes and regions so that they can purify all decisions from these cockroaches"; he left no doubt that "any Libyan who takes arms against Libya will be executed" (quoted in ABC 2011). From Gaddafi's perspective, his grip on power was at stake.

Alarmed by the events in Libya, leading UN officials employed the RtP discourse in order to provide a framework for their stipulations. On February 22, for instance, the High Commissioner for Human Rights called on Libya to refrain from shooting demonstrators since this "may amount to crimes against humanity" (quoted in Bellamy and Williams 2011:839). On the following day, the Secretary General insisted that Libya's actions amounted to crimes against humanity and that the country comply with its commitment to RtP of 2005. Without much controversy, the permanent as well as the elected members of the UN Security Council unanimously passed Resolution 1970 on February 26, condemning "the gross and systematic violation of human rights, including the repression of peaceful demonstrators...[and also] rejecting unequivocally the incitement to hostility...made from the highest level of the Libyan government" (UNSC 2011a:1). Furthermore, "[r]ecalling the Libyan authorities' responsibility to protect its population" (UNSC 2011a:2), the resolution demanded an immediate end to the force used against Libyans. In diplomatic terms, the resolution represented a standard act of condemnation and, thus, had no real "bite".

The *United States* supported the efforts of the United Nations, though reluctantly. On February 23, President Obama stressed that "this [i.e. Libya] is not simply a concern of the United States"; moreover, in the shadow of Iraq and its Middle East experiences more broadly, he hastened to add that "this change [inside Libya] doesn't represent the work of the United States" (White House 2011a). Nonetheless, the US government partly adopted the RtP discourse to condemn Gaddafi. "Like all governments, the Libyan government has a responsibility to refrain from violence...and respect the rights of its people. It must be held accountable for its failure to meet those responsibilities" (ibid.). It was, therefore, not difficult for the administration to endorse the stipulations of, the rather light, Resolution 1970, including an arms embargo, asset freeze of and a travel ban for individual members of the Libyan regime (UNSC 2011a:3–4, 8–10). Besides, it was widely assumed that the support for the UNSC's resolution on the part of the Arab League and the African Union further persuaded the United States to endorse the resolution (Guardian February 28, 2011).

Similarly, *China* accepted the resolution and voted in its favor. International observers were somewhat surprised to see China agreeing with its text, which made explicit references to RtP and referred those Libyans in charge, that is, the incumbent president and his close aides, to the International Criminal Court (ICC), of whose statute Beijing was not a member (UNSC 2011a:2–3). Nevertheless, apart from attempting to improve its international image, China's position was far more nuanced than its pro-RtP stance might otherwise suggest.[10] First, it was absolutely clear to Beijing that the conflict could only be solved by political means, for instance, by reminding Gaddafi of his duty to protect his citizens (i.e. RtP's Pillar I). In order to achieve this goal, some light punishment of the government was accepted; however, this approach left no doubt that China resolutely rejected any forceful means to interfere in Libyan affairs (Bellamy and Williams 2011:840). In fact, while the resolution had explicitly endorsed Libya's "responsibility to protect its population", just four paragraphs later it had also reaffirmed its "strong commitment to the sovereignty, independence, [and]...territorial integrity" (UNSC 2011a:2). Doubtlessly, this was a clear indicator of where some UNSC members, including China, saw the limits of the resolution despite the fact that the resolution concluded with the "readiness to consider taking additional appropriate measures, as necessary" (UNSC 2011a:7). Second, Gaddafi's outspoken sympathies for and close ties with Taiwan and his well-known policy to raise resentments among African states against China's economic engagement on the continent made it somewhat easier for Beijing to vote in favor of the resolution (Oertel 2011:2). Finally, , there was mounting domestic pressure to successfully save the lives of some 35–40,000 Chinese working in Libya. In fact, according to China's UN ambassador, Li Baodong, another key driver behind China's condemnation of Gaddafi via the UNSC resolution was to protect its citizens, thereby proving its ability to project naval power far away from the mainland (Economist January 3, 2011).

Gaddafi's unsurprising defiance in the following weeks further escalated the situation in Libya. Challenged by the rebels' establishment of a "Transitional National Council" (TNC) in Benghazi on February 27, 2011, Libya's president drastically intensified his military efforts. While the rebels failed to take the capital of Tripoli at an early stage, the fighting in the West of the country was extremely fierce, with Gaddafi's troops, for instance, firing indiscriminately at residents of Zawiya on March 9, including at ambulances. In the beginning of March, it appeared as if Gaddafi, together with his son, had successfully regrouped loyalist forces after several defeats in the West (IISS 2011:16).

The growing intensity of the conflict prompted states, mainly Western, to think about further measures to stop the atrocities. Since Resolution 1970 seemed to have had no major impact on Gaddafi's intentions, the British Prime Minister Cameron ventured the imposition of a no-fly zone on Libya already on February 28 in order to prevent the latter's air force from bombarding the rebels. Put briefly, Cameron wanted to extend the available measures and use military force to support the anti-Gaddafi forces. Without using RtP terms, Cameron's suggestions hinted at Pillar III of the concept. As a consequence, the weeks between the UNSC's acceptance of Resolution 1970 and of Resolution 1973 (March 17, 2011) were to provide plenty of evidence of US and

Chinese motives regarding their RtP-related decision-making processes, respectively.

As for the *United States*, the process of its positioning occurred in two phases. The first lasted from the beginning of March to March 12; the second one culminated on March 15, which prepared the ground for its vote at the UNSC two days later. Similar to previous debates about interventions abroad, the political spectrum within the administration stretched from strict anti-interventionists (e.g. Robert Gates) to less strict ones (e.g. John Kerry) and committed liberal interventionists (e.g. Susan Rice; Samantha Power), with the first two having the slight domestic upper hand until mid-March. The cautious US President, focused on economic rebuilding, did not take sides until March 15.

Reflecting the overstretch of the US military as well as a broad unwillingness in the population, Defense Secretary Gates succinctly summarized the arguments of the anti-interventionists in regard to Libya: "I don't think it's a vital interest of the United States..." (quoted in WSJ March 27, 2011). By narrowing US national interests to the security of the homeland, Gates revealed his deep-seated anxiety about yet again, actively pursuing (and getting caught up in) a military intervention abroad.[11] Referring to plans of establishing a no-fly zone, he continued, "[l]et's call a spade a spade. A no-fly zone begins with an attack on Libya to destroy the air defenses.... that's the way it starts" (ibid.). His insinuation that such a no-fly zone would require "a big operation in a big country" left no doubt about what he thought of such plans (quoted in NYT February 3, 2011). In that, he was supported by another senior official who warned that "as soon as we become a military player, we are at risk of falling into the old trap that Americans are stage-managing events for their own benefit" (quoted in WSJ March 27, 2011). Gates' judgment was also supported by two neorealist IR scholars.[12] The late Kenneth Waltz, for instance, plainly said that he was against any kind of US intervention because "no American national interest was at stake"; and John Mearsheimer was equally against any military intervention "because Qaddafi was not engaged in or planning mass murder" (Foreign Policy 2012). Others, for instance, John Kerry, then chairman of the Foreign Relations Committee, seemed equally reluctant, merely suggesting that "a no-fly zone ought to be an option" which "we should not remove... from the table" (quoted in NYT February 3, 2011). In stark contrast to Gates, Samantha Power, who was a member of the National Security Council, drew from her book on genocide (2003) to argue against those (e.g. Gates) who insisted on America's national safety as the only guideline for action or, more likely, inaction. Previously shaped by the events in Bosnia, which she covered as a young news reporter, she invoked America's liberal values and rights and underlined the need to support those values with force, wherever they were under threat (NYT March 18, 2011).

Events on the ground and US decision-making were by now inextricably linked. With Gaddafi's forces recapturing cities such as Zawiya, Ras Lanuf and Ajdbiya and repeatedly brutally attacking unarmed civilians, the pressure on the United Nations to act increased on a daily basis. From the perspective of the US anti-interventionists, it came as a surprise, after Iraq, that, if unwanted, an Arab League meeting in Cairo on March 12 unanimously called on the United Nations to immediately impose a no-fly zone over Libya.[13] France and the United Kingdom had also managed to put the debate about such a zone onto the agenda of NATO (NATO 2011). Furthermore, by that time the sheer brutality of the civil war had already caused some 200,000 people to flee their country to neighboring Egypt and Tunisia (IISS 2011:16, 68). The impact of the new mass flight on the politics of the revolution, especially in Egypt, was yet unclear, though. Since Cairo remained the United States' strongest ally in the region, further instability at the Nile could not be in Washington's interest.

In any event, even if Bellamy and Williams exaggerate when they state that it was the Arab League's resolution which "brought the US on board" (2011:846), the League's decision tremendously strengthened the hand of the interventionists (UNSC 2011a). This was all the more the case since during the days of the 12th and the 15th Gaddafi's forces made headway into the East, rolling back the rebels and "regain[ing] most of the territory lost"; most critically, marching toward Benghazi, the growing fear was that, due to Gaddafi's brutal tactics throughout, the rebels' stronghold would be put under siege and a massacre could then not be avoided (IISS 2011:68). Whereas the cautious US president had until then not sided with either camp, he was eventually more convinced by the arguments of the "interventionists" in an "extremely contentious" meeting at the White House on March 15 (Bellamy and Williams 2011:843). The atrocities, it seemed, had cleared away existing legitimacy concerns in the region toward the United States; in fact, the Arab League's plea to the United Nations was directed at no one more than the United States. It was this implicit invitation from within the region, together with a strong US interest in preventing any further destabilization of its ally Egypt (with an eye on its strategic peace treaty with Israel), that permitted Obama to promote the – always contested – reconciliation of the protection of (universal) values with the United States' national interests. Early on, though, Obama had made it very clear that the United States, quite unprecedented, would "lead from behind" and that its "role would be limited" in the event of military operations (White House 2011b).

These observations allow us to more easily understand the eventual justifications provided by the US government for its decision to vote in favor of UNSC Resolution 1973 on March 17.[14] The resolution itself authorized the use of "all measures... to protect civilians and civilian populated areas under threat of attack in Libya [.]..., including Benghazi while excluding a foreign occupation force of any form", predicated on the enforcement of "a ban on all flights in the airspace of... Libya[.]" (UNSC 2011b:3). In his remarks, Obama explicitly stressed that the United States had to "*always* measure our interests against the need for action" (White House 2011b). On the one hand, notably using RtP's Pillar III terminology, neglecting "our responsibilities to our fellow human beings under such circumstances would have been a betrayal of who we are"; on the other, he insisted, "America has an important strategic interest in preventing Gadhafi from overrunning those who oppose him. A massacre would have driven thousands of additional refugees across Libya's border, putting enormous strains on the peaceful... transition[.] in Egypt" (White House 2011b).[15] He summed up his reasoning by stressing that there are "times... when our safety is not directly threatened, but our interests and values are" (ibid.). Gates put it more narrowly, "I don't think it is a vital interest of the United States, but we clearly have an interest here", noting that the events in Libya might further destabilize its ally in Egypt (quoted in WSJ March 27, 2011).

The *Chinese position* did traditionally not have the room to maneuver between policies supporting action or inaction. Rather, except for its one-time support for the US invasion of Afghanistan in 2001, the Chinese position was strictly based on the principle of non-interference in domestic affairs. Thus, regardless of its vote in favor of all three pillars of the UN General Assembly (UNGA) proposal of the "Responsibility to Protect" norm in 2005, China's attitude was shaped by three factors: first, its domestic and post-colonial view prompted it to vigorously insist on non-intervention; second, China's economic interests in Africa required it to take into account its image both as patron of the African G77 states and as an increasingly critically viewed large-scale foreign investor and aid giver; third, China was keen to avoid a situation in which it stood out alone as defying a widely held consensus.

To begin with, as it was shown, China had agreed to UNSC Resolution 1970 at the end of February. One key feature of the resolution had been that its agreed-on measures did not include military ones. Resolution

1973, in contrast, endorsed the use of force, for instance, to install a no-fly zone over Libya. While the Chinese ambassador to the United Nations, Li Baodong, declined to give an answer to a journalist asking him about China's position in regard to a potential no-fly zone when Western powers discussed the issue at the beginning of March (CNN March 8, 2011), the government's position was very clear after the vote on the resolution was concluded on March 17.

Li, who acted as the president of the UNSC at that time, first gave a general statement in which he reminded the other members of the Council that "China is always against the use of force in international relations" (UNSC 2011b:10). What he had in mind, was, of course, force used as a means of intervening in the domestic affairs of nation-states. While he was concerned about "acts of violence against civilians" in Libya, he stated China's clear preference for "resolv[ing] the current crisis in Libya through peaceful means" (ibid.). Later in his short address, he stated which peaceful means would be conducive to prevent the Libyan president from continuing his course of action. First, though, he presented the essence of the Chinese position when he suggested that "China has always emphasized that, in its relevant actions, the Security Council should follow the United Nations Charter and the norms governing international law, respect the sovereignty, independence, unity and territorial integrity of Libya" (ibid.). His statement indicated how China preferred to interpret the RtP norm: it endorsed Pillar I, but left especially Pillar III unmentioned. As a consequence of this interpretation, China had, as he put it, "serious difficulty with [those] parts of the resolution" that legitimated the application of force (ibid.).[16]

China's fear to stand out as the only power not agreeing was relieved early on in March. A powerful, if politically diverse, group of states (e.g. Germany, Brazil, Russia and India) had publicly indicated many days before the actual vote that it would not support any resolution that included the use of force in Libya. Nonetheless, while this made the Chinese government more comfortable to present its international position as a largely accepted one, its decision not to vote against the resolution, but merely to abstain from it, revealed less so a remaining feeling of discomfort with its position - but rather something else. Whereas China certainly saw no need to even partly endorse the resolution or to verbally grant respect to the RtP norm, it felt obliged to accommodate those states that had hosted it, however grudgingly, as their main investor and aid giver. Needless to say, such an accommodation was cheap but nonetheless diplomatically wise in order to protect China's economic interests on the continent. Showing great respect for, without formally agreeing with (i.e. "attaching great importance") the important efforts undertaken especially by the Arab League but, equally, taking into account the African Union's earlier advances, Li publicly appreciated both of their efforts: "..., China attaches great importance to the relevant position by the 22-member Arab League on the establishment of a no-fly zone over Libya. We also attach great importance to the position of African countries and the African Union" (ibid.).

At its core, China's abstention was, therefore, motivated by its economic interests in Africa, which is why it tried pressing those, who had voted in favor of the resolution, to stop using military means. Employing China's insistence on the principle of non-interference, Li went on to say: "We support the Secretary-General's Special Envoy for Libya, as well as the continuing efforts by the African Union and the Arab League to address the current crisis in Libya *by peaceful means*" (ibid.). As a consequence, when NATO started its airstrikes on March 19, the Chinese government voiced its "regret" (quoted in Guardian March 30, 2011) and was quick to announce its fear of a looming "humanitarian disaster" (quoted in NYT March 22, 2011).[17]

Naturally, despite talking about humanitarian disasters, the rebels were not mentioned at all in Chinese statements because the Communist Party was most afraid of setting a precedent domestically. But the virtual non-existence of the rebels in the statements also proved something else. In fact, by denying the key rationale provided by Evans and Thakur, it nicely confirmed that China was intrinsically opposed to RtP. Thus, since Evans and Thakur had stressed that the norm was explicitly "victim- and people-centered" (2013:202), this implied that, for China, such a view on "the people" did not exist. At least, as it turned out, the people did not exist until it became impossible to deny their imminent and future role in Libyan politics even for Beijing's government. Again, the key motive behind its pragmatic turn "to respect the choice of the Libyan people" (China Times August 22, 2011) after the rebels had taken Tripoli in August was an economic one since, at that point, China revealingly feared that "Libya's new authorities will make it pay for its support for the old regime by discriminating against it in business deals, including potentially lucrative ones related to the oil industry" (Economist November 10, 2011).

The politics of RtP 2: Syria

The case study on Syria differs from the previous one on Libya in that no military intervention has occurred and now, after what has happened thus far, seems unlikely. Nevertheless, the similarities both between the Libyan and Syrian governments' responses to their national uprisings as well as between the discussions held internationally make their trajectories at least partly comparable. This is despite the fact that Russia's role in the opposition against intervention in Syria was far more prominent than China's.[18]

For the purposes of this chapter, the internationally contested debates about intervention in Syria (2011–14) need to be viewed against a three-layered background. First, the United States experienced substantial domestic struggles in social (e.g. National Health Care Reform) and, relatedly, financial terms (e.g. government shutdown). Exacerbating these domestic struggles, the debates about both issues also need to be seen in light of the presidential election and the campaign that preceded it (2011–12). The domestic stalemate on economic reform unabatedly continued thereafter. Second, China underwent its transformation of the Communist Party's politbureau. Accordingly, heightened nationalistic sentiments further underpinned its well-known conservative stance on sovereignty. Moreover, this political atmosphere exacerbated, and was exacerbated by, the growing "strategic distrust" between China and the United States. Third, Syria enjoyed a long-standing alliance with Iran and played a major role in the support of non-governmental anti-Israeli forces. The politically charged, sectarian strife among Syria's complex fabric of ethnic and religious groups also involved a Saudi–Iranian/Sunni–Shia struggle over regional hegemony and was further intensified by radical Islamist fighters joining the conflict from Iraq and elsewhere. This latter point on regional dynamics accounts for the most significant difference to the Libyan case. With military options self-consciously limited to airstrikes, the international implications of sectarian-geographical context had a major impact on the policies of the great powers, especially Western ones.[19]

When Libya's Gaddafi was already fighting for his political survival in March 2011, Syrians just began protesting for the release of political prisoners in the capital Damascus and for more freedom and less corruption in Deraa in the South (BBC 2013). Answering the protesters, Syria's president, Assad, issued a strong warning in his first speech on March 30. Aside from the conventional references made to the influence of conspiracies, he stated: "Sedition is worse than killing, as the Holy Quran says. Anyone who is involved in it, willfully or not, is working to kill his country. Therefore, there is no place for anyone to stand in the middle" (translated in CFR 2011:465). Similar to the previous developments in Libya, the peaceful protests were immediately met with harsh responses from the Syrian police. Equally similar, by mid-2011 protests were observable throughout the country and began to develop into a broader uprising. In turn, Assad quickly sensed the danger of losing his grip on power and immediately sent out tanks to the cities of Hama (July 31, 2011) and Latakia (August 14, 2011); additionally, he also instructed some of his warships to attack the latter city (IISS 2012:6).

Against this background, the *United States* called on the Syrian president to step down on August 18 (IISS 2012:7). At that time, some 2,700 protesters had already been killed by the regime's security forces (UNSC 2011b:2). Consequently, the United States supported the preparation of a draft resolution for the United Nations Security Council (UNSC 2011a, all quotes). Notably, the draft first recalled "the Syrian government's primary responsibility to protect its population". At its core, it "condemn[ed] the continued grave and systematic human rights violations and the use of force against civilians by the Syrian authorities" and "demand[ed] an immediate end to all violence" (ibid.:1,2). The peaceful reconciliation of the country was envisioned as "an inclusive Syrian-led political process", which, as the draft stressed, was based on the "strong commitment to the sovereignty, independence, territorial integrity and national unity of Syria" (ibid.:1). Making reference to Article 41 of the UN Charter, the draft precluded any involvement of military force but suggested the imposition of economic sanctions in the future, if Syria did not comply with the draft's demands within 30 days (ibid.:3). In essence, the Western draftees of the resolution employed Pillar 1 of the RtP norm to frame their demands.

However, the Security Council failed to adopt the resolution on October 4.[20] The United States' representative stated, quite unusually, that her government was "outraged that this Council has utterly failed to address an urgent moral challenge"; explicitly pointing at China and Russia, she reminded the audience that "several members have sought for weeks to weaken and strip bare any texts that would have defended the lives of innocent civilians"; those two countries had, thus, vetoed an already "vastly watered-down text" (UNSC 2011b:8). More specifically outlining the US position, Ambassador Rice said that her government instead had wished to "impose tough, targeted sanctions and an arms embargo on the Assad regime, as we have done domestically" (ibid.). Such a more "principled stand", if desirable, did not imply, as Rice clarified, "military intervention" (ibid.:9, 8).

Though the United States had made it clear that it respected Syria's sovereignty and did not desire a forceful intervention, the arguments explaining *China's veto* were of a different nature. In particular,

Ambassador Li's remarks, at the same meeting, powerfully underlined Beijing's conservative attitude to RtP. In particular, while Li called "on the various parties in Syria... to avoid more bloodshed and all forms of violence", he insisted that this could only be facilitated by "a Syrian-led and inclusive political process" (ibid.:5). While the UNSC and the international community could provide assistance to facilitate such a process, as Li continued, the key to the question whether the Council would take further action should "depend on whether it complies with the Charter of the United Nations and the principle of non-interference in the internal affairs of states" (ibid.). In order to leave no doubt in this respect, he added that the "Chinese government's position on those questions has been consistent and firm" (ibid.). He went on to suggest how China wanted to influence the developments in Syria. Precisely because China did not believe that "sanctions or threat thereof does... help... " but would "further complicate the situation", Li instead promised to "continue to support... mediation efforts... in the region" (ibid.).

In the meantime, while most likely intended as a way to regroup his increasingly unsuccessful forces, Assad accepted a roadmap of the Arab League on November 3, 2011. The peace plan demanded that the government withdraw its army from cities, free political detainees and start talks with the rebels. However, after only a few days the ceasefire broke down and presidential troops quickly resumed attacking protesters, killing several hundreds of them in the following days (IISS 2012:11). For the moment, it seemed that the rebel forces' momentum would not cease; in fact, they made headway into the regime' power bases, reaching the suburbs of Damascus early in January 2012. In any event, since the government's military was capable of breaking their resistance due to overwhelming material capabilities, the less coordinated and less well-armored rebels had to retreat from the capital and from prominent strongholds, such as Homs, by February 2012 (ibid.:222). At the same time, the strong efforts of the Arab League, supported by China and the United States, failed at two occasions. First, a second agreement between Assad and the Arab League, signed on December 19, 2011, failed by January 2012. Second, similar to the one presented earlier to Mubarak, a proposal by the League of January 22, suggesting that Assad should give up power and leave the country, was rejected by the president. As a consequence, the Arab League forwarded the issue again to the UNSC (IISS 2012:224). By then, some 5,000 people had been killed (IISS 2012:13).

On February 4, the United States (together with several Arab and European states, among others) submitted a draft resolution to the

Security Council (UNSC 2012a). In sum, the draft restated the proposal of the Arab League from the previous December. More specifically, the Council demanded that the "Syrian government, in accordance with the Plan of Action of the League of Arab States of 2 November 2011 and its decision of 22 January", inter alia, "cease all violence and *protect* its population", "release all persons detained arbitrarily" and "withdraw all Syrian military... from cities and towns" (UNSC 2012a:2). Moreover, the draft also supported the League's decision to offer Assad his departure into exile, which, in turn, would "facilitate a Syrian-led political transition to a democratic, plural political system" (ibid.). Therefore, the draft saw no contradiction to expressing respect to "the sovereignty, independence... and territorial integrity of Syria" (ibid.:1). In fact, it went out of its way to note "that nothing in this resolution authorizes measures under Article 42 of the Charter", that is, forceful means (ibid.). Conspicuously reflecting the United States' restrained conduct in regard to authoritarian regimes after Iraq, the draft resolution left no doubt that the notion of sovereignty was the core principle framing it. Therefore, the text only implicitly pointed to Pillar I of the RtP norm. Nevertheless, China and Russia strongly disagreed with the draft and voted against it on the same day.[21]

As for the *United States*, Ambassador Rice repeated its dissent with the Chinese (and Russian) vote in the same strong wording, as she had done the previous October. "The United States", she said, "was disgusted that a couple of members of this Council continue to prevent us from fulfilling our sole purpose here, which is to address an ever-deepening crisis in Syria" (UNSC 2012b:5). Not making any (verbal) reference to the RtP norm, her disappointment originated from the fact that the draft had "simply supported an Arab League plan... and the subsequent Arab League decision toward a peaceful resolution of the crisis" (ibid.), that is, Assad's voluntary departure into exile. Unsurprisingly, albeit supporting the resolution, she reminded the members of the actual US preferences: "to impose tough, targeted sanctions and an arms embargo on the Al-Assad regime, as many countries have already done" (ibid.). In other words, the United States had hoped to apply measures of Pillar III of the RtP norm, though, without making explicit reference to it.

China, on the other hand, straightforwardly defended its conservative attitude toward the notion of sovereignty. Calling "on all parties in Syria to stop the violence and in particular to avoid casualties among innocent civilians" as well as "to respect the request of the Syrian people for reform", Ambassador Li reiterated his advocacy of an "inclusive political process led by the Syrian people... to peacefully resolve differences...through dialogue and negotiations" (ibid.:9). Perhaps unwittingly making reference to Pillar II of the norm, he encouraged the "international community [...] to provide constructive assistance to help achieve these goals" (ibid.). In all of this and without exception, "the sovereignty, independence and territorial integrity of Syria should be fully respected" (ibid.). Some two weeks later, speaking in front of the General Assembly, he restated his whole-hearted decline of any actions that would interfere in the domestic affairs of sovereign states: "We do not approve of armed intervention and...do not believe that sanctions or the threat of sanctions are helpful" (UNGA 2012a:8–9). Besides nationalist and anti-hegemonic domestic sentiments that needed to be accommodated, China's voting behavior reflected the deep "trust deficit" that had emerged between Washington and Beijing since 2008/9 and which Xi Jinping had unmistakably stressed before his first visit to the United States as the unofficial future head of the CCP in February (Reuters February 7, 2012). As a result, notwithstanding the fact that the resolution precluded measures based on Article 42 of the UN Charter, it was difficult to see how such a principled stance could be squared with the interventionist character that Evans and Thakur had attributed to RtP earlier (2013).

Well aware of the international disputes surrounding the debates at the UNSC that came to his help, Assad reconquered the city of Homs at the beginning of March, having used artillery and helicopter gunships. When the UN under-secretary for humanitarian affairs came to Homs a few days later, she found it completely devastated (IISS 2012:223). Unsurprisingly, neither an almost unanimously adopted UNGA resolution on February 16 (NGA 2012a:8)[22] nor a Human Rights Council deploring the regime's "brutal" acts and calling for an end of the attacks could halt Assad at this point (IISS 2012:224). Furthermore, knowing full well that China (and Russia) wanted him to stay in power, the Syrian president eventually agreed to a six-point plan to stop the violence and to have the United Nations monitor the cessation. The plan was unanimously adopted by the Security Council on April 21, 2012 (UNSC 2012c). However, after mass executions near Homs in May,[23] the UN envoy leading the monitoring, Annan, had to admit that the government was unwilling to implement the six-point plan on May 25, 2012. Assad's unrestrained freedom to act was further underlined four days later when some 80 people were reportedly killed close to Hama and, tellingly, UN inspectors were fired at, while attempting to reach the town. On June 16, the patrols of the United Nation's monitoring mission were altogether suspended due to growing violence throughout

Syria (IISS 2012:19). The civil war that was now underway had cost the lives of 17,000 Syrians thus far, with 100 civilians being killed every day (UNSC 2012c:2). While it is unclear how much responsibility foreign forces carry in this war, the ancient Sunni–Shia and the political Iranian–Saudi rivalry in the Middle East heavily exacerbated the events on the ground.[24]

Similar to the pretext of the February draft resolution in terms of the sanctioning of non-compliance, Western states attempted to tighten the framework, through which Kofi Annan had tried to implement his peace plan, by putting it under Chapter VII of the UN Charter. The latter move, as the draft of UNSC resolution 2043 suggested, implied "that, if the Syrian authorities have not fully complied ... within ten days, then [the Council] shall impose immediately measures under Article 41", that is, non-military sanctions (UNSC 2012c:4). Even though the protection of civilians was the discernible subtext and overarching goal of the resolution, no verbal reference was made to RtP. Neither did the wording mention the "responsibility of the government", nor did it spell out the government's obligation to "protect" its population. Significantly, the second paragraph of the draft underlined that the authors had no interest in influencing the eventual course of domestic affairs from outside. Rather, their impetus was to provide the conditions for a "comprehensive political dialogue between the Syrian authorities and the whole spectrum of the Syrian opposition" (UNSC 2012c:3). Therefore, as they stressed, the draft reaffirmed "its strong commitment to the sovereignty, independence, unity and territorial integrity of Syria" (UNSC 2012c:1). Equally similar, however, China (and Russia) vetoed the draft resolution on July 19, 2012.[25] After the vote, the debates became extremely heated, while the concept of RtP did not seem to have any implications for the rhetorical exchanges between China and the United States.

As for the *United States*, Ambassador Rice repeated that the "draft resolution just vetoed demanded that all parties cease violence"; therefore, as she explained, it "invoked Chapter VII to make more binding on the parties their obligation to implement the six-point plan ... ". Nonetheless, "it would not even impose sanctions at this stage and ... would in no way authorize ... foreign military intervention" (UNSC 2012c:10). Hinting at a revival of the Kosovo option, that is, to act without a UNSC mandate, she laid out plans, though unspecified, "to intensify our work with a diverse range of partners outside the Security Council to bring pressure to bear on the Al-Assad regime" (ibid.:11). Albeit common to US institutional behavior, suggesting the breakaway from the UN framework was in and of itself indicative of how little the RtP norm seemed to affect US thinking in view of the realities on the ground in Syria and at the UNSC and, thus, how little it was globally accepted. In this vein, Rice stated at the end of August that it was "our goal" to achieve "a peaceful, Syrian-led transition to democracy", tellingly adding that this "should be the goal of all nations of goodwill" (UNSC 2012d). On the other, the main reason why President Obama did not use force without UN approval was that he was, at that time, too deterred by the unique geographical and sectarian context in which the Syrian crisis occurred. While Libya was, all things being equal, an issue that could be limited to the country, Syria had been allied with Iran and Hezbollah against Israel since 1979. In other words, while notwithstanding the then slowly beginning thaw between the United States and Iran, Syria was part of a highly intricate web of regional tensions which could easily mean the spillover of war from one regional center to another. This is the background to Obama's cautious remarks: "what's happening in Syria is...outrageous...And the actions that he's [i.e. Assad] now taking against his own people is inexcusable, and the world community has said so in a more or less unified voice....On the other hand,...this is a much more complicated situation....We've got to think through what we do through the lens of what's going to be effective, but also what's critical for U.S. security interests" (White House March 6, 2012).

As for *China*, its ambassador's account of why Beijing had vetoed the draft resolution merely confirmed the lack of RtP's global acceptance. His main sticking point remained, as before, the principle of non-intervention. In particular, while China generally shared the view that Annan's plan needed to be implemented, it saw the draft's "unbalanced content seek[ing] to put pressure on only one party. Experience has shown that such a practice would not help resolve the Syrian issue" (UNSC 2012c:13). This statement alone showed how far China's views were from Evans' and Thakur's stress that their concept of RtP gave much preference to the party of the "victims". Critically, China based its veto on "sovereign equality and non-interference in the internal affairs of other countries...[as] the basic norms governing inter-state relations" (ibid.). Therefore, only a "Syria-led political process", "rather than [a process] imposed by outside forces", should henceforth "independently decide [on] the future and fate of Syria" (ibid.:14, 13). In contrast, the "invocation of Chapter VII...and the threat of sanctions" ran completely counter to the Chinese view of a political solution for Syria (ibid.:14). In other words, China did not hesitate to veto the resolution based on its own politico-historical convictions. Moreover, precisely because Russia had reliably opposed interventionist policies and seemed inclined to do so in the future, Beijing did not have to worry about its international image, concerned that it would stand alone, but could comfortably take the back seat while Moscow was taking the driver's seat of the opposition at the UNSC.

When the UNSC adopted resolution 2059 a day after it had publicly presented its deep divisions, it became obvious that those disagreements had come at the expense of more immediate measures to stop the violence in Syria. The short resolution was unanimously adopted and laid its focus singly on the formal extension of the UN monitoring team's mandate (UNSC 2012d). Nonetheless, Annan's judgment as to how he could further influence the process as the United Nations' envoy led him to resign on August 2, 2012. His main reasons were political impasse, militarization of the conflict and, somewhat revealingly, inadequate international action (IISS 2013:6).[26]

As Li had said time and again in his statements, China indeed tried to urge Syria to be more receptive to the United Nations' mediation efforts and, therefore, pressed the Syrian envoy when she visited Beijing in mid-August (IISS 2013:318). Nevertheless, even though another mass killing in the suburbs of Damascus on August 20 showed the deficits of its approach (IISS 2013:7), the Chinese government, quite unsurprisingly, remained steadfast in its conviction that "national governments should bear the primary responsibility for protecting their own civilians" (UNSC 2013a). In other words, Beijing singled out one element, that is, Pillar I of the concept, to support RtP. Ambassador Wang, who made the statement at a UNSC "Open Debate on Protection of Civilians in Armed Conflict" in 2013, underlined the Chinese non-intervention rationale when he said: "While the international community can render constructive assistance, it cannot replace the responsibility of national governments and parties to conflict" (ibid.). Lakhdar Brahimi, a very experienced diplomat, who took over from Annan at the end of August, thus, faced an unabatedly deteriorating situation.

Moreover, China's and the United States' exclusive focus on their domestic power transitions, respectively, withdrew much of the international attention from the conflict.[27] Consequently, the months from September 2012 through March 2013 did not see any meaningful international activity with regard to Syria, even if the United Nations reported in January that 60,000 people had been killed and in March that one million Syrians had been displaced thus far (IISS 2013:11–12). In the case of the United States, the stalemate in Congress about how to resolve the financial and economic crisis at home approached the so-called fiscal cliff and even led to a government shutdown at the end of September 2013 (AP October 1, 2013). In the case of China, the new president's harsh policies aimed at addressing corruption within (not only the upper) the ranks of the CCP *and* the military was, similarly, one of the main reasons that distracted Beijing from non-regional aspects of international politics. For an extremely prominent case, a former top-ranking cadre of the CCP, Bo Xilai, was dismissed from his offices early in 2012 and given a lifelong sentence in September 2013 (Economist September 22, 2013). None of this is to say, however, that neither country followed the developments in Syria, especially Brahimi's efforts; rather, this is to highlight the prioritization of domestic policy issues that inevitably affected the treatment of international concerns. Needless to say, both China's long-standing passivity with regard to the issue as well as US domestic recession-based resistance against foreign interventions more generally reflected the little impact which the RtP norm had on either side.

The discussions about how to deal with the Syrian crisis intensified again in the spring. In April 2013, US observations of the situation in Syria tentatively revealed that Assad might have used chemical weapons against the rebels, albeit on a small scale (IISS 2013:14). And when the European Union eventually decided to supply the rebels with arms in May, in which it was joined by the United States in June, Russia's statement, that it would stock Assad with anti-aircraft missiles (to prevent a thus far not mentioned) no-fly zone, showed, among other things, that the RtP norm did not play a role in either party's considerations (IISS 2013:14–15).

The new impulse came from US intelligence agencies which found that the Syrian regime had used chemical weapons in its attacks on suburbs of Damascus on August 21 (White House August 30, 2013). Events in the following weeks submitted the US reaction to several changes. To begin with, based on "human, signals and geospatial intelligence as well as a significant body of open source reporting", the White House concluded that "a chemical weapons attack took place in the Damascus suburbs on August 21" (ibid.). At the same time, it was assumed that the rebels did not have the capabilities to prepare and execute such an attack. With over 1,000 people having been killed through the use of internationally prohibited weapons, the US president stated on August 31 that, "after careful deliberation, I have decided that the United States should take military action against Syrian regime targets" (White House August 30, 2013). To be safe, he reassured the public that while US forces were ready to attack, he would exclusively do so with airstrikes, at a point in time that was still to be determined.

In terms of RtP, how did Obama attempt to justify the use of military force? Clearly, he stressed that Assad's "attacks on [his] own people" had, more broadly, also been directed against "human dignity"; moreover, he stated that since Assad's actions went against "international fundamental rules", that is, the prohibition of chemical weapons, those rules needed to be upheld which, in turn, required US leadership (ibid.). Interestingly, while these justifications could be read as a reference to the RtP norm, Obama put another, more important, reason upfront in his remarks. Key to his justification was safeguarding "national security" since chemical weapons could endanger allies bordering Syria, such as Israel, Jordan or Turkey, and could also proliferate terrorists (ibid.). He added that national security was at stake since failing to deter Assad from using chemical weapons could inspire other tyrants to use them elsewhere, possibly against US soldiers (White House September 10, 2013).[28] In essence, Obama decided to not merely rely on the "Responsibility to Protect", which had been violated, but more on the security implications that its violations might have for the United States. Only in conjunction, with security aspects taking the lead, were "our security and our values" employed as justification for military intervention (White House August 31, 2013). Another aspect further highlighted the lack of support that RtP had received on the global stage. Precisely because the UNSC "has been completely paralyzed and unwilling to hold Assad accountable", Obama stated that he was "comfortable going forward without the approval" of the former (ibid.). In other words, while Pillar III of RtP could be employed by Western states, such as the United States, the latter's actions would, inevitably, come at the expense of the norm's legitimacy on the global plane. The contested nature of the norm, which had been accepted globally in 2005, could not have been exposed more clearly.

In addition to the domestic factors shaping the attention of both great powers, another factor came into play with regard to RtP, though limited to the United States. Obama knew, as he said, that the American people were "weary of war" and, thus, "after Iraq and Afghanistan the idea of any military action ... is not going to be popular" (White House August 31, 2013; September 10, 2013). Important in regard to the domestic support which is merely assumed by RtP advocates, he admitted that "Americans want all of us in Washington – especially me – to concentrate on the task of building our nation at home: putting people back to work, educating our kids, growing our middle class" (White House September 10, 2013). In fact, a survey in the fall of 2013 showed that some 52% of Americans wanted the United States to "mind its own business internationally", which was the "highest figure in five decades of polling" (Economist March 5, 2014:9). Therefore, while he was convinced of the arguments he had put forward in favor of the intervention, Obama's second statement reflected the broad and deep-seated resistance of the population, which was why it gave the "national security" aspects in the debate considerably more weight than his first statement. Here he made it much clearer that "in the absence of a direct or imminent threat to our security" he would search for authorization from Congress (White House September 10, 2013). Curiously, Obama employed the narrow conception of national security that Gates had used when he had argued against military intervention in Libya two years earlier; logically, his wording was also diametrically opposed to what ambassador Power, posted at the NSC, had argued for regarding Libya. Needless to say, the US president's self-confidence to forge ahead, and into military intervention, may have been affected by the UK prime minister losing his vote on Syria on August 30 (BBC August 30, 2013). As a result, US national security aspects as well as a feared lack of domestic support characterized the debate that was to foster followership, if indirectly, for the implementation of the RtP norm.

China, on the other hand, was consistently and vehemently opposed to the United States' serious military considerations. Xi Jinping told President Obama during a G20 meeting on September 6 in Russia that a "political solution is the only right way out for the Syrian crisis" while it was inconceivable to him that "a military strike can[.] solve the problem from the root" (quoted in Time September 13, 2013). Repeating China's principled position of non-intervention, a spokesman of the Foreign Ministry stated that China has "always oppose[d] the use of force in international relations"; therefore, any US plans of military intervention would run counter to "international law and the basic norms governing international relations" (Time September 13, 2013). In other words, the analytical omission of a non-interventionist rising power in Evans' and Thakur's account revealed what negative impact China had on the RtP norm.

As for the following weeks, since this is not the place to describe the diplomatic moves and calculations that came to shape *US* foreign policy, here it may suffice to say that the president's hesitation to act at the end of August, if well justified, created room for Russian diplomatic finesse. In turn, viewed against the backdrop of Russia's record during the crisis, it also considerably lowered the chances for RtP to be implemented. Put briefly, probably motivated by the US threat to use force, Russia could easily press Assad to internationally admit the possession of chemical weapons (which he had thus far denied) and to agree to their immediate destruction. As a consequence, Obama postponed a(n uncertain) vote to authorize the use of force by Congress on September 10 (White House September 10, 2013).

Four days later, a deal was struck between Russia and the United States in Geneva.[29] At its core, the two parties agreed, inter alia, that UN teams would be sent into Syria to secure chemical weapons stocks and factories and, after that, would verify that the inventories were complete and the poison destroyed. Having effectively prevented US airstrikes, Russian diplomacy had in many ways been conducive to the fact that "in Western capitals the sigh of relief over Syria is audible" (Economist September 10, 2013). As much as the administration had seemed committed to military intervention, the domestic obstacles, which Obama had mentioned in his address on September 10, had already drawn most of his attention away from Syria and to the stalemate in Congress over the president's healthcare program. The latter implicated that, if the parties could not find a compromise before the beginning of the new fiscal year on October 1, no spending legislation could be enacted and, as a result, a partial federal government shutdown would become inevitable (Associated Press October 1, 2013).[30] This was the domestic US context in which the preparations for the UNSC resolution occurred, through which the bilateral Geneva deal was to be implemented.

Two and a half years into the Syrian civil war, the wording and the discussion of the "historic resolution" (UNSC 2013:2) at the Security Council, as the secretary general put it on September 27, provided a good way of measuring Chinese and US support for RtP. Unanimously adopted, Resolution 2118 was framed by its reference to the Convention on the Prohibition of Chemical Weapons.[31] Consequently, it made two legally binding demands: first, it demanded from Syria to "not use … or retain" any chemical weapons (UNSC 2013:2); second, the Council decided that Syria must provide the weapons inspectors "with immediate and unfettered access to and the right to inspect … all sites" (UNSC 2013:3). In terms of RtP, though, it was most interesting to see that the resolution did not attribute responsibility for the gas attacks explicitly to the Syrian government. In fact, while the resolution "condemn[ed] in the strongest terms any use of chemical weapons", it did so by merely suggesting that this use had occurred *"in* the Syrian Arab Republic" (UNSC 2013:2), instead of saying "use of chemical weapons *by* the Syrian Arab Republic". Neither did the resolution entail an RtP-like imposition of sanctions under Chapter VII in case Syria did not comply.[32]

Following the remarks of the Russian foreign secretary, his US counterpart applauded the "single voice" with which the world had spoken and imposed for the "first time binding obligations on the Al-Assad regime"

(UNSC 2013:4). Even though President Obama had kept the use of military force on the table, John Kerry was convinced that "tonight's resolution in fact accomplishes more" (ibid.:5). Effectively taking US military means off the table, Kerry insisted that the call "for a transfer of power to a transitional governing body" (UNSC 2013:5) remained a US aim, even if Annex II of the resolution outlined a non-binding roadmap. Reflecting this, Kerry could merely remind his audience that "when it comes to those who murder their own citizens, the world's patience needs to be short"; therefore, the "same determination and the same cooperation" that had led to Resolution 2118 should lead the way forward (ibid.). Perhaps unwittingly, thereby Kerry acknowledged that the resolution and the diplomacy that had preceded its formulation had effectively limited the debate to the non-use of chemical weapons. Notwithstanding the merits of the resolution, the drivers of, and the responsibility for, the civil war had not been addressed. The key goal of ending the fighting, as opposed to merely ruling out the use of some of the means employed in it, was not accomplished, allowing "both sides [to] find other ways to continue the killing" (Economist October 28, 2013). At this time, it seemed that the great powers' underlying divergences on the notion of sovereignty had been brushed aside. Inevitably, such a change came at the expense of the politics of RtP, which had always put first the responsibility underlying the sovereignty of states. Remarkably, John Kerry admitted that, two and a half years into the civil war, this was not the time for high-aiming solidarist goals in global politics, as pursued by Samantha Power among others. Singling out the driver of global governance approaches as the main obstacle to political progress, however tilted and morally questionable, he concluded: "when we put aside the politics for the common good, we are still capable of doing big things" (ibid.).

Throughout the crisis, China's passivity had not put any obstacles in the way of this kind of traditional pluralist great-power politics. Representing Beijing, the Chinese Foreign Secretary Wang Yi was "heartened by the . . . adoption today of resolution 2118", precisely because "China suffered deeply from the use of chemical weapons by Japanese invaders during the Second World War" (UNSC 2013:9). Pointing to previous US plans, he said that "several weeks ago dark clouds of war overshadowed the Syrian issue" and went on to reiterate Beijing's position that "China opposes the use of force in international relations", which was why it believed "that military means cannot solve the Syrian issue" (ibid.). In contrast, the resolution presented a "new opportunity to find a political settlement to the issue", a process which "should take place in parallel with the process of destroying Syria's chemical weapons (ibid.). Somewhat oddly, though, Wang acknowledged, in light of the history of the Syrian crisis, that achieving "a ceasefire and the cessation of violence" based on the "principle of the peaceful settlement of disputes" would not resemble "smooth sailing" (ibid.:10). Similar to Kerry's remarks, though unsurprisingly, China was content with the fact that an agreement on chemical weapons in regard to Syria had been found, while it envisioned no further steps effectively addressing the sources of the civil war. Conspicuously, Chinese and US understandings of sovereignty had merged, or, as Cochran had put it earlier, the United States and China found "ideas of right and wrong... within a practice of states".

To conclude, both the United States and China have undercut the RtP norm to such an extent that its transformation into a customary norm of international law has failed. While China has remained steadfast in its support for the principle of non-interference in domestic affairs throughout, the United States' commitment to cases of RtP first and foremost depended on the protection of national security interests. It seems almost indisputable today that RtP has "turn[ed] out to be an instance where a norm retreats rather [than] advances" (Foot and Walter 2011:61). In particular, the United States' more reluctant attitude in Libya and Syria was heavily shaped by its immense domestic socioeconomic problems and, relatedly, its recent experiences in Iraq and Afghanistan. Though willing to employ sanctions against both states, Washington saw no automaticity that would, due to a perceived violation of RtP, involve it into military efforts to solve either crisis. The permissive condition for its involvement was the justification of its actions as defending "national security", albeit not in a "vital" sense. Unless moral purposes could be framed by harder, interest-based motivations of security, the administration was unwilling to act. This held true even in the case of the Syrian gas attack in August 2013. China, on the other hand, was wedded to the notion of non-interference throughout. In both case studies, China repeatedly underlined the fact that the prime responsibility to protect its people lies with the respective state, which was why only a political process that was free of foreign intervention could guarantee a balanced outcome. In Libya, China abstained primarily for economic interests. Concerned about its image, in both cases other BRIC or Western states helped China not to find itself in a situation in which it would have been alone in its opposition.

Part IV
Conclusions

9
Conclusion

This book argued that the financial crisis of 2008/9 has established China as the key challenger to the United States amidst a process of order transition, in which the latter has been far from acting as a status quo power. Their subsequent disagreements about the future shape of the global order's legitimacy have manifested themselves in their intense competition with regard to spheres of influence in East Asia, the environment- and ideology-related aspects of the order. In particular, *both* have undercut the related regional and international institutional mediation efforts (e.g. UNCLOS, ASEAN), the impact of TNAs on climate negotiations (e.g. UNFCCC) and emerging norms of international law (e.g. RtP), respectively. Crucially, since *both* sides have vigorously pursued their national self-interests in this contest, their revisionist antagonism has consequently led to manifold deadlocks in today's institutionalized world of global governance. In turn, their competition has prevented a new political grand bargain that could underlie a new order. As a result, the ongoing process of order transition has reaffirmed the critical role of great powers and the powerful notion of sovereignty in a systemic process that has played out to the detriment of global and transnational governance ambitions and institutions. The conclusion addresses this final result in the first section and stresses the implications that the book's analysis ought to have for the discipline. Essentially, it argues that the discipline can no longer sustain its well-nourished notion of global governance in its current form. The second section succinctly summarizes the key theoretical failures that led to a new thinking about the systemic meaning and conceptual implications of widespread deadlocks in global politics in the first place.

The politics of sovereignty and the failure of the global governance concept

In an exemplary fashion, Barnett and Sikkink had told us that "the concept of governance" had successfully established itself as "a worthy alternative to anarchy" (2008:78). Viewed from today, however, this process has largely been reversed. Inevitably, the disciplinary rapprochement between accounts of global governance and of more anarchic great-power politics is overdue. In the meantime, the rules of the engagement, it seems, have been set by the latter.

In a condensed form, global governance advocates have long thought that, since states faced global challenges and were, therefore, inextricably integrated in networks of legalized regime complexes, it would merely take the constitutionalizing of fragmented policy issue areas to produce well-functioning global governance structures and processes. By transferring governance from sovereign states to global systems of knowledge and expertise, public goods could be provided globally (Koskenniemi 2011:61–65). However, these flawed attempts at *depoliticizing quintessentially political processes*, that is, processes of negotiating global collective action, have altogether failed. Disguised as the promotion of "common social purposes" for "the international community", global governance accounts failed to explain who was represented by them (and who was not), for whom the provision was, why the output-oriented arrangements were portrayed as legitimate (and thus left no sovereign choice to decline them) and, finally, why the political impact of material power had been made negligible by technical expertise. Strikingly, despite their solidarist and often cosmopolitan normative leanings, theorists of global governance revealingly could not answer the question, "why...the world [is] not better" (Koskenniemi 2011:63). Some more caution or humility, as classical realists would have it, as to how to conceive of, judge and operationalize the possibilities (and limits) of shaping international politics would have most likely been more conducive. As Carr had classically warned (1946:179), institutions "cannot be understood independently of the political foundations on which [they] rest[.] and of the political interests which [they]...serve[.]". Conversely, the practical consequences of these conceptual failures have been exposed most clearly in the deadlocks and the systemic political contestation that has characterized international political life since 2008.[1] In fact, these failures have led to the return of the politics of sovereignty with a vengeance. And this is precisely what this book has been about: understanding politics in relation to order transition.

The flagrant denial of politics, moreover, needed to be attributed to two further disciplinary developments since the end of the Cold War. First, the deeply entrenched, strict compartmentalization of the discipline had been conducive to highly evolved theoretical work on disconnected subjects. Second and related, the strong contestation of structural theories in the 1990s, partly (but not only) derived from end-of-history announcements, led the all-too-willing discipline to believe that systemic questions had lost their importance. *Serious contemplation about profound systemic challenges, such as the nature of the global order and the role of power in this process, received little to no theoretical interest and seemed outdated. This is precisely why one of the book's main aims was to carefully identify and present an innovative framework that could demonstrate "what makes the world hang together".*[2] *The notion of order transition, conceptualized as the renegotiating of the global order's legitimacy, successfully did that.* It captured both the limits which the world of global governance had faced, as embodied in the deadlocks of international regimes, and the systemic implications of the political competition between China and the United States that had caused them in the first place. By employing a first-order perspective, the analysis was able to look closely at the renegotiations of the underlying "rules of the game that establish the parameters of the system" (Gamble 2011:42). The key actors in this process, central to world politics, were two great powers that had engaged in a fierce political competition. At its conceptual core, this competition was about the internal layer of great-power management, much neglected by the related theoretical bodies, which had mistakenly still been concerned with how the United States would re-arrange its rights and duties vis-à-vis the remainder of international society. In contrast, today this is about how China and the United States would negotiate those responsibilities in various policy areas exclusively *among themselves*. In doing so they present themselves as equally sovereignty-protective great powers or, as Morgenthau classically put it, "[nations] ... pursuing their respective interests defined in terms of power" (1973:5). Except for the minimum goal of peaceful coexistence, their interaction shared no common social purpose. Not even their economic interdependence, as the related theories would have it, managed to lower the strategic distrust between them. Polarity was not adversarial, though; rather, the best way to describe the nature of the relationship between the two most important poles was to view it as reciprocally instrumental.

Thus far, it remains unclear where the renegotiations of the global order's legitimacy will head. While the possibility of a war cannot be eliminated, two other, potentially consecutive, developments seem more likely in the meantime. First, the current stalling of the structures and processes of the institutionalized world continues as long as the great powers have not found ways to agree on the aforementioned "rules of the game". Due to the contestation of the global order's systemic legitimacy, this seems to be the logical consequence flowing from the analysis presented in this book. Hu Jintao's unwittingly first-order admonition that it is "imperative that we [i.e. the US and China] stand on a higher plane, transcend differences on specific issues... [and] move beyond short-term considerations" (2011) could indeed show the way forward. Second, this pragmatic path, however rocky and incremental, could eventually lead to a new "bargained consensus" and, thus, another "constructed peace" in global politics (Trachtenberg 1999). Nevertheless, such a sanguine assessment needs to confront those formidable obstacles that already stand in its way or could derive from existing tensions, for instance, in the ECS or SCS. Moreover, neither the United States nor China has yet heeded to Hu's admonition in any way. Therefore, the opposite seems to be a more accurate description.[3]

As a final remark, if we tried to carefully imagine which conceptual features the more realistic first development, mentioned above, might have, a revised categorization of the mental maps prevailing in the discipline seems apt. In this regard, David Lake recently suggested a spectrum of three global theoretical frameworks (2013). At one end of the spectrum, he found that the debates in relation to US unipolarity reflected largely US-centric views. At the other end, he saw the "European model of the post-national state", if currently under strain, "foretelling a future in which multi-level governance is matched by multi-level political identities that mitigate... twentieth century nationalisms"; this vision, he observed, was "as Eurocentric as... unipolarity is American-centric" (2013:570). Between these centric poles, he suggested, resided the more balanced assumption that "international relations... [remain] massively affected by cooperation and competition between the great powers" (ibid.). In principle, this book sympathizes with Lake's concise depiction of the three models. While the first two may reflect powerful, if too narrow, American- and Euro-centric constituencies of researchers, it is the third one which most accurately captures the overall pluralist dynamics shaping global politics today. To begin with, the middle model rightly points to the significance of nationalism(s) in global politics, that is, superior worldviews, as well as the self-regarding nature in which China and the United States will negotiate the terms of global legitimacy for the foreseeable future, most likely dismissing European positions.

Equally central, Lake's position reaffirms the crucial impact which the great powers have on the nature of the political practices evolving in global politics. Therefore, when he suggests that world affairs continue to be "massively affected" by the great powers, he implicitly confirms one of the key premises of this book: without the support of the great powers no social purpose underlying a global order can be achieved.

Nevertheless, in light of the approach chosen for this book, two important conceptual improvements are necessary to critically sharpen the main features of Lake's spectrum. First, the notions of the China dream and of the modern versions of the tribute system underlying much of today's Chinese theorizing have made it, if unwittingly but also revealingly, as Chinese-centric as the former two are Euro- and American-centric. Second, the crucial focus on great-power politics should not employ parsimony as a methodological means to conveniently withdraw to the blank slate of exclusively state-based views in which all actors but states are epiphenomenal. Instead, based on pragmatist methodology, future research about order transition should not only be firmly grounded in great-power frameworks but also systematically examine the analytical and theoretical tensions that arise from the fact that the great powers are situated in a highly institutionalized world. While great-power disagreements will undoubtedly continue to come at the expense of the impact of institutions and post-Westphalian actors alike, the latter ones build the foil against which the intensity and tactics of the great powers' instrumental use and, often, factual disregard of them can be measured.

Summary of the book's key results

To begin with, though partly predating, but strongly exacerbated by, the financial crisis of 2008/9, processes of socializing China and enmeshing the United States (and China) in global governance structures largely failed. Remembering that social constructivism stood out after 1989/91 as the emerging school that argued ontologically for a much larger role of agency in IR, it is striking that the same theory failed in the case of China because it considered the socializee as merely a passive object. It was inconceivable for constructivists, such as Wendt, Risse or Johnston, that a state would first accept the norms it encountered because it had either no other choice or wanted to, but after a while, most likely after an increase in material power, changed its identity over time without showing the expected and self-sustaining signs of socialization at that later stage. However, China's international evolution from the 1970s through 2014 appears to reflect just that (Narlikar 2010b). If socialization was indeed "central to constructivists" and was "the one process concept in IR that is uniquely constructivist" (Johnston 2008:xvi), then not much of its central character had stood the test of time. Equally, the evolution of China's foreign policy put Finnemore's and Sikkink's (1998) cascade model on its head. Striving to become a member of international organizations and regimes at first, then partly internalizing some of the prevailing norms but, eventually, becoming much more powerful, so that China is now in a position to choose what is, and what is not, in its interest (to internalize), also mirrored the failure of the passivity assumption. Furthermore, these failures were caused by the built-in progressive bias of socialization theory. Conventional theorists seemed convinced that since socialization had worked after the Cold War with regard to smaller East European states, it would equally work with rising powers. Nonetheless, not only did such thinking fail to see the material differences between these states, but, more importantly, neither did the socialization of socialization theory in a Western-centric cognitive milieu geared at cooperation among "like-minded" states (Keohane 1984) appear to present a potential hindrance in the eyes of IR theorists with regard to China.

Similarly, theories of institutional enmeshment may have enveloped China in a web of relationships; however, they clearly failed to redefine the target state's interests and did not alter its identity. Taking into account China's increasingly less integrative behavior within IOs, Ikenberry's mantra that the "American-led open-democratic political order", offering "public good provision, rule-based cooperation, and voice opportunities and diffuse reciprocity" is "easy to join, but hard to overturn" (2011), had turned out to be much less convincing in recent years. China undoubtedly "joined", but it remains unclear how it is to be further included in international organizations and regimes, if the "ultimate guardian", comprising a "liberal complex of states", is necessary to protect "the rules, institutions, and progressive purposes of the liberal order" (2011). If the latter complex is exclusively liberal, Ikenberry's question as to "who precisely is the international community" is elusive.

Moreover, the book also found that enmeshment theories had failed with regard to the United States. While often (and mistakenly) portrayed as a status quo power, the United States has never hesitated to employ its more revisionist foreign policy traditions, if it deemed them apt to secure its sovereignty. Especially in the context of an emerging challenger, Washington has often resisted enmeshment in order to retain its freedom to act and thus to maintain the conditions that have facilitated its exceptional role in global politics. Defending this state of "just disequilibrium", the United States has never fully tied its search for effectiveness and the protection of its interests to global governance structures, precisely because "no international order can be supported by international institutions alone" (US NSS). Consequently, this implied that the United States could not "simply be working inside formal institutions" (ibid.). In practice this has meant that the United States has employed great-power practices such as unilateral disengagement, creating new institutions, switching allegiance to an alternative regime or informalizing international organizations or forum-shopping. Lastly, whereas most European theorists have been socialized into theories of integration and supranationality, the interventionist-state impetus, underlying much of the history of global governance theories, has further undermined the likelihood that it will find acceptance in traditionally anti-statist US domestic politics. Taken together, China and the United States were seen as revisionist powers, as opposed to Ikenberry's insistence that both were, indeed, status quo powers (2011:341).

Against this background, the book went on to ask what the consequences of the implied global governance failures were. Before this step was taken, though, for the purposes of our analysis it was necessary to put into context the impact of the financial crisis. In fact, it turned out that a new perspective on the theory of hegemonic stability was required to account for the events. Notwithstanding the differences among existing accounts, the position of the provider underpinning the order has conventionally been regarded as steady. But what if the provider is, even temporarily, incapable of materially underpinning the order? This is precisely what occurred in the fall of 2008. With China spending some 600 billion USD or four trillion yuan as a domestic stimulus, its economic policies assumed systemic importance and, thereby, prevented the world economy from crumbling (Lebow and Reich 2014). What did it mean for the status of other actors, if they could substitute for the material underpinnings and thereby prevent the order from collapsing? Regardless of whether it did so for reasons of domestic regime security, ultimately, the accomplishment of the system's maintenance meant the tacit recognition of China as a great power (Buzan 2004). But when and how exactly would a new great power effectively stake its claims? Conventional wisdom largely considers wars the most important expressions of "turning points" (Nye 2011). It has, thus, been widely taken for granted that the absence of a war and "no [subsequent] general meeting of states to remake the institutions of public life" (Kennedy 1994), that is, an "ordering moment", implies that there was no need to renegotiate the "basic rules of the system". However, the near dysfunction of the system and inability of the incumbent provider to fully satisfy its responsibilities, if temporarily, can be seen as the functional equivalent to the end of a major war. The book therefore suggested that the maintaining of the system by an actor other than the incumbent hegemon needed to be viewed, in analogy, as a turning point. Importantly, precisely because "no general meeting" was held to provide China with "voice opportunities", and, instead, the United States remained extremely passive regarding the implementation of systemic changes, Beijing consequently displayed a new assertiveness.

Thus, the foundations for a systemic competition between the United States and China, if buffered by their economic interdependence, were laid. Inevitably, this state of affairs led to the worsening of global institutional cooperation. In particular, key international institutions, such as the WTO, the IMF and other organizations, were increasingly affected by deadlocks in the negotiations intended to reform those regimes. A group of formerly leading practitioners of global governance and scholars succinctly summarized the common sense, stating that they held "one broadly accepted view", according to which "existing institutions and arrangements are mostly deadlocked in the attempt to solve some of the outstanding global issues", notwithstanding the varying degree of contestation among those issues (CIGI 2012).

Thus far, it was not difficult to recognize that material aspects had facilitated a good deal of the theoretical accounting. But existing theories had failed to take into account the notion of worldview. Looking at the deadlocks, liberal rationalist theorists admitted that their theories of cooperation had already reached their limits and, consequently, referred back to underlying power structures. Accordingly, the key explanation could only be found in "a greater divergence of interests, weighted by power" (Keohane 2012), since "as the distribution of tangible resources...becomes more equal, international regimes...weaken" (Keohane 1989). And yet, the underlying notion of material power was too narrow to account for China's non-socialization. Conspicuously, even though Beijing had been offered more voting rights in the WTO and the IMF, it had not changed its attitude toward these institutions. For instance, when a Chinese top delegate to the climate summit in Copenhagen was asked what, in essence, had determined its position, he answered that the politics underlying the negotiations were "much more important" than the climate regime itself; combined with its later rhetoric of its "return to normalcy", this explains why Keohane's theory failed (2012). Keohane overlooked the fact that China's worldview had re-emerged with a self-perception of its own superiority. This was similar to US views of itself, and, thus, could not be disregarded. Put differently, the possible implication that international cooperation worked earlier because it was dominated by Western states and that this same reason might explain why this was increasingly less the case today was not explored.

At this point, the book had to halt and acknowledge that, since theories of socialization and enmeshment had largely failed and deadlocks had come to characterize international cooperation, the explanatory power of prevailing global governance accounts had immensely weakened. Instead, global politics had (yet again) come to be shaped by great-power politics. Three features stood out. Firstly, a politico-military competition between China and the United States had ensued, even if their economic ties reflected a state of complex interdependence. Despite over a dozen meetings between the US president and his Chinese counterpart in the Strategic and Economic Dialogue between 2009 and mid-2014, the relationship had evolved from Chinese hedging and "biding its time", US pivoting and bilateral attempts to strengthen strategic trust, into an era of merely managing and controlling their "trust deficit", as China's new leader Xi Jinping put it (Guangjin and Yingzi 2012). Secondly, the United States and China were involved in a process of *reciprocal* socialization (Terhalle 2011). This meant that the two countries had come to mutually influence each other to such an extent that each warily observed the other's behavior toward international institutions; in doing so, their main focus was, respectively, on how the other's actions affected one's own position in the global power hierarchy. This process made the contest between the United States and China central to world politics, in that "the global order and the attitudes and behavior of these two important states are a mutually constitutive social phenomenon" (Foot and Walter 2011). Most conspicuously, this was reflected in a recent, substantial, change in great-power hierarchies; while P5 consultations were still substantial at the UNSC, "bilateral U.S.-China consultations outside the Council chambers have become far more important" (Prantl 2012). Thirdly, both China's failed socialization and the United States' interest-based selectivity concerning its engagement in global institutions had come at the expense of governance patterns of global order. As Keohane put it, "[a]s a generalization, it seems that... what could have been seen in the mid-1990s as a progressive extension of international regimes, with stronger rules and larger jurisdictions, has been halted if not reversed" (2012). This development, in turn, further strengthened the great-power competition that has already ensued. Pointedly, "on balance", it "eroded the willingness of *both* to accept global normative frameworks as legitimate standards of appropriate behavior" (Foot and Walter 2011). Signposts of this evolution toward great-power-based politics could be observed in both countries. Since 2012, Chinese leaders have conceived global governance as a "new type of great-power relations" to which US officials have responded in kind.

The order framework

One of the central methodological problems of the book was now to identify an appropriate framework which could capture the systemic nature of the problem. Much had been written that assumed a China-centric or a US-centric view on global affairs, often in one way or another arguing for the endurance or at least prolongation of US hegemony or, conversely, for the whole-scale and inevitably urgent overhaul of existing governance structures on China's terms (e.g. Ikenberry 2011; Jacques 2011). Others were propeled into thinking, too deterministically, that the US–China competition would naturally evolve into the direction of classic power transition that had historically ended with systemic wars (Ross and Feng 2008; Tammen et al. 2000; Thompson and Rapkin 2003). In contrast, with the aforementioned theoretical limitations and failures in mind, wide theoretical room needed to be carved out in order to better understand how the newly required *political* consensus on the "basic rules of the game" (Gamble 2011) could be achieved. Since what was at stake was the notion of global order, the English School provided the appropriately broad framework through which, first, the problem at hand and, subsequently, its theoretical elaboration, could be filtered. In particular, four elements of the order-based theory seemed to be advantageous.

First, by offering a broad spectrum-based view on state practices, it suggested a framework that could incorporate the changes from global governance-derived politics to the revived dynamics of great-power politics. Practices in this sense were "fundamental and durable [and] .... evolved more than designed"; they were "constitutive of actors and their patterns of legitimate activity in relation to each other" (Buzan 2004). Second, understanding order transition as system-relevant changes in the main practices pertaining to the nature of the global order's governance permitted to conceptually link the notions of order transition and systemic legitimacy. Third, by distinguishing between primary (practices) and secondary institutions (IOs, regimes), the theory pointed to the degree to which the latter reflected "frozen decisions", which "history [had] encoded into rules" and were, thus, built on a power-political and normative consensus negotiated *earlier* (March and Olsen 1984). Precisely because they merely reflected such an earlier agreement, it was, in turn, quintessential to identify some of the "deeper and more lasting causes" of why deadlocks had occurred in the first place (Narlikar 2011). Fourth, the English School's synthesis of material and ideational components captured the broadness of the contestation which the existing order had undergone. In this way, the theory fruitfully put itself at the juncture of logics of appropriateness and logics of consequences (March and Olson 1998).

A theory of negotiating systemic legitimacy

Having established the overall framework for the book, the analysis needed to identify theories of systemic legitimacy which could address the overall nature of legitimacy, on the one hand, and the analytical complex of negotiations and transition which surrounded the former, on the other. It chose the, complementary, works of Ian Clark (2005) and Robert Gilpin (1981) as its conceptual starting points. The former explained the elements that shaped the politics of legitimacy as the dynamic interplay between the notions of legality, morality, constitutionality and balance of power, while the latter offered the main patterns that needed to be renegotiated during order transition (e.g. rules concerning the economic- and security-related aspects of an order, its underlying worldview, the special rights great powers are endowed with, agreement on key spheres of influence and on the overall balance of power). Nevertheless, while Clark and Gilpin provided the broad concepts that were the most apt and fluid ones in order to capture the dynamic "(re-)negotiating" and "transitioning" aspects of global order, their accounts shared three weaknesses that required broad conceptual revisions. As with many other contemporary theories, their state-based models were firmly embedded in the assumptions of an uncontested US hegemony. The decisive conceptual challenge was therefore to carefully adapt their accounts to the current order transition in order to improve the scope for theoretically analyzing the dynamics of systemic legitimacy. In particular, three adaptations were introduced that referred to the notions of the global order's hybrid environment, common culture and its effectiveness.

Firstly, building on the English School's broad spectrum-based view on state practices opened up space for the analysis of a hybrid global environment in which more solidarist foundations of global multi-level governance had to cope with incursions of the more pluralist and anarchic great-power politics of US–China relations. Therefore, the revised model should be able to explain to what extent the processes and structures of global governance have been able to retain a degree of their supposed autonomy. Secondly, broadening Clark's and Gilpin's notions of morality by drawing on the English School's principal suggestion of a plurality of values and historical identities, that is, worldviews, helped to better account for whether the absence of a "common culture" among (today's) great powers inevitably led to the impossibility of peaceful order transition. Finally, the US–China competition accompanying order transition also made it necessary to rethink the notion of effectiveness in a hybrid environment. The revision of Clark's original parameter of constitutionality as a new model of effective management could then answer the question what kind of hegemony was needed to provide effective leadership. Curiously, such an all-encompassing reconceptualization had been lacking in the literature.

The elaborations of the conceptual part of the book (Chapters 3–5) led to three main results. First, Clark's exclusively state-based framework remained incomplete as long as it did not include post-Westphalian elements. Therefore, the related literatures had correctly depicted those elements as important to any sensible explanation of an institutionalized world. In an exemplary fashion, theorists of transnationalism saw "institutional access... as a central determinant of TNA influence" (Tallberg 2013). However, while Clark's theory needed to be revised in light of today's hybrid global order, the aforementioned theorists failed to ask what their accounts could tell us when confronted with the current order transition. In other words, what if the structural and normative foundations on which Tallberg's institutions were built were substantially shifting? The answer was that the influence of non-state actors was *dependent* on a particular institutional context in which the key political questions framing the social order were settled by major powers at an earlier time. "Institutional access" was, therefore, precisely not a "central determinant" as long as the framing patterns of those secondary institutions (in English School terms) were not agreed upon.

Second, Clark's "morality" and Gilpin's "ideology" underlying the international order were firmly based on liberal values. This normative bias was partly responsible for the deadlocks in international negotiations and partly for the ideological underpinnings of the US–China trust deficit. Conceptually, the analysis found that two underlying assumptions prevented their accounts from broadening the order's normative underpinnings. To begin with, the logic of the transfer of the hegemon's idiosyncratic values onto the international plane remained intact only as long as the hegemon's position was not disputed. Logically, if the group of leading states was viewed as less ideologically homogenous than originally assumed by Clark and Gilpin, then this would require us to view the nature of the transfer mechanism as politically more amenable. Moreover, the liberal nature of the basic patterns of US worldviews was taken to be static. Thus, Clark and Gilpin overlooked the degree to which new systemic processes might affect the level of the hegemon's otherwise unspoken acceptance. For instance, an increasing degree of legalization-promoting globalization might contribute new layers to the common culture, which may still be informed by the liberal ideology, but might go beyond its conventional practices in a way that does not necessarily cohere with the leading power's understanding of the application of its worldview. This suggested that while today's global governance processes and structures are indeed underpinned by liberal worldviews, the growing institutionalization and efforts of legalization shaping those processes were often not accepted as common culture by the predominant actor. Taken together, acknowledging these weaknesses facilitated a new understanding of the problem. It permitted the conceptual analysis to identify and accommodate the existence of *two* superior worldviews. Furthermore, as opposed to large parts of the literature, the assessment found that US and Chinese worldviews were indeed involved in an ideological competition. In turn, in light of the notion of order transition this triggered the important question as to whether the two were incommensurable. While not evading the possibility of a war, the analysis concluded that middle-ground "ideas of right and wrong found within a practice of states", which did not presuppose any kind of a "moral community", provided the worldview-based stability necessary to renegotiate global order.

Third, Clark's interrelated notions of "constitutionality" and "power relations" as well as Gilpin's notion of effectiveness were predicated on understandings of a US single hegemony. However, not only had China become a great power in the financial crisis, but both countries, aware of the fiercely competitive elements in their relationship, had also engaged in a discussion about a "new type of great power relations". While they had not agreed on any particular features which this "type" might have, the mere existence of such a discourse, however lofty, together with China's great-power status urged the analysis to re-examine managerial theories. According to them, great powers "contribute to international order in two main ways: by managing their relations with one another; and by exploiting their preponderance in such a way as to impart a degree of central direction to the affairs of international society as a whole" (Bukovansky et al. 2012; Bull 2002). However, viewed against the backdrop of today's global governance failures, the analysis needed to admit that China and the United States had not "impart[ed] a degree of central direction", precisely because they had not "manag[ed] their relations" with each other in a way that was conducive to providing "central direction" in global politics. In other words, when managerial theories assumed that leading great powers had "grave obligations...to each other" (Claude 1986), they implied that recognizing these internal "obligations" occurred somewhat naturally between the leading great powers. Nevertheless, since this was traditionally achieved at peace conferences after systemic wars, but is conspicuously not the case today, how would the reconceptualization of single-hegemony understandings proceed? A closer look at these underlying assumptions found that managerial theories failed to address what was dubbed here as the *hierarchical* relationship between the internal (among the great powers) and external (between the hegemons and the remainder of international society) layers of great-power management. While existing research primarily focused on the external layer, looking at the former revealed two things. First, it showed that there could be no special responsibilities without the agreement within the peer group of great powers. Second, it found that an outstanding agreement on special responsibilities prevented any proper steering of international society as such. Therefore, Clark's and Gilpin's frameworks needed to incorporate the necessity for the great powers to negotiate the scope of their respective special responsibilities *among each other, before* any thinking about how to provide leadership to the remainder was possible at all. Without adopting this analytical hierarchy, no deeper conceptual understanding of the problem could be advanced.

Three case studies

Based on the key assumption of this book that the competition between the leading great powers had come at the expense of global governance structures and processes and, thus, prevented the large-scale institutional redesign required to remove the manifold deadlocks in international negotiations, the analysis explored the three conceptual innovations to Clark's and Gilpin's frameworks as follows: firstly, the argument that special responsibilities were exclusively (re)negotiated among leading great powers was explored through an account of the degree to which renegotiations of spheres of influence had come at the expense of global regimes as well as East Asian regionalism (Chapter 6); secondly, the proposition that the environmental rules of today's hegemonic order needed to be viewed in light of hybrid sets of actors was explored through an analysis of the degree to which the impact of TNAs was neutralized due to the prevailing disagreements among the great powers (Chapter 7); finally, the argument that the competitive encounter between two superior worldviews was accommodated through middle-ground "ideas of right and wrong found within a practice of states" was explored through an assessment of the degree to which the RtP has been rejected as a norm of customary international law, because the two powers have not been able to agree on common standards to make it such (Chapter 8).

Regarding spheres of influence, despite the largest Strategic and Economic Dialogue convened between the United States and China thus far in the spring of 2010, Beijing's new assertiveness led it (based on its own demarcations) to mark the South China Sea as its "national interest", which prompted the United States to follow suit shortly after. Conspicuously, speaking in front of ASEAN, whose overall goal it was to resolve political disputes in the region consensually, China's foreign minister bluntly indicated the Thucydidean terms, according to which those differences had to be treated: "China is a big country and other countries are small countries and that is just a fact." The severe impact, which the US–China contestation over spheres of influence had gained on ASEAN, for instance, was unmistakably put on display at its annual meeting in Hanoi 2012. Precisely because ASEAN states failed to politically agree on whether to include a diplomatically phrased condemnation of China's recent assertiveness, the deeply split membership concluded their meeting without a consensual communique for the first time in 45 years. The United States, for its part, did not take any serious initiatives to buttress existing multilateral mediation structures, but conveniently relied on, and reaffirmed its bilateral security treaties through, the "pivot" to Asia (as much as Beijing based its regional approach on bilateral diplomacy). If spheres of influence are indeed revealed "through tests and probes" of diplomatic clout and military strength (Waltz 1979), this was what tellingly happened when China unilaterally declared an Air Defense Identification Zone late in 2013 in the East China Sea. Only a few days later, the United States responded by flying two B52 bombers through the ADIZ without having given advance notice to China. Thereby the United States made it clear that it did not accept the changes imposed on its sphere of influence. The fact that China, in turn, did not try to enforce the ADIZ against the United States turned the two-day event into a classic example of a "tacit understanding" between the two antagonists about the scope of their spheres of influence. As this event clearly showed, there was little room for governance structures to provide regional public goods such as dispute settlement. Moreover, attempts by smaller states to refer their sovereignty disputes with China over islands in the SCS to the International Tribunal for the Law of the Sea equally failed. Beijing made it clear that if, for instance, the Philippines or Vietnam decided to do so, it would "ignore" those international arbitration efforts altogether. Strikingly, insisting on self-attributed historical rights to those dispersed islands, it left no doubt that "[t]hose rights do not derive from UNCLOS" (Gao and Jia 2013). Unwittingly, China thereby forcefully confirmed that UNCLOS was no more than one of the status quo supporting instances Martin Wight had described as "pseudo-institutions" (1991); similarly, Bull had found that precisely because the "UN is not the source" of the rights and duties of the great powers, the key determinants of the latter needed to be found *"prior* to international law, or to any particular formulation of international law" (Bull 2002). Put differently, notwithstanding the United States' and China's participation in manifold ASEAN-related meetings, their negotiations of the scope of the East Asian sphere of influence were exclusively undertaken *among them.* Ultimately, both great powers had de facto agreed that neither UNCLOS nor ASEAN had a role in sovereignty issues.

Concerning the UNFCCC, while Clark's state-based account made the omission of TNAs most tangible in this case study, it also demonstrated that the systemic disagreements between China and the United States on climate-related questions minimized the institutional impact of TNAs. The latter confirmed Drezner's assumption of the "inverse correlation between NGO influence and the public visibility of these actors" (2007) before Copenhagen; although TNAs decisively changed their tactics after Copenhagen in order to become more "efficient", by launching broad transnational initiatives that were aimed at rule setting and the provision of funding, their impact remained minimal. While the TNA literature had long believed that non-state actors could directly govern environmental issues, in fact, that they were part of an emerging class of global governors which transformed international life, the meager outcomes of the summits since Copenhagen pointed into quite the opposite direction. Responsible for this state of affairs were, inter alia, two interrelated sets of factors. First, China's and the United States' governments uncompromisingly pursued their national interests, such as economic growth, to further their global competitiveness at the expense of environmental concerns. Second, the strategic rivalry between the two great powers had turned climate-related issues into a "deeply political problem in that it was part of the much larger problem of reorganizing the global order" (Bräuner 2010). In fact, China believed that the United States, albeit no member, tried to manipulate the Kyoto Protocol to Beijing's disadvantage, for instance, through the United States' insistence on more distributional fairness with regard to the CDR (Common but Differentiated Responsibilities and respective capabilities), which the latter perceived as heavily imbalanced. In turn, the United States repeatedly stated in public that China should be more willing to accept international environmental obligations. If unspoken, the driver behind such statements was to slow China's economic growth. Consequently, their disagreements came extremely close to a zero-sum game in which neither wanted to move forward, "unless the other accepts that it too must play its part" (Foot and Walter 2011). As a result, TNAs remained dependent on a well-functioning order, if hybrid, provided and orchestrated by states. Since such an environment was elusive in times of order transition, TNAs were neutralized.

As for the RtP, albeit accepted by an overwhelming majority at the UN General Assembly in 2005, including China and the United States, and though viewed by many as the "normative instrument of choice" in humanitarian crises, the latter two great powers (but not only those two) have prevented the norm from becoming part of customary international law. An external indicator of this was that only very few references to RtP were found in the UNSC resolutions which were examined; and, in those rare cases where notions of responsibility did appear, they referred to the sovereignty-protecting Pillar I of the concept. As for China, it vigorously declined to vote in favor of several resolutions that included (non-military) sanctions against Libya and Syria; its voting behavior in regard to three critical resolutions was first and foremost based on the unwavering defense of the principle of non-interference in domestic affairs. It made small concessions, as it was often overstressed in the aftermath of the Libyan case, when the target state was merely condemned or minimally punished (e.g. asset freeze). As for the United States, while it was traditionally more willing to use the classic tools of intervention, such as economic sanctions, the key characteristic of its support for the resolutions was not normative in nature. To the contrary, while its rhetoric was sympathetic to "the people" on the ground, Washington saw no automaticity that would, due to a perceived violation of RtP, involve it in military efforts to resolve the crises, respectively. Unless moral purposes could be framed by harder, interest-based motivations of national security, the administration was unwilling to act. Other domestic, socio-economic reasons as well as concerns related to the geographic setting (Syria) also played into the United States' reluctance to get involved. Having said that, China's and the United States' attitudes to RtP were most clearly put on display in their reactions to the gas attack of the Syrian government in August 2013. As in previous instances, the US president framed his justification for intervention in national security terms (and not in RtP terms) but felt uneasy to go ahead without the, uncertain, positive vote of Congress. China, on the other hand, constantly repeated its preference for a peaceful solution to the crisis. A crystallizing moment for the prevailing mood among the leading great powers came when, after Russia and the United States had struck a deal on the destruction of chemical weapons in Syria, the UN Security Council unanimously adopted the according resolution. In fact, it was the US foreign secretary who tellingly summarized the unspoken moral limits set by great-power politics: "when we put aside the politics for the common good, we are still capable of doing big things". Strikingly, since he did not insert a moderating phrase, such as *for the moment*, behind his "when we put aside the politics for the common good", the implications were of a truly pluralist nature.

Notes

1   Global Orders: Contestation and Transition

1. Alternatively, Koskenniemi (2012).
2. With great self-confidence the United States and the European Union are publicly exhorted to fix their domestic problems (Noesselt 2012).
3. Wade (2013); Patrick (2010:53).
4. On "threshold effects" and "tipping points", Gladwell (2000); Granovetter (1978).
5. In terms of its Gross Domestic Product (GDP), China was ranked second in 2010 and even overtook the United States in 2014. Obviously, the analysis looks much different when based on per capita ratios or Gross National Income (GNI). For GDP and GNI numbers, http://siteresources.world bank.org
6. Interviews with senior Western officials, in charge of Security Council (SC) issues at the United Nations, strongly confirmed this argument (New York, March 2011).
7. Doubtlessly, government positions and the direction of state-funded research go hand in hand.
8. This was preceded by "a series of special lectures ... convened by Chinese academics and the country's top leadership between 2003 and 2006. ... These lectures were subsequently elaborated into *The Rise of Great Powers*, a twelve-part film series aired on Chinese national television ... and watched by hundreds of millions of viewers" (Kissinger 2011:498).
9. The more serious political commentary literature has, equally, proposed US–China re-negotiations of the global order (White 2012).
10. Similarly, three organizations underlined the empirical finding of deadlocks: Oxford University's "Martin Commission for Future Generations" (Economist 2013); the UNDP's report on "Transforming Global Governance for the 21st Century" (Woods et al. 2013) and the World Economic Forum which identified the WTO deadlock as one of the major "global governance failures" (2011:11).
11. Bernstein (2000).
12. Alternatively, Johnson/Urpelainen (2012). The term contestation, as employed here, focuses on consensus-seeking, however complicated; it is distinct from Tilly's "contentious politics" (2008:5), which refer to disruptive measures employed by actors to trigger change.
13. Absorbed by their concerns about security, neo-realists have equally failed to think about how the great powers develop systemic agreements (Little 2007:165).
14. Contrary to Peerenboom et al., Kratochwil 2014.
15. Alternatively, Khong 2014:167–168.
16. Alternatively, a former US top official (Catherine Kelleher) reminded a group of scholars at the 2013 ISA convention that between 1920 and 1930 the

British cabinet reassured itself and the public every year that there would be no war in the next ten years. The implicit reason given was that everybody had an interest in the international system's continuation because of its economic benefits. While that "everybody" could not embody the then Soviet Union or Weimar Germany, it reflected a widely held view in Europe's societies (Steiner 2007).

17. Critically, Levy 2008:17–25.
18. For a sophisticated critique of Barnett/Duvall (2005), Mattern (2008); Baldwin (2012) alternatively, Beck (2006).
19. Hurd seems to follow this path (2007:7).
20. The ICC's head attorney, Fatou Bensouda, underlined Clark's conclusion (Scheen 2012): "We [the ICC] are a juridical institution, nonetheless, we have to operate within a political environment."
21. Alternatively, Scharpf (1993) on "blockades" in international negotiations.
22. In contrast to positivist methods prevailing in the United States, IR, non-positivist approaches, available since the Enlightenment era and in constant struggle with the former, have been taught and applied throughout.
23. Similarly, George/Bennett had warned: "The choice of real-world problems ... is often deemed of secondary importance, and problems are framed to permit adherence and contributions to sound methodology" (2005:264).

2 Order Transition, Systemic Legitimacy and Institutionalization

1. Alternatively, Schimmelfennig (2005); Waltz (1979). The former employs the notion of socialization as "a process characterized by exogenous, self-interested political preference and instrumental action" (830). For Waltz, socialization, which is driven by competition among states, is meant to produce their "sameness" (128; 74–77; critically, Mearsheimer 2011:138 n. 23). The obvious problem with both accounts is that neither can explain why China has, nonetheless, not been socialized. The main reason for this is that both address smaller states.
2. Ironically, the same authors now criticize the underlying assumptions of global goods theories, asking who defines what the goods are (Avant et al. 2011).
3. Such passivity has also characterized cosmopolitan liberal theory. As Hurrell noted: "Post-cold war liberal discourses on global justice often appear to be discourses about what the rich and powerful owe to the poor, weak, and oppressed. The weak and oppressed appear mostly as the passive objects of (potential) benevolence" (2013:197).
4. The Risse-Sikkink model is based on the same, mistaken, linear assumptions (1999).
5. Author's interview with a top-ranking Western diplomat, Washington, March 2011.
6. Alternatively, for postcolonial perspectives on socialization, Epstein et al. (2014).
7. Ironically, even before the advent of constructivism, Honneth (1987:355) had leveled his charges against conventional critical theory's views of

conceptualizing culture. He reminded his peers that "socialized subjects are not simply passively subjected to an anonymous steering process but rather actively participate... in the complex processes of social integration".

8. This also holds true when it is taken into account that China is suspicious about getting involved in informal groupings. The main reasons are its closed domestic governance system and the legacy of Western imperialism (Huang 2010:33–38).

9. Chinese behavior very much resembles the US approach (Nye 2011:227).

10. A confidential conversation between Singapore's Mentor Minister Lee, and the US ambassador, Herbold, reflects this. Lee suggested, "China tells the region, 'come grow with me'. At the same time, China's leaders want to convey the impression that China's rise is inevitable and that countries need to decide if they want to be China's friend or foe when it 'arrives' " (WikiLeaks 2007a).

11. Ikenberry echoes here official US wording, which spoke of "a single model for national success" (US-NSC 2002, quoted in Clark 2005:174).

12. Neither do those accounts answer the question "good for what purpose"? This, in turn, opens space for normative theories.

13. Similarly, Cox (1996:55–56).

14. US claims that regimes require it to do more than any other state are exaggerated, as Foot and Walter (2011:12) have shown.

15. Similarly, in the case of China, Cai states (2013:767): "In order to maintain their national development, (...) [China] will take advantage of both the effectiveness and weakness of international law as much as possible."

16. Buzan/Hansen (2009:207) reminded Critical Security Studies theorists that "[e]mancipated individuals are in need of a resolution at the collective level, and to envisage this as unproblematically flowing from the individual level leads one back to a Classical utopian position".

17. It took Olson to remind liberal rational choice theorists that it is not "true that the idea that groups will act in their self-interest follows logically from the premise of rational and self-interested behavior". Such be not the case, "unless there is coercion or some other special device to make individuals act in their common interest, rational, self-interested individuals will not act to achieve their common or group interests" (quoted in Amadae [2003:177]).

18. Narlikar (2010) for a wide-ranging number of examples confirming the deadlocked nature of international regimes.

19. Arguing that the hegemon's key tasks were, for a limited time, taken on by China and that, therefore, the critical weight attached to the hegemonic actor by HST can be questioned is *altogether different from* arguing that this did not hinder the operation of the capitalist system. Thus, when Drezner (2014) suggests that, in economic terms, "the system worked" because other states heavily invested in the United States when the latter went into recession, he does not tell us *who* did the system's "working" in the meantime to make the system "work".

20. For a better sense of the size of the Chinese spending, the entire German Federal Budget (2009) stood only at 450 billion USD and at 490 billion USD in 2010.

21. For various concepts of recognition and social order, Bartelson (2013); Kessler and Herborth (2013).

22. Norloff (2010:249) argues that the United States' "relative weakening", caused by the financial crisis, is, at its core, characterized by a "supreme irony". Precisely because "the world's leading economies are inextricably bound up with the American economy, coordinating a soft landing of the US economy has always had a clear economic rational" (186). It is those built-in "automatic stabilizers to cushion America's fall" (249) that explains why the United States is "too big to fail" (186). In essence, Norloff suggests that the internal logic of the capitalist system is American and, therefore, no other power but the United States can be the hegemon.

    However, as it is argued here, while Norloff might account for both why the United States has a "global advantage" and reaps more benefits from the economic order than others, she overlooks two things. First, America is not self-sufficient in economic terms, contrary to her own description of the key attribute which a hegemon must have (251); rather, it is dependent on other states' critical material underpinning of the system (if less dependent than others), even if supporters, such as China, are driven by economic self-interest. Second, Norloff overlooks that she is tied to the conception of a single hegemon as provided by HST.

23. This led one key US negotiator to consider the G20 "useless" (author's interview, Berlin June 2, 2012).

24. China's voting rights were supposed to rise from 3.65% to 6.39% between 2009 and 2011 (Hearn 2012:158), but still stood at 3.81% in January 2014 (http://www.imf.org/external/np/sec/memdir/members.aspx#U, January 14, 2014). With the US holding 16.75% of the votes on the Executive Board, China's rising number of voting rights still does not come anywhere near the voting power to block major reforms, which stands at 15.01%.

25. Some global public goods theorists acknowledge the role of values regarding what should be considered a global good (Kaul et al. 1999:6).

26. McMahon and Zou (2011:117) rightly question why theories that are indebted to a Western historico-political environment should be applicable across time and space. For a good analytical outline of varieties of value sets, Tamanaha (2004:9); also Mayntz (2010:8); for a highly contested account of diverging value sets, Huntington (1996).

27. On the variety of available national US narratives, Smith (1993).

28. On the notion of modernization during the Cold War, Hunt (2007); Ekbladah (2010); on the US origins of modernization theory, Gilman (2003).

29. More nuanced, Dunoff/Trachman 2009.

30. Alternatively, Marxist approaches to world order or the Stanford School predicated on the spread of Western rationality (e.g. Wallerstein 1974; 1980; 1989; Meyer et al. 1997); alternatively, Young (1982); for a sociological understanding of negotiated orders, Fine (1984).

31. Here, Buzan follows Searle (2010, 1995). One conspicuous example of a property to which a non-physical, social status is attributed is money.

32. Historically, Carr (in Buzan 2007:238).

33. This presupposition was "the home of various forms of inter-war legal idealism. It underlay...a naturalist perspective that saw the world always already united by basic values, the principles of 'reason'...that remained unchanging through space and time" (Koskenniemi 2012:306).

34. Little's links to the English School indicate that his quote should not be confused with IR bargaining theory (Fearon 1995; Blainey 1988; Lake 2010). The latter theory represents the "rationalist approach to war" and is "the dominant approach in conflict studies, providing the workhorse model for many theories of crisis, escalation, and civil and interstate war" (Lake 2010–11:7). Neither should it be conflated with non-coercive negotiation theory (Narlikar 2010); Odell (2013).
35. The fact that Gilpin attributes legitimacy/prestige such centrality in his account closely resembles Richelieu who accorded it, that is reputation, with the highest priority in his political testament (Mommsen 1923:215).
36. Jervis (1991–2:53) suggested the notion of meta-power that showed some resemblance to the broader understanding of power implied in Clark's account. Though, Jervis did not explore the concept.
37. Constitutionality should not be confused with constitutionalization (see Chapter 3).
38. Relatedly, Hurd views legitimacy as one of the "three currencies of power" (1999:379).
39. Mayntz (2010:8); Bukovansky (2002:39–40). While Clark does not mention domestic politics, Gilpin does. However, he views the domestic perspective merely as a source of internal growth (1981:152) and as a limit to great-power expansion (146).
40. Recent attempts at transferring democratic legitimacy standards to the global plane, reflected in patterns of good governance such as transparency, accountability, inclusion or responsibility, not only reveal a strongly Western bias but also, more importantly, fail to recognize the global political dynamics driving the negotiations on legitimacy. For instance, democratization, as stressed by Hu, means strengthening sovereignty internationally (Jintao 2012). In marked contrast to these theoretical extensions, the US view and its pragmatic and instrumentalist application have reflected similarities to the Chinese approach to sovereignty.
41. Confirming the system-level approach, a similar view has resonated in China's Department of State Security (SWP 2012:4–5).
42. For a more recent power-transition perspective on this, though less on systemic legitimacy, Ross and Feng (2008:295–305).
43. Similarly, Schroeder 2004:249.

3 Order Transition in a Hybrid Environment

1. TNAs are defined as private actors, operating on a for-profit or non-profit basis regarding international institutions (Risse 2012). They comprise NGOs, multinational corporations, philanthropic foundations and scientific communities. International institutions recruit TNAs as compliance watchdogs, stakeholder representatives, service providers and policy experts (Raustiala 1997; Scholte 2011).
2. For the important role of Poland's Solidarnosc movement, fostering civil disobedience against Communist rule, see the work of "transnational" historians (Snyder 2011:ch. 8).
3. For the question whether TNAs have made IOs more legitimate, Take 2013.

4. Abbott and Snidal (2000); Hawkins (2006); Keohane (1984).
5. Johnston (2008).
6. Contrary to Tallberg (2010:53), ECOSOC's often supposedly positive role of connecting civil society to IOs has been much less conducive than often thought. De Frouville (2008) showed that the emergence of government-oriented TNAs, which he terms "servile society" (72), serves the respective states, not civil society. This is due to ECOSOC's 1996 reforms so that more national-level TNAs could participate. The critical problem has become that the committee's review process can be used to intimidate TNAs "considered too critical" (92) of affected states by "threatening to have their UN status suspended or withdrawn" (Charnovitz 2009:779). Similarly, Roy (2005, 2008).
7. Gruber (2000); Krasner (1991).
8. Raustialaand Victor 2004.
9. Alternatively, Pfeil (2011).
10. Transnational historians have confirmed these similarities for the nineteenth century (Nehring 2012:131).
11. Chapter 2.
12. Here leadership is understood as concerted political activity of one or a group of great power(s), including its/their course of planned and executed action.
13. Avant et al. (2011:23) speak of leadership as agenda-setting, that is input, but overlook the implications of the distinction between input and outcome.
14. Also, Mayntz (2008:46, 57).
15. Avant et al.'s "leadership" refers to personal leadership inside the "global governors" (2010:23).
16. For an exception, Nolte (2005), Held et al. (1999:16) had preceded Barnett/Duvall in demanding such changes. The crux with most other global governance accounts (e.g. Bevirand Rhodes (2010); Ferguson and Mansbach (2004); McGrew (2013); Weiss and Wilkinson (2013)), which have thought about power and how to better integrate it in the literature, is that they have failed to influence the mainstream.
17. Equally, historians have collected powerful evidence showing that the adoption of progressive ideas by great powers is a critical precondition for their success (Mazower 2011).
18. A different case is TNAs that choose to walk out from negotiations. For instance, members of the Gates Foundation, who were offered to participate in sessions of the G20, determined to leave the forum when issues, in which the Foundation was not interested (e.g. Greece's financial crisis), were on the table. I would like to thank Andrew Cooper for sharing this with me (San Francisco, April 5, 2013).
19. Busby (2010), Raustalia (1997), Smithand Wiest (2005).
20. Alternatively, Bob (2005).
21. For exceptions analyzing the state/IGO–NGO relationship, Cooper (2013), Wiseman (2004), Steffek (2013).
22. Japan and Australia have followed the US model, whereas Chinese officials insist that they have adopted their NSC model from Russia (Qin 2014:5).
23. In contrast, without employing standard forms of positing law based on state consent, that is treaties or customary law, the UNSC's P5 implemented two

resolutions on terrorism and weapons of mass destruction, which strongly impinge on domestic politics and can be executed against the will of the respective state (Cohen 2012:ch. 5).

4 Order Transition, Common Culture and Exceptional Worldviews

1. Critically, Bukovansky (2009:161); Shambaugh (2013:131).
2. For an exclusionary example of a Western common culture, see the historic "standard of civilization" and, as some see it, its contemporary extension (Gong 1984). This is why African leaders see the actions of the ICC as a civilizational imposition. This is tellingly confirmed by the remarks of the French negotiator at the Rome Conference made to his US counterpart: "David, I'm going to sign this treaty...because we know that no French national will ever appear before the International Criminal Court. We will ensure that our courts take the case first" (quoted in Nolte and Aust 2013:417).
3. Foot et al. 2003:267; a similar view is held by some international lawyers: "the values of a particular country should be reflected in the norms of international law" (Bradford and Posner 2011:7).
4. Hartz (1955); but, Smith (1988, 1993) for a whole-scale revision.
5. For instance, Mahbubani strongly cautioned against the "presumptuous Western belief" that "when India emerges as a great power, it will join the Western community of states" since it is "the world's largest democracy" and represents "a natural addition to the Western community" (2008:165).
6. Prantl (2013) termed this approach as the so-called SCO spirit. It strongly resembles, though, the Chinese "Five Principles of Peaceful Coexistence". Recently, Russia's President Putin has expressed the underlying ideas of this spirit at the height of the (then aborted) US plans to bomb Syria's military facilities (NYT September 12, 2013).
7. Friedman (2012).
8. Some acknowledgement of this development can be found in Katzenstein (2010:3).
9. Westad 2012:6 – A good example of the implied insularity is the minimal use of the "international card" in domestic politics by either player in order to support policy proposals. For the US, Foot and Walter (2011:283); Geyer (2005:226); Patrick (2001:27) for China, Khong (2001:55). For resistance of US judges to use international materials, Nolteand Aust 2013:429.
10. On *Chinese exceptionalism*: Schweller and Pu (2011); Callahan (2012, 2008); Zhang (2011); Yongjin and Buzan (2012); Noesselt (2011); Nau and Ollapally (2012). On *US exceptionalism*: Smith (1993); Hoff (2008); Ignatieff ed. (2005); Hodgson (2009); Malone and Khong (2003).
11. Such notions of justice are altogether different from normative theory, either in its cosmopolitan or communitarian version (Beitz 1999; Nagel 2005; Pogge 1989; Rawls 1999).
12. Curiously, Foot and Walter do not address this conceptual issue; they only loosely locate it in the respective realms of domestic politics (2011:3, 8, 30).
13. Critically, McGregor (2010).

14. Yahuda (2011:270) argues that China does not want to export its domestic ideals. But this view is only accurate to the extent that China does militarily impose its ideas on others. China promotes, however, its ideals of a (domestic) harmonious society to the outside world. For instance, China's notion of a "harmonious world" has made it into joint declarations of China and India (2005) or China and African leaders (2009). www.fmprc.gov.cn

15. For critical (Chinese) assessments of the "harmony ideology", Davies (2007:19, 69); Shambaugh (2013:212–313).

16. Jiechi's remarks (foreign minister until May 2013 and as such not a member of the politbureau) carry special authenticity due to his promotion to a state councilor (member of the politbureau) since then.

17. Revealingly, by making reference to a Chinese position paper for the 65th session of the UN's General Assembly (September 13, 2010), Cai stated that China does "not dare, openly at least, to challenge the international rule of law" (2013:766).

18. Gat 2010:82.

19. In December 2010, as state councilor, Bingguo was the highest-ranking official supervising Beijing's foreign policy due to his membership in the politburo. His remarks also served the purpose of countering the international/regional impression of China's more assertive approach in 2009 and 2010.

20. Racial connotations are, historically, not limited to China. The racial origins of the aforementioned 200-year myth have been traced in-depth by constructivist scholars. They showed the "racialized identity of the Anglosphere"; as Vucetic put it, with respect to its perceived "moral superiority", the "Anglosphere is a product of its racial past" (2011:4). Whether or not such notions are politically revived today points to a difficult process of nationalistic self-assurance in view of perceived, and culturally disguised, politico-economic threats.

21. For instance, the Chinese ambassador stated at a "Luncheon of Asia-Pacific Ambassadors" with regard to "China's Perception of Itself and the World" (Chinese Embassy Berlin 2010): "In 1799 . . . , [w]e could say that China used to be a world power."

22. China is likely to become the economic number one within a decade, if measured by market exchange rates (Economist November 23, 2013, Special Report:4). In per capita terms, the picture looks vastly different.

23. Zhang states that this superiority is "an essential part of the worldview of the Chinese government" (2011:307).

24. I would like to thank Liwen Qin (MERICS) for the translation of Keqiang's speech. The notion of justice used here is altogether different from China's earlier leanings toward notions of distributive justice (Mitter 2003).

25. Though Waltz is frankly not a normative scholar, his remarks point to those made by normative pluralists (Walzer 1983). For an excellent overview, Hurrell (2007:300–308).

26. Critics argue that Callahan's article misleads the readers in terms of the real weight that should be attributed to Mingfu's work. I would challenge such arguments drawing on two, diametrically opposed, writers' accounts. First, Jacques' China-centric and atrociously titled book "When China Rules the World" suggests that he "highly recommend(s)" Callahan's work precisely

because it "seeks to understand (China)...on its own terms" (440). Second, Kissinger, who can safely be disregarded as an uncritical observer of China, devotes an entire section on Mingfu in his "On China". He indicates that the latter's book should by no means be underestimated, both in its public reach and its reflection of parts of the establishment's mindsets. Since Kissinger is closely linked up to the CCP's top echelon, his judgment seems authoritative.

27. This observation is related to the US in two ways: the deep anti-intellectualism among practitioners and the disconnect between IR and the practice of US diplomacy.

28. In contrast, politico-historical accounts, which take into account the multiple traditions of Chinese history, are, in terms of quantity, "overwhelmed by the epic discussions of the Chinese century" that are most clearly expressed in and, partly, collapsed into, the so-called "Sino-speak" (Callahan 2012:49; also Sachsenmaier 2011:229). Alternatively, Zhang 2011:306; Liqun 2010.

29. Employing a considerable dose of symbolism, the first occasion at which Xi presented his (Mingfu's) China dream of the "great revival of the Chinese nation" was at the national museum in Tiananmen Square in November 2012, where "an exhibition called 'Road to Revival' portrayed China's suffering at the hands of colonial powers and its rescue by the Communist Party" (Economist April 5, 2013:11).

30. Reportedly, Xi has installed himself as the leader of a small CCP group in charge of naval operations against Japan, including the disputed islands (Rajan 2014). Moreover, Xi's course of action in the East China Sea in 2013, also contradicts the strategic gist of the 2012 White Paper: http://www.gov.cn/jrzg/2011-09/06/content_1941204.htm.

31. Critics, who argue that Mingfu's book does not help to reveal the assumptions of superiority in Chinese thinking or that the author has no standing in the establishment, overlook three points. First, intellectual processes preparing the grounds for arguments, which may (or may not) be spread more widely at a later stage, do not immediately turn into mainstream. In fact, leaders are usually happy to see such authors not insisting on their intellectual property more fervently. Nonetheless, Mingfu became a popular author shortly after the book's publication. Secondly, Mingfu's pamphlet, despite the fact that it contradicted parts of the official Chinese parlance, successfully passed the governmental review process and, thus, must have reflected the mindsets of a growing portion of China's administration (Kissinger 2011:505). Thirdly, it is hard to believe that the sameness of the two titles, that is, of Mingfu's book and Xi's statement, is entirely coincidental.

32. Shambaugh 2013:129.

33. As the author could observe, professor Zhang Weiwei (Fudan) resented any critical engagement with his notion of Chinese "cultural superiority" when he attended the panel discussions of a summer school in 2013. Also, Davies (2007:25); Yongjin and Buzan (2012:14).

34. Ironically, Mingfu would find ample support from key European thinkers such as Marx, Hegel or Mill. All of them axiomatically believed in a hierarchy of states in which only a few nations had the morally superior greatness to assume responsibility in global affairs. Thus, when Hurrell believes that it "was in relation to the non-European world that differentiation and

hierarchy were clearest. Hence the widely-held belief in the concept of civilization and in a hierarchy of races...and 'standards of civilization'" (2013:191), the study of Mingfu proves that such thinking has become very modern again.

35. The resemblance between Mingfu's concept and the strong racial connotations of the Japanese government's "Investigation of Global Policy with the Yamato Race as Nucleus" in 1943, underpinning Japan's "Greater East Asia Co-Prosperity Sphere", is disconcerting (Buzas 2013; Hotta 2013).

36. Leffler identified four broad similarities between the three presidents Obama, G.W. Bush and Clinton (2011:42–43): overarching global military superiority, the essential importance of democratic values, a critical commitment to the open-door policy and global free trade, and the reservation of any US president's right to act independently.

37. Regardless of the accuracy of Ikenberry's assumption, the important point is that he echoes official US wording, which speaks of "a single model for national success" in global politics (US NSS 2002, quoted in Clark 2005:174). What is remarkable, therefore, is that Ikenberry's liberal thoughts are reflected in the wording of a Republican administration for which he worked during a stint in 2001/2. In essence, his assumptions confirm a bipartisan worldview prevailing in the American domestic spectrum.

38. Obviously, the United States did not win either World War alone. As for WW I, its entry in 1917 gave the Western powers the decisive material edge over the middle powers. As for WW II, it shared the military burden with Stalin's Soviet Union.

39. However, the NSS exposes itself to "India fallacy", that is, the mistaken belief that cooperation with any democratic state is naturally beneficial.

40. Explicitly, see the 1996 and 2000 versions of "America's National Interests: A Report from the Commission on America's National Interests", published by Harvard University's Belfer Center (which is said to have close ties to the administration).

41. Xuetong (2011:16) confirms Mingfu, bluntly stating that the "goal of strategy must be...to provide a better model for society than that given by the United States".

42. Xuetong (2011:245) turns Mingfu's remarks into a straightforward stipulation according to which (especially Chinese) students of IR should look at "how to replace one hegemony with another".

43. Thomas Kuhn's earlier use of the term incommensurability was different because it referred to incomparable theories (1962).

44. What Carr meant was the "moral" reasons why Britain rejected German peace offers in 1940. Churchill preferred American predominance over German hegemony.

45. Later in the book, Friedberg, who also used to work as a top US official, tellingly highlights his cognitive proximity to the (democratic) 200-year myth and the continued US role in it: "In the long run, the United States can learn to live with a democratic China as the preponderant power in East Asia, much as Great Britain came to accept America as the dominant power in the Western Hemisphere.... Having kept the peace, encouraged the transition of all the major regional players from authoritarianism to democracy, and overseen the re-emergence of Asia as a leading center of world wealth

and peace, Washington will be free to call home its legions" (2011:251–252). For a systemic critique of Friedberg, Jervis (2006).
46. If not an IR theorist, Nagel 1991.
47. For solidarist critiques, Linklater and Suganami (2006:136–147); for further cosmopolitan proponents, Held (2004); Giddens (2000). For a well-balanced refutation of pluralism, Hurrell (2007:292–298).
48. White 2012:112–114,161–162; Kissinger 2013:xvi. Conspicuously, Bush's letter to Deng in the immediate aftermath of Tiananmen in May 1989 reflects such an approach (quoted in Jackson and Towle 2006:70).
49. Adler and Pouilot suggest five patterns that any kind of "practice" needs to fulfill in order to be counted as such (2011:7–8). Since the English School's institutions "certainly comes quite close" to the essence of the practice literature (Adler and Pouilot 2011:4), the links between the two approaches are not spelt out.
50. Bukovansky (2011) and Katzenstein (2011) also disagree with the cosmopolitan bias of many accounts.
   The former refers to "the broader purpose of human dignity and flourishing" (176), the latter to the "material and psychological well-being of all humans" (242) in order to identify the key characteristics of international practices. The questions remains, though, who defines what exactly this means or what it can achieve on the international/global level?

5 Order Transition and Effectiveness

1. Insisting on unaltered US global responsibilities, Kagan (2008:57).
2. This is distinct from the use of constitutionality in domestic/international law.
3. Also, Shambaugh (2013:121).
4. Alternatively, Xuetong argues that a single Chinese hegemony is bound to arise (2011:216–221).
5. For an authoritative treatment of the topic, Bukovansky et al. 2012. Albeit erudite, its key weakness lies in its exclusive "focus on the US" (viii). While affiliated with Columbia University, I once asked Robert Jervis how he would suggest that one might think about the reinterpretation of US and Chinese special responsibilities. His answer that "this is the big question, of course, and I wished I had even the start of an answer" further inspired me to pursue this research agenda (e-correspondence, May 4, 2012).
6. This chapter does not support the idea of a G2 (ch. 1).
7. On US–Chinese leaders, Rudd (2013); more generally, Nye (2008).
8. This thinking permeates Ikenberry's entire book (2, 15, 16 n.16, 59, 60 n.37, 275, 339, 340). For a rare exception, Nye 2011:155–157.
9. Early on, the supposedly smooth "handover" of the United Kingdom's hegemony to the United States in the Americas in 1898 received critical reviews (Barraclough 1978). Among historians, Niall Ferguson (2003:160), who is the most ardent defender of the 200-year thesis, argues that O'Brien overlooked the large extent to which British and American economic and political leaders have underlined the notion of Anglo-Saxon leadership. Ironically, Ferguson thereby powerfully mirrors the strength of the widely spread internalization of the 200-year narrative.

10. Chapter 2.
11. Alternatively, Williams' study of realism asks how prudent statecraft acts as "ethic of responsibility" to limit national interests (2005:ch. 5).
12. Daase (2012:14–15). Obviously, this resembles the dialectic between logics of appropriateness and of consequences.
13. Similarly, Rapkin (1990). For a good summary of the literature on political leadership as state or party leaders.
14. Chapter 2.
15. Posen suggested that the material growth rates of the BRICS make unipolarity's transition to multipolarity more likely. Alternatively, Wohlforth (1999, 2008).
16. Buzan's use of the term "superpower" for the United States is not adopted in this study.
17. The global governance literature has put forward an alternative "managerial" strand (Koskenniemi 2011). This chapter addresses, inter alia, the question why the latter has been sharply criticized.
18. Alternatively, Bisley (2012); Mearsheimer (2001). The former views great-power management as outdated for reasons of interdependence and global challenges (12–13), but cannot say where leadership is going to come from; the latter denies any managerial aspects altogether, since great powers only aim at singlehegemonies.
19. Alternatively, leading IR theorists of East Asia (Goh 2005; Kang 2003) have suggested that hierarchy (and, thus, special responsibilities) was formally accepted in Asia and the equality of actors treated as informal. However, it remains unclear why this should make any difference today, when notions of a hierarchical regional system, with China at the helm, invariably encounter two substantial challenges. First, in contrast to the times before the "age of humiliation", today's world has been organized along formal sovereignty. Post-colonial states, in particular, have been extremely defensive about their newly gained independence. Second, East Asia has been penetrated by a very sticky and powerful web of US treaty-based alliances. Neither did exist when those hierarchical Chinese views were first conceived. Any plans to rethink the current status of world politics must start from here. Otherwise, analysts commit what I would call the "umma fallacy", that is, an attempt to draw a map of the world based on a political reality that went by long ago. Yan Xuetong argues in a similar direction, but admits the hypocrisy that has come to characterize Chinese proposals of "democratizing" international politics. Those suggestions aim at broadening the membership of international institutions, but cannot hide China's conservative support for its hierarchical position in the UN Security Council. In fact, China cannot but "openly recognize that it is a dominant power in a hierarchical world, but this sense of dominance means that it has extra responsibilities" (Xuetong 2011:16).
20. Claude (1986:722–724) quotes Truman, Acheson and Shultz for further examples.
21. This is true for two of the English School's leading theorists (Buzan 2006; Little 2007).
22. This runs counter to the prevailing sociological-constructivist view that, once the black box of the state is opened, there is room for non-state

actorsand so on to shape the preferences of states. While this argument may be accurate in times when preferences are open to challenge in day-to-day politics, in our contrary case, states are about to determine the foundational "rules of the game" underlying day-to-day politics of contesting preferences.

23. Curiously, while he talks about the necessity of the "management of international affairs", he can do so only at the expense of very considerably deviating from his core rationalist propositions (1979:80, 197). Waltz is here a prime example of what Gaddis called "The Tyranny of Method over Subject" (1992/93:25–26). Already in 1966, Deutsch, a leading behavioralist scholar of peace studies, had made suggestions (in his "Future of World Politics") that offered causes of the future transformation of the global system. Gaddis, thus, correctly asked why behavioralists did not "accomplish anything like this" in the 25 years that followed, since one of their key aims had been to predict major events (26). Gaddis' answer has not lost any validity: " Deutsch was prepared to depart from quantitative analysis when that technique was inappropriate: for him, subject determined method, rather than the other way around. Too many other behavioralists let method determine subject, with the consequences one might expect in any situation in which means are allowed to overshadow avowed ends" (ibid.).

24. Little (2007:155–158), who has provided the most comprehensive assessment of Bull's great-power management, has not recognized this point either.

25. The caution in relation to the G2 idea remains untouched.

26. The main difference between Vabulas and Snidal (2013) and Prantl (2013) is that the latter operationalized the formal-informal continuum, whereas the former did not.

27. Holbraad (1979:98). Holbraad usefully discusses five ways of containing threats to intra-hegemonic management (104–107).

28. For the penetration of highly institutionalized environments by aspects of power politics, Gruber (2000); Drezner (2007).

29. Gerring 2010; Mahoney 2010; Collier et al. 2010.

6   Renegotiating the Security-Related Rules of Global Order

1. The term's usage is highly politicized. While the Organization for Security and Co-operation in Europe (OSCE) has expressly rejected it in 1994, 1996 and 1999 (Neuhold 2009), as have top politicians (Biden 2009; Clinton 2009) and scholars (Foot 2009) alike, its current practical application has reoccurred nonetheless (e.g. 2010–14: South/East China Seas; 2009: Georgia; 2013–4: Ukraine). As the great powers did not want to see their special responsibilities explicitly manifested in the UN Charter after World War II, a similar reluctance characterizes today's talk about spheres of influence, while its factual reflection as a rationale of great-power politics remains unchanged.

2. The chapter cannot discuss the large literature on the ways in which the management has been conceived, that is, as a concert, power-sharing deal or a group of two (Ayson 2012; White 2012).

3. In 2011, China still denied that it pursued the goal of a sphere of influence ("White Paper of China's State Council", quoted in Economist October 9, 2011:78). However, this outright denial has recently been moderated because China *now* possesses "developmental interests" in the SCS that needed to be guarded ("White Paper" 2013). Curiously, the paper does not say why these interests should remain uncontested in the region.
    Rather, it slowly became clear(er) that the Monroe Doctrine (1823), in which the United States had declared the entire Western Hemisphere as its sphere of influence, was a standing model.
4. Similarly, IISS 2009:73.
5. *ASEAN Regional Forum* (ARF) comprises Brunei, Cambodia, Indonesia, Laos, Malaysia, Myanmar, Philippines, Singapore, Thailand, Vietnam and has added the United States, China, Japan and South Korea; the *East Asia Summit* (EAS): ASEAN, China, Japan, South Korea, Australia, New Zealand, India, the United States and Russia; *ASEAN Defence Ministers' Meetings Plus* (ADMM+); *Asia-Pacific Economic Cooperation* (APEC): Australia, Brunei, Canada, Chile, China, Hong Kong, Indonesia, Japan, Republic of Korea, Malaysia, Mexico, New Zealand, Papua New Guinea, Peru, Philippines, Russia, Singapore, Taiwan, Thailand, the United States and Vietnam.
6. Dung's comment was matched by earlier statements by other Southeast Asian observers (Frankenberger April 30, 2009:10). Theorists have confirmed this finding. For instance, while Japan–China relations were lightly improving between 2004 and 2008, scholars have suggested that they have failed to deliver *afterwards*. The main obstacle was that "a solution to the dispute (had not been) predicated on increasing *political trust* between the conflicting parties" (Emmers 2010:114).
7. As this analysis suggests, China has recently further extended the territory covered by the nine-dash line toward the north, that is, sea-based territory partly claimed by Japan, which China has tried to make part of its ADIZ. Both seas carry the greatest stock of fish worldwide and contain extremely vast and unexplored quantities of natural resources (e.g. oil, gas). The nine-dash line carves out most of the SCS for China. Starting in the north, it runs from east of Vietnam down to the north of Indonesia, passes Brunei and Malaysia in the west and goes up north again leaving the Philippines to its right.
8. There is no room to discuss the political meaning of the Transpacific Partnership (TPP). Suffice to say that its free-trade character is to undermine Chinese plans to further the economic dependence of SCS states (and beyond) on Beijing. Already in 2011, China was the largest trading partner of the ASEAN states, Japan, South Korea and Australia (Khong 2013/14:162 n. 17). No less than 90% of Beijing's trade (and 80% of its crude oil) arrive at/depart from its ports and, thus, underline the importance of international sea lanes. So do the 20% of US trade that flows through the two seas (Raine and Le Miere 2013:12).
9. Talks about further joint undertakings were briefly resumed in June 2010, but were abandoned shortly afterwards due to renewed tensions between Japan and China (IISS 2011:361–362).
10. More critically, Ba (2009).

11. Leading Chinese military leaders gave the impression that the meager outcomes of recent US interventions further contributed to the change of climate (author's interviews, fall 2013).
12. The two were Jeff Bader (senior director of Asian Affairs at the National Security Council) and James Steinberg (Deputy Secretary of Defense).
13. China has since then used any opportunity to repeat its sovereignty claim. Yang (who became state councilor in 2013) chose his – global – audience well when he underlined the Chinese claim right in front of the UN General Assembly in 2012 (Jiechi 2012) or when he did so a few weeks earlier at a joint press conference with Clinton in Beijing (Clinton 2012).
14. It should be noted that unexpectedly critical Chinese voices, such as the *Global Times*, argued on July 27 that China should avoid "arbitrarily expanding" the definition of its core interests (quoted in Economist July 31, 2010: 32), if without any impact.
15. Author's interview late 2012. Domestically, Chinese school books advance the notion that China deserves thousands of square miles in the adjacent seas today (Shambaugh at the 2013 ISA Convention).
16. So, too, Russia, France, Canada and South Korea.
17. On Yang, Chapter 5.
18. Indonesia was the main driver behind the United States' inclusion into ASEAN.
19. The US sphere of influence has three characteristics: geographically, it covers the entire SCS and ECS; militarily, it is based on bilateral alliances and a heavy naval presence; furthermore, though much objected to by China. For instance, in the Defense Ministry's "interpretation" of the ADIZ [Defense Ministry 2013], this military presence includes the self-acclaimed right to pursue naval and aerial reconnaissance inside the sovereign (sea-based) territory of other states, that is, the EEZs (Dutton 2010); functionally, though all-encompassing in its coverage, it allows free passage for any participant of world trade. From the US perspective, this is central to sustaining the (sea lanes for the) global commons (Posen 2003).
20. Author's interview, June 10, 2011.
21. This statement reflected the status of the discussions between the US head of the Joint Chiefs of Staff, admiral Mullen, and his counterpart, General Guanglie, member of the Central Military Commission, state councilor and defense minister. When they met a week prior to the ARF, their disagreements about SCS-related events remained unresolved (Buchensteiner July 21, 2011:7).
22. Certainly, the United Sates had accepted UNCLOS as customary international law (Raine and Le Miere 2013:221–222); however, China saw no reason why it should submit itself to a convention from which the United States had formally abstained. Hence, Beijing's opt-out.
23. Documenting the political atmosphere in which ASEAN found itself, one of China's immediate reactions was to publicly announce the ready deployment of anti-aircraft carrier missiles in the SCS (IISS 2012:336).
24. Alternatively, observers from the region insisted that ASEAN members knew very well that they had to better balance their relationships with China and the United States, respectively. Accordingly, the "ASEAN split-up scenario

is out of the question" (author's interview with Prof. Panaspornprasit, Bangkok, May 20, 2014).

25. Reflecting the degree to which great powers commonly use their material means to achieve their political goals, China announced that it would support Cambodia with more than 500 million USD in soft loans (Economist April 27, 2013:48). In a leaked cable, the former Singaporean prime minister, Lee, confirmed China's underlying strategy: "Lee claimed, China tells the region 'come grow with me'. At the same time, China's leaders want to convey the impression that China's rise is inevitable and that countries need to decide if they want to be China's friend or foe when it arrives" (WikiLeaks October 19, 2007). The similarities with the United States' instrumental uses of foreign aid elsewhere are striking and telling at the same time (Schade 2005).

   Regardless of whether or not these actions were coordinated with the United States, the fact that Japan canceled Myanmar's 1.8 billion USD debt and offered to provide some 500 million USD in aid loans certainly reflected, and further cemented, the underlying political divisions within ASEAN (Economist June 1, 2013:52). Moreover, Japan pledged some 20 billion USD to ASEAN states in 2013 (FAZ December 14, 2013).

26. Obviously, this is another example that disproves Ikenberry's mantra that the US order is "easy to join".

27. This does not imply that the SCS began to resemble calm waters. For instance, in March a large group of Chinese warships appeared merely 50 miles off the coast of Malaysia and undertook exercises. In a similar pattern, China's PLAN conducted a vast ten-day exercise in the SCS, involving warships, aircrafts, submarines and marine soldiers (IISS 2013:357). It is hard to believe that those excursions were intended to strengthen UNCLOS or the outstanding "code of conduct".

28. When Japan formally named ten uninhabited islands as part of its territorial waters (May 2011), China's Navy sent its (thus far) largest squadron of 11 warships, including a large-scale destroyer, close to Japan's Okinawa Prefecture a month later (IISS 2012:367).

29. More accurately, while China did indeed suffer immensely from Japanese occupation, it did not, as Potsdam implies, militarily contribute to the defeat of Germany, Japan and Italy.

30. The carrier is currently designed for combat helicopters. Experts estimate that it would not take too much to transform it into a carrier for fighter jets.

31. Similarly, a scholar from the region, Prof. Panaspornprasit (Bangkok), called the Chinese move a "political barometer instrument" (author's interview May 20, 2014).

32. For instance, a joint Japan–ASEAN statement published in December barely mentioned the ADIZ-related crisis (asean.org, December 29, 2013).

33. US constant reference to international law was, of course, in itself partial in that if Japan was so sure of its claims, why did it not take the issue to court?

34. Author's interviews with Chinese and Southeast Asian top military commanders, winter 2013.

35. This is why recent, authoritative analyses suggest that drawing from US–USSR crisis management lessons is a necessary way forward in channeling US–China relations today (IISS 2012:398).

36. Abe's embracing of US military support showed how much China's behavior had changed Japan's domestic setting (which had tried to reach greater strategic freedom from Washington in 2009 [IISS 2012:363]).
37. Clinton told her Japanese counterpart in September 2010 that this was the case, only to be confirmed by the secretary of defense, Gates, shortly afterwards in public (IISS 2011:347).
38. Author's interview, summer 2013. In particular, the Western diplomatic source described Xi's remarks as "unmistakably strong", while Obama's reaction was "uncompromising" regarding the security guarantees.
39. Indeed, this was exactly what happened at the 2014 Shangri-La Dialogue, where Abe and Hagel, in a somewhat coordinated manner, infuriated the PLA's deputy chief of staff, Wang Guanzhong (FAZ June 2, 2014).
40. It is no coincidence that the authors published the political analysis of their legal arguments in a prestigious US journal, that is, the *American Journal of International Law*.
41. Author's interview, fall 2012.

7 Renegotiating the Environmental Rules of Global Order

1. Carbon dioxide, the most dominant, man-made greenhouse gas (GHG), remains in the atmosphere for 100 years and is only extremely slowly absorbed by nature. Other fluorocarbons have lifetimes of over a thousand years, for instance, hydrofluorocarbons (HFCs).
2. In an earlier draft, the authors had been even clearer, suggesting the willingness "to steer and direct the behavior of members ... of a broader community" (2012).
3. All numbers (in percent) are in relation to world total, based on statistics of the US Energy Information Administration (eia.gov): US energy consumption 17.8 (2013), GHG emissions: 17.7 (2013); Chinese energy consumption 19.7 (2013), GHG emissions: 25.4 (2013).
4. For a balanced account of this fiercely contested event, Hurrell/Gupta (2012).
5. NGOs had already become more critical of the often ineffective UNFCCC process in the years before Copenhagen.
6. Attempts at strengthening the effectiveness after Copenhagen by larger governments, such as US-driven (though half-hearted) approaches via the Major Emitters Forum (MEF), remained as short-lived as China's rejection of binding responsibilities was constant.
7. This large number includes, among others, business/research NGOs and environmental NGOs. The focus below is on the latter while their activities cannot be neatly separated from the activities of other activists outside the conference halls.
8. In contrast to the United States and China, the world's least developed states strongly rely on NGO advice due to their lack of capacities.
9. At the final (and decisive) day only 90 observers were admitted. This observation runs counter to the views held by earlier research (Betsill and Corell 2001:70; Weiss and Gordenker 1996).
10. China has never been a member of the G77, though it has been its self-appointed spokesperson since Bandung. "Leading" the G77 does not imply

that China has been successful in convincing smaller countries of the positions it has taken. Especially its rows with the Least Developed Countries (LDCs) at Copenhagen have revealed the splits within the group.

11. A Western top-level delegate dryly suggested to the author after Doha that "typically, bilateral agreements are the way to get things done" (December 9, 2012). If one-sided, the comment revealed the large degree of frustration among many negotiators regarding the sheer size of the summits, both in terms of NGOs and governments.

12. As a former UNFCCC staff member and attendee of the summit explained: "the" de-facto exclusion of most ENGOs from the conference center in the second week further contributed to their disillusionment with the negotiations (interview with Joanna Depledge, July 1, 2014).

13. For the full list of initiatives, Bulkeley et al. (2012:598).

14. Reports are voluntary only for LDCs; though for non-Annex I parties reporting is conditional on receipt of financial support (non-Annex I parties need to report every two years, which was one of the few accomplishments of Copenhagen/Cancun).

15. Developed countries (save the US) promised to transfer 100 billion USD per year to developing countries by 2020; also, a climate fund, partly run by the World Bank, was to be established; finally, a deal was concluded that outlined the financial conditions for the support of maintaining national forests (Economist December 16, 2010).

16. While Canada has withdrawn from the entire Protocol, Japan and Russia remain parties to it, but will not sign up to the second commitment period. Japan had hinted at this political move for some time.

17. Tellingly, Foot and Walter could show that China's and the United States' "mutually destructive stance" "may even have led to forms of collusion between the two governments, such as when both appeared to work together at negotiations in 2005 to weaken attempts to work out post-Kyoto arrangements" (2011:224).

18. At that time, China had just finished preparing its five-year plan to cut emissions, followed by South Korea and Mexico (FAZ November 29, 2011; Held et al. 2013:23, 42–46). The central question of enforcement, though, remained unanswered in the Chinese case (Hallding et al. 2011:72).

19. The MEF, bringing together the world's 15 major polluters, accomplished only very little. The main reason was that the majority did not want it as an addition to the UNFCCC process, fearing that this would come at the expense of historic responsibilities; similarly, the majority was against linking energy security and climate-change issues (Foot and Walter 2011:208).

20. The European Union, Australia, Norway and a few others accepted new carbon-cutting targets under Kyoto, extended to 2020. While poor countries could not strike a deal on new funds for their adaptation process, their "loss and damage" claim was formally adopted.

21. Critically, Steffek et al. (2008:11).

22. ICLEI establishes exact GHG emission reduction targets for local governments, sets standards for community-scale GHG registries and provides reporting of local climate efforts. The Gold Standard measures projects according to its environmental integrity criteria and certifies only those that

provide benefits for the societies that host the projects. The GHG Protocol supports mainly businesses in their efforts to produce measurements and reports of their impact on the global climate in order to improve cross-business monitoring (and possibly facilitate the reduction of GHG emissions).
23. Alternatively, Compagnon et al. (2012:237–264).
24. Correspondence with Joanna Depledge (Cambridge, UK), June 2, 2014.
25. This is not to say that the United States and China are opposed to the UNFCCC's ultimate objective of avoiding dangerous climate change. They are not, if only because such a move would, even for great powers of their caliber, unnecessarily damage their international images, respectively. Rather, this section intends to probe into why the two countries have often objected to solutions offered on the negotiation tables worldwide.
26. The film was entitled "An Inconvenient Truth" (2006).
27. For a nuanced account of US foreign environmental policy, Eckersley (2012:351–374).
28. In 2013, while unable to convince Congress, President Obama overcame the pressure of business lobbies and instructed the EPA to limit the amount of vast GHG emissions produced by power plants in the United States. Nonetheless, the downside of Obama's plans to circumvent the (opposed) legislative branch was that, while the EPA could suggest such plans to the states, it had to wait for each state to provide a plan of how to implement it, including compliance terms. Not only would this procedure last several years, the decisions eventually made could both be taken to court and reversed by future administrations (Economist June 29, 2013:43).
29. Alternatively, Brunnee and Streck (2013); Abeysinghe and Arias (2013). For an in-depth exploration of justice-related concerns, Brooks (2013).
30. There is no room to discuss China's concerns about its international image in depth. Suffice to say that that both its insistence on its status as a developing country and the persistent lack of implementing its well-communicated goals related to environmental protection have put, as this author sees it, other more image-friendly interpretations of its behavior in a negative light.
31. Admittedly, the numbers predate the time frame set out for this analysis. Nevertheless, since no more recent data were available and no major change in China's environmental behavior was discernible, this move seemed acceptable.
32. Note that due to both its participation at the inaugural conference in Stockholm 1972 and its policy input to the 1992 UN Conference on Environment and Development (UNCED), China has been a "norm-maker rather than norm taker" (Foot and Walter 2011:187). In this sense, China has not been a challenger that aims to overturn an institution because it has not been given "voice" in it, but rather a revisionist challenger that strikes the hegemon on its involuntarily "common but differentiated" turf.
33. This does not rule out that China and the United States will conclude (further) non-binding agreements, for instance, in Paris 2015. Interview with Charlotte Streck, June 25, 2014.
34. In contrast, experts closely linked to the UNFCCC insist that the pledging of targets by China (India and others) represent "major breakthroughs". They also see progress in the fact that the climate summitry itself has not broken

down and thus believe that, according to the nature of the climate negotiations in the past, no deal can be expected until much closer to the next summit in 2015 (interview with Joanna Depledge, July 1, 2014). The problem with such thinking is that it underestimates the deeper and underlying causes of great-power disagreements that cannot be resolved by piecemeal progress.

35. For a slightly more optimistic account, Held et al. (2013:1–25).

8   Renegotiating the Ideology-Related Aspects of Global Order

1. Luck 2011; Foot 2011.
2. Also, Thakur (2006); Evans (2008); alternatively, Reinold 2013; Stahn 2007. Secretary General Ki-Moon suggested in September 2011 that "our debates are now about how, not whether, to implement the Responsibility to Protect. No government questions the principle" (2011). Needless to say, the statement is far from being uncontested (Welsh 2011:106; Niemelä 2008).
3. Of course, smaller powers have also taken advantage of the "declaratory tradition" (e.g. Libya and Syria). Nevertheless, the great powers' deliberate failure to live up to the obligations of the respective norms has usually had a much larger impact on the effectiveness of those institutions and norms.
4. Other cases, such as Cote d'Ivoire (2010–11), which – quite revealingly – received much less international attention than Libya, were similar in terms of the fatalities accrued ahead of the eventual military intervention (Bellamy and Williams 2011:829–838). Most importantly, with regard to the case selection, China and the United States were not engaged at all in the operations, apart from passing the respective resolutions in *2011* (2000, 1992, 1980, 1981, 1975, 1968, 1967) and *2010* (1962, 1951, 1946, 1942 and 1933).
5. This is not to say that the Cold War contained all civil wars, as Westad's erudite study showed to the contrary (2006). Rather, after 1989/91 there was, in theory, for the first time sufficient political room to raise awareness for this problem and to facilitate international actions.
6. According to UN estimates, 300,000 people died in the Sudanese War (Guardian April 23, 2008).
7. RtP has been endorsed by several UNSC resolutions since 2006. The fact that the change was made from the formerly prevailing term "humanitarian intervention" to stressing the responsibility underpinning sovereignty was due to the manifold criticisms by developing states (Mani and Weiss 2011).
8. Ironically, when Evans and Thakur suggest that the "principled underpinnings for adopting R2P . . . are reinforced by the reality of the gradual but steady shift of power and influence from the West to the rest" (2013:203), they seem to assume that this "shift" supports the RtP norm. As this case study shows, this underlying assumption is mistaken. If their intention was to stress that the "shift" might prevent intervention in the less developed world, they might be right. But, again, this does not lead to the deepening of the normative stances that are conducive to RtP.
9. For authoritative Middle East studies, Fawcett 2013; Gause 2010; Lawson 2006. Especially on Libya, Vandewalle 2012; on Syria, Hinnebusch 2012.

10. At the beginning of 2011, China had portrayed the protesters against Egypt's Mubarak as "lawless troublemakers" (Economist September 10, 2011).
11. Remarkably, precisely because Gates had been the head of the CIA for many years and had, thus, overviewed manifold operations abroad to protect America's "national" security, his stance in 2011 reflected the overwhelming readiness to abstain from foreign interventions and limit US forces to the protection of the homeland. In his memoirs, he outright despised Power's military demands (Washington Post, May 7, 2014).
12. Others supported the military intervention (e.g. Nye, Wendt, Keohane, Finnemore [Foreign Policy 2012]).
13. The Gulf Cooperation Council (3/7/2011) and the Organization of Islamic Countries (March 8, 2011) had demanded a no-fly zone (Bellamy/Williams 2011:841). Cynically, after just having advocated all three organizations' demands, Saudi Arabia militarily invaded Bahrain to crush Shia protests on March 14.
14. *In favor*: Bosnia and Herzegovina, Colombia, France, Gabon, Lebanon, Nigeria, Portugal, South Africa, the United Kingdom and Northern Ireland, the United States; *against*: none; *abstaining*: Brazil, China, Germany, India, Russian Federation (UNSC 2011b:3).
15. According to UN estimates, by April 10 some 500,000 people had fled Libya (IISS 2011:20).
16. Needless to say, this quasi-pacifist attitude sits uncomfortably with China's approach to its own region in recent years. However, it fits squarely with the official advocacy of a "harmonious world".
17. The rhetorical condemnations of Western use of force partly derived from the need to satisfy Chinese nationalists and their anti-hegemonic resentments (People's Daily March 22, 2011).
18. Many accounts have argued that since Western powers extended their Libya mandate in a way that permitted regime change, this was key to China's and Russia's decision to veto resolutions on Syria (Evans and Thakur 2013:200, 206; alternatively, Bellamy 2014:26–27). Suffice to say that this case study could not identify any such evidence in the examined documents.
19. For an excellent study on the strategic and interest-based context of humanitarian interventions, Seybolt 2007.
20. *In favor:* Bosnia and Herzegovina, Colombia, France, Gabon, Germany, Nigeria, Portugal, the United Kingdom, the United States; *against:* China, Russia; *abstentions:* Brazil, India, Lebanon, South Africa.
21. *In favor:* Azerbaijan, Colombia, France, Germany, Guatemala, India, Morocco, Pakistan, Portugal, South Africa, Togo, the United Kingdom, the United States; *against:* China, Russia.
22. *In favor:* 137 votes, *against:* 12, *abstentions:* 17.
23. A US-Arab resolution put forward to the UN Human Rights Council was rejected by China, Russia and Cuba (IISS 2012:337–338).
24. Viewed from Riyadh, the US withdrawal from Iraq left the Middle East in Shia hands.
25. *In favor:* Azerbaijan, Colombia, France, Germany, Guatemala, India, Morocco, Portugal, Togo, the United Kingdom, the United States; *against:* China, Russia; *abstentions:* Pakistan, South Africa.

26. His successor, the Algerian diplomat Brahimi, was appointed on August 18 and took office on September 1 (Reuters 2012).
27. Obama was reelected on November 6; Xi was appointed as head of the CCP and the military on November 15, 2012. Obama was sworn in on January 15, Xi succeeded Hu Jintao as president in March 2013 (IISS 2013:9–10).
28. Concerning RtP, various authors have confirmed the critical importance of hard security-related reasons for US decisions to use force (Luck 2011:14; Foot 2011:61).
29. In one of his rare statements before the resolution was discussed, Wang cryptically suggested that the deal "will enable tensions in Syria to be eased" (quoted in BBC September 15, 2013).
30. The government was indeed shut down for a short period of time, causing Obama to cancel significant trips to East Asia promoting the US pivot (Reuters October 4, 2013).
31. *In favor*: Argentina, Australia, Azerbaijan, China, France, Guatemala, Luxembourg, Morocco, Pakistan, Republic of Korea, Russia, Rwanda, Togo, the United Kingdom, the United States.
32. The measures under Chapter VII were limited to the "unauthorized transfer ... or any use of chemical weapons by anyone" in Syria (UNSC 2013:4).

9   Conclusion

1. This is notwithstanding the crises related to the Ukraine and Crimea, Syria, Palestine/Israel, Nigeria's Boko Haram and Islamic State and other dreadful developments that have occurred in the non-OECD world.
2. Here "world" referred to both the state of global politics since 2008 and, somewhat optimistically, to IR theory as such. Obviously, this new filling of Ruggie's path-breaking phrase showed no similarities to the original (1998).
3. On a positive note, for instance in environmental terms, both states have made intermittent progress on a national level, respectively.

Bibliography

Abbott, Andrew. *Time Matters: On Theory and Method.* Chicago: University of Chicago Press, 2001.

Abbott, Kenneth W. and Snidal, Duncan. "Hard and Soft Law in International Governance." *International Organization* vol. 54, no. 3 Summer (2000): 421–456.

Abeysinghe, Achala and Arias, Gilberto. "CBDR as a Principle of Inspiring Actions Rather than Justifying Inaction in the Global Climate Change Regime." In *Climate Change: International Law and Global Governance*, edited by Oliver Ruppel et al., Baden-Baden: Nomos, 2013.

Acharya, Amitav. "Can Asia Lead? Power Ambitions and Global Governance in the Twenty-first Century." *International Affairs* vol. 04, no. 87 (2011): 851–869.

Acharya, Amitav. *Speech on Global IR, held as New President at ISA 2014*, April 27, 2014.

Acharya, Amitav, and Johnston, Iain. *Crafting Cooperation: Regional International Institutions in Comparative Perspective.* Cambridge: Cambridge University Press, 2007.

Adler, Emanuel and Pouliot, Vincent, eds. *International Practices.* Cambridge and New York: Cambridge University Press, 2011.

Adler, Emanuel and Pouliot, Vincent. *International Practices.* Cambridge: Cambridge University Press, 2012.

Albright, Madeline. "Interview on NBC-TV 'The Today Show' with Matt Lauer." http://www.state.gov/1997–2001-NOPDFS/statements/1998/980219a .html, 2/19/1998 (accessed December 3, 2010).

Albright, Madeleine K. "Interview on NBC-TV 'The Today Show' with Matt Lauer." Columbus, OH, February 19, 1998. http://www.state.gov/1997-2001 -NOPDFS/statements/1998/980219a.html

Amadae, Stephen. *Rationalizing Capitalist Democracy: The Cold War Origins of Rational Choice Liberalism.* Chicago: Chicago University Press, 2003.

Aron, Raymond. *Frieden und Krieg: Eine Theorie der Staatenwelt.* Frankfurt: S. Fischer, 1986 [1962].

Aron, Raymond. *Frieden und Krieg: Eine Theorie der Staatenwelt.* S. Fischer Publishing, Frankfurt, 1966.

Associated Press. "2013 Government Shutdown Timeline: Congress' Path to Gridlock." October 1, 2013. http://dyn.politico.com/printstory.cfm?uuid= 980A0888-F713-45B463AA8FAB58B0A751 (accessed August 7, 2014).

Association of Southeast Asian Nations. "ASEAN-CHINA Dialogue Relations." http://www.asean.org/news/item/asean-china-dialogue-relations (accessed May 19, 2014).

Avant, Deborah, Martha, Finnemore and Susan, Sell, eds. *Who Governs the Globe?* New York: Cambridge University Press, 2011.

Ayson, Robert. "Formalizing Informal Cooperation?" In *Effective Multilateralism: Through the Looking Glass of East Asia*, edited by Prantl, Jochen, ed., Basingstoke: Palgrave Macmillan, 196–211, 2013.

Ayson, Robert. *Hedley Bull and the Accommodation of Power*. Basingstoke: Palgrave Macmillan, 2012.

Ba, Alice. *(Re)Negotiating East and Southeast Asia: Region, Regionalism, and the Association of Southeast Asian Nations*. Stanford: Stanford University Press, 2009.

Bader, Eric. *Obama and China's Rise: An Insider's Account of America's Asia Strategy*. Washington, D.C.: Brookings Institution Press, 2012.

Baldwin, David. *Paradoxes of Power*. New York: Basil Blackwell, 1989.

Baldwin, David. "Power and International Relations." In *Handbook of International Relations*, edited by Walter Carlnaes, Thomas Risse and Beth Simmons, 273–296. Los Angeles: SAGE, 2012.

Bang, Guri, Hovi, Jon and Sprinz, Detlef F. "US Presidents and the Failure to Ratify Multilateral Environmental Agreements." *Climate Policy* vol. 12 (2012): 755–763.

Barnett, Michael. "Social Constructivism." In *The Globalization of World Politics. An Introduction to International Relations*, edited by John Baylis and Steve Smith, 251–270. New York: Oxford University Press, 2006.

Barnett, Michael, and Duvall, Raymond. *Power in Global Governance*. New York: Cambridge University Press, 2005.

Barnett, Michael, and Sikkink, Kathryn. "From International Relations to Global Society." In *The Oxford Handbook of International Relations*, edited by Christian Reus-Smit and Duncan Snidal, 62–83. New York: Oxford University Press, 2008.

Barraclough, Geoffrey. *An Introduction to Contemporary History*. London: Penguin 1978.

Bartelson, Jens. "Three Concepts of Recognition." *International Theory* vol. 5, no.1 (2013): 107–129.

Bartelson, Jens. *Visions of World Community*. Cambridge: Cambridge University Press, 2009.

Baumgart, Winfried. *Europäisches Konzert und nationale Bewegung, 1830–1878*. Schöningh: Paderborn, 1999.

BBC News. "Cameron Loses Commons Vote on Syria Action." August 30, 2013. http://www.bbc.com/news/uk-politics-23892783?print=true (accessed August 7, 2014).

Beck, Ulrich. *Cosmopolitan Vision*. Cambridge: Polity Press, 2006.

Beck, Ulrich. *Der kosmopolitische Blick*. Suhrkamp: Frankfurt a. M., 2004.

Beckman, Robert. "The UN Convention on the Law of the Sea and the Maritime Disputes in the South China Sea." *American Journal of International Law* vol. 107 (2013): 142–163.

Beeson, Mark. *Institutions of the Asia-Pacific: ASEAN, APEC and Beyond*. London: Routledge, 2009.

Beetham, David. *The Legitimation of Power*. Basingstoke: Palgrave Macmillan, 1991.

Beitz, Charles. *Political Theory and International Relations*. Princeton: Princeton University Press, 1999.

Bellamy, Alex, and Williams, Paul. "The New Politics of Protection? Cote d'Ivoire, Libya and the Responsibility to Protect." *International Affairs* vol. 87, no. 4 (2011): 825–50.

Bender, Thomas. *A Nation among Nations: America's Place in World History*. New York: Hill & Wang, 2006.

Berlin, Isaiah. *The Crooked Timber of Humanity: Chapters in the History of Ideas.* London: Pimlico, 1990.

Bernstein, Steven. "Legitimacy in Intergovernmental and Non-State Global Governance." *Review of International Political Economy* vol. 18, no. 1 (2000): 17–51.

Betsill, Michele, and Corell, Elisabeth. "NGO Influence in International Environmental Negotiations: A Framework for Analysis." *Global Environmental Politics* vol. 1, no. 4 (2001): 65–85.

Betts, Alexander. *Protection by Persuasion: International Cooperation in the Refugee Regime.* New York: Cornell University Press, 2009.

Bevir, Mark, and Rhodes, Richard. *The State as Cultural Practice.* Oxford: Oxford University Press, 2010.

Biden, Joe. "U.S. Rejects 'Sphere of Influence' for Russia." February 7, 2009. http://www.nytimes.com/2009/02/07/world/europe/07iht-07munich.20001384.html?_r=0.

Bisley, Nick. *Great Powers in the Changing International Order.* Boulder: Lynnie Rienner, 2012.

Blainey, Geoffrey. *The Causes of War.* New York: The Free Press, 1988.

Bob, Chris. *The Marketing of Rebellion: Insurgents, Media, and International Activism.* Cambridge: Cambridge University Press, 2005.

Bobbitt, Philip. *The Shield of Achilles: War, Peace and the Course of History.* New York: Knopf, 2002.

Boesenecker, Aaron, and Vinjamuri, Leslie. "Lost in Translation? Civil Society, Faith-Based Organizations and the Negotiation of International Norms." *The International Journal of Transitional Justice* vol. 5 (2011): 345–365.

Börzel, Tanja, and Risse, Thomas. "Governance without a State: Can It Work?" *Regulation & Governance* vol. 4, no. 2 (2010): 113–134.

Boyle, Alan, and Chinkin, Christine. *The Making of International Law.* Oxford: Oxford University Press, 2007.

Bradford, Anu and Posner, Eric. "Universal Exceptionalism in International Law." *Harvard International Law Journal*, vol. 52, no. 1 (2011): 3–54.

Brady, Henry, and Collier, David, eds. *Rethinking Social Inquiry: Diverse Tools, Shared Standards.* Lanham: Rowman, 2004.

Bräuner, Oliver. *Der Klimagipfel von Copenhagen aus der Sicht Chinas. Aus Chinesischen Fachzeitschriften.* Berlin: SWP, 2010.

Braumoeller, Bear. *The Great Powers and the International System.* New York: Cambridge University Press, 2012.

Breitmeier, Helmut. "Institutionelles Design und effektive Problemlösung zum Schutz der Ozonschicht und des globalen Klimas." In *Die Umwelt. Konfliktbearbeitung und Kooperation*, edited by Gerald Mader et al., 50–62. Münster: Agenda Verlag, 2011.

Bremmer, Ian, and Roubini, Nouriel. "A G-Zero World: The New Economic Club Will Produce Conflict, Not Cooperation." http://www.foreignaffairs.com/articles/67339/ian-bremmer-and-nouriel-roubini/a-g-zero-world (accessed May 19, 2011).

Brenton, Anthony. "Great Powers in Climate Politics." In *The Changing Geopolitics of Climate Change. Climate Policy. Special Issue*, edited by Terhalle, Maximilian, and Streck, Charlotte, 541–546. 13:5 (2013).

Brooks, Stephen, and Wohlforth, William. *World Out of Balance: International Relations and the Challenge of American Primacy*. Princeton: Princeton University Press, 2008.

Brooks, Thom. "Introduction to Climate Change Justice," *Political Science and Politics* vol. 46 (2013): 9–12.

Brown, Chris. "The Poverty of Grand Theory." *European Journal of International Relations* vol. 19, no. 3 (2013): 483–497.

Brown, Garrett. "The Constitutionalization of What?" *Global Constitutionalism* vol. 2, no. 1 (2012): 201–228.

Brunnee, Jutta, and Streck, Charlotte. "The UNFCCC as a Negotiation Forum: Towards Common, but More Differentiated Responsibilities." In *The Changing Geopolitics of Climate Change: Special Issue*, edited by Maximilian Terhalle, and Charlotte Streck, 589–607. 13:5 (2013).

Buchanan, Allen, and Keohane, Robert. "The Legitimacy of Global Governance Institutions." *Ethics and International Affairs* vol. 20, no. 4 (2006): 405–437.

Buchsteiner, Jochen. "Entspannungssignale in Bali. Konflikt im Südchinesischen Meer." *Frankfurter Allgemeine Zeitung*, July 21, 2011: 7.

Buchsteiner, Jochen. "Was der EU Fehlt. ei Allen Schwierigkeiten Blickt die Asean Wohlgefällig auf ihr Wirken." *Frankfurter Allgemeine Zeitung*, July 25, 2011: 10.

Busby, Joshua. *Moral Movements and Foreign Policy*. New York: Cambridge University Press, 2010.

Bukovansky, Mlada. "Cynical Rascals or Conscientious Objectors? Interpreting Noncompliance with International Norms." In *On Rules, Politics and Knowledge: Friedrich Kratochwil, International Relations, and Domestic Affairs*, edited by Oliver Kessler et al., 158–177, Basingstoke: Palgrave, 2009.

Bukovansky, Mlada. *Legitimacy and Power Politics*. Princeton: Princeton University Press, 2002.

Bukovansky, Mlada, Clark, Ian, Eckersley, Robyn, Price, Richard, Reus-Smit, Christian, Wheeler, Nicholas J. *Special Responsibilities: Global Problems and American Power*. Cambridge: Cambridge University Press, 2012.

Bulkeley, Harriet, Andonova, Liliana, Bäckstrand, Karin, Betsill, Michele, Compagnon, Daniel, Duffy, Rosaleen, Kolk, Ans, Hoffmann, Matthew, Levy, David, Newell, Peter, Milledge, Tori, Paterson, Matthew, Pattberg, Philipp, and VanDeveer, Stacy. "Governing Climate Change Transnationally: Assessing the Evidence from a Database of Sixty Initiatives," *Environment and Planning C: Government and Policy* vol. 30 (2012): 591–612.

Bull, Hedley. *The Anarchical Society. A Study of Order in World Politics*. New York: Columbia University Press, 1977.

Bull, Hedley. *The Anarchical Society. A Study of Order in World Politics*. New York: Columbia University Press, 2002.

Bull, Hedley. "The Great Irresponsibles? The United States, the Soviet Union, and World Order." *International Journal* vol. 35, no. 3 (1979–80): 438–447.

Buzan, Barry. "Culture and International Society." *International Affairs* vol. 86, no. 1 (2010): 1–25.

Buzan, Barry. *From International to World Society? English School Theory and the Social Structure of Globalisation*. Cambridge: Cambridge University Press, 2004.

Buzan, Barry. "From International System to International Society: Structural Realism and Regime Theory Meet the English School." *International Organization* vol. 47, no. 3 (1993): 327–352.

Buzan, Barry. *People, States and Fear. An Agenda for International Security Studies in the Post-Cold War Era*. Colchester: ECPR Press, 2007.

Buzan, Barry. "The Inaugural Kenneth N. Waltz Annual Lecture. A World Order without Superpowers: Decentered Globalis." *International Relations* vol. 25, no. 1 (2011): 3–25.

Buzan, Barry. *The United States and the Great Powers: World Politics in the Twenty-first Century*. Cambridge: Polity Press, 2004.

Buzan, Barry, and Hansen, Lene. *International Security Studies*. Cambridge: Cambridge University Press, 2009.

Buzan, Barry and Waever, Ole. *Regions and Powers the Structure of International Security*. Cambridge: Cambridge University Press, 2003.

Buzas, Zoltan. "The Color of Threat: Race, Threat Perception, and the Demise of the Anglo-Japanese Alliance. (1902–1923)," *Security Studies* vol. 22, no. 4 (2013): 573–606.

Cable News Network (CNN). "Security Council Discusses Libya No-Fly Zone." March 3, 2011. http://edition.cnn.com/2011/WORLD/africa/03/08/un.libya/ (accessed July 28, 2014).

Callahan, William. "Chinese Visions of World Order: Pots-hegemonic or a New Hegemony." *International Studies Review* vol. 10 (2008): 749–761.

Callahan, William. "Sino-Speak: Chinese Exceptionalism and the Politics of History." *The Journal of Asian Studies* vol. 71, no. 1 (2012): 33–55.

Calleo, David. *Beyond American Hegemony: The Future of the Western Alliance*. New York: Basic Books, 1987.

Campbell, Kurt, "Watch the Rise of Asia's National Security Councils", *Financial Times*, 9 January, 2014. http://blogs.ft.com/the-a-list/2014/01/09/watch-the-rise-of-asias-national-security-councils/ (accessed January 18, 2014).

Carpenter, Chad. "Businesses, Green Groups and the Media: The Role of Non-Governmental Organizations in the Climate Change Debate." *International Affairs* vol. 77, no. 2 (2001): 313–328.

Carr, E.H. *The Twenty Years Crisis, 1919–1939: An Introduction to the Study of International Relations*. London: Palgrave Macmillan, 1946.

Casey, Steven, and Wright, Jonathan, eds. *Mental Maps in the Era of Two World Wars*. London: Palgrave Macmillan, 2008.

Centre for International Governance Innovation (CIGI). "An Unfinished House. Filling the Haps in International Governance" October 29, 2011. http://www.cigionline.org/publications/2012/6/unfinished-house-filling-gaps-international-governance (accessed July 28, 2014).

Chan, Steve. *China, the U.S., and the Power-Transition Theory: A Critique*. London and New York: Routledge, 2008.

Charnovitz, Steven. "Recent Scholarship on NGOs: Review Essay." *American Journal of International Law* vol. 103, no.4 (2009): 777–784.

Charlesworth, Hilary and Coicaud, Jean-Marc, eds. *Fault Lines of International Legitimacy*. New York: Cambridge University Press, 2009.

Charlesworth, Henry and Coicaud, Jean-Marc. *Fault Lines of International Legitimacy*. Cambridge: Cambridge University Press, 2010.

Chayes, A., and Chayes, A. *The New Sovereignty: Compliance with International Regulatory Agreements*. Cambridge: Harvard University Press, 1995.

Chayes, Abram and Chayes, Antonia Handler. "On Compliance." *International Organization* vol. 47, no. 2 (1993): 175–205.

Checkel, Jeffrey. "International Institutions and Socialization in Europe. Introduction and Framework." *International Organization* vol. 59, no. 4 (2005): 801–826.

Chen, Ian, and Yang, Alan. "A Harmonized Southeast Asia? Explanatory Typologies of ASEAN Countries' Startegies to the Rise of China." *The Pacific Review* vol. 26, no. 3 (2013): 265–288.

Christoff, Peter, and Eckersley, Robyn. *Globalization and the Environment.* New York: Rowman & Littlefield, 2013.

China Central Television (CCTV). "Japanese Politicians Begin 3-day-visit to Beijing." May 5, 2014. http://english.cntv.cn/2014/05/05/VIDE 1399281840333301.shtml (accessed May 14, 2014).

China Times. "Respect the Choice of the Libyan People." August 22, 2011. http://thechinatimes.com/online/2011/08/1123.html (accessed July 28, 2012).

Clark, Ian. *Hegemony in International Society.* Oxford: Oxford University Press, 2011.

Clark, Ian. *Legitimacy in International Society.* Oxford: Oxford University Press, 2005.

Clark, Ian. *The Hierarchy of States: Reform and Resistance in the International Order.* Cambridge: Cambridge University Press, 1989.

Claude, Inis. "The Common Defense and Great-Power Responsibilities," *Political Science Quarterly*, vol. 101, no. 5 (1986): 719–732.

Clinton. "Remarks with Chinese Foreign Minister Yang Jiechi," September 5, 2012. http://www.state.gov/secretary/20092013clinton/rm/2012/09/197343.htm

Cochran, Molly. "Charting the Ethics of the English School: What 'Good' Is There in a Middle-Ground Ethics." *International Studies Quarterly* vol. 53, no. 1 (2009): 203–225.

Cohen, Jean. *Globalization and Sovereignty: Rethinking Legality, Legitimacy, and Constitutionalism.* New York: Cambridge University Press, 2012.

Cohrs, Patrick. *The Unfinished Peace.* Cambridge: Cambridge University Press, 2006.

Collier, David. "Typologies: Forming Concepts and Creating Categorical Variables." In *The Oxford Handbook of Political Methodology*, edited by Janet M. Box-Steffensmeier, Henry E. Brady, and David Collier, 152–173. Oxford: Oxford University Press, 2010.

Compagnon, Daniel, Cham, Sander and Mert, Asyem. "The Changing Role of the State." In *Global Environmental Governance Reconsidered*, edited by Frank Biermann, and Philipp Pattberg, 237–263. Cambridge, MA: MIT Press, 2012.

Conceicao-Heldt, Eugenia da. *Negotiating Trade Liberalization at the WTO.* London: Palgrave Macmillan, 2011.

Conrad, Björn. "China in Copenhagen: Reconciling the 'Beijing Climate Revolution' and the 'Copenhagen Climate Obstinacy'." *The China Quarterly* vol. 210 (2012): 435–455.

Conrad, Sebastian, and Sachsenmaier, Dominic. *Competing Visions of World Order. Global Moments and Movements, 1880s–1930s.* London: Palgrave Macmillan, 2007.

Cooley, Alexander, and Ron, James. "The NGO Scramble: Organizational Insecurity and the Political Economy of Transnational Action." *International Security* vol. 27, no. 1 (2002): 5–39.

Cooper, Andrew. "Civil Society Relationship with the G20: An Extension of the G8 Template or Distinctive Pattern of Engagement?" *Global Society* vol. 27, no. 2 (2013): 179–200.

Cooper, Helene. "Hagel Spars with Chinese Over Islands and Security." *New York Times*, April 9, 2014: 6–7.

Council on Foreign Relations (CFR). "ASEAN's Six-Point Principles on the South China Sea." July 20, 2012. http://www.cfr.org/asia-and-pacific/aseans-six-point-principles-south-china-sea/p28915 (accessed July 29, 2014).

Council on Foreign Relations, ed. *The New Arab Revolt. What Has Changed, What It Means, and What Comes Next.* Washington DC, 2011.

Cox, Robert. *Approaches to World Order.* New York: Columbia University Press, 1996.

Cox, Robert. "Gramsci, Hegemony and International Relations: An Essay in Method." In *Gramsci, Historical Materialism and International Relations*, edited by Stephen Gill, 49–66. Cambridge: Cambridge University Press, 1993.

Craig, Gordon, and George, Alexander. *Force and Statecraft. Diplomatic Challenges of Our Time.* New York: Oxford University Press, 1995.

Daase, Christopher. "Die Englische Schule." In *Theorien der Internationalen Beziehungen*, edited by Siegfried Schieder and Manuela Spindler, 243–268. Opladen: Verlag Barbara Budrich, 2006.

Daase, Christopher. "Die Informalisierung internationaler Politik – Beobachtungen zum Stand der internationalen Organisation." In *Die Organisierte Welt: Internationale Beziehungen und Organisationsforschung*, edited by Klaus Dingwerth, Dieter Kerwer and Andreas Nölke, Baden-Baden: Nomos, 2009.

Daase, Christopher. "Theorie der Internationalen Beziehungen." In *Politikwissenschaft in Deutschland*, edited by Irene Gerlach et al., 317–338. Baden-Baden: Nomos Verlag, 2010.

Daase, Christopher, Geis, Anna and Nullmeier, Frank. "Der Aufstieg der Legitimitätspolitik. Rechtfertigung und Kritik politisch-ökonomischer Ordnungen." *Leviathan Sonderband* vol. 40, no. 27 (2012), 11–40.

Daase, Christopher, and Junk, Julian. "Problemorientierung und Methodenpluralismus in den IB." *Zeitschrift für Internationale Beziehungen* vol. 18, no. 2 (2011): 123–136.

Damrosch, Lori, Henkin, Louis, Murphy, Sean and Smit, Hans. *International Law, Cases and Materials.* Los Angeles: West Academic Publishing, 2009.

Darwin, Jacob. *The Empire Project: The Rise and Fall of the British World System, 1830–1970.* Cambridge: Cambridge University Press, 2009.

Davies, Gloria. *Worrying about China: The Language of Chinese Inquiry.* Cambridge: Harvard University Press, 2007.

Declaration of the Heads of State of the Member States of the Shanghai Cooperation Organization on Building a Region of Lasting Peace and Common Prosperity. June 7. http://www.sectsco.org/EN123/show.asp?id=442

De Frouville, Olivier. "Domesticating Civil Society at the United Nations." In *NGOs in International Law: Efficiency in Flexibility?* edited by Pierre-Marie Dupuy and Luisa Vierucci, Cheltenham: Edward Elgar, 2008.

Deudney, Daniel, and Meiser, Jeffrey. "American Exceptionalism." In *US Foreign Policy*, edited by Cox, Michael, and Stokes, Doug, 21–39. Oxford: Oxford University Press, 2012.

Defense Ministry. "Spokesman on China's ADIZ." December 3, 2013. http:// eng.mod.cn/TopNews/2013-12/03/content_4477632.htm (accessed August 7, 2014).

Della Porta, Donatella, and Tarrow, Sidney, eds. *Transnational Protest and Global Activism*. New York: Rowman & Littlefield, 2004.

Deng, Francis, Kimaro, Sadikiel, Lyons, Terrence, Rothschild, Donald and Zartman, William. *Sovereignty as Responsibility: Conflict Management in Africa*. Washington: Brookings, 1996.

Deng, Yong, and Moore, Thomas. "China Views Globalization: Toward a New Great-Power Politics?" *The Washington Quarterly* vol. 27, no. 3 (2004): 117–136.

Depledge, Joanna. "The Outcome from Copenhagen: At the Limits of Global Diplomacy. *Environmental Policy and Law* vol. 40, no. 1 (2010): 17–24.

Dessler, David, and Owen, John. "Constructivism and the Problem of Explanation: A Review Article." In *Perspectives on Politics* vol. 3, no. 3 (2005): 597–610.

Dikötter, Frank. *The Discourse of Race in Modern China*. Stanford, CA: Stanford University Press, 1992.

Dingwerth, Klaus, Kerwer, Dieter, and Nölke, Andreas, eds. *Die Organisierte Welt: Internationale Beziehungen und Organisationsforschung*. Baden-Baden, 2009.

Ditchley Foundation. *The Condition of International Law*. http://www.ditchley.co .uk/conferences/past-programme/2010-2019/2010/international-law, 2010.

Donnelly, Jack. *Realism and International Relations*. Cambridge: Cambridge University Press, 2000.

Doran, Charles. *Systems in Crisis: New Imperatives of High Politics at Century's End*. Cambridge: Cambridge University Press, 1991.

Downie, Christian. "Transnational Actors: Nongovernmental Organizations, Civil Society and Individuals." In *Handbook of Global Environmental Politics*, edited by Paul Harris, 176–186. London: Routledge, 2014.

Doyle, Michael. "Liberalism and World Politics." *American Political Science Review* vol. 80-4 (1986): 1151–1169.

Drezner, Daniel. "The Realist Tradition in American Public Opinion." *Perspectives on Politics* vol. 6, no. 1 (2008): 51–70.

Drezner, Daniel. *The System Worked*. New York: Oxford University Press, 2014.

Drezner, Dan. *All Politics Is Global. Explaining International Regulatory Regimes*. Princeton: Princeton University Press, 2007.

Dueck, Colin. *Reluctant Crusaders: Power, Culture, and Change in American Grand Strategy*. Princeton: Princeton University Press, 2006.

Dung, Nguyen. Keynote Address (12th IISS Asia Security Summit, Shangri-La Dialogue), May 31, 2013. www.iiss.org (accessed September 11, 2013).

Dunne, Tim. "The English School." In *The Oxford Handbook of International Relations*, edited by Christian Reus-Smit and Duncan Snidal, 267–285. Oxford: Oxford University Press, 2008.

Dunne, Tim. *Inventing International Society: A History of the English School*. Basingstoke: Macmillan 1998.

Dupuy, Florian, and Dupuy, Pierre-Marie 2013. "A Legal Analysis of China's Historic Rights Claim in the South China Sea." *The American Journal of International Law* vol. 107, no. 1 (2013): 124–141.

Dunoff, Jeffrey, and Trachman, Joel, eds. *Ruling the World? Constitutionalism, International Law, and Global Governance*. New York: Cambridge University Press, 2009.

Dutton, Peter, ed. "Military Activities in the EEZ: A US-China Dialogue on Security and International Law in the Maritime Commons." Newport: US Navy War College, 2010. https://www.usnwc.edu/Research--Gaming/China-Maritime-Studies-Institute/Publications/documents/China-Maritime-Study-7_Military-Activities-in-the-.pdf (accessed August 7, 2014).

Dutton, Peter. "The Sino-Philippine Maritime Row: International Arbitration and the South China Sea." In *East and South China Seas Bulletin # 10 (2013)*. http://www.cnas.org/files/documents/publications/CNAS_Bulletin_Dutton_TheSinoPhilippineMaritimeRow_0.pdf (accessed August 7, 2014).

Dyer, Geoff, and Anderlini, Jamil. "China's Lending Hits New Heights." January 17, 2011 (accessed January 28, 2011), http://www.ft.com/intl/cms/s/0/488c60f4-2281-11e0-b6a2-00144feab49a.html#axzz3EuBxetXR2011

Eckersley, Robyn. "Global Environment." In *US Foreign Policy*, edited by Cox, Michael, and Stokes, Doug, 351–373. Oxford. Oxford University Press, 2012.

Economist. "An Interview with Hillary Clinton." March 22. http://www.economist.com/blogs/lexington/2012/03/foreign-policy 2012

Economist. "A Special Report on China's Place in the World." December 4, p. 3. 2010.

Edmondson, Beth, and Levy, Stuart. *Climate Change and Order: The End of Prosperity and Democracy*. New York: Palgrave Macmillan, 2013.

Eichengreen, Barry. "Hegemonic Stability Theories of the International Monetary System," *NBER Working Papers* vol. 2193, (1987): 1–30.

Ekbladah, David. *The Great American Mission: Modernization and the Construction of an American World Order, 1914 to the Present*. Princeton: Princeton University Press, 2010.

Emmers, Ralf. *ASEAN and the Institutionalization of East Asia*. London: Routledge, 2012.

Emmers, Ralf. *Geopolitics and Maritime Territorial Disputes in East Asia*. New York: Routledge, 2010.

Emanuel Adler and Vincent Pouliot, eds. *International Practices*. Cambridge and New York: Cambridge University Press, 2011.

Epstein, Charlotte. "Forum: Interrogating the Use of Norms in International Relations: Postcolonial Perspectives." *International Theory* vol. 6, no. 2 (2014): 293–390.

Epstein, Charlotte. "Stop Telling Us How to Behave: Socialization or Infantilization?" *International Studies Perspectives* vol. 13, no. 2 (2012): 135–145.

Evans, Gareth. *The Responsibility to Protect: Ending Mass Atrocity Crimes Once and For All*. Washington: Brookings Institution Press, 2008.

Evans, Gareth, Thakur, Ramesh, and Pape, Robert. "Correspondence: Humanitarian Intervention and the Responsibility to Protect." *International Security* vol. 37, no. 4 (2013): 199–214.

Falk, Richard, Juergensmeyer, Mark and Popovski, Vesselin eds. *Legality and Legitimacy in Global Affairs*. New York: Oxford University Press, 2012.

Fawcett, Louise. *International Relations of the Middle East*. Oxford: Oxford University Press, 2013.

Fawcett, Louise and Hurrell, Andrew. *Regionalism in World Politics: Regional Organization and International Order*. Oxford: Oxford University Press, 1995.

Fearon, James. "Rationalist Explanations for War." *International Organization* vol. 49, no. 3 (1995): 379–414.

Ferguson, Niall. *Empire: How Britain Made the Modern World*. London: Penguin, 2003.

Figueres, Christiana. "Climate Policy: A New Foundation of Stability and Prosperity." In *The Changing Geopolitics of Climate Change*. *Special Issue*, edited by Maximilian Terhalle, and Charlotte Streck, 538–540. 13:5 (2013).

Finnemore, Martha and Sikkink, Kathryn. "International Norm Dynamics and Political Change." *International Organization* vol. 52, no. 4 (1998): 887–917.

Fisher, Dana. "COP-15 in Copenhagen: How the Merging of Movements Left Civil Society Out in the Cold." *Global Environmental Politics* vol. 10, no. 2 (2010): 11–17.

Florini, Ann ed. *The Third Force: The Rise of Transnational Civil Society*. Washington, DC: Brookings, 2000.

Foley, Michael. "Bringing Realism to American Liberalism: Waltz and the Process of Cold War Adjustment." In *Realism and World Politics*, edited by Ken Booth, 35–49. London: Routledge, 2011.

Foot, Rosemary. "Asia's Cooperation and Governance: The Role of East Asian Regional Organizations in Regional Governance: Constraints and Contributions. Japanese." *Journal of Political Science* vol. 13, no. 1 (2012): 133–142.

Foot, Rosemary. "China and the United States: Between Cold and Warm Peace." *Survival* vol. 51, no. 6 (2009): 123–146.

Foot, Rosemary, and Walter, Andrew. *China, the United States, and Global Order*. Cambridge: Cambridge University Press, 2011.

Foreign Policy. "Nine of the World's Top International Relations Scholars Weigh in on the Ivory Tower Survey." January/February 2012. http://www.foreignpolicy.com (accessed July 30, 2014).

Franck, Thomas. *The Power of Legitimacy among Nations*. New York: Oxford University Press, 1990.

Frankfurter Allgemeine Zeitung. "China fühlt sich von Amerika und Japan provoziert." June 2, 2014.

Frankfurter Allgemeine Zeitung (FAZ). "China kritisiert Waffengeschäft mit Taiwan." September 23, 2011, p. 6.

Frankfurter Allgemeine Zeitung (FAZ). "Chinas Militär warnt vor einem 'zufälligen' Krieg." February 7, 2013 (www.faz.net)

Frankfurter Allgemeine Zeitung (FAZ). "Südchinesisches Meer: Unfallgefahr in der Badewanne. " April 26, 2012 (www.faz.net/-gq5-6zf7c)

Frankfurter Allgemeine Zeitung. (FAZ). "Vor dem G-20-Gipfel: Das Ende der Chinesischen Zurückhaltung. March 31, 2009." http://www.faz.net/aktuell/politik/ausland/vor-dem-g-20-gipfel-das-ende-der-chinesischen-zurueckhaltung-1920555.html (accessed August 7, 2014).

Frechette, Louise. "International Governance, the G8 and Globalization." www.g8.utoronto.ca/scholar/frechette-2007.pdf, 2007.

Freeden, Michael, Sargent, Lyman Tower and Stears, Marc. *The Oxford Handbook of Political Ideologies*. Oxford: Oxford University Press, 2013.

Friedman, Edward. "Power Transition Theory: A Challenge to the Peaceful Rise of World Power China." In *China's Rise – Threat or Opportunity?* edited by Yee and Herbert, 11–32. London : Routledge, 2011.

Friedman, Max. *Re-thinking Anti-Americanism: The History of an Exceptional Concept in American Foreign Relations*. Cambridge: Cambridge University Press, 2012.

Foot, Rosemary and MacFarlane, Neil. *US Hegemony and International Organizations: The United States and Multilateral Institutions*. Oxford: Oxford University Press, 2003.

Gamble, Andrew. "The Politics of Deadlocks." In *Deadlocks in Multilateral Negotiations: Causes and Consequences*, edited by Amrita Narlikar, 25–46. Cambridge: Cambridge University Press, 2011.

Gao, Zhiguo, and Jia, Bing. "The Nine-Dash Line in the South China Sea: History, status and Implications." *The American Journal of International Law* vol. 107, no. 1 (2013): 98–124.

Gat, Azar. *Victorious and Vulnerable: Why Democracy Won in the 20th Century and How It Is Still Imperiled*. New York: Rowman & Little, 2010.

Gause, Gregory. *The International Relations of the Persian Gulf*. Cambridge: Cambridge University Press, 2010.

Gelpi, Christopher. *The Power of Legitimacy. The Role of Norms in Crisis Bargaining*. Princeton: Princeton University Press, 2003.

German Federal Budget (2009), "Bundestag Verabschiedet Rekordhaushalt." http://www.faz.net/aktuell/politik/inland/290-milliarden-euro-bundestag -verabschiedet-rekordhaushalt-1728111.html (accessed January 18, 2013).

German Federal Budget (2010), "Bundestag Beschließt den Haushalt 2010." http://www.bundestag.de/dokumente/textarchiv/2010/28886051_kw11 _vorschau/201244.

German Federal Budget. www.bundestag.de (accessed May 19, 2011).

Gerring, John. *Case Study Research: Principles and Practices*. Cambridge: Cambridge University Press, 2007.

Gerring, John. *Case Selection for Case-Study Analysis: Qualitative and Quantitative Techniques. The Oxford Handbook of Political Methodology*, edited by Janet M. Box-Steffensmeier, Henry E. Brady, and David Collier. Oxford UP, 2010.

Geyer, Michael, and Bright, Charles. "Regimes of World Order: Global Integration and the Production of Difference in Twentieth Century World History." In *Interactions: Transregional Perspectives on World History*, edited by Jerry H. Bentley et al., 202–238. Honolulu: University of Hawai'i Press, 2005.

Giddens, Anthony. *Runaway World: How Globalization Is Reshaping Our Lives*. London: Routledge 2000.

Gilman, Nils. *Mandarins of the Future: Modernization Theory in Cold War America*. Baltimore: Johns Hopkins University Press, 2003.

Gilpin, Robert. *The Multinational Corporation and the National Interest (Prepared for the Committee on Labor and Public Welfare, United States Senate)*. Washington: U.S. Government Printing, 1973.

Gilpin, Robert. "The Politics of Transnational Economic Relations." In *Transnational Relations and World Politics*, edited by Robert Keohane and Joseph Nye, 48–69. Cambridge: Harvard University Press, 1972.

Gilpin, Robert. *War and Change in World Politics*. Princeton: Princeton University Press, 1981.

Gladwell, Malcolm. *The Tipping Point: How Little Things Can Make a Big Difference*. New York: Little Brown, 2000.

Goh, Evelyn. *Constructing the US Rapprochement with China, 1961–1974: From Red Menace to Tacit Ally*. Cambridge: Cambridge University Press, 2005.

Goh, Evelyn. "Great Powers and Hierarchical Order in Southeast Asia. Analyzing Regional Security Strategies." *International Security* vol. 32, no. 3 (2007): 113–157.

Goh, Evelyn. "Institutions and the Great Power Bargain in East Asia: ASEAN's Limited 'Brokerage' Role." *International Relations of the Asia-Pacific* vol. 11, no. 3 (2011): 373–401.

Goh, Evelyn. *The Struggle for Order: Hegemony, Resistance and Transition in Post-Cold War East Asia*. Oxford: Oxford University Press, 2013.

Goldstein, Judith, Kahler, Miles, Keohane, Robert O. and Slaughter, Anne-Marie. "Introduction: Legalization and World Politics" *International Organization* vol. 54, no. 3 (2000): 385–399.

Goldstein, Judith, Kahler, Miles, Keohane, Robert, and Slaughter, Anne-Marie, eds. *Legalization and World Politics*. Cambridge: MIT Press, 2001.

Goldstein, Judith, and Keohane, Robert. *Ideas and Foreign Policy: Beliefs, Institutions, and Political Change*. Ithaca: Cornell University Press, 1993.

Gong, Gerrit. *The Standard of Civilization in International Society*. Oxford: Oxford University Press, 1984.

Goodrich, Lloyd, and Carroll, Matthew, eds. *Documents on American Foreign Relations* vol. 3. Princeton: Princeton University Press, 1947.

Gourevitch, Peter et al. *The Credibility of Transnational NGOs: When Virtue Is Not Enough*. New York: Cambridge University Press, 2012.

Granovetter, Marc. "Threshold Models of Collective Behavior." *American Journal of Sociology* vol. 83, no. 6 (1978): 1420–1443.

Grieco, Joseph. *Cooperation among Nations*. Ithaca: Cornell University Press, 1990.

Gruber, Lloyd. "Globalization with Growth and Equity: Can We Really Have It All?" *Third World Quarterly* vol. 32, no. 4 (2011): 629–652.

Gruber, Lloyd "Power Politics and the Institutionalization of International Relations." In *Power in Global Governance. Cambridge Studies in International Relations*, edited by Barnett Michael and Duvall Raymond, 102–129. London: Cambridge University Press, 2005.

Gruber, Lloyd. *Ruling the World: Power Politics and the Rise of Supranational Institutions*. Princeton, NJ: Princeton University Press, 2000.

Guangjin, Cheng, and Yingzi, Tan. "Vice-President's Trip to Address 'Trust Deficit' with US." *China Daily*, February 10, 2012. http://www.chinadaily.com.cn/cndy/2012/02/10/content_14573690.htm (accessed July 30, 2014).

Gungwu, Wang. *The Chineseness of China*. Hongkong: Oxford University Press, 1991.

Habermas, Jürgen. *Faktizität und Geltung. Beiträge zur Diskurstheorie des Rechts und des demokratischen Rechtsstaats*. Frankfurt: Suhrkamp, 1992.

Hallding, Karl, Olsson, Marie, Vihma, Anton and Carson, Markus. *Together Alone: BASIC Countries and the Climate Change Conundrum*. Stockholm: Environment Institute, 2011.

Halliday, Fred. "International Relations in a post-hegemonic age." *International Affairs* vol. 85, no. 1 (2009): 37–51.

Halper, Stefan. *The Beijing Consensus: How China's Authoritarian Model Will Dominate the 21st Century*. New York: Basic Books, 2010.

Hartz, Louis. *The Liberal Tradition in America*. New York: Harcourt, 1955.

Haslam, John. *Russia's Cold War: From the October Revolution to the Fall of the Wall*. New Haven: Yale University Press, 2011.

Haufler, Virginia. "Transnational Actors and Environmental Governance." In *Governing the Environment: Interdisciplinary Perspectives*, edited by Magali Delmas and Oran Young, 119–134. New York: Cambridge University Press, 2009.

Hawkins, Darren. *Delegation and Agency in International Organizations*. New York: Cambridge UP, 2006.

Hearn, Adrian. "China, Global Governance and the Future of Cuba." *Journal of Current Chinese Affairs* vol. 41, no. 1 (2012): 155–179.

Held, David. *Global Covenant: The Social Democratic Alternative to the Washington Consensus*. Cambridge: Polity, 2004.

Held, David and Hale, Thomas. *Gridlock: Why Global Cooperation Is Failing when We Need It Most*. Polity: Cambridge University Press, 2013.

Held, David and McGrew, Antony. *Global Transformations: Politics, Economics and Culture*. Stanford: Stanford University Press, 1999.

Hellmann, Gunther. "Pragmatismus." http://www.fb03.uni-frankfurt.de/48145 591/Pragmatismus_Hellmann.pdf, 2003.

Hickmann, Thomas. *The Reconfiguration of Authority in Global Climate Policy-Making: The Interplay between Bottom-Up Governance Arrangements and the International Climate Change*. Unpublished manuscript, Presented at the ECPR General Conference. Bordeaux September, 2013.

Hinnebusch, Raymond. "Syria: from Authoritarian Upgrading to Revolution?" *International Affairs* vol. 88, no. 1 (2012): 95–113.

Hochstetler, Kathryn. "Civil Society." In *The Oxford Handbook of Modern Diplomacy*, edited by Cooper, Andrew, Heine, Jorge, Thakur, Ramesh. Oxford: Oxford University Press, 2013, 176–191.

Hodgson, Godfrey. *The Myth of American Exceptionalism*. New Haven: Yale University Press, 2009.

Hoff, Joan. *A Faustian Foreign Policy from Woodrow Wilson to George W. Bush: Dreams of Perfectibility*. New York: Cambridge University Press, 2008.

Holbraad, Carsten. *Superpowers and International Conflict*. London: Palgrave Macmillan, 1979.

Holsti, Kal. "Exceptionalism in American Foreign Policy: Is It Exceptional?" *European Journal of International Relations* vol. 17, no. 3 (2010): 381–404.

Honneth, Alex. *Critical Theory, in: Anthony Giddens und Jonathan Turner (Hg.): Social Theory Today*. Cambridge: Polity Press, 1987, 347–382.

Hotta, Eri. *Japan 1941: Countdown to Infamy*. New York: Knopf, 2013.

Hovi, Jon, Bang, Guri, and Sprinz, Detlef. "Why the United States Did Not Become a Party to the Kyoto Protocol: German, Norwegian and U.S. Perspectives." *European Journal of International Relations* vol. 18 (2012): 129–150.

Huang, Jing. "China's Approach and Perception Towards Informal Multilateral Groupings." October 2010. http://www.icrier.org/pdf/Jing-Heiligendamm _Paper_1.pdf (accessed August 5, 2014).

Hughes, Christopher. *Chinese Nationalism in the Global Era*. London: Routledge 2006.

Hunt, Michael. *The American Ascendancy: How the U.S. Gained and Wielded Global Dominance*. University of North Carolina Press, 2007.

Huntington, Samuel. *The Clash of Civilizations and the Remaking of World Order*. New York: Simon & Schuster, 1994.

Huntington, Samuel. *The Clash of Civilizations*. New York: Simon & Schuster, 1996

Hurd, Ian, and Cronin, Bruce, eds. *The United Nations Security Council and Global Governance*. New York, 2008.

Hurd, Ian. *After Anarchy: Legitimacy and Power in the United Nations Security Council*. Princeton: Princeton University Press, 2007.

Hurd, Ian. "Legitimacy and Authority in International Politics." *International Organization* vol. 53, no. 2 (1999): 379–408.

Hurrell, Andrew. "ESIL Keynote Speech. International Law 1989–2010: A Performance Appraisal." August, 2010. http://www.esil-en.law.cam.ac.uk/Media/papers/Hurrell_ESIL2010_Keynote.pdf (accessed August 5, 2014).

Hurrell, Andrew. "Hegemony, liberalism and global order: What Space for Would-Be Great Powers." In *International Affairs* vol. 82, no. 1 (2006): 1–19.

Hurrell, Andrew. *On Global Order: Power, Values, and the Constitution of International Society*. Oxford: Oxford University Press, 2007.

Hurrell, Andrew. "Order and Justice." In *Order and Justice in International Relations*, edited by Rosemary, Foot et al., 24–48. Oxford: Oxford University Press, 2003.

Hurrell, Andrew. "Power Transitions, Emerging Powers, and the Shifting Terrain of the Middle Ground." In *Ethical Reasoning in International Affairs: Arguments from the Middle Ground*, edited by Cornelia Navari, 222–245. Basingstoke: Palgrave Macmillan, 2013.

Hurrell, Andrew. "Security and Inequality." In *Inequality, Globalization, and World Politics*, edited by Andrew Hurrell and Ngaire Woods, 248–271. Oxford: Oxford University Press, 1999.

Hurrell, Andrew, and Gupta, Sandeep. "Emerging Powers, North–South Relations and Global Climate Politics." *International Affairs* vol. 88, no. 3 (2012): 463–484.

Ignatieff, Michael, ed. *American Exceptionalism and Human Rights*. Princeton: Princeton University Press, 2005.

Ignatieff, Michael. "We're So Exceptional." http://www.nybooks.com/articles/archives/2012/apr/05/were-so-exceptional/ 4/5/2012.

IISS. *Strategic Survey*. London: Routledge, 2010.

IISS. *Strategic Survey*. London: Routledge, 2011.

IISS. *Strategic Survey*. London: Routledge, 2012.

Ikenberry, John. *After Victory. Institutions, Strategic Restraint, and the Rebuilding of Order after Major Wars*. New Jersey: Princeton University Press, 2001.

Ikenberry, John. *Liberal Leviathan. The Origins, Crisis, and Transformation of the American World Order*. New Jersey: Princeton University Press, 2011.

Ikenberry, John. "The Myth of the Autocratic Revival. Why Liberal Democracy Will Prevail." *Foreign Affairs* vol. 89, no. 3 (2009): 90–96.

Ikenberry, John and Slaughter, Anne-Marie. "Forging a World of Liberty Under Law." Final Report of the Princeton Project on National Security. 2006. http://www.world-governance.org/IMG/pdf_080_Forging_a_world_of_liberty_under_law.pdf

Iriye, Ariya. *Global Community*. Berkeley: University of California Press, 2002.

Jacques, Martin. *When China Rules the World*. London: Penguin, 2009.

Jacques, Martin. *When China Rules the World: The End of the Western World and the Birth of a New Global Order*. London: Penguin Books, 2011.

Jackson, Patrick. *The Conduct of Inquiry in International Relations*. New York: Routledge, 2010.

Jackson, Robert. *Sovereignty: Evolution of an Idea*. Cambridge: Polity Press, 2007.

Jackson, Robert. *The Global Covenant: Human Conduct in a World of States*. Oxford: Oxford University Press, 2000.

Jackson, Robert J. and Towle, Philip. *Temptations of Power: The United States in Global Politics after 9/11*. Houdmills: Palgrave, 2006.

Jakarta Post. "Guidelines Prove that ASEAN and China Can Deliver Results: Marty." July 21, 2011. http://www.thejakartapost.com/news/2011/07/21/guide lines-prove-asean-china-can-deliver-results-marty.html (accessed August 5, 2014).

James, Harold. "International Order after the Financial Crisis." *International Affairs* vol. 87, no. 3 (2011): 525–537.

Jervis, Robert. "A Political Science Perspective on the Balance of Power and the Concert." *American Historical Review* vol. 97 (June 1992): 716–724.

Jervis, Robert. "From Balance to Concert: A Study of International Security Cooperation." *World Politics* vol. 38, no. 1 (October 1985): 58–79.

Jervis, Robert. *Perception and Misperception in International Politics*. Princeton: Princeton University Press, 1976.

Jervis, Robert. "The Future of World Politics." *International Security* vol. 16, no. 3 (1991–1992), 39–73.

Jervis, Robert. "Theories of War in an Era of Leading-Power Peace: Presidential Address, American Political Science Association, 2001." *American Political Science Review* vol. 96, no. 1 (2002): 1–14.

Jervis, Robert. "The Remaking of a Unipolar World." *Washington Quarterly* vol. 17, no. 3 (2006): 51–70.

Jervis, Robert. "Unipolarity: A Structural Perspective." *World Politics* vol. 61, no. 1 (2009): 188–213.

Jetschke, Anja. "ASEAN." In *Handbook of Asian Regionalism*, edited by Mark Beeson and Richard Stubbs, 338–349. New York: Routledge, 2010.

Jetschke, Anja. "ASEAN." In *Routledge Handbook of Asian Regionalism*, edited by Mark Beeson and Richard Stubbs, 327–338. New York: Routledge, 2011.

Jiechi, Yang. "China Underlines Fairness, Effectiveness in Conducting Global Governance." September 27, 2012. http://english.cntv.cn/20120928/103421 .shtml (accessed April 14, 2014).

Jiechi, Yang. "Statement in Front of the UN General Assembly." September 27, 2012. http://daccess-dds-ny.un.org/doc/UNDOC/GEN/N12/523/49/PDF/ N1252349.pdf?OpenElement, pp. 25–29.

Jing, Huang. "China's Approach and Perception Towards Informal Multilateral Groupings." *The Indian Council for Research on International Economic Relations (ICRIER)* vol. 1 October 2010. http://www.icrier.org/pdf/Jing-Heilegendamm _Paper_1.pdf

Jintao, Hu. "Continuing to Promote the Noble Cause of Peace and Development of Mankind: Full text of Hu Jintao's report at 18th Party Congress." November 17, 2012. http://news.xinhuanet.com/english/special/18cpcnc/ 2012-11/17/c_131981259_12.htm (accessed December 30, 2012).

Jintao, Hu. "Chinese President Hu's Speech at G20 Summit in Cannes." http:// news.xinhuanet.com/english2010/china/2011-11/04/c_131228470.htm, 2011 (accessed November 9, 2012).

Jintao, Hu. "Promote Growth through Win-Win Cooperation." November 3, 2011. www.fmprc.gov.cn/eng/zxxx/t875041.htm (accessed August 7, 2014).

Johnson, Tana, and Urpelainen, Johannes. "A Strategic Theory of Regime Integration and Separation." *International Organization* vol. 66, no. 3 (2012): 645–677.

Johnston, Alastair. *Social States*. Princeton: Princeton University Press, 2008.

Johnston, Iain, Chen, Dingding, and Pu, Xiaoyu. "Correspondence: Debating China's Assertiveness." *International Security* vol. 38, no. 3 (2014): 176–183.

Kagan, Robert. "The September 12 Paradigm." *Foreign Affairs* vol. 87, no. 5 (2008): 53–60.

Kahler, Miles. "Multilateralism with Small and Large Numbers." In *Multilateralism Matters*, edited by John Gerard Ruggie, 295–326. New York: Columbia University Press, 1993.

Kang, David. "Getting Asia Wrong: The Need for New Analytical Frameworks." *International Security* vol. 27, no. 4 (2003): 57–85.

Katzenstein, Peter. *Anglo-America and Its Discontents: Civilizational Identities beyond West and East*. Routledge: London, 2011.

Katzenstein, Peter, ed. *Civilizations in World Politics: Plural and Pluralist Perspectives*. New York: Routledge, 2010.

Katzenstein, Peter and Sil, Rudra. *Beyond Paradigms: Analytic Eclecticism in the Study of World Politics*. New York: Palgrave Macmillan, 2010.

Katzenstein, Peter and Sil, Rudra. "Eclectic Theorizing in the Study and Practice of International Relations." In *The Oxford Handbook of International Relations*, edited by Duncan Snidal and Cristian Reus-Smit, 109–130. New York: Oxford University Press, 2008.

Kaul, Inge, Grunberg, Isabelle and Stern, Marc A. *Global Public Goods: International Cooperation in the 21st Century*. New York: Oxford University Press, 1999.

Keal, Paul. *Unspoken Rules and Superpower Dominance*. London: Macmillan, 1983.

Keck, Margaret, and Sikkink, Kathryn. "Transnational Advocacy Networks in International and Regional Politics." *International Social Science Journal* vol. 159 (2000): 25–42.

Kennan, George. *The Decline of Bismarck's European Order: Franco-Russian Relations 1875–1890*. Princeton: Princeton University Press, 1979.

Kennedy, David. "Challenging Expert Rule: The Politics of Global Governance." *Sydney Journal of International Law* vol. 27 (2005): 5–28.

Kennedy, David. "New World Order: Yesterday, Today, and Tomorrow." *Transnational Law & Comtemporary Problems* vol. 4 (1994): 329–379.

Kennedy, David. "The Mystery of Global Governance." *Ohio Northern University Law Review* vol. 34 (2008): 827–860.

Keohane, Robert. *After Hegemony*. New Jersey: Princeton University Press, 1984.

Keohane, Robert. "Governance in a Partially Globalized World." *American Political Science Review* vol. 95, no. 1 (March 2001): 1–13.

Keohane, Robert. *International Institutions and State Power: Essays in International Relations Theory*. Boulder: Westview, 1989.

Keohane, Robert. *Power and Interdependence in a Partially Globalized World*. Routledge: New York, 2002.

Keohane, Robert. "Twenty Years of Institutional Liberalism." *International Relations* vol. 26, no. 2 (2012): 125–138.

Keohane, Robert and Buchanan, Charles. "The Preventive Use of Force: A Cosmopolitan Institutional Proposal." *Ethics and International Affairs* vol. 18, no. 1 (2004): 1–22.

Keohane, Robert, and Victor, David. "The Regime Complex for Climate Change." *Perspectives on Politics* vol. 9, no. 1 (2011): 7–23.

Kessler, Oliver, and Herborth, Benjamin. "Recognition and the Constitution of Social Order." *International Theory* vol. 5, no. 1 (2013): 155–160.

Keqiang 2014, *Speech Given in February* (translated by Liwen Qin, MERICS).

Khong, Yuen, "Negotiating Order during Power Transitions." In *Power in Transition: The Peaceful Change of International Order*, edited by Kupchan, Charles, 34–67. Tokyo: United Nations University Press, 2001.

Khong, Yuen. "Primacy or World Order? The United States and China's Rise – A Review Essay." *International Security* vol. 38, no. 3 (2014): 153–175.

Ki-Moon, Ban. "Address to Ministerial Roundtable." *Responsibility to Protect: Responding to the Imminent Threats of Mass Atrocities*. New York City, September 23, 2011. http://www.un.org/news/press/docs/2011/sgsm13838.doc.htm (accessed August 5, 2014).

Kindleberger, Charles. *The World in Depression, 1929–1939*. Berkeley: University of California Press, 1973.

King, Gary, Verba, Sidney, and Keohane, Robert. *Designing Social Inquiry: Scientific Inference in Qualitative Research*. Princeton: Princeton University Press, 1994.

Kingsbury, Benedict and Krisch, Nico, "The Emergence of Global Administrative Law." *Law and Contemporary Problems* vol. 68, no.1 (2005).

Kingsbury, Damien, and Avonius, Leena. *Human Rights in Asia: A Reassessment of the Asian Values Debate*. New York: Palgrave Macmillan, 2008.

Kissinger, Henry. *On China*. New York: Penguin, 2011.

Kissinger, Henry. *On China*. New York: Penguin, 2013.

Klabbers, Jan. "Global Governance at the ICJ: Re-reading the WHA Opinion." *Max Planck Yearbook of United Nations Law* vol. 13 (2009): 1–28.

Koh, Tommy. "Asian Values Reconsidered." *Asia-Pacific Review* vol. 7, no. 1 (2000): 131–136.

Koppell, Jonathan. "Review Article." *Perspectives on Politics* vol. 11, no. 1 (2013): 222–224.

Koppell, Jonathan. *World Rule: Accountability, Legitimacy, and the Design of Global Governance*. Chicago. 2010.

Koremenos, B., Lipson, Charles, and Snidal, Duncan. *Rational Design of International Institutions*. Cambridge: Cambridge University Press, 2004.

Koremenos, Barabara et al. "The Rational Design of International Institutions." *International Organization* vol. 55, no. 4 (2001): 761–799.

Koskenniemi, Martti. "Hegemonic Regimes." In *Regime Interaction in International Law: Facing Fragmentation*, edited by Margaret A. Young, 305–324. Cambridge: Cambridge University Press, 2012.

Koskenniemi, Martti. "The Politics of International Law: Twenty Years Later." *European Journal of International Law* vol. 20 (2009): 7–19.

Koskenniemi, Martti. *The Politics of International Law*. Oxford: Oxford University Press, 2011.

Krämer, Ludwig. "Transnational Access to Environmental Information." *Transnational Environmental Law* vol. 1, no. 1 (2012): 95–104.

Krasner, Stephen. "Global Communications and National Power: Life on the Pareto Frontier." *World Politics* vol. 43, no. 3 (1991): 336–366.

Krasner, Stephen D. *Sovereignty. Organized Hypocrisy.* New Jersey: Princeton University Press, 1999.

Krasner, Stephen D. "State Power and the Structure of International Trade." *World Politics* vol. 28, no. 3 (1976): 317–347.

Kratochwil, Friedrich. *The Status of Law in World Society: Meditations on the Role and Rule of Law.* New York: Cambridge UP, 2014.

Kratochwil, Friedrich and Ruggie, John. "International Organization: A State of the Art on an Art of the State." *International Organization,* vol. 40, no. 4 (Autumn, 1986), pp. 753–775.

Krieger, Leonard, and Stern, Fritz. *The Responsibility of Power: Historical Essays in Honor of Hajo Holborn.* New York: Palgrave Macmillan, 1967.

Kuhn, Thomas. *The Structure of Scientific Revolutions.* Chicago: Chicago UP, 1962.

Kurth, James. "The United States as a Civilizational Leader." In *Civilizations in World Politics: Plural and Pluralist Perspectives,* edited by Peter Katzenstein, 41–66. London: Routledge, 2010.

Lake, David. "Great Power Hierarchies and Strategies in Twenty-First Century World Politics." In *Handbook of International Relations,* edited by Walter Carlnaes, Thomas Risse and Beth Simmons, 555–577. Los Angeles: Sage, 2013.

Lake, David. "International Economic Structures and American Foreign Economic Policy, 1887–1934." *World Politics* vol. 35, no. 4 (July 1983): 517–43.

Lake, David. "Two Cheers for Bargaining Theory: Assessing Rationalist Explanations of the Iraq War." *International Security* vol. 35, no. 3 (2010/11): 7–52.

Lawson, Fred. *Constructing International Relations in the Arab World.* Stanford: Stanford University Press, 2006.

Lawson, Fred. "Syria's Relations with Iran: Managing the Dilemmas of Alliance." *Middle East Journal* vol. 61, no. 1 (2007): 186–205.

Layne, Christopher. "US Decline." In *US Foreign Policy,* edited by Michael Cox. Oxford: Oxford University Press, 410–420. 2012.

Lebow, Ned. "Review article: Philosophy and International Relations." *International Affairs* vol. 87, no. 5 (2011): 1219–1228.

Lebow, Ned, and Reich, Simon. *Good-Bye, Hegemony! Power and Influence in the Global System.* Princeton: Princeton University Press, 2014.

Le Yucheng. "On the Peaceful Rise of China." The Script of Remarks by Mr. Le Yucheng, Director General of Policy Planning Department, Chinese Ministry of Foreign Affairs in the Center for International & Strategic Studies, Peking University, June 11, 2011. http://www.ciss.pku.edu.cn/En/DocumentViewForMac.aspx?id=700 (accessed August 5, 2014).

Lee, F.E. "Senate Representation and Coalition Building in Distributive Politics." *American Political Science Review* vol. 94, no. 1 (2000): 59–72.

Legro, Jeff. *Rethinking the World: Great Power Strategies and International Order.* Ithaca: Cornell University Press, 2007.

Levy, Jack. "Power Transition Theory and the Rise of China." In *China's Ascent: Power, Security, and the Future of International Politics,* edited by Robert S. Ross and Zhu Feng, 11–33. Ithaca, NY: Cornell University Press, 2008.

Liang, Zhi. *Recent Trends in the Study of Cold War History in China.* Woodrow Wilson Center, Washington, DC. October, 2012. http://www.wilsoncenter.org/sites/default/files/ECNU-WWICS_Occassional_Paper__Recent_Trends_in_the_Study_of_Cold_War_History_in_China.pdf (accessed August 5, 2014).

Lieberthal, Kenneth and Jisi, Wang. *Adressing US_China Strategic Distrust.* 2012. http://www.brookings.edu/~/media/research/files/papers/2012/3/30% 20us%20china%20lieberthal/0330_china_lieberthal.pdf

Lieberthal, Kenneth, and Sandalow, David. *Overcoming Obstacles to U.S.-China Cooperation on Climate Change.* Washington: Brookings Institution, 2009.

Linklater, Andrew. *The Transformation of Political Community: Ethical Foundations of the Post-Westphalian Era.* Cambridge: Polity Press, 1998.

Linklater, Andrew, and Suganami, Hidemi. *The English School of International Relations: A Contemporary Reassessment.* Cambridge: Cambridge University Press, 2006.

Lipset, Seymour. *American Exceptionalism: A Double-edged Sword.* W.W. Norton, 1997.

Little, Richard. "International Regimes." In *The Globalization of World Politics: An Introduction to International Relations,* 369–386. Oxford: Oxford University Press, 2006.

Little, Richard. *The Balance of Power in International Relations. Metaphors, Myths, and Models.* Cambridge: Cambridge University Press, 2007.

Little, Richard, and Wohlforth, William. *The Balance of Power in World History.* London: Palgrave Macmillan, 2007.

Luck, Edward. "The Responsibility to Protect: The First Decade." *Global Responsibility to Protect* vol. 3, no. 4 (2011).

Mahbubani, Kishore. *The New Asian Hemisphere: The Irresistible Shift of Global Power to the East.* New York: Public Affairs, 2008.

Mahoney, James. "After KKV: The New Methodology of Qualitative Research." *World Politics* vol. 62, no. 1 (2010): 120–147.

Malloch-Brown, Mark. *The Unfinished Global Revolution: The Limits of Nations and the Pursuit of a New Politics.* London: Penguin, 2011.

Malone, David, and Khong, Yuen, eds. *Unilateralism and U.S. Foreign Policy: International Perspectives.* Boulder: Lynne Rienner, 2003.

Mani, Rama, and Weiss, Thomas, eds. *Responsibility to Protect: Cultural Perspectives from the Global South.* New York: Routledge, 2011.

Manicom, James. *Sources of Tension in the Asia-Pacific: Strategic Competition, Divided Regionalism and Non-Traditional Security Challenges.* Barton: ASPI, 2014.

Mansbach, Richard, and Ferguson, Yale. *Remapping Global Politics.* New York: Cambridge University Press, 2004.

Mansfield, Edward D. and Milner, Helen V. "The New Wave of Regionalism." *International Organization* vol. 53, no. 3 (1999): 589–627. March, James, and Olsen, Johan. *Rediscovering Institutions. The Organizational Basis of Politics.* New York: Routledge, 1989.

March, James, and Olsen, Johan. "The Institutional Dynamics of International Political Orders." *International Organization* vol. 52, no. 4 (1998): 943–969.

March, James, and Olsen, Johan. "The New Institutionalism: Organizational Factors in Political Life." *American Political Science Review* vol. 78, no. 3 (1984): 734–749.

Mattern, Janice. "The Concept of Power and the (Un-)Discipline of International Relations." In *The Oxford Handbook of International Relations,* edited by Christian Reus-Smit, and Duncan Snidal, 691–698. New York: Oxford University Press, 2008.

Mayntz, Renate. "Legitimacy and Compliance in Transnational Governance." *MPIfG Working Paper* vol. 10, no. 5 (2010).

Mayntz, Renate. "Von der Steuerungstheorie zu Global Governance." In *Governance in einer sich wandelnden Welt*, edited by Gunnar Folke Schuppert and Michael Zürn, 43–61. Wiesbaden: Springer Verlag, 2008.

Mayntz, Renate, and Scharpf, Fritz. Politische Steuerung – Heute? *Zeitschrift für Soziologie* vol. 34, no. 3 (2005): 236–243.

Mazower, Mark. *Governing the World: The History of an Idea.* New York: Penguin Press, 2011.

McGregor, Richard. *The Party: The Secret World of China's Communist Rulers.* New York: Non Basic Stock Line, 2010.

McGrew, Anthony. "Globalization and Global Politics." In *The Globalization of World Politics. An Introduction to International Relations*, edited by John Baylis and Steve Smith, 19–44. Oxford: Oxford University Press, 2006.

McMahon, Patrice, and Zou, Yue. "Thirty Years of Reform and Opening Up: Teaching International Relations in China." In *Political Science & Politics* vol. 44, no. 1 (January 2011): 115–121.

Mead, Walter R. *Special Providence: American Foreign Policy and How It Changed the World.* New York: Routledge, 2002.

Mearsheimer, John. "Reckless States and Realism." In *Realism and world Politics,* edited by Ken Booth, 124–140. New York: Routledge, 2011.

Mearsheimer, John. *The Tragedy of Great Power Politics.* Norton: New York, 2001.

Mearsheimer, John. *The Tragedy of Great Power Politics.* Norton: New York, 2014.

Mearsheimer, John, and Walt, Stephen. "Leaving Theory Behind: Why Simplistic Hypothesis Testing Is Bad for International Relations." *European Journal of International Relations* vol. 19, no. 3 (2013): 427–457.

Meyer, John, Boli, John, Thomas, George M. and O Ramirez, Francisco. "World Society and the Nation-State." *American Journal of Sociology* vol. 103, no. 1 (1997): 144–181.

Miles, Edward L., Andresen, Steinar, Carlin, Elaine M., Skjærseth, Jon Birger, Underdal, Arild and Wettestad, Jørgen. *Environmental Regime Effectiveness: Confronting Theory with Evidence.* Cambridge: MIT Press, 2001.

Miller, Bejamin. *When Opponents Cooperate: Great Power Conflict and Collaboration in World Politics.* Ann Arbor, MI: The University of Michigan Press, 1995.

Miller, B. ABC Australia. "Defiant Gaddafi Issues Chilling Threat." February 23, 2011.   http://www.abc.net.au/worldtoday/content/2011/s3146582.htm (accessed July 23, 2014).

Ministry of Foreign Affairs (MFA). "Foreign Minister Yang Jiechi Refutes Fallacies on the South China Sea Issue." July 26, 2010. www.fmprc.gov.cn/eng/zxxx/t719460.htm# (accessed August 5, 2014).

Mitchell, Ronald. *International Politics and the Environment.* New York: Sage Publications, 2010.

Mitter, Rana. *A Bitter Revolution: China's Struggle with the Modern World.* Oxford: Oxford University Press, 2004.

Mitter, Rana. "An Uneasy Engagement: Chinese Ideas of Global Order and Justice in Historical Perspective." In *Order and Justice in International Relations*, edited by Rosemary Foot, John Lewis Gaddis, and Andrew Hurrell. Oxford: Oxford University Press, 2003.

Mommsen, Hans. "Richelieu als Staatsmann." *Historische Zeitschrift* vol. 127, no. 2 (1923): 210–242.

Moravcsik, Andrew. "Liberal International Relations Theory: A Scientific Assessment," In *Progress in International Relations Theory: Appraising the Field*, edited by Colin Elman and Miriam Fendius Elman, 159–204. Cambridge: MIT Press, 2003.

Morgenthau, Hans. *Politics among Nations: The Struggle for Power and Peace*. New York: W.W. Knopf, 1973/1993.

Nagel, Thomas. *Mortal Questions*. Cambridge: Cambridge University Press, 1991.

Nagel, Thomas. "The Problem of Global Justice." *Philosophy and Public Affairs* vol. 33, no. 2 (2005): 113–147.

Narlikar, Amrita. *Deadlocks in Multilateral Negotiations. Causes and Consequences*. Cambridge: Cambridge University Press, 2011.

Narlikar, Amrita. *New Powers. How to Become One and How to Manage Them*. London: Columbia University Press, 2010.

Nathan, Andrew, and Scobell, Andrew. How China Sees America. http://www.foreignaffairs.com/articles/138009/andrew-j-nathan-and-andrew-scobell/how-china-sees-america (accessed November 9, 2012).

Nau, Henry, and Ollapally, Deepa, eds. *Worldviews of Aspiring Powers*. Oxford: Oxford University Press, 2012.

Navari, Cornelia. "The Terrain of the Middle Ground." In *Ethical Reasoning in International Affairs: Arguments from the Middle Ground*, edited by Eadem, 1–12. Basingstoke: Palgrave Macmillan, 2013.

Nehring, Holger. "Transnationale Bewegungen." In *Dimensionen internationaler Geschichte*, edited by Jost Dülffer and Wilfried Loth. München: Oldenbourg Verlag 2012.

Neuhold, Hanspeter. "Spheres of Influence." 2009. http://opil.ouplaw.com/view/10.1093/law:epil/9780199231690/law-9780199231690-e991?rskey=B3rbKL&result=9&prd=EPIL

Never, Babette. "Power in Global Climate Governance." In *Climate Change: International Law and Global Governance vol. 2*, edited by Oliver Ruppel et al., 217–234. Baden-Baden: Nomos Verlag, 2013.

New York Times. "China Urges Quick End to Airstrikes in Libya." March 22, 2011 http://www.nytimes.com/2011/03/23/world/asia/23beiijing.html?_r=0&pagewanted=print (accessed August 5, 2014).

New York Times. "Gates Warns of Risks of a No-Flight Zone." March 2, 2011 http://www.nytimes.com/2011/03/03/world/africa/03military.html?_r=1&pagewanted=print (accessed August 5, 2014).

New York Times. "Obama Takes Hard Line with Libya after Shift by Clinton." March 18, 2011. http://www.nytimes.com/2011/03/19/world/africa/19policy.html?pagewanted=all&_r=0 (accessed August 7, 2014).

Niemelä, Peter. *The Politics of the Responsibility to Protect*. Helsinki: Erik Castren Institute, 2008.

Ninkovich, Frank. *Global Dawn: The Cultural Foundation of American Internationalism, 1865–1890*. Cambridge: Harvard University Press, 2009.

Noesselt, Nele. Die Grenzen ,nicht-westlicher' Theorien der Internationalen Beziehungen: Eine Rekonstruktion der Metaebene der chinesischen Theoriedebatte. Zeitschrift für Internationale Beziehungen vol. 21, no. (2014): 79–107.

Noesselt, Nele. *Alternative Weltordnungsmodelle? IB-Diskurse in China.* Wiesbaden: VS Verlag, 2010.

Noesselt, Nele. Zeitenwende in der internationalen Politik? *GIGA Focus* 6 (2012).

Nolte, Georg, ed. *European and US Constitutionalism.* Cambridge: Cambridge University Press, 2005.

Nolte, Georg, and Aust, Helmut. "European Exceptionalism?" *Global Constitutionalism* vol. 2, no. 3 (2013): 407–436.

Norloff, Carla. *America's Global Advantage: US Hegemony and International Cooperation.* New York: Cambridge University Press, 2010.

Nullmeier, Frank et al. *Der Aufstieg der Legitimationspolitik. Rechtfertigung und Kritik politisch-ökonomischer Ordnungen.* Baden-Baden: Nomos Verlag, 2012.

Nye, Joseph. *The Future of Power.* New York: Public Affairs, 2011.

Nye, Joseph. *The Powers to Lead.* New York: Oxford University Press, 2008.

Obama, Barack. "Remarks by the President at the Acceptance of the Nobel Peace Prize, Oslo 2009." http://www.whitehouse.gov/the-press-office/remarks-president-acceptance-nobel-peace-prize (accessed October 3, 2009).

O'Brien, Patrick, and Pigman, Garreth. "Free Trade, British Hegemony, and the International Economic Order in the 19th Century." *Review of International Studies* vol. 18, no. 2 (1992): 89–114.

Odell, John and Tingley, Dan. "Negotiating Agreements in International Relations." *Negotiating Agreement in Politics: American Political Science Association,* edited by Jane Mansbridge and Cathie Martin, 144–82. Task Force Report, December 2013.

Oertel, Janka. "China und das Sanktionsregime der Vereinten Nationen: Pragmatische Positionierung im Sicherheitsrat." *SWP-Aktuell* vol. 23 (2011): 1–4.

Osiander, Andreas. *The States System of Europe, 1640–1990 Peacemaking and the Conditions of International Stability.* Oxford: Clarendon Press, 1994.

Osterhammel, Jürgen. "Weltordnungskonzepte." In *Dimensionen internationaler Geschichte,* edited by Jost Dülffer and Wilfried Loth, 409–27. München: Oldenbourg, 2012.

Paterson, Matthew. "Post-hegemonic Climate Politics?" *British Journal of Politics and International Relations* vol. 11 (2009): 140–158.

Patrick, Stewart. "Irresponsible Stakeholders? The Difficulty of Integrating Rising Powers." *Foreign Affairs* vol. 89, no. 6 (2010): 45–55.

Patrick, Stewart. "Multilateralism and Its Discontents: The Causes and Consequences of US Ambivalence." In *Multilateralism and US Foreign Policy: Ambivalent Engagement.Boulder,* edited by Stewart Patrick and Shepard Forman, 1–44. Lynnie Rienner, 2001.

Peerenboom, Randall et al. *Rule of Law Dynamics in an Era of International and Transnational Governance.* Cambridge: Cambridge University Press, 2011.

Peerenboom, Randall, Zürn, Michael and Nollkaemper, André, eds. *Rule of Law Dynamics in an Era of International and Transnational Governance.* Oxford: Hart Publishing, 2012.

People's Daily. "Chinese FM Meets Syrian President's Special Envoy (Xinhua)." August 17, 2012. http://english.peopledaily.com.cn/90883/7913622.html (accessed August 7, 2014).

People's Daily. "How Humanitarian Is Western Intervention in Libya?" March 22, 2011. http://english.peopledaily.com.cn/98670/102055/7327885 .html (accessed August 7, 2014).

Pentagon. "Joint Press Conference with Secretary Hagel and Minister Chang in Beijing, China." April 8, 2014. http://www.defense.gov/Transcripts/Transcript .aspx?TranscriptID=5411

Pfeil, Florian. *Globale Verrechtlichung*. Baden-Baden: Nomos, 2011.

Pigman, Garreth. "Hegemony and Trade Liberalization Policy. Britian and the Brussels Sugar Convention of 1902." *Review of International Studies* vol. 23, no. 2 (1997): 185–210.

Pogge, Thomas. *Realizing Rawls*. Ithaca: Cornell University Press, 1989.

Pomfret, John. "US Takes Tougher Tone with China." *Washington Post*, June 30, 2010.

Popovski, Vesselin et al. *Governance through Civil Society Engagement in Asia*. United Nations University Press, Policy Brief No. 7. Availabe at: http:// i.unu.edu/media/unu.edu/publication/783/pb07–08-governance-through -civil-societyengagement-in-asia.pdf, 2008 (accessed October 10, 2012).

Posen, Barry. "Command of the Commons: The Military Foundation of U.S. Hegemony." *International Security* vol. 28, no. 1 (2003): 5–46.

Posen, Barry. "From Unipolarity to Multipolarity: Transition in Sight?" In *International Relations Theory and the Consequences of Unipolarity*, edited by Ikenberry, John, and Wohlforth, William, 317–341. Cambridge: Cambridge University Press, 2011.

Power, Samantha. *A Problem from Hell: America and the Age of Genocide*. New York: Harper, 2013.

Prantl, Jochen. *Effective Multilateralism: Through the Looking Glass of East Asia*. London: Palgrave Macmillan, 2013.

Prantl, Jochen. "Rise of the East, Decline of the West? Global Security Governance in Transition." *School of Public Policy*. Policy Brief Series 6 (March 2012).

Prantl, Jochen. *The UN Security Council and Informal Groups of States*. Oxford: Oxford University Press, 2006.

Qin, Liwen. Securing the "China Dream": *What Xi Jinping Wants to Achieve with the National Security Commission (NSC)*. China Monitor 4(2014), http://www .merics.org/fileadmin/templates/download/china-monitor/China_Monitor _No_4.pdf (accessed March 1, 2014).

Rabkin, Jeremy. *Law without Nations? Why Constitutional Government Requires Sovereign States*. New Jersey: Princeton University Press, 2005.

Raine, Sarah, and Le Miere, Christian. *Regional Disorder: The South China Sea Disputes*. London: Routledge, 2013.

Rajan, D. S. "China: Can Xi Jinping's 'Chinese Dream' Vision Be Realized? – Analysis." 2014. http://www.eurasiareview.com/04012014-china-can-xi-jinpings -chinese-dream-vision-realized-analysis/.

Rajan, D. "China: Xi Jinping's 'Chinese Dream' – A Critique." September 16, 2013 http://www.southasiaanalysis.org/node/1354, 2013 (accessed December 30, 2013).

Rapkin, Dave, ed. *World Leadership and Hegemony*. Boulder: Lynne Rienner, 1990.

Raustalia, Kal. "States, NGOs, and International: 'Environmental Institutions'." *International Studies Quarterly* vol. 41, no. 2 (1997): 719–740.

Raustiala, Kal, and Victor, David. "The Regime Complex for Plant Genetic Resources." *International Organization* vol. 58, no. 2 (2004): 277–309.

Rathbun, Brian. "Interviewing and Qualitative Field Methods: Pragmatism and Practicalities." In *Oxford Handbook of Political Methodology*, edited by Box-Steffensmeier, Janet, and Brady, Henry, 685–701. New York: Oxford University Press, 2008.

Raustalia, Kal. "States, NGOs, and International: 'Environmental Institutions.' " *International Studies Quarterly* vol. 41, no. 2 (1997): 719–740.

Ravenhill, John. "Regional Trade Agreements." In *Global Political Economy*, edited by idem, 173–211 Oxford: Oxford University Press, 2013.

Rawls, John. *A Theory of Justice.* Cambridge: Harvard University Press, 1999/1971.

Reinold, Theresa. *Sovereignty and the Responsibility to Protect: The Power of Norms and the Norms of the Powerful.* London: Routledge, 2013.

Reus-Smit, Christian. *The Moral Purpose of the State: Culture, Social Identity, and Institutional Rationality in International Relations.* New Jersey: Princeton University Press, 1999.

Reuters. "China sees 'trust deficit' before Xi's U.S. trip." February 7, 2012. http://www.reuters.com/article/2012/02/07/us-china-usa-idUSTRE8160AV20120207 (accessed August 7, 2014).

Risse, Thomas. "Let's Argue! Communicative Action in World Politics." *International Organization* vol. 54, no. 1 (2000): 1–39.

Risse, Thomas. *Governance Configurations in Areas of Limited Statehood: Actors, Modes, Institutions and Resources.* Berlin: SFB-Governance Working Paper Series 32, 2012.

Risse, Thomas. "Transnational Governance." In *Handbook of International Relations*, edited by Walter, Carlnaes et al. (Hrsg.), 426–452. New York: Oxford University Press, 2013.

Risse, Thomas, Carnaes, Walter and Simmons, Beth, eds. *Handbook of International Relations*, 2nd edition, Thousand Oaks, CA: Sage Publications, 2012.

Rittberger, Volker, Kruck, Andreas and Romund, Anne. *Grundzüge der Weltpolitik. Theorie und Empirie des Weltregierens.* Wiesbaden: VS Verlag für Sozialwissenschaften, 2010.

Rittberger, Volker, and Zangl, Bernhard. *Internationale Organisationen. Politik und Geschichte, 3rd edition.* Wiesbaden: VS Verlag für Sozialwissenschaften, 2003.

Roberts, Christopher. *ASEAN Regionalism: Cooperation, Values and Institutionalization.* London: Routeledge, 2013.

Rosenau, James. "Governing the Ungovernable: The Challenge of a Global Disaggregation of Authority." *Regulation & Governance* vol. 1, no. 1 (2007): 88–97.

Rosenau, James. *Turbulence in World Politics: A Theory of Change and Continuity.* Princeton: Princeton University Press, 1990.

Ross, Robert, and Zhu Feng, eds. *China's Ascent Power, Security, and the Future of International Politics.* Ithaca: Cornell University Press, 2008.

Roy, Oliver. "Civil Society in Central Asia and the Greater Middle east." *International Affairs* vol. 81, no. 5 (2005): 79–96.

Roy, Oliver. *The Politics of Chaos in the Middle East.* New York: Columbia University Press, 2008.

Rubin, Herbert, and Rubin, Irene. *Qualitative Interviewing: The Art of Hearing Data.* Thousand Oaks, CA: Sage Publications, 2005.

Rudd, Kevin. "Beyond the Pivot: A New Road Map for U.S.-Chinese Relations." 2013. http://www.foreignaffairs.com/articles/138843/kevin-rudd/beyond-the -pivot?page=2&cid=rss-comments-beyond_the_pivot-000000

Rudd, Kevin. "Fault Lines in the 21st Century Global Order: Asia Rising, Europe Declining and the Future of 'the West'." Speech at Chatham House http://www.foreignminister.gov.au/speeches/Pages/2012/kr _sp_120124.aspx?ministerid=2 (accessed June 24, 2012).

Ruggie, John. *Constructing the World Polity.* New York: Routledge, 1998.

Russett, Bruce. *Grasping the Democratic Peace: Principles for a Post-Cold War World.* Princeton: Princeton University Press, 1993.

Sachsenmeier, Dominic. *Global Perspectives on Global History: Theories and Approaches in a Connected World.* Cambridge: Cambridge University Press, 2011.

Schade, Jeanette. *Soft Superpower: Die Rolle der Zivilgesellschaft in der US-Außen- und Entwicklungspolitik.* Baden-Baden: Nomos, 2005.

Scharpf, Fritz. "Demokratieprobleme in der europäischen Mehrebenenpolitik." In *Demokratie in Ost und West. Für Klaus von Beyme,* edited by Wolfgang Merkel und Andreas Busch, 672–694. Frankfurt: Suhrkamp, 1999.

Scharpf, Fritz. "Positive und negative Koordination in Verhandlungssystemen." In *Policy Analyse. Kritik und Neuorientierung. Politische Vierteljahresschrift Special Issue 24,* edited by Adrienne Héritier, 57–83. Opladen: Westdeutscher Verlag, 1993.

Scheen, Thomas. *Will Verändern: Frankfurter Allgemeine Zeitung,* September 6, 2012, 10.

Schelling, Thomas. *Strategy of Conflict.* Cambridge: Harvard University Press, 1960.

Scheuermann, William. *Hans Morgenthau: Realism and Beyond.* Cambridge: Polity Press, 2009.

Schimmelfennig, Frank. *Internationale Politik.* Paderborn: Schöningh, 2013.

Schimmelfennig, Frank. "Strategic Calculation and International Socialization: Membership Incentives, Party Constellations, and Sustained Compliance in Central and Eastern Europe." In *International Organization* vol. 59, no. 4 (2005): 827–860.

Schmidt, Brian. "Realist Conceptions of Power." In Felix Berenskoetter ed. *Power in World Politics,* London: Routledge, 2007: 43–63.

Schroeder, Paul. *Systems, Stability, and Statecraft: Essays on the International History of Modern Europe.* New York: Palgrave Macmillan, 2004.

Schroeder, Paul. *The Transformation of European Politics, 1763–1848.* Oxford: Clarendon Press, 1994.

Schweller, Randall. "Emerging Powers in an Age of Disorder." *Global Governance* vol. 17 (2011): 285–297.

Schweller, Randall, and Pu, Xiayou. "After Unipolarity: China's Visions of International Order in an Era of U.S. Decline." *International Security* vol. 36, no. 1 (2011): 41–72.

Searle, John. *Making the Social World: The Structure of Human Civilization.* Oxford: Oxford University Press, 2010.

Seybolt, Taylor. *Humanitarian Military Intervention: The Conditions for Success and Failure.* Oxford: Oxford University Press, 2007.

Shafer, Byron. "American Exceptionalism." *American Review of Political Science* vol. 2 (1999): 445–463.

Shambaugh, David. *China Goes Global. The Partial Power.* New York: Oxford University Press, 2013.

Shanghai Cooperation Organization. Declaration of the Heads of State of the Member States of the Shanghai Cooperation Organization on Building a Region of Lasting Peace and Common Prosperity. June 7, 2012. http://www.sectsco.org/EN123/show.asp?id=442 (accessed August 5, 2013).

Siemons, Mark. „Die Verweigerte Kosmopolitisierung." December 3, 2013. http://www.faz.net/-hxb-7k0xj (accessed August 7, 2014).

Simmons, Beth, Dobbin, Frank and Garrett, Geoffrey. "Introduction: The International Diffusion of Liberalism." *International Organization* vol. 60, no. 4 (October 2006): 781–810.

Simpson, Gerry. *Great Powers and Outlaw States: Unequal Sovereigns in the International Legal Order.* Cambridge: Cambridge University Press, 2004.

Sing, Lam. "A Short Note on ASEAN-Great Power Interaction." *Contemporary Southeast Asia*, vol. 15, no. 4 (1994): 451–463.

Smith, Jackie, and Wiest, Dawn. "The Uneven Geography of Global Civic Society: National and Global Influences on Transnational Association." *Social Forces* vol. 84, no. 2 (2005): 621–652.

Smith, Roger. "Beyond Tocqueville, Myrdal, and Hartz: The Multiple Traditions in America." *American Political Science Review* vol. 87 (1993): 549–566.

Smith, Rogers. "The 'American Creed' and American identity: The Limits of Liberal Citizenship in the United States." *The Western Political Quarterly* vol. 12, no. 4 (1988): 225–251.

Smith, Steve. "Is the Truth Out There? Eight Questions about International Order." In *International Order and the Future of World Politics*, edited by T.V. Paul, and John Hall, 99–119. New York: Cambridge University Press, 1999.

Snidal, Duncan. "The Limits of Hegemonic Stability Theory." *International Organization*, vol. 39, no. 4 (1985): 579–614.

Snidal, Duncan, and Abbott, Kenneth. "Strengthening International Regulation through Transnational New Governance." *Vanderbilt Journal of Transnational Law* vol. 42 (2009): 501–578.

Snyder, Jack. *Power and Progress: International Politics in Transition.* New York: Routledge, 2012.

Snyder, Sarah. *Human Rights Activism and the End of the Cold War: A Transnational History of the Helsinki Network.* New York: Cambridge University Press, 2011.

Spence, Jonathan. *The Search for Modern China.* New York: W.W. Norton, 1990.

Stahn, Carsten. "Responsibility to Protect: Political Rhetoric or Emerging Legal Norm." *American Journal of International Law* vol. 101 (2007): 99–120.

Steffek, Jens. "Explaining Cooperation between IGOs and NGOs – Push Factors, Pull Factors, and the Policy Cycle." *Review of International Studies* vol. 39, no. 4 (2013): 993–1013.

Steffek, Jens, and Hahn, Kristina, eds. *Evaluating Transnational NGOs: Legitimacy, Accountability, Representation.* Basingstoke: Palgrave Macmillan, 2010.

Steffek, Jens, Kissling, Claudia and Nanz, Patrizia. *Civil Society Participation in European and Global Governance: A Cure for the Democratic Deficit?* Basingstoke: Palgrave Macmillan, 2008.

Steiner, Zara. *The Lights that Failed: European International History 1919–1933.* Oxford: Oxford University Press, 2007.

Steiner, Zara. *The Triumph of the Dark: European International History 1933–1939.* Oxford: Oxford University Press, 2013.

Stone, Randall. *Controlling Institutions. International Organizations and the Global Economy*. New York: Cambridge University Press, 2011.

Strategic Survey 2009–2013. *The Annual Review of World Affairs*. London: Routledge, 2013.

Stroup, Sarah. *Borders among Activists: International NGOs in the United States, Britain, and France*. Ithaca: Cornell University Press, 2012.

Suchman, Matt. "Managing Legitimacy: Strategic and Institutional Approaches." *Academy of Management Journal* vol. 20, no. 3 (1995): 571–610.

Suganami, Hidemi. *The Domestic Analogy and World Order Proposals*. Cambridge: Cambridge University Press, 1989.

SWP, Berlin. *China und die ‚Rückkehr' der USA nach Asien: Aus chinesischen Fachzeitschriften des ersten Halbjahrs 2012*. Berlin: SWP, 2012.

SWP, Berlin. "Der Klimagipfel von Kopenhagen aus der Sicht Chinas: Aus chinesischen Fachzeitschriften vom Januar 2010." *Zeitschriftenschau* vol. 2 (March 2010). Berlin: SWP, 2010.

Take, Ingo. *Globales Regieren auf dem Prüfstand. Nicht demokratisch aber legitim?* Baden-Baden: Nomos, 2013.

Taliaferro, Jeffrey, Ripsman, Norrin M. and Lobell, Steven. *The Challenge of Grand Strategy: The Great Powers and the Broken Balance between the World Wars*. Cambridge: Cambridge University Press, 2012.

Tallberg, Jonas, and Jönsson, Christer, eds. *Transnational Actors in Global Governance: Patterns, Explanations and Implications*. Basingstoke: Palgrave Macmillan, 2010.

Tallberg, Jonas, Sommerer, Thomas, Squatrito, Theresa, and Jönsson, Christer. *The Opening Up of International Organizations: Transnational Access in Global Governance*. Cambridge: Cambridge University Press, 2013.

Tallberg, Jonas and Smith, James McCall. "Dispute Settlement in World Politics: States, Supranational Prosecutors and Compliance." *European Journal of International Relations Online*, vol. 20, no. 1 (2014): 118–144.

Tamanaha, Brian. *On the Rule of Law*. New York: Cambridge University Press, 2004.

Tammen, Ronald, and Kugler, Jacek, and Lemke, Douglas. *Power Transitions: Strategies for the 21st Century*. New York: Chatham House Publ Inc., 2000.

Tarrow, Sidney. *The New Transnational Activism*. New York: Cambridge University Press, 2005.

Teitel, Ruti. *Humanity's Law*. Oxford UP, 2011.

Tellis, Ashley, and Tanner, Travis, eds. *Strategic Asia 2012–13: China's Military Challenge*. National Bureau of Asian Research. 2012.

Terhalle, Maximilian. "Reciprocal Socialization." *International Studies Perspectives* vol. 12, no. 4 (2011): 341–361.

Terhalle, Maximilian. "Transnational Actors and Great Powers during Order Transition." *International Studies Perspectives* vol. 16 (2015): forthcoming.

Thakur, Ramesh. *The United Nations, Peace and Security: From Collective Security to the Responsibility to Protect*. New York: Cambridge University Press, 2006.

The Economist. "Bo Xilai's life sentence: End of the Road?" September 22, 2013. http://www.economist.com/node/21586707/print (accessed June 7, 2014).

The Economist. "The Libyan Dilemma." September 10, 2011. http://economist.com/node/21528664/print (accessed January 18, 2012).

The Economist. "The Summit: Barack Obama and Xi Jinping Have a Chance to Recast this Century's Most Important Bilateral Relationship." June 8, 2013. p. 10.

The Economist. "What Would America Fight for?" March 5, 2014.

The Guardian. "Darfur dead could number 300,000." April 23, 2008. http://www.theguardian.com/world/2008/apr/23/sudan.unitednations (accessed July 30, 2014).

The Guardian. "David Miliband: China ready to join US as world power." May 17, 2009. http://www.theguardian.com/politics/2009/may/17/david-miliband-china-world-power

The Guardian. "Libya Conflict: Reactions Around the World." March 30, 2011. http://www.theguardian.com/world/2011/mar/30/libya-conflict-reactions-world/print (accessed July 30, 2014).

The Guardian. "Libya No-fly Resolution Reveals Global Split in UN." March 18, 2011. http://www.theguardian.com/world/2011/mar/18/libya-no-fly-resolution-split/print (accessed July 30, 2014).

The Guardian. "Russia and China Join West in UN War Crimes Ruling as Britain Revokes Immunity for Leader and Family." February 28, 2011. http://www.theguardian.com/world/2011/feb/27/libya-gaddafi-pressure-russia-china/print (accessed July 30, 2014).

The White House. "Remarks by President Obama to the Australian Parliament. Canberra." November 17, 2011. http://www.whitehouse.gov/the-press-office/2011/11/17/remarks-president-obama-australian-parliament (accessed August 5, 2014).

The White House. "U.S.-China Joint Statement. Beijing, China." November 17, 2009: http://www.whitehouse.gov/the-press-office/us-china-joint-statement (accessed August 5, 2014).

The White House. "United States National Security Strategy 2010." http://whitehouse.gov/nsc/nss/2010 (accessed August 5, 2014).

Thompson, David, and Rapkin, "William. Power Transition, Challenge and the (Re)Emergence of China." vol. 29, no. 4 (2003): 315–342.

Time. "China's View on Syria Crisis: America's 'Hidden Motivations' Are Leading It Astray." September 13, 2013. http://world.time.com/2013/09/13/chinas-view-on-syria-crisis-americas-hidden-motivations-are-leading-it-astray/print/ (accessed August 7, 2014).

Tomes, Robert. "American Exceptionalism in the Twenty-First Century." *Survival* vol. 56, no. 1 (2014): 27–50.

Trachtenberg, Marc. *A Constructed Peace: The Making of the European Settlement, 1945–1963*. Princeton: Princeton University Press, 1999.

Tsebelis, George. *Veto Players. How Political Institutions work*. Princeton: Princeton University Press, 2002.

Tucker, Robert. *The Inequality of Nations*. New York: Basic Books, 1977.

U.S. Department of Defense. "Joint Press Conference with Secretary Hagel and Minister Chang in Beijing, China." April 8, 2014. http://www.defense.gov/Transcripts/Transcript.aspx?TranscriptID=5411 (accessed July 29, 2014).

U.S. Department of State. "Strategic and Economic Dialogue." July 27–28, 2009. http://www.state.gov/e/eb/tpp/bta/sed/2009/ (accessed August 5, 2014).

United Nations General Assembly. "Resolution adopted by the General Assembly 60/1. 2005 World Summit Outcome." October 24, 2005. http://unpan1.un.org/

intradoc/groups/public/documents/un/unpan021752.pdf (accessed August 5, 2014).

United Nations Security Council (UNSC). "Letter Dated 14 March 2011 from the Permanent Observer of the League of Arab States to the United Nations addressed to the President of the Security Council, UN Doc S/2011/137." March 15, 2011. http://de.scribd.com/doc/58134121/Council-of-the-League -of-Arab-States-Resolution-7360–Libya-no-fly-zone (accessed August 5, 2014).

United Nations Security Council (UNSC). "SC/10403, 6627th Meeting (Night)." October 4, 2011. http://www.un.org/News/Press/docs/2011/sc10403.doc.htm (accessed August 5, 2014).

United Nations Security Council (UNSC). "SC/10536, 6711th Meeting." February 4, 2012. http://www.un.org/News/Press/docs/2012/sc10536.doc.htm (accessed August 5, 2014).

United Nations Security Council (UNSC). "S/PV.7038." September 28, 2013. http://www.un.org/en/ga/search/view_doc.asp?symbol=S/PV.7038 (accessed August 5, 2014).

United Nations Security Council (UNSC). "S/PV.7180, 7180th Meeting." May 22, 2014. http://www.un.org/en/ga/search/view_doc.asp?symbol=S/PV .7180 (accessed August 5, 2014).

United Nations Security Council (UNSC). "S/RES/1970." February 26, 2011. http://daccess-dds-ny.un.org/doc/UNDOC/GEN/N11/245/58/PDF/N1124558 .pdf?OpenElement (accessed August 5, 2014).

United Nations Security Council (UNSC). "S/RES/1973." March 17, 2011. http:// daccess-dds-ny.un.org/doc/UNDOC/GEN/N11/268/39/PDF/N1126839.pdf? OpenElement (accessed August 5, 2014).

United Nations Security Council (UNSC). "S/RES/2059." July 20, 2012. http:// www.un.org/en/ga/search/view_doc.asp?symbol=S/RES/2059%282012%29 (accessed August 5, 2014).

United Nations Security Council (UNSC). "United Nations S/PV.6498 Security Council Sixty-sixth year 6498th Meeting, Thursday, 17 March 2011, 6 p.m., NY." http://responsibilitytoprotect.org/Security%20Council%20meeting% 20on%20the%20situation%20in%20Lybia%2017%20March%202011.pdf (accessed August 5, 2014).

US National Security Strategy May 2010. http://www.whitehouse.gov/sites/ default/files/rss_viewer/national_security_strategy.pdf

US Energy Information Administration. "China – Country Analysis Brief Overview." May 30, 2013. http://www.eia.gov/countries/country-data.cfm? fips=CH&trk=m (accessed August 5, 2014).

US Energy Information Administration. "Overview Data for United States." May 30, 2013. http://www.eia.gov/countries/country-data.cfm?fips=US&trk=m (accessed August 5, 2014).

Vabulas, Felicity and Snidal, Duncan. "Informal Intergovernmental Organiza-tions (IIGOs) and the Spectrum of Intergovernmental Arrangements." *Review of International Organizations*, vol. 8, no. 2 (2013): 193–220.

Vandewalle, Dirk. *A History of Modern Libya*. Cambridge: Cambridge University Press, 2012.

Voeten, Eric. "Unipolar Politics as Usual." *Cambridge Review of International Affairs* vol. 22, no. 3 (2011): 30–46.

Wade, Robert. "Protecting Power: Western States in Global Organizations." In *Global Governance at Risk*, edited by David Held and Charles Roger, 77–110, Cambridge: Polity Press, 2013.

Waever, Ole. "Still a Discipline After all These Debates?" In *International Relations Theories: Discipline and Diversity*, edited by Tim Dunne, and Milja Kurki, and Steve Smith, 306–327. Oxford: Oxford University Press, 2013.

Wall Street Journal. "Gates Says Libya Not Vital National Interest." March 27, 2011. http://m.europe.wsj.com/articles/SB10001424052748704308904576226704261420430?mobile=y (accessed August 5, 2014).

Wallerstein, Immanuel. *The Modern World-System, Bd. I–III*. Academic Press: New York, 1974, 1980, 1989.

Walt, Stephen. "The Myth of American Exceptionalism." *Foreign Policy*, 2011, 72–75, October 11, 2011, http://foreignpolicy.com/2011/10/11/the-myth-of-american-exceptionalism/.

Waltz, Kenneth. *Theory of International Politics*. Boston: McGraw-Hill, 1979.

Waltz, Kenneth. "Globalization and Governance." In *Realism and International Politics*. New York: Routledge, 2008 [1999], 230–245.

Waltz, Kenneth. "Realist Thought and Neorealist Theory." In *Realism and International Politics*. New York: Routledge, 2008 [1990], 67–82.

Wang, Yamei. "China's Peaceful Development." http://news.xinhuanet.com (accessed February 9, 2012). 2011.

Washington Post. "Clinton Urges Continued Investment in U.S." February 22, 2009. http://www.washingtonpost.com/wp-dyn/content/article/2009/02/22/AR2009022200468.html (accessed August 7, 2014).

Washington Post. "Robert Gates, Former Defense Secretary, Offers Harsh Critique of Obama's Leadership in 'Duty'." January 7, 2014. http://m.washingtonpost.com/world/national-security/robert-gates-former-defense-secretary-offers-harsh-critique-of-obamas-leadership-in-duty/2014/01/07/6a6915b2-77cb-11e3-b1c5-739e63e9c9a7_story.html (accessed August 5, 2014).

Walzer, Michael. *Spheres of Justice: A Defence of Pluralism and Equality*. Oxford: Blackwell, 1985.

Watson, Adam. Hegemony and History. London: Routledge, 2007.

Watson, Adam. *The Evolution of International Society: A Comparative Historical Analysis*. New York: Routledge, 1992.

Weeramantry, Christopher. *Universalizing International Law. Nijhoff*. Leiden: Brill, 2004.

Weiss, Thomas, and Gordenker, Leon, eds. *NGOs, the UN, and Global Governance*. Boulder: Lynne Rienner, 1996.

Weiss, Thomas, and Wilkinson, Rorden. "Rethinking Global Governance? Complexity, Authority, Power, Change." *International Studies Quarterly* vol. 58, no. 1 (2014): 207–215.

Welch, David. *Justice and the Genesis of War*. New York: Cambridge University Press, 1993.

Welsh, Jennifer. "Who Should Act? Collective Responsibility and the Responsibility to Protect." In *The Routledge Handbook of the Responsibility to Protect*, edited by Andy Knight, Frazer Egerton, 103–114. London: Routledge, 2011.

Wendt, Alexander. "Anarchy Is What States Make of It: the Social Construction of Power Politics." *International Organization* vol. 46, no. 2 (1992): 394.

Wendt, Alexander. "Collective Identity Formation and the International State." In *American Political Science Review* vol. 88, no. 2. (1994): 384–396.

Wendt, Alexander. "The Agent-Structure Problem in International Relations Theory." *International Organization* vol. 41, no. 3 (1987): 335–370.

Wertheim, Stephan. "A Solution from Hell: The United States and the Rise of Humanitarian Interventionism, 1991–2003." *Journal of Genocide Research* vol. 3, no. 12 (2010): 149–172.

Westad, Odd. *Restless Empire: China and the World Since 1750.* London: Bodley Head, 2012.

Westad, Odd. The Global Cold War. *Third World Interventions and the Making of Our Times.* Cambridge: Cambridge University Press, 2006.

White, Hugh. *The China Choice: Why America Should Share Power.* Collingwood: Black Inc., 2012.

White House. "Press Conference by the President." March 06, 2012. http://www.whitehouse.gov/the-press-office/2012/03/06/press-conference-president (accessed August 7, 2014).

Wiener, Antje, Lang, Anthony, Maduro, Miguel and Kumm, Mathias. "Why a New Journal on Global Constitutionalism?" *Global Constitutitonalism* vol. 1, no. 1 (2012): 1–15.

Wight, Martin. *Power Politics.* Leicester: Bloomsbury Academic, 1991.

Willetts, Peter. *Non-Governmental Organizations and World Politics.* New York: Routledge, 2011.

Williams, Michael. *The Realist Tradition and the Limits of International Relations.* Cambridge: Cambridge University Press, 2005.

WikiLeaks 2007. "Lee Kuan Yew on Burma's 'stupid' Generals and the Gambler Chen Shui-Bian." October 19, http://wikileaks.ca, no longer available.

Wiseman, Gerald. "Polylateralism and New Modes of Global Dialogue." In *Diplomacy Volume III*, edited by C. Jonnson, and Langhorne, Richard, 36–57. London: Sage, 2004.

Woods, Ngaire et al. *Transforming Global Governance for the 21st Century.* UN Development Program: New York, 2013.

Woods, Ngaire and Mattli, Walter. Edited by Walter Mattli & Ngaire Woods. Princeton: Princeton UP, 2009.

Wohlforth, William "The Stability of a Unipolar World." *International Security* vol. 24, no. 1 (1999): 5–41.

Wohlforth, William. "US Primacy." In *US Foreign Policy*, edited by Michael Cox, 421–430. Oxford: Oxford University Press, 2012.

Wohlforth, William et al. *The Balance of Power in World History.* Palgrave: New York, 2007.

Wolfers, Arnold. *Discord and Collaboration. Essays on International Politics.* Baltimore, MD: Ulan Press, 1962.

Wolfrum, Rüdiger. *Legitimacy in International Law.* Berlin: Springer Verlag, 2008.

Xue, Huang. "Chinese Observation on International Law." *Chinese Journal of International Law* vol. 6, no. 1 (2007): 83–93.

Xuetong, Yan. "Ancient Chinese Thought, Modern Chinese Power", edited by Daniel Bell and Sun Zhe. Princeton: Princeton University Press, 2011.

Yahuda, Michael. *The International Politics of the Asia Pacific.* New York: Routledge, 2011.

Yew, Lee Kuan. *The Grand Master's Insights on China, the United States, and the World.* Cambridge: MIT Press, 2013.

Yongjin, Zhang. "Understanding Chinese Views of the Emerging Global Order." In *China and the New International Order*, edited by Y. Zheng, 149–161. London: Routledge, 2008.

Yongjin, Zhang, and Buzan, Barry. "The Tributary System as International Society in Theory and Practice." *Chinese Journal of International Politics* vol. 5 (2012): 3–36.

Young, Margaret, ed. *Regime Interaction in International Law: Facing Fragmentation.* Cambridge: Cambridge University Press, 2012.

Young, Oran. "Regime Dynamics: The Rise and Fall of International Regimes." *International Organization* vol. 36, no. 2 (1982): 277–297.

Yucheng, Le. "Foreign Ministry Policy Planning Chief Gives Speech at the MASI Annual Meeting." June 11, 2011. http://www.ciss.pku.edu.cn/en/documentviewformac.aspx?id=700 (accessed August 7, 2014).

Yuzawa, Takeshi. *Japan's Security Policy and the ASEAN Regional Forum: The Search for Multilateral Security in the Asia-Pacific.* Routledge: London, 2007.

Yuzawa, Takeshi. *Japan's Security Policy and the ASEAN Regional Forum.* Abingdon: Routledge, 2010.

Zhang, Feng. "The Rise of Chinese Exceptionalism in International Relations." *European Journal of International Relations* vol. 19, no. 2 (2011): 305–328.

Zhang, Zhongxiang. "How Far can Developing Country Commitments Go in an Immediate Post-2012 Climate Regime?" *Energy Policy* vol. 37, no. 5 (2009): 1753–1757.

Zhao, Suisheng. *China and the United States: Cooperation and Competition in Northeast Asia.* New York: Palgrave Macmillan, 2008.

Zoellick, Robert B. "The End of the Third World?" Speech at Woodrow Wilson Center. Voltaire Network, Washington D.C. April 14, 2010. http://www.voltairenet.org/article164965.html (accessed August 5, 2014).

Zoellick, Robert. "The End of the Third World?" April 14, 2010. http://web.worldbank.org/WBSITE/EXTERNAL/NEWS/0,,contentMDK:22541126~pagePK:34370~piPK:42770~theSitePK:4607,00.html (accessed August 7, 2014).

Zürn, Michael, and Joerges, Christian, eds. *Governance and Law in Postnational Constellations. Compliance in Europe and Beyond.* Cambridge University Press, (2005).

Zürn, Michael. "Global Governance as an Emergent Political Order. The Role of Transnational Non-Governmental Organisations." In *Global Governance and the Role of Non-State Actors*, edited by Gunnar Schuppert, 31–45. Baden-Baden: Nomos Verlag, 2006.

Zürn, Michael. "Global Governance as Multi-Level Governance." In *Oxford Handbook of Governance*, edited by David Levi-Faur, 730–744. Oxford: Oxford University Press, 2010.

Zürn, Michael. "Global Governance under Legitimacy Pressure." In *Government and Opposition* vol. 39, no. 2 (2004): 260–287.

Zürn, Michael. "Globalization and Global Governance." In *Handbook of International Relations, 2nd edition*, edited by Thomas Risse et al., Chapter 16. Thousand Oaks, CA: Sage Publications, 2013.

Zürn, Michael, and Joerges, Christian. *Law and Governance in Postnational Europe: Compliance beyond the Nation-State. Themes in European Governance.* New York: Cambridge University Press, 2011.

Zürn, Michael, and Joerges, Christian, eds. *Governance and Law in Postnational Constellations. Compliance in Europe and Beyond.* Cambridge University Press, 2005.

Index

CPSIA information can be obtained
at www.ICGtesting.com
Printed in the USA
LVOW04*2019190416

484338LV00018B/307/P